Day In, Day Out

Women's Lives in North Dakota

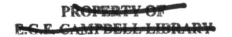
Edited by Bjorn Benson, Elizabeth
Hampsten and Kathryn Sweney
University of North Dakota,
Grand Forks

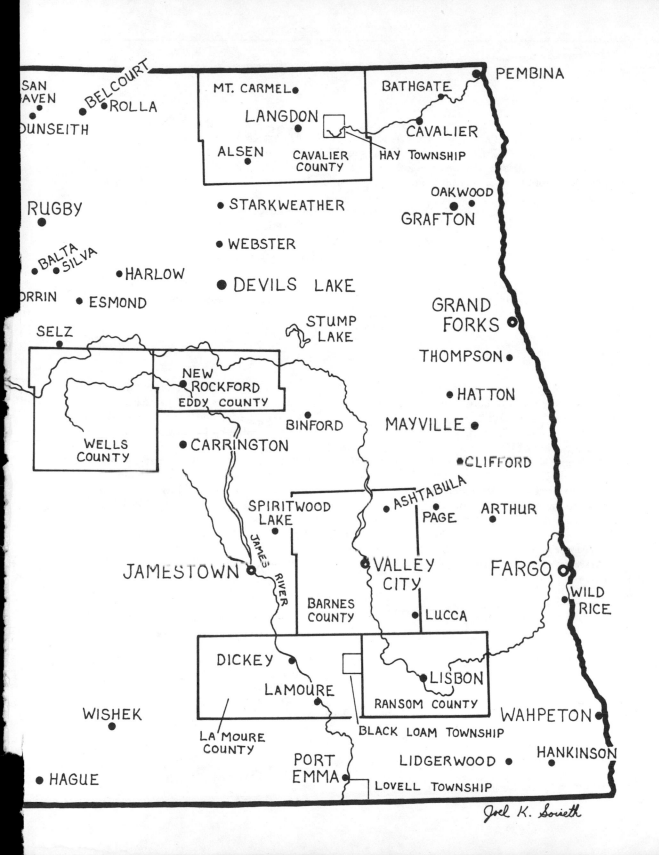

SAN
HAVEN
DUNSEITH
BELCOURT
ROLLA
MT. CARMEL •
LANGDON
ALSEN
CAVALIER
COUNTY
HAY TOWNSHIP
BATHGATE
CAVALIER
PEMBINA
OAKWOOD
GRAFTON
RUGBY
STARKWEATHER
BALTA
SILVA
HARLOW
WEBSTER
ORRIN
ESMOND
DEVILS LAKE
STUMP
LAKE
GRAND
FORKS
THOMPSON
SELZ
NEW
ROCKFORD
EDDY COUNTY
BINFORD
WELLS
COUNTY
CARRINGTON
SPIRITWOOD
LAKE
MAYVILLE
CLIFFORD
ASHTABULA
PAGE
ARTHUR
HATTON
JAMES RIVER
JAMESTOWN
VALLEY
CITY
FARGO
WILD
RICE
BARNES
COUNTY
LUCCA
DICKEY
LAMOURE
LISBON
RANSOM COUNTY
WISHEK
LA MOURE
COUNTY
BLACK LOAM TOWNSHIP
WAHPETON
HAGUE
PORT
EMMA
LOVELL TOWNSHIP
LIDGERWOOD
HANKINSON

Joel K. Sorieth

The publication of this book has been sponsored by the Committee for the North Dakota History of Women Project, Ruth Meiers (chair): Everett Albers, Kathie Anderson, Thomas J. Clifford, Elizabeth Hampsten, Elaine Lindgren, Sharon Monilaws, Susan Peterson, Ann Rathke, and Ann Whalen. Funding for the writing and production of this book has come from the Office of the President, University of North Dakota.

Cover (chalk) by Jacquelyn McElroy-Edwards.
North Dakota maps by Joel Soiseth.
Index prepared by Joyce McWilliams.
Cover Design by James Hughes.

Special thanks to the following: The University of North Dakota Office of the President, Department of English, School of Communication, Special Collections, and University Relations.
The North Dakota State Historical Society.
The Minot Daily News.
Team Electronics, Grand Forks.

Writers and editors wish to thank the following individuals who have been helpful in the many stages of this book: Patricia Jackson-Benson, Sr. Borgia, Jean A. Brookins, Joyce Burr, Tom Duval, Fr. T. William Coyle, Gwen Crawford, John Crawford, Marion Eckes Early, Fred Eldridge, Ralph Erdrich, Rita Erdrich, Ellen Erickson, Virginia Esslinger, John Evenson, Sr. Felicitas, Grace Fisher, Don Fisk, Srs. Rita and Teresa Fitzgerald, Jean Cooper Fuschillo, Nancy Gilliland, Kathy Grantham, Rod Grantham, David Gray, Keith Gunderson, Sarah Hampsten, Sr. Mary Jo Hasey, Kathryn Hefti, Thomasine Heitkamp, Deborah Hodges, Iva Dell Honeyman, Esther Horne, Sadie Bartz Horvey, Ursula Hovet, Linda Johnson, Roger Johnson, Fr. Terrence Kardong, Ethel Knudsen, Mary Anne Lach, Mabel Landeene, Gretchen Lang, Muriel McBeth, Mavis McKelvey, Shirley Lee Moe, Sr. Mary Margaret Mooney, Francis Nermyr, Deborah Nichols, Lenore Nordwall, Sandra Parsons, Fr. Benedict Pfaller, Sr. Ria, Benjamin Ring, Lola Ruff, Dianne Sheppard, Loney Tassi, Mark Thiel, Stephen Trosley, Sr. Angele Tufts, James Vivian, Jean Wick, Sr. Kathryn Zimmer.

The University of North Dakota, Grand Forks, 58202

Contents

I

II

III

IV

Ruth Meiers

To Ruth Olson Meiers
(1925-1987)

Ruth Olson Meiers was born in Parshall, North Dakota, on November 6, 1925. Her parents were Axel and Grace Olson; her mother was active in church and community affairs and in the Women's Christian Temperance Union, and her father organized for the Farm Holiday Association and the Non-Partisan League. Ruth was the youngest of nine children.

She graduated from the University of North Dakota in 1946 with a degree in social work, and for the next six years held several positions with the Mountrail County Welfare Board. In 1950 she married Glenn Meiers; they raised four sons and a foster son from Paraguay, and for a number of years Ruth worked part time in social services. She was active in church and community affairs: American Lutheran Church Women, Sew and So Homemaker's Club, Mountrail County Historical Society. She taught Sunday School for 25 years.

In 1974 Ruth Meiers was elected to the North Dakota House of Representatives, the first woman to be elected from District 4, exactly 40 years after her father had served his first legislative term in 1935. During her ten years in the State House of Representatives, she worked especially on social service and child welfare issues, serving on the Appropriations and on the Social Services and Veterans' Affairs Committees.

On November 6, 1984 (her 59th birthday) she was elected Lieutenant Governor. She chaired the Commission on Children and Adolescents at Risk, formed in 1985. She proposed and convened the North Dakota History of Women Project, and in February 1987 was selected as the first recipient of the North Dakota Citizen Award by the North Dakota Hall of Fame. Ruth Meiers died of cancer on March 19, 1987, at Medcenter One Hospital in Bismarck.

Ruth Meiers once spoke of a life that many in North Dakota can recognize:

I was a little girl during the Depression years. I suppose by today's standards we lived in poverty. But I didn't know we were poor — I thought we went barefoot in the summer because it was fun — I really wasn't aware that my parents could not afford shoes for nine children. But I had parents who helped us appreciate the things we had. We learned to share the load — we learned responsibility — we learned about integrity and honor — we learned about cooperation. We had the freedom to explore. We helped our neighbor and our neighbor helped us. We loved, respected, and feared our parents. We learned discipline — we learned to do "without." We learned to be resourceful. We learned to fail and to succeed. We learned the difference between pride and false pride. We learned to be independent — to walk alone."

Her own life was the inspiration for her idea of a centennial project that would focus on the contributions of women to the history and development of our state. She explained these connections in her speech to the Centennial Planning Conference in October 1985.

I know the heartaches and the hardships my mother endured. She was the first one up in the morning and the last one in bed at night. Nearly all of the food on our table was the result of endless hours of canning from a garden that had to be watered constantly to produce. And yet she found time to nurture her family and instill in them the love of beauty, literature and the arts. Her contributions can be multiplied hundreds of times by your mothers and your grandmothers. The women in those early days were the impetus behind the churches that were built for worship and the schools that provided an education for their children.

During this North Dakota Centennial let us celebrate women. Let us celebrate our early homemakers and our homemakers of today. Let us celebrate the early teachers who overcame many adversities to bring learning to our prairies. Let us celebrate the women who took up the cause of women's suffrage. Let us celebrate the women who raised their children alone with courage and strength. We have much to celebrate.

Our history should celebrate the woman who chose to be a homemaker, who saw that role as creative and exciting. Our history should celebrate the professional women — those who used their talents to heal, to advocate, to nurture. Our history should celebrate the women who, side by side with their husbands, shared in the work and responsibility on the small farms and businesses in this state. Our history should celebrate the women who reared their children alone with courage and determination.

But let us remember when we are writing history, that there were women who hurt, who were unemployed, who were ravaged, who were disturbed, and who were abused. Let us commit ourselves to remembering them and today to giving women in those situations help and to giving them hope.

If all "men are brothers," then all "women are sisters," and we should be supportive of each other and our efforts to improve, enhance, and sustain a better quality of life for the future."

Prepared by Janis S. Cheney and Carol Jean Larsen, Bismarck, N.D.

Introduction:
In A White Room

North Dakota is a fragile state. The grass cover is gone now, where roots once were thick and deep enough to make sod building blocks. Trees grow on their own only along river banks. Little offers protection— low buttes and hills in the west, but in the east a glacial lake bed so flat you think you can see the earth curve. Temperatures in a year may vary by as much as 150 degrees. The wind is unremitting, rain uncertain, snow and ice long-lasting. In dry seasons, the air can become black with soil moved by the wind.

The state's economy, based mainly on wheat and oil, is fragile too, and barely sustains education and social services even for the small population. In a year of low oil prices and drought, the talk is of farmers leaving the land and faculty leaving the universities. A hundred or so years ago, letters arrived at real estate offices from states like Pennsylvania and New Jersey inquiring whether the country would be good for families, and whether peach trees grew here. There are no peach trees in North Dakota, and while it is too late to wonder whether a place that cannot support peaches is fit for children and women (or men for that matter), there is no doubt this is, physically and economically, a precarious place to live.

Yet the landscape that looks so bleak and uninteresting the first time teaches one to see more carefully. A slight rise lifts out of the glacial lake-bed river valley, the beach ringed with gravel and sometimes shells of water creatures. Going west, one does not so much anticipate the mountains still several hundred miles away, as marvel that the land should rise and fall at all in open grassy hills. Fields of snow can look pale blue and reflect rainbow colors, corrugated by the wind. Children grow up thinking they deserve a 360-degree horizon. It is an exotic land. And, where people are few and far between, they may sometimes have a tolerance for difference that can be absent in urban areas.

While many are genuinely glad to be living here, and value opportunities they are pretty sure they would not find elsewhere, the more popular view is to complain. Derision is almost a local sport. North Dakota may be the least memorable of the fifty states, and the one that some people, when they arrive for a public appearance, are likely to say is the last of the states they had not visited. (They also are apt to think they are in South Dakota.)

For some who find themselves here, North Dakota is not a place that particularly stimulates the mind or fills the heart with a desire to remain. Young people, the state can claim, are its primary export. North Dakota has one of the nation's lowest high school drop-out rates, and while its graduates are sought after in other regions for being honest and hard working, within North Dakota young people tend to feel undervalued, claiming that little is done to encourage their talents.

Mental health counselors speak of a "North Dakota Syndrome," the conviction that nothing good can come from North Dakota, and that something must be wrong with anyone who is living here (let alone glad to be). To make sure that local talent is not over-valued, we tend to hold each other to higher standards than we would someone else, judging a thing worthy "even though" it was produced within the state. We find it hard to believe in ourselves, to take anyone seriously who persists in being North Dakotan. There is economic boosterism — and those who urge MX missile-shuttling installations because they will "stimulate the economy" — but little recognition given to artists, writers, artisans, or people who quietly have achieved any number of endeavors. Individual accomplishments are more likely to be recognized nationally or internationally than in one's home town. Era Bell Thomp-son, as an example, is better known nationally as an editor of *Ebony* magazine than she is in North Dakota, where her name is given to the Era Bell Thompson Black Cultural Center in Grand Forks. Apart from people who frequent the Center, few North Dakotans take notice of her, nor of her family who were early Black settlers.

These attitudes may well have historical foundations. The region was among the last to be settled, and became a refuge for the rural poor. For the most part, people with any wealth financed their way to the coastal and mountain states, or if they undertook the journey west soon enough, found land in the more southern plains. For a great many people who settled here, North Dakota was the end of the line. They came because their lives were so bad where they were — in economically or politically oppressed regions of Europe, or on failed farms in the eastern and midwestern U.S. — that they could not imagine the move to promise anything but improvement.

The precariousness of so many of these arrivals adds to the sense of fragility one can feel about the state, regardless of the much-touted toughness attributed to pioneers. Some realized their hopes, many did not. The considerable wealth that lies in farming and mining comes less from individual small farmers, the inheritors of the 160-acre homesteads, than from national and multi-national corporations. In spite of state regulations that try to limit corporate farming, land increasingly is being absorbed by fewer and fewer owners. But even apart from farming, the state's economy from its beginnings has been largely controlled by such corporate industries as railroads, coal and oil companies, and the military: two strategic defense airbases allow North Dakota to brag that it is the world's third largest nuclear power. We can imagine ourselves colonials, in a land belonging to someone else.

For some women, settlement may have seemed a double colonization. Women came to settle in North Dakota usually with families — husbands and fathers and sons, and while one needn't suppose that they were particularly "reluctant" pioneers, neither are many likely to have been the ones in the family to make the decision to come. A few women homesteaded on their own, although of those a good number filed claims only immediately before marriage in order to combine their acres with their husbands', as women after marriage could not file a homestead claim. Some women, often single or married and without children, report adventures and good times in coming here (dances, picnics, church socials) but for most women the generally harsh and sparse conditions were much harder to endure than for men. Women were often confined in small houses many miles apart without a community of friends; they did not have the mobility of men who worked often with other men and were likely to be the ones to make trips to town. The absence of doctors and other health services in rural areas was particularly difficult on women's childbearing, even though women healers, midwives, and neighbors did what they could to help each other.

In some ways, the agricultural frontier presented women with a step backwards, for, from the mid-nineteenth century on, life elsewhere was becoming more diverse, healthier, and less physically demanding, even for working class women. In more populated areas women were attending women's colleges, joining women's voluntary and cultural organizations, and moving to cities to find jobs as teachers, nurses, factory workers, and undertaking careers in a profession that had opened to them because of a new technology. Women were being employed as "type-writers." In cities women of all ages could enjoy cultural activities and social contacts; cities were important in the social and economic advances women made at the turn of the century.

The closeness of rural life, where most people know each other and many are related, provides easy social contact, but also acts as a check. Abuse against women, for instance, is thought to be even more under-reported in rural areas than in cities because of the lack of anonymity. Although North Dakota divorce rates have doubled in the last ten years, they still are lower than national averages, but not, probably, because marriages are that much happier here than elsewhere. While in the larger towns in the late 1980s gay and lesbian groups have begun to organize (mainly on college campuses), it still is more difficult here than in urban settings to sustain open lesbian relationships.

It is not that living in North Dakota is all that different from living elsewhere in the U.S. (many say), it merely exaggerates ordinary vicissitudes of life. It isn't different, it's just more so — more violent weather, greater isolation, less human response. But for all the difficulties, many, and we think women especially, feel a passionate attachment to their lives in the state. Sometimes people's narratives, whether recent or from a generation or two ago, sound contradictory. They will detail hardships — economic failure, bad weather, illness and family deaths — and also insist that those were wonderful years. If it is true that North Dakotans do not sufficiently appreciate talent in their midst, the same relative indifference tends also to mean that one is seldom interfered with. Often you can do pretty much what you want while no one is noticing, as it were (a state of affairs that reportedly has not escaped the notice of some survivalist and para-military groups). And it is easy to make contacts. In a total state population of 650,000 it takes a very few jumps to find someone who knows someone you want to contact. The results have been often imaginative, original, and fruitful undertakings — the NPL political movement of the 1910s, the "New School" innovations in education of the early 1970s, Chautauqua performances of the state Humanities Council, all models of innovation. In the rural regions of North Dakota, nurses' training programs, teachers' colleges and training institutes, and Catholic sisterhoods have provided important communities. There are good reasons for the strong loyalty and affection and fascination that many, women and men alike, feel about living in the subtle and complex region of North Dakota.

It is that kind of attachment and curiosity that brought us as editors to this book on women's lives in North Dakota, even as, somewhat in the ingenious manner of other improvisations in the state, we have invented the book as it went along. Its beginnings were auspicious. In October 1986, the North Dakota Centennial Commissions invited citizens to an open meeting to plan celebrations in 1989 for one hundred years of statehood. Thomas J. Clifford, President of the University of North Dakota, and Lieutenant Governor Ruth Meiers both suggested that the centennial was none too soon for a history of women in North Dakota. Ruth Meiers spoke to the gathering in the Senate chambers about women who had been important to North Dakota since the last century. Soon afterwards, she and President Clifford called a meeting of scholars and members of groups with interests in women's issues to initiate a project that, two years later, has evolved into this book.

Those of us who became its editors were fairly clear about the kind of book we envisioned: a reflection of the diversity of experiences of women in the state, to be read and enjoyed by the diverse women who were its authors and subjects, who would see places they knew, hear familiar voices and recognize their own lives. We became even more certain, as work progressed, about the kind of book we did not want. It would not be an auxiliary to text-book histories (as in "meanwhile the women . . ."). We did not want to give the impression that women's experience is adequately accounted for merely by tacking their doings onto a narrative otherwise primarily told about men — what is known as the add-women-and-stir method of compensatory history.

Nor would this book be a who's who of notable women; we were not willing to select a few with claims to notability from a multitude who, by omission, would be assumed to have none. The book does include some individual "lives," for a collective story partly depends on them. But these emphasize, we hope, the ways that an individual person reflects some part of the common experience. A physician named Helena Wink, for instance, would appear to have overcome prejudices against professional women, especially those who practiced medicine, by being not only extraordinarily competent, but also extraordinarily kind, lady-like, and just eccentric enough to be thought harmlessly amusing. She performed one of the first appendectomies (successfully) on her kitchen table, herself nursed and cleaned house for patients, and drove her buggy and then automobile recklessly. She created about her an aura of admiration and affection that virtually elevates her to folk hero. Dr. Helena Wink illustrates how one woman negotiated a life and career in what might have been an unfriendly place but for her special luster. The tactics that worked for her have certainly been useful to others. (The prostitute Little Casino similarly charmed her way into legend.)

A hundred writers answered a call for proposals, and the writings of over fifty are included here. The reflective essays by Lois Phillips Hudson and Louise Erdrich came at our request. The rest came in response to our call, and we have been mainly guided by them, seeing their variety as well as sometimes their incompleteness as reflecting the manner in which a "history" necessarily begins. For some that history is a family story, or the sequence of events leading to the founding and maintenance of an institution. And, for other writers, women's experiences in the state and region lead to analyses of the lives of women, and of the state in larger contexts. The several kinds of interests and points of view, we think, can respond conversationally to each other on the page. Because responses were so varied, so are the forms of these essays, and we have tried to design the pages to reflect these differing forms. There are essays that describe and analyze topics in fairly broad and comprehensive detail — as on groups of nuns. A second kind describe single aspects of the broader categories — Grey nuns, a handicapped child. Some of these appear on the page beneath a more general essay that they supplement and help to illustrate. A third form we think of as "snap-shots" — a few sentences that bring to life the particulars of an event. These varying modes, we hope, will reflect how people indeed think about experience: sometimes applying critical analysis to broad issues; sometimes accumulating details that are vital to appreciation and understanding but do not necessarily, at the moment, suggest abstract reflections. And sometimes a short, vivid story is whole by itself. We have tried to honor the variations of these perceptions.

It has also been our hope as editors to design a book that would be useful to those who wanted to continue studies of their own. The history of a hospital in Bismarck that focused on the work of the woman who first organized it might lead someone to write about the founder of a hospital or other institution in another town.

While we are gladdened to have found so many opportunities awaiting other investigators, there are some subjects, we freely admit, we wish might have been attempted for this volume. There is no systematic essay about women who taught in elementary and secondary schools, or about nurses, two omissions that surprise us when nursing and schoolteaching have been primary professions for women from earliest days of settlement to the present. (However, in the recent scholarship on women these topics, surprisingly, have not been well addressed either.) We regret not having more attention given to Black women and women of Hispanic descent, but would hope that as more women of minority groups other than Native Americans move into the state, writers will emerge to record their experiences. Women's business enterprises also need recording, especially weekly newspapers that in many towns are edited and staffed by women.

Some interesting issues and ventures are so recent in women's experience in the state that it may still be too soon to think of writing their history, but it is not too soon to keep track of documents that will become archival sources. Women have been active in the founding and staffing of alternative businesses, such as food co-ops, and in alternative schools, such as a "fresh air" school in Bismarck on Fannie Dunn Quain's front porch. A "history," properly speaking, of lesbian women may be just beginning in North Dakota, and while the presence of lesbians is hardly new, women feeling able to declare themselves in the more exposed atmosphere of a rural state is fairly recent here. Adult abuse centers, women's centers, and feminist groups and publications have been gaining strength and acceptance in the twenty years of the women's movement, and they deserve their chroniclers.

In all this variety and rich experience, how to order a book? If history can be described as a narrative of what people do, then what women mainly do, and have done in North Dakota, is work. There are a number of ways that one might arrange discussions about work: by kinds of work (housework, work caring for children, wage work, professional work), or by places of work (home, farm, office, school, hospital). But these divisions did not seem to us to fit the ways that women during the course of a life-time, or even a single day, moved among the quite varied categories of work they performed. We needed a more fluid principle to account for the various kinds of work women have done, whether for love, for duty or for money.

Thus women who are partners in a farm or ranch, according to their own reporting, do almost all of the housework, but typically they also "help" with field work, and often contribute a wage or salary to the family income from an off-farm job. The farm earns money but they presumably do not receive a wage; their housework is essentially for the maintenance of family and farm; and wage or salary from off-farm work goes into the kitty. How are such women to be described as workers? Work/non-work, earning or not earning money are fluid and complicated terms; nevertheless, we have wanted to pay attention to the way work flows in and around questions of earnings. The primary question is not whether or not women "work" — they do, one way or another — or even whether they work for money, for much, if not most, of the work they do is paid for, even if the women are not, or not enough.

The principle we are exploring in the arrangement of essays, the degree to which women are paid for the work they do, involves a movement from purely domestic work, which (depending on one's frame of mind at the moment), is done either for love or because it has to be done, to questions about work that women do for pay, and debates of equity and comparable worth that follow them into the labor force. A section on families portrays several generations of a single family, as well as shorter glimpses into the idea of family. The next group describes women's work mainly outside the context of family but still for "love" and little or no pay — what is termed "volunteer," and extends family obligations to the community. These include the volunteer work of women and some of the political causes women have worked for, like the anti-suffrage movement. Another category contains work for which the women themselves receive little or no pay, but the work itself may produce income. Sisterhoods of nuns have founded and operated hospitals and schools; the nuns receive support but not much cash, although the school or hospital charges for services.

Then there is work for which women do expect to be paid a wage or salary. Nurses, writers, artists, seamstresses, teachers and others are often not paid as much as men would be for similar effort or as their work ought to be worth; nevertheless, some of this work brings income. Women have sometimes found inventive ways of earning money, like barnstorming. The increased professionalization of women's involvement in politics illustrates a movement from volunteer to career commitments; women no longer exclusively support men who run for office, they prepare for and run themselves and look forward to careers in politics and government service.

Work then, we find, is an element that hardly varies among women who speak of their lives in North Dakota. "Work was everything," they say. In the early years, for settler women, work meant survival and was unremitting; it defined day-to-day lives and women's aspirations. Those who spoke of work as "survival" seemed to mean a degree of drudgery and exhaustion that barely kept one in the same place. For others, exerting great effort led to movement and change; it brought visible accomplishment: a woman might have founded a hospital and kept it running, begun a school for business students, organized fundraising for the building of a church. Native American women have solidified the political strength of their entire community by keeping solid the ties of their families. Of course there were, and are, pleasures as well — dances and parties and a great deal of visiting — but few speak of leisure and no one says she had nothing to do.

Physicists say that "work" occurs when there is a combination of "force and displacement in the same direction." Lifting an object is work, but holding it is not (there is no displacement); moving something on a plane back and forth does not qualify as work, for the displacement (sidewise) is not in the same direction as the force (upward). Stasis is the opposite of work.

North Dakota history, its settlement and continued habitation, evokes images of both stasis and work, and abounds as well as in moral, physical and economic contradictions. The state contains soil as rich as any on the globe; but in it are planted missile silos more thickly than almost anywhere else — the work of producing wheat cancelled by the stasis of non-productive bomber squadrons. Settlers made their strenuous moves, they often said, so that their children might have a fuller life than their parents had, yet the state has not sustained later generations of children, who leave again to settle in more hospitable places. But the greatest contradiction for any narrative that hopes to be part of a collective celebration involves the juxtaposition of Native Americans and Anglo-Europeans, the "history" of one marking the displacement of the other. There are countless ways that the language of this purported collective history has erased the Native American populations. Indians are listed with the weather and high shipping costs as one of the menaces of the settlement period; we hear of "the first white child" or "the first white woman" to appear in a given town or county, as though "white" were the only group that mattered. Early records about women at army forts, in religious missions, in hospitals and schools almost always assume that these institutions were exercising necessary, if not always benevolent services among Native Americans. It is difficult for critical scholars to ask why the Anglo-Europeans were there at all, and what difference would it have made to Native Americans if they had not been disturbed.

The complexion of the state has changed drastically in the last one hundred years in at least two differing patterns: from a sparse, diffuse population of native Indian people and early settlers, to a burgeoning of activity in towns and farmsteads (and some "boom" growth in western oil towns), then more reduction of population in the countryside during gradual although not very extended expansion of a few larger towns. Many of the losses since the end of World War II — the depopulation of villages and farmsteads — have erased the more visible signs of women's work, and what should have remained as women's public contributions to the state. Force and displacement of women's energies have ceased to move in the same direction. The village schools, the country churches, the square, two-storied, sometimes gabled farmhouses — these architectural monuments to women's presence are disappearing quickly from the North Dakota landscape. If women described in the pages of this book were to wonder how lasting was the work they did, there would not be a lot to reassure them.

The farmhouses are empty, the school districts consolidated and schoolhouses left unused, and rural churches moved to museum settings. Such social institutions as Ladies Aid, WCTU, the missionary societies became state-funded social service agencies, and book clubs and music clubs gave way to arts and humanities councils, usually directed by men (although women by federal statute sit on the councils and staff the agencies, especially at the lower ranks). Few may actually decry the loss of quilting bees and teacher institute picnics, but there hardly is enthusiasm for proposals to the legislature that it ensure "comparable worth" in workers' pay. Women's reward is martyrdom; they will not be remembered by the rural institutions which, chiefly, they built, nor are they likely soon to receive a full share in the major urban-based institutions that now employ them.

Too much of what does remain is spoiled in sentimentality. A hushed, awed silence falls like dust over the starched and ironed christening gowns, the wedding dresses, enamel coffee pots, iron bedsteads, ancestral portraits, sometimes a toy or two — all the brick-a-brack of historical society displays and antique shops. How are we to interpret these brave, sad remnants? Among the group of buildings clustered around one town's museum — a church, a school, a barbershop, postoffice — is a "pioneer home." The ceilings are low, the rooms small, floors uneven, and narrow stairs lead to a hot attic on a hot day.

To the side and under the stairway downstairs is a bedroom, the bed tucked under the slant of the stairs. Everything in the room is painted white: the walls, floor and ceiling are white; there is a white bedspread on a white bed; a side table, with bowl and jug, are white. The room had been prepared, the museum manager explains, for a sister of the woman who lived there and farmed with her husband. The sister had been told she would die in six months, but actually lived seven years, all of them nursed in that room. What must those years have been for her and for the farming couple, and why the daze of white?

Whether or not the family were imitating a hospital setting, the room and the fragmented story cannot help but make one think of suffering and sacrifice. The room could stand as a shrine to the one reward, of martyrdom, that rural agrarian communities freely bestow to women, in return, as it were, for the dismembered institutions they worked so hard to found.

But martyrdom is not good enough, nor is thinking that whatever anyone might do in North Dakota won't be worth much. To know what we are worth, it will help to tell of our past as fully and fairly as we can, trying to understand and not merely venerate what an entirely white room might have meant to the woman who lived and died in it.

Elizabeth Hampsten
Bjorn Benson
Kathryn Sweney
Summer 1988

Marjorie Nelson Peterson, daughter of
homesteader Grace Jacobson Nelson

The Child is Mother of the Writer

by Lois Phillips Hudson

In June of 1937, defeated by drought, Depression, and dust, my family left our rented half-section south of Cleveland, North Dakota, and moved to a farm in a valley fifteen miles east of Seattle. I was nine, and it was eleven years before I looked again at the spacious horizons of my native state. I had flown over it in the night, on my first airplane ride, to attend the National Intercollegiate Press Convention in Minneapolis, but I took the Empire Builder back to Seattle, and spent one of the most memorable days of my life gazing out of the train window. I felt as though I must not even let myself blink, so precious was this time to gaze and gaze at the earth that had made me.

I was totally alone in my enthrallment. All around me, the other passengers complained, ever more irritably as the hours passed, about the "boring" view. When, at last, we sighted the foothills of the Montana Rockies, the car was filled with sighs of relief: Thank heaven! Back in God's country!

Forty years later, I catch my jaws clenching when I remember how much I wanted to stand up in the middle of the Empire Builder and deliver a few crisp observations on the intellectual and spiritual limitations of persons who could appreciate only landscapes that go precipitately up and down. At that time I had not yet read many wise thoughts that could make my speech even better today. For example, "Nature never wears a mean appearance" (Emerson, *Nature*). Or Oliver Wendell Holmes: "Intelligence is not so much the capacity to learn as the capacity to wonder."

These two premises sum up nearly all that I want to say in what follows, but first I must speak of the savage response which mindless statements about my native state evoke in me. It was my own "savage," "wild," most "natural" time — my time for learning to love my birthplace as every animal learns to love it — that I spent on the northern Great Plains. My response to inane dismissals of that lovely part of my planet, where I first learned to love all of my planet, is the response of a creature who senses that its very survival is being threatened. For I do not doubt that persons who do not know that nature never wears a mean appearance are persons who have taken the first step toward dismissing the rest of their planet. Souls that cannot respond to the subtle planes and colors of the prairie earth or the grandeur of a prairie sky are souls that have lost much of their capacity to wonder, and who are, therefore, unconscious participants in the madness of a species which is destroying its own habitat.

On that train I was like Mole, in *The Wind in the Willows,*

> . . . when suddenly the summons reached him, and took him like an electric shock.
> We others, who have long lost the more subtle of the physical senses, have not even proper terms to express an animal's intercommunications with his surroundings, and have only the word "smell," for instance, to include the whole range of delicate thrills which murmur in the nose of the animal night and day, summoning, warning, inciting, repelling. It was one of those mysterious fairy calls from out the void that suddenly reached Mole in the darkness, making him tingle through and through with its very familiar appeal. . . .He stopped dead in his tracks, his nose searching hither and thither in its efforts to recapture the fine filament, the telegraphic current, that had so strongly moved him. A moment, and he had caught it again; and with it this time came recollection in fullest flood.
> Home!

We can see how deep is our need to *feel* "home" in this elemental sense when we see the appalling distortions of this instinct in city ghettos. (To me, our contemporary megalopolises are *all* ghetto, but I'm speaking here of those areas which we all recognize as ghettos.) Here we have adolescent gangs fighting over "territories," marking them with arcane graffiti, like animals branding trees and rocks with musk and urine, fiercely defending a perimeter of slum streets indistinguishable from any other slum streets, having to pretend that they have a *place,* a home that is worth defending. Seen in such a context, my furious reaction to my companions in the railroad car does not seem so very extreme, does it?

Why do great stretches of relatively unpopulated, relatively "flat" land seem to need a disproportionate amount of defending? My guess is that my species has so overcrowded its home with its own kind that most of us no longer grow up *placing* ourselves in relation to any landmarks other than ourselves and objects constructed by ourselves. Hence, most of us find a landscape relatively free of ourselves and our constructions unbearably "lonely." Further, most of us growing up deprived of natural variety are not able to appreciate any but the most extreme stimulations of our imaginations and senses. I believe Wordsworth was absolutely right, when he wrote in the *Preface to the Lyrical Ballads* (1800):

> The human mind is capable of being excited without the application of gross and violent stimulants; and he must have a very faint perception of its beauty and dignity who does not know this. . . .It has therefore appeared to me that to endeavor to produce or enlarge this capability is one of the best services in which, at any period,

a writer can be engaged....A multitude of causes, unknown to former times, are now acting with a combined force to blunt the discriminating powers of the mind....The most effective of these causes are the great national events which are daily taking place, and *the increasing accumulation of men in cities*, where the *uniformity of their occupations* produces a craving for extraordinary incident, which the rapid communication of intelligence hourly gratifies. (My italics)

What would Wordsworth have said of X-rated television channels, movies of chainsaw murders, and telephone pornography! How lucky I was to live my most formative years on the North Dakota prairie instead of next-door to a shopping mall, where all the strivings of the businesses to out-unique each other result always in more sameness. "The health of the eye," said Emerson, "seems to demand a horizon. We are never tired so long as we can see far enough." What kind of jaded, undiscriminating minds are being nurtured in horizonless mall arcades of beeping, popping, exploding video games? I tremble, thinking of the kind of readers and writers such an early environment may produce. All I know for certain, of course, is that I as a writer was completely shaped by growing up on farms, and that I certainly would not be the sort of writer I am if I had not spent my very most impressionable years in North Dakota. (As Teddy Roosevelt said, "I never would have been President if it had not been for my experiences in North Dakota.")

My mother kept not one, but three, "baby books" chronicling all the remarkable events in the life of her first-born. When I was three or four months old, she wrote, "No matter how fussy you are, if I take you outside, you will always stop crying and begin to gaze happily at the big world around you." That entry is accompanied by a snapshot of me in my grandmother's arms, swaddled in a bundle of blankets the size of a bushel basket, peeping out from under a ruffled bonnet at my grandparents' frozen farmyard. It must have been tedious to do all that bundling of us on a December day, but apparently it was the only amusement that would shut me up. Sixty years later, I still am infinitely more interested in being *out*side than *in*side, and I find that, generally speaking, it is much harder for me to describe the interior of a room or building than to picture for the reader any natural setting. And what could possibly be a healthier first horizon for the focus of an embryo writer than the Psalmist's "circle of the earth" as seen from the breast of a sweeping North Dakota hill?

Do most people born and raised in Megalopolis ever acquire the love for their planet that I felt by the time I was three or four years old? In *Nature and Madness*, Paul Shepard says,

Among those relict tribal peoples who seem to live at peace with their world, who feel themselves to be guests rather than masters, the ontogeny of the individual has some characteristic features. I conjecture that their ontogeny is more normal than ours and that it may be considered to be a standard from which we have deviated. Theirs is a way of life to which our ontogeny was fitted by natural selection, fostering a calendar of mental growth, cooperation, leadership, and the study of a mysterious and beautiful world where the clues to the meaning of life were embodied in natural things, where everyday life was inextricable from spiritual significance.

I have never doubted that living my most malleable years in North Dakota taught me, besides my love for this earth, that I am, indeed, a guest here. (In fact, when I was a college freshman, I wrote a poem in which I said, to the earth, "this flesh owes thanks of a beholden guest.") One genuine North Dakota blizzard can do more than millions of words to reveal the true relationship between my species and its planet!

For a number of years I stopped writing fiction and wrote articles about threats to our environment instead. I have a "brilliant" acquaintance who has a Ph.D. in American Literature from Harvard. One day she said to me, in complete serious-ness, "They can cover the whole earth with concrete for all I care. I care only about *people*." She grew up the daughter of a wealthy gynecologist in Los Angeles. I grew up in a two-room hut without electricity, plumbing, or other supposedly necessary "amenities," but I grew up enormously richer than she. Even in the home of a well-to-do doctor, she grew up in concrete, her eyes filled with smog, irredeemably jaded by the time she was twelve, and, by the time I met her, blinded by the hubris that so often seems to accompany what Paul Shepard would call "the abnormal ontogeny" of children surrounded by a man-made landscape. They call their world the "real world," the "big world," when, of course, it is a very *un*real, very *small* — and frequently very lonely world.

My companions on the train found the great stretches of land without people depressingly "isolated." Yet my guess is that most of them were unwitting members of David Riesman's "lonely crowd." "The greatest delight which the fields and woods minister," said Emerson, "is the suggestion of an occult relation between man and the vegetable. I am not alone and unacknowledged. They nod to me and I to them. The waving of the boughs in the storm is new to me and old. It takes me by surprise, and yet is not unknown." In *Arctic Dreams* Barry Lopez writes, "The land retains an identity of its own, still deeper and more subtle than we can know. Our obligation toward it then becomes simple: To intend from the beginning to preserve some of the mystery within it as a kind of wisdom to be experienced, not questioned. And to be alert for its openings, for that moment when something sacred reveals itself within the mundane, and you know the land knows you are there." During treaty negotiations with Washington state's first governor, Chief Seattle asked in his famous 1854 oration, "What will we do if the animals all die? Man will die of loneliness."

Sometimes I can't help wondering if many of the people in the lonely crowd have not already died of loneliness. Perhaps it is impossible for us to relate normally to each other if we don't grow up relating normally to a normal habitat. Perhaps growing up in concrete so isolates us from our own spiritual selves that we are like animals in concrete zoos, so alienated from their "normal ontogeny" that they refuse to obey that most basic "natural law," mothering their own offspring.

I know I did not feel at all lonely, standing beside my father on the one-plank platform of the drill, clinging to the long box filled with wheat, watching the working haunches of the horses, the wondrous grains trickling down through the cylinders planting them in the harrowed field. In those economically grim years, my parents could not give me fancy clothes or a fancy house, but they did give me a horizon.

Some years ago we took our small daughters to visit Yellowstone Park. I am still haunted by the words of a little boy about their age — seven or eight — who said, in strong, cynical, Brooklyn accents, "I bet they made that." We were watching an eruption of Old Faithful. I cannot help dreading that he, and millions like him, see all man-made and natural forces as part of some nebulous "they" ("'they' can cover the whole earth with concrete") against which all of us are equally powerless. I think that those of us who grew up with the natural forces in North Dakota acquired not only a decent humility I often find lacking in city-bred people, but also a much better sense than many of them have of what *nature* is responsible for and what our own species is responsible for. In my case, at least, this lesson from North Dakota wind and North Dakota sky has resulted not in pessimism but in optimism — and the energy to work to save my planet from, and *for*, my species.

The more I observe Megalopolis-bred people who have never experienced *space* as children, the more I fear for the earth. I wonder how a sufficient number of us will so love our birthplace that we will mature into a love of our planet fierce enough to contend successfully with the destroyers of our planet. The July/August 1988 *Greenpeace* reports, "One of the rivers flowing into Lake Michigan is so polluted with oil and grease that Landsat mapping satellites no longer recognize it as water." If the people living in the cities along that river understood, as I do, how precious water is, I think they would be marching on the polluters and demanding an economic system that does not insist on trading the destruction of the earth for jobs.

Speaking of those monotonous jobs that Wordsworth blamed for so much dulling of human sensibilities, I submit that the average farmyard of my childhood offers us incomparably more variety than can any ten-block area of Megalopolis. Take chickens, for example. Take the chickens of the greatest mock epic in English. I find that when I teach Chaucer's grand tale of Chauntecleer and Pertelote, I must spend at least one class period just talking about chickens. This I can do very well, as I have enough chicken stories to fill two or three weeks of class periods. However, the number of English professors who have spent years of Saturdays scraping the droppings from the floor of a chicken house is rapidly dwindling. When the last of us is gone, I wonder if any class reading "The Nun's Priest's Tale" will ever come close to a decent appreciation of it. Without firsthand experience or the help of us who have been there, will they possibly see and hear Pertelote prescribing for her lord and master "digestifs of wormes. Pekke hem right up and ete hem in." Or truly picture the wild climax of the "epic":

> Ran cow and calf, and eek the verray hogges,
> Sore aferd for berking of the dogges
> And shouting of the men and wommen eke.
> They ronne so hem thoughte hir herte breke;
> They yelleden as feendes doon in helle;
> The dokes criden as men wolde hem quelle;
> The gees for fere flowen over the trees;
> Out of the hive cam the swarm of bees.

Chaucer himself was dubious about the survival of his young language for more than a few generations. Yet that language can still be heard and understood across six centuries, and what Chaucer never even dreamed of has happened: it is the poor widow's farmyard that has nearly disappeared.

"Fiction depends for its life on place," says Eudora Welty in *The Eye of the Story*. She goes on to speak repeatedly of the "mystery" and "magic" in *place*:

One element is surely the underlying bond that connects all the arts with place. All of them celebrate its mystery. . . .From the dawn of man's imagination, place has enshrined the spirit; as soon as man stopped wandering and stood still and looked about him, he found a god in that place; and from then on, that was where the god abided and spoke from.

What kind of a god speaks to us from rows of glass and steel monoliths? What mystery or magic can a normal spirit feel in these lifeless horrors?

Welty goes on to say that "place can focus the gigantic, voracious eye of genius and bring its gaze to a point. . . .The art of focusing itself has beauty and meaning; it is the act that, continued in, turns into meditation, into poetry." Mystery plus magic plus surprise equal curiosity, discovery, and creation. As J. Bronowski put it in *Science and Human Values*, "The discoveries of science, the works of art are explorations — more, are explosions, of a hidden likeness" resulting in a new theory or a new metaphor. I feel quite sure that I would not have developed my particular kind of focusing power if I had spent my first ten years in a city — or even on the Washington farm where I finished my growing up. Paradoxically, living in so much unbroken space *requires* focusing in a way that living in a city or in very lush rumpled country may not. (Our twenty-acre farm in the Sammamish Valley was composed of five long steep hills — "not a level square foot on the property," as my grandmother observed.) But living in North Dakota space, one *must* wonder, one cannot escape, it seems to me, feeling oneself in the presence of the Infinite Mystery.

I remember sitting on the wind-seared steps of our paintless cottage, looking out across our pastures and the cornfield sloping up to the great sky, and wondering. If God made the earth and the stars, then who made God? Where did *He* come from? Like many small children I was fascinated by tiny things, always looking for the very tiniest things. I came to the conclusion that God must have begun as something like the tiniest living thing I had ever seen — the bright red spider mites skittering across a green leaf. God must have started out as a very strong little creature, perhaps even smaller than the spider mite, and then just made Himself grow and grow and grow until He was big enough to make the Universe. I was six or seven when I arrived at this answer to the question that none of my Sunday School teachers ever answered. Now we have the Big Bang theory of the creation of the Universe — the beginning of it all from one unimaginably small seed. As Blake would say, "To see the world in a grain of sand." That's focusing.

Of course I don't mean to imply that the North Dakota prairie is the *only* place that nurtures a sense of universal mystery. I can speak only of what shaped *my* imagination, *my* focusing, *my* uniqueness, for it is really impossible for one human being ever to understand completely the workings of another human being's imagination — which is why each of us truly lives her/his life in the solitude of that imagination. (An excellent reason for launching it in a natural setting, as Shepard insists.) Starting out in the prairie space taught me early this truth, and taught me early to begin dealing with it.

To some of us, this image of our solitary selves in space is almost unbearable. Pascal said, "The eternal silence of those infinite spaces terrifies me." When I was five, my mother began teaching me the constellations above us in the wide prairie night, and I have always felt even more *wonder* than terror contemplating space.

Einstein, in *Out of My Later Years*, described the way I feel about those infinite spaces: "I live in that solitude which is painful in youth, but delicious in the years of maturity." I learned to listen to that "eternal silence" in a world filled with transcendental experiences.

When I first read Wordsworth's "Intimations of Immortality" in high school, I felt a dazzling recognition. Here, exactly, was my own early childhood,

> when meadow, grove, and stream,
> The earth, and every common sight,
>   To me did seem
>   Appareled in celestial light,
> The glory and the freshness of a dream.
>
>   . . .
>
>   Those shadowy recollections,
>   Which, be they what they may,
> Are yet the fountain light of all our day,
> Are yet a master light of all our seeing.

"Surprised by joy," I wandered across the fields or prowled the groves of our north and south windbreaks, my heart leaping up at the dash of a baby rabbit I frightened from behind a clod; the fairy wonder of newly hatched killdeer, perfect miniatures of their mother, making their first excursion into the stubble; the breath-taking nearness of a brown creeper pecking its way up a tree trunk; the swoop of an angry king-bird brushing my hair; the astounding beauty of a nest of robin's eggs; the glorious music of blackbirds and meadowlarks ringing from slough and fence; the gallant clump of lavender crocuses suddenly appearing on the sunny side of a glacial boulder; the single prairie rose blooming against so many odds — as precious to me as was the Little Prince's one rose on his unique planet: entranced by the mystery of every wind-shadow moving in the wheat, every snowbank melting into shimmering new grass, every far-off curve of the earth spinning out of the radiant northern twilight.

Now, in my later years, I am different from Wordsworth in one marvelous way. I do not grieve that "there hath passed away a glory from the earth." I wonder if that is because my landscape-teacher taught me how to focus so intensely. "The light of common day" is still more than enough to bring me those transcendental moments Wordsworth describes so magnificently in "Intimations." A couple of years ago I drove to Mount Rainier and hiked all day along the trails on its awesome lower flanks. Though the mountain is only a hundred miles away, I seem to manage a trip there only about once every three or four years, and this day had been so fine that I couldn't bear to leave, even though I knew that the longer I lingered, the wearier the long drive home would be. With every step down the trail to the lodge parking area, I felt sadder and sadder. Heavy with the pain of parting, I climbed into the car and gazed one last time up at the snowy peak reflecting the pink of the sunset far to the west. Then that "electric shock," that "moment when something sacred reveals itself within the mundane" seized me. I heard that transcendental voice that has spoken on great occasions since I was little: You are not leaving it behind. The mountain is inside you.

I'm sure that it was all that space outside and inside my solitary self when I was six or seven (Welty talks of "these inner and outer surfaces [of place and person] that lie so close together and so implicit in each other") which made it so simple for me to discover that Mount Rainier has always been inside me.

Since the mountain is inside me, it makes no sense at all to think of "conquering" it — just as the idea of "conquering space" seems the acme of witless — and dangerous—hubris. Why *do* we think we must "conquer space"? Is it because those of us who are obsessed by this idea grew up in cities, and space is something foreign, to be feared? Perhaps the reason I can't work up any enthusiasm for blasting our resources off to "conquer" space is that from my beginnings I have known myself to be *of* space.

One thing I am certain of is that Wordsworth was right when he said, "The child is father of the man." Even more certainly, the child is mother of the writer. "Should the writer, then, write about home?" asks Eudora Welty.

> It is both natural and sensible that the place where we have our roots should become the setting, the first and primary proving ground, of our fiction. Location . . . is to be discovered, as each novel itself, in the act of writing, is discovery. Discovery does not imply that the place is new, only that we are.

I cannot state, any better than that, the mystery of the life-long re-discovery of place, of one's roots.

One bleak November day when I was seven, my father came home with two weighty packages — a radio stuffed with wires and tubes, and the big battery that powered it. He set it on a shelf, connected the wires, and turned the knob. I entered the Electronic Age to Xavier Cugat's orchestra playing "The Isle of Capri." Most of the words meant little to me, but how I was enchanted by that nostalgic simple melody! How filled with undreamed-of wonders, of gorgeous colors and strange animals, of new tastes and smells and adventures must be the Isle of Capri! For many years I was haunted by the Isle of Capri.

Now I know that the Little Prince was right. The mystery is that "What is essential is invisible to the eye." In the Twelfth Century, Hugh of St. Victor wrote, "From boyhood, I have lived in exile, and I know with what grief the spirit sometimes deserts the narrow limits of the poor man's hut, and with what a sense of freedom it afterwards despises marble halls and panelled ceilings." The splendid spaces of North Dakota helped me to understand what Hugh of St. Victor meant. If we are honest, we admit that ultimately we all live in a certain irreducible measure of solitude and that there would be no possibility of human dignity if this were not true. With what a sense of freedom my spirit, nurtured in the wide horizons of the Great Plains, despises our planet-destroying fantasies.

Whatever enchantments the Isle of Capri might offer, I would not trade them for the enchantments of half a square mile of earth two miles southeast of Cleveland, North Dakota.

Lois Phillips Hudson lives in Seattle, where she teaches in the University of Washington English Department. She is the author of the novel *Bones of Plenty,* **1962, and a collection of stories** *Reapers of the Dust,* **1965, set in North Dakota.**

Winter 1977. Photo by Jeff Green. Courtesy of UND Special Collections.

Louise Erdrich crowned "Queen of the Wops," Wahpeton High School, 1972.

Conversions

by Louise Erdrich

On the road to Damascus, Saint Paul of Tarsus was struck with blinding light and converted to belief in one true God. In more humble and hometown circumstances, I, too, was the victim of a bolt. Only mine occurred in 1961, on the Ninth Street sidewalk on the way to Zimmerman School in Wahpeton, North Dakota, and the bolt itself was unhurled, which meant it hung over me a good many years.

It is impossible to remember back and calculate the order of ideas going through my seven year old brain in order to produce the thought that stopped me cold on that threatening, overcast morning. Whatever they were, I suddenly wondered if God, about whom I'd heard so much, was real. There were already ominous rumors adrift on the Indian School Campus, where my family worked and lived, regarding Santa Claus, the Easter Bunny. So far, however, no one had mentioned God.

I stood for a long moment, before a deep pink house upon which a small white sign was hung advertising the services, within, of a licensed Swedish masseuse. Times were innocent. People went there and just got their shoulders kneaded. I looked up into the sky, regarded the darkening assembly of clouds, and then my heart beat fast. I knew I was about to say something aloud, and I did. When the words came out, I awed myself.

"You're not really up there!" I whispered.

I expected a jag of lightning, a bolt of thunder, some sign of outrage, if not an immediate sizzling direct hit that would, as my cousin convinced me lightning did to humans, turn me to hamburger. But absolutely nothing broke the stillness except, from a distance, the electrical jangle of the first bell.

I was just a year short of making my first confession and receiving Holy Communion, about which I mainly remember the struggle not to lose balance and become overwhelmed by the yellow spots that danced before my eyes, not to faint into the aisles of Saint John's church. For by then I had begun to swoon at every Mass that I attended, always right after the congregation shuffled to the front and received the Host on their tongues. In that hush of suspension, when the priest muttered to himself and everyone was silent and reflective around me, I seemed to feel the clouds pressing down. The ornate chandeliers hung, fragile and immense, above me on linked chains and I would try to keep certain thoughts from entering my mind: how were the lightbulbs changed? What ladders could reach that high? Who in the world had the courage to climb them?

If I visualized a climber on the spindly and impossible rungs, the golden haze would spread, the strength would flood from my limbs, and I would collapse. So over time, and with the help of ordinary events, the days of school and summer that came and went, the warmth of my busy parents, the necessities of fitting in among my classmates, I controlled my fantasies. I stopped thinking things that made me dizzy. I grew up. Years went by and I grew increasingly adept at this, until, finally, at the other end of my undistinguished school career, which was mainly a struggle to fit somehow, anyhow, into the ornate schemata of female social alliances, I could almost congratulate myself on not having thoughts at all.

How else to explain the zeal and determination with which, a decade later as a high school senior, I tried to become the Queen of the Wops?

There are confessions I make, even now, late at night, only to those who love me for myself. The first is the name of my hometown team, the Wahpeton Wops; the second is my short but unforgettable reign as their homecoming queen.

At the time, the fall of 1971, I was terribly proud, ecstatic even when my name was announced over the school P.A. system along with the other members of the Royal Court. It did not occur to me that, should I actually win the title, I'd be queen of an ethnic slur.

Of course, to Wahpetonians, the Wop was a mascot of rather undeterminate smurflike nature. A friend of mine had even constructed a costume to represent the Wops at games. It consisted of a dark purple bedsheet into which eyeholes were cut. Years later, an Italian friend visiting the community was astonished and then pained to hear the words of our defiant song issue from a passing schoolbus . . . *We are the Wops, the mighty mighty Wops, everywhere we go, people want to know, who we are, so we tell them, WE ARE THE WOPS !*

I could tell by the bewildered look in his eyes, the shamed anger, that the word didn't just amuse people but could actually hurt.

I was a long shot for the title because I didn't belong to the popular group of girls, the ones who swung their hair, stood in clumps, slept at each other's houses and vacationed in "DL" (short for Detroit Lakes), and partied. Our school was carefully stratified, relationships between girls were calibrated and maintained. My friends and I were those whom hard work drew together — the yearbook editor, the newspaper columnists, those who took advanced typing, set up scenery for school plays, joined Chemistry Club, and decorated the gym for prom — the serious girls.

These were the days before girl's sports were organized; indeed, we were not allowed to do the splits lest our virginity suffer. Every gym day, we stood in line, and those who had their periods stepped out and, sheepishly, said the word "observing" as though menstruation were a thing happening to our bodies, not ourselves. "Observers" were permitted to sit on the stage and gossip, and the word itself was a euphemism known throughout the school, snickered at when teachers used it in a lecture. Because we girls had no athletic teams or activities to democratize us, as boys did, we were forced to rely for status solely on our grooming, our clothing, and the cultivation of something that I never got the hang of — cuteness.

Cute was a combination of things, not just a certain look, not just money or a quick wit or self-confidence. It also involved, as I now realize, the final suppression of every original thought. Still, after years of trying, I had come no closer to cuteness than that fluke nomination, which, however, decided me in my aspirations. Desperately, wholly, and with a passion beyond myself, I wanted to be elected the Queen.

"This is the greatest challenge of my life," I wrote solemnly in my journal, never realizing that the very act of keeping a journal, of having secret thoughts, was what barred me from cuteness in the first place and made the whole enterprise so difficult. Later in that notebook I meditated on the word "popular" and it came as a kind of revelation that the definition meant, simply, having lots of friends. Lots and lots! Then it also dawned on me that there were many potential friends (voters) in Wahpeton High School that the designated popular girls did not notice in their daily pre-class perambulations through the hallways. So I did notice them. Homecoming candidates did not campaign with posters, with slogans. They were never so crass. Instead, charm was used, constantly applied, full pressure. But where my opponents ricochetted it mainly off each other, I spread around whatever charm I could muster.

The young, for instance: Those innocent ninth graders who did not understand the subtleties of senior class distinctions, might welcome a little attention. And how about the wild-eyed junior botanists who discovered North Dakota ditchweed before the widespread use of herbicides? They had a vote apiece, if they remembered to cast it. And the guys who only cared to work on their cars? I'd admire their lifters, their fancy grills. The members of the chess club? I knew (embarrassing admission for a girl at the time) how to play chess. And the choir members, the piano accompanists, the doggedly but somehow unsuccessfully "cute," the earnest "personality girls" — would I, could I, win their votes?

I tried. I became the first populist homecoming candidate, even if nobody else was aware of it. I brought my campaign to the masses and gave up for lost those elite few who would vote for other members of their group no matter what.

I did have one ally on the court, a surprise nominee, like me, but predictable also since she was absolutely gorgeous — tall, with dreamy blue eyes, a rose and cream complexion. Her problem, the reason she was not in the in-group, was that she was somehow too nice to be cute. She blushed constantly and her figure stunned grown men in their tracks. I'd seen it happen on Dakota Avenue, during Krazee Daze, a man dropping a drumstick right out of his hand at the barbecued chicken feed, when she walked past him. But this friend was so nice that she wouldn't have believed it, too kind to have any vaulting ambitions.

Other problems: Royal courtesans required a boy on their arms, and I was thwarted in my first escort idea. I wanted my brother Mark, a junior, to walk down the floodlit aisle with me on Homecoming Night, before the big football game. He was handsome, about my height, too, and a lettered cross country runner. But he did not play football and so was automatically vetoed by the contest organizers, who were strict on protocol.

On the rebound, I chose the person with the broadest based support imaginable. An eagle scout. If I couldn't have a blood relation for support, I would get the whole pack's vote.

I make my plans sound thoroughly premeditated, energetic and ridiculous, but in a way I think of this whole time of my social life as sad. The proof is in my journal, filled with words of angst, of conviction that the prettier and nicer you are, the better the world will treat you, of absolute reliance on female cunning, a learned response that, later in life, would cause me to set my hair with electric steam rollers during the very first stages of labor.

I assumed that if I "looked nice" while delivering my daughter, I would be treated better in the hospital. Perfectly styled hair would dispel pain. Yes, absurd. By the time I was panting and pushing, no one was the slightest bit interested in the upper end of me, least of all myself. I had quickly become so absorbed that I did not even get the chance to comb out my curls. My hair is lumpy in the first pictures of mother and daughter, but I look like I am having thoughts all over the place, and so does she.

As homecoming inexorably neared, the royal gowns were constructed with insane amounts of wrangling. Purple velvet was the material of choice, the style Empire, decorated at the bodice with tiny purple ruffles and a band of hotly contested silver braid. I bought silver lame bedroom slippers, and planned my coif like an architect. I also began to overeat from nervousness so that, on The Night, the zipper burst and my mother had to sew me into my dress by hand. And then there followed a claustrophobic, blank, uncertain hour in which I wished all of this had never taken place. Standing in the girl's locker room, looking at myself in the mirror, I hardly recognized or much liked the young woman who pushed at her lacquered ringlets.

God should have struck me then, having saved His chance for all those years. It had occasionally crossed my mind that He might have held back because He was, by my own reasoning, All Merciful. At this moment, however, I really deserved no mercy. In a frenzy of ambition I had denied everything but victory. I kept such ideas at a distance by humming Pomp and Circumstance as I walked down the aisle and stood before the dias that my own hardworking friends had lovingly decorated. The stage was all tin foil, purple streamers, and for the royalty, antique wooden chairs made to resemble actual thrones. The auditorium blurred, my parents and sisters and brothers were somewhere out there, and a hush fell as the world waited for the fateful announcement.

There was a strange moment, when it happened, as I felt the crown descend and fit onto my skull. What was happening to me was not completely wonderful, as I had imagined, but rather in a faint way, it was a push to the edge of some unexpected boundary. A proof. If I tried hard enough I could garner things I craved, but I wouldn't be the same once I got them. Nothing, nothing is quite as untarnished as one imagines, except the actual and true exchange of love.

In a photograph of that night, taken by our school photographer and given to me by his daughter, a member of the Wopanin Yearbook staff, I am screaming, "No, no, no!" This is not the picture of a person proud of what she's done, or even very pleased with what's happening. It's an image of a young woman afraid of her own power, soon to be surprised that the crown, which looked so glittery from below the stage last year, is welded from scrap metal and glued with bits of blue glass. The longstem roses, thrust into her arms, bristle now, but by morning they'll be deader than nails.

I should have put the roses in water. I should have done a lot of things. The thorns scratched, but I clutched them as I approached the microphone, and said:

"I'd like to thank the other members of the Royal Court, to say to the football team, 'We're Gonna Win!', to thank my teachers and thank everyone, my family, my friends, and especially the members of the high school band and those of you parents who will be observing . . . (here I stop, in horror, swallow and retrieve myself) . . . the game."

Louise Erdrich lives in Cornish Flats, New Hampshire. She is the author of *Love Medicine* (1984), *The Beet Queen* (1986), and *Tracks* (1988), published by Holt, Rinehart & Winston.

Nellie G. Sparling, 1914

It was then moved by Mr. Fox, seconded by Mr. Kelly, that the Council express their appreciation for the very excellent services of the ladies of the Women's club, and particularly the committee of which Mrs. Arthur Sparling is chairman, for their efforts towards improving the City Park and that a record of same be incorporated in the minutes of this meeting. Motion carried, all voting in favor.

Minutes of Langdon City Council, May 4, 1925.
(Contributed by Audrey Mahoney Will
Dayton, Ohio.)

Members of the Fargo branch of the American Pen Women in the 1950s.

Professing Culture: A History of North Dakota Clubwomen

by Sheryl O'Donnell

Must we claim unalienated self, body, labor? Or should we denounce and undo the reigning illusion that projects alienation onto one class and represents and rationalizes another as in command?
Jane Gallop, "The Mother Tongue" 1981

At various intervals in our lives it is well to reexamine the roots of our present culture; it keeps us from being too intrigued with the fantasies of success, forgetting that all destinies cannot be controlled by our educated selves.
Historian's Records, Fargo Fortnightly Club, 1976-1981

More than one way to skin a cat, my dears!
Edna LaMoore Waldo, *The Pen-Gram*, 1937

Not until the last two decades have professional and academic historians noticed women's clubs. Of course, women's clubs have kept their own records since their inception. And many of them have found their way to libraries and archives. But these records are haphazardly collected and maintained. They lie in boxes marked "Miscellaneous" or "Women," suffering the same obscurity that Virginia Woolf lamented in 1929, when she looked in a British library for information on Women and Fiction. Women's clubs, when noticed at all by academics, are not sympathetically viewed. Here, for instance, is a description of a Friendship club for women convening in rotation at the homes of eight Midwestern women after World War II:

The food served is not only competitive but unwise, since all members are striving to preserve their figures. After a luncheon of lobster or crab meat, tuna baked in shells, chicken patties, lavish salads, and New York ice cream, they settle down to bridge with their hats on and their shoes pushed off under a card table. Their voices rise higher and higher, their short-range view of human events becomes crueler and crueler as they double and redouble one another's bids, make grand slams and quarrel over the scoring. No reputation is safe with them, and every member must be present to preserve her own. The innocent are thrown to the wolves, the kind made fun of, the old stripped of the dignity which belongs to their years. "They say" is the usual phrase when a good name is auctioned off the block. "They say" she has cancer; "they say" that he was running around; "they say" (Maxwell 1954).

This fictional account comes from William Maxwell's novel, *Time Will Darken It*, written in 1948, and is quoted by the sociologist of Midwestern town life, Lewis Atherton, who spends a total of three pages on women's clubs in his 423-page social analysis, and presents this fantasy as an accurate portrayal of female culture in the American Midwest. Today, academic historians such as Gerda Lerner (1979), Karen Blair (1980), and Anne Firor Scott (1982) have demonstrated how the formation of middle-class women's clubs after the Civil War led to every major social and humanitarian reform dubbed "The Progressive Era" by traditional historians. The settlement house movement, the public health movement, the push for civic and humanitarian reform, the education of immigrants, the improvement of sanitary conditions, the installation of orphanages and hospitals and public parks and libraries and art museums may be traced to women's clubs and associations. These facts stand in stark rebuttal to the fiction just quoted, where a circle of women threatens civilization. The mythical Friendship Club of Maxwell's novel is a witches' coven of rage and nakedness and gluttony, a sinister black hole of death-dealing chaos, an anti-community. Pope's drawing-room scenes in *The Rape of the Lock* serve as a tutor text for this quotation. Now the Cave of Spleen is aboveground and on Main Street, Middle America.

But I want to move beyond corrective criticism of this passage, beyond the progressive theories of women's history which "save" women from men's horrified gaze by explaining their pleasures away. Men's stories of women's clubs have at least one advantage over Scott's careful history: they are paranoid, and therefore make the very connections which Scott must sever. Indeed, my study of North Dakota clubwomen in part confirms the destructive power of women's groups, a power often noted by clubwomen themselves. Maude Krake Backlund, whose column "Deuces Wild" ran each Thursday in her husband Charles' *Benson County Gazette*, summed up her forty years of covering the Lisbon, North Dakota, social scene thusly in 1941:

It was during the first week of our married life, our wedding having been neatly sandwiched between two Thursdays, I learned that something more than his [her husband's] ardent affection for me had urged him toward a speedy marriage. I discovered what all wives of young country-weekly editors learn sooner or later: someone must write up the weddings, "obits," programs, and parties, dig up items for the local page, read proof, and it is cheaper to marry a reporter than to hire one. The ghost must walk for the rest of the forces on Saturday night, but wives are easily paid in a little feasting, flattery and affection.

In the lively young years of our Northwest town, the social side of life was stressed unduly. When Mrs. Astor gave a party, the editor's wife received her invitation in a true Tommy Tucker spirit. She expected to sing for her supper in next Thursday's issue. Then Mrs. Vanderbilt would give a dinner meant far to outdo Mrs. Astor's, and poor Cinderella of the country press would be there. Midnight would find her shorn of her finery, pounding out upon a balky typewriter a quarter of a column of small-town stuff, and cursing Noah Webster for failing to record enough synonyms for delicious as applied to food.

Backlund, herself a North Dakota clubwoman and correspondent of Sinclair Lewis, provides a valuable glimpse of some complex ironies here, ironies which invariably arise when clubwomen themselves tell their stories. Connections between private lives and public duty, between the call to civic duty and the zeal for moral reform, are uneasy. My purpose in this essay is to clarify some of these connections by asking how clubwomen themselves have told their stories. I will explore how they have used the tools of speech and writing, necessarily associated with the assumption of public, male, discourse, for their own purposes and their own pleasures. The approach I will use was inspired by a Wisconsin clubwoman's notes on North Dakota clubwoman Edna LaMoore Waldo, whose book, *Leadership for Today's Club Woman* appeared, with an introduction by the editor of *Woman's Home Companion*, in 1939: "Mrs. Waldo took down the club women's hair, combed out the snarls, and put it back up again." The self-consciousness of this analogy — its attention to craft, to private arrangement for public style — directs my remarks.

I want to argue that the work of North Dakota clubwomen was public, overt, and self-dramatizing. They linked the state's women writers, artists, journalists, teachers, librarians, social reformers, and lecturers to a national network of self-consciously professional women who clearly saw their work as a means to uplift themselves by educating American society. While giving lip service to the centers of male power — banks, the legislature, the War Department — North Dakota clubwomen shifted public attention away from these male-dominated institutions to aesthetics and moral improvement, realms where women could prevail. That these realms were utterly genteel and utterly racist must be faced and accounted for. That North Dakota clubwomen have a paradoxical history which is both maddening and sad must be admitted. Yet, in the telling of their history lies much hope for a better understanding of women as producers, not mere consumers, of culture.

North Dakota women have recorded their histories in "official" ways for nearly 100 years. Here is a typical biography of a clubwoman, entered anonymously, perhaps by the subject herself in the April 1927, Fargo "State Record":

Miss Christin Corse (Mrs. Robert M. Pollock), a native of Racine, Wisconsin, born December 1854, moved to Fargo in 1897 and with her husband, became identified with every moral movement for the betterment of city and state — particularly the WCTU, the State Enforcement League and Fargo College. Mrs. Pollock is a pioneer member of the Fortnightly Club, the State Federation of Women's Clubs, a member of the Fargo Board of Education, teaches Women's Bible Class and is a Deacon in the First Presbyterian Church, and for twenty years the managing editor of the White Ribbon Bulletin, the organ of the state WCTU. She is an enthusiastic Suffragist and contends that she can exercise her "legal right" and cast her vote on public questions without interfering with her duties to her home. She is the faithful Mother of five sons and two daughters.

This "official" biography makes clear a characteristic rhetorical strategy of North Dakota clubwomen. Mrs. Pollack's public accomplishments are capped by a pious nod toward her private duties. The last sentence justifies her monumental efforts to reorganize American culture from a woman's point of view. And here is the source of both power and paradox in clubwomen's self-portrayal: rather than serving as apologists for female oppression, they used the culture's favorite myths about women to change the world.

Clubwomen were informally organized in Dakota Territory days, and they used genteel gatherings to raise money for their various charities. In 1887, for instance, a Mrs. Sate from Fargo organized a "Living Whist" entertainment to raise money for what became the North Dakota Children's Home. She hired a group of Chicago entertainers to train sixty men and women, dressed as playing cards, for a performance of drills and dances. Her extravaganza attracted the attention of one Colonel Morton, who donated lots, on the outskirts of Fargo on 10th Street South, for the orphanage.

In 1890, North Dakota legislators gave women the right to vote for state and school officials, although they used separate ballot boxes until 1923. The North Dakota Federation of Women's Clubs was organized in July 1897, under the leadership of Mary Whedon, editor and manager of the WCTU newspaper, *Western Womanhood*. When Whedon suggested a Woman's Day be held at the Devils Lake

---

After my younger brother was delivered by Dr. Helena Wink (of Jamestown), a woman from Homer Township in Stutsman County was hired to cook and clean and tend my mother and baby brother for a couple of weeks. Her name was May Warren, and this was how she helped supplement the income for her farm and large family. I can remember seeing her wash the sheets every day in a wash tub, wring them out by hand, and hang them on the clothesline in the freezing February weather. She still found time to clean the house and cook delicious meals.

Lorraine Fairfield
Eldridge, N. D.

Chautauqua, eight women's clubs attended. And a ninth was quickly added in compliance with the General Federation of Women's Clubs rules for organizing state chapters. The NDFWC mission was to "bring women of the state into communication for acquaintance, mutual helpfulness, and the promotion of higher intellectual, social, and moral conditions." All clubs in the state who were "organized for literary, artistic, musical, philanthropic, scientific, or other educational purposes, who owed allegiance to no political or sectarian control," were welcome. Standing committees of the newly-formed NDFWC included music, sweat shops, library, household economics, education, and forestry (Alsop 1975).

Of course not everyone was pleased by the statewide organization of North Dakota clubwomen, particularly because they insisted upon being thought of as professionals. One disgruntled Fargo town luminary, Colonel C. A. Lounsberry, himself an amateur historian, complained in a November 1897 issue of the *Fargo Record:*

> Women are engaging in all business and professional pursuits to such an extent that they are making serious inroads on the opportunities of men to gain a means of livelihood — tramps, hoboes and crooks are recruited from those thrown out of employment because women have taken their place. . . .I don't mind having women in such jobs as nursing, teaching, and domestic service, but, doggone it, they are getting so uppity they insist on doing stenographic work and engaging in business activities.

Since Colonel Lounsberry's own wife was president of the Bunker Hill Chapter of the DAR, formed in 1897, his household was no doubt tainted by clubwomen's activities. Even the Great Flood of that year seemed powerless against the new upsurge. Several Fargo women's clubs agitated for a public library, a plan mostly opposed by men. The question was put on a city ballot in the form of a one mill levy, but many polling places were submerged by flood waters. Since one of the polling places, the Water Works, was approachable by rowboat, many women stuffed their ballots down the chimney. When their efforts proved vain, they started a library anyway, buying books to donate, giving from private collections, and storing the books in the office of Fargo Mayor Johnson and later in the basement of the Masonic Temple (Alsop).

From 1899 to 1918, the North Dakota WCTU introduced a women's suffrage bill in every legislature. International feminists, including the British radical Sylvia Pankhurst, visited North Dakota at the invitation of clubwomen. In 1907 the General Federation of Women's Clubs urged its members to study the conditions of working women and children in their sessions, since, claimed the GFWC, "there is little intelligent interest in the matter." That year the Fargo Fortnightly Club resolved to work for

1. 10 hours maximum per day, 60-hour work week.
2. No work in industry before 6 AM or after 9 PM .
3. Chairs for workers and adequate toilet facilities.
4. Sufficient inspectors to enforce labor laws.
5. Hours of labor posted in workrooms (Schroeder 1983).

And at its 1914 state convention in Jamestown, NDFWC delegates heard a keynote speech, "The Woman's Movement," by Mrs. Robert LaFollette of Wisconsin. The delegates pledged to promote:

1. Fly-proof barn boxes for manure.
2. Hunting up foreign-born women and encouraging them to keep up lace work, weaving, etc.
3. No spitting on sidewalks or floors of streetcars.
4. Milk inspection.
5. Hot lunch at school.
6. Studying English literature from its origins to the present.
7. Working to eradicate the causes of TB, childhood's greatest menace.
8. Moral training in the public schools (North Dakota Federated Women's Club, Miscellaneous File 1913-14 and 1916).

North Dakota clubwomen lobbied local, state, and national levels of government for social reform. In 1911, for instance, the Round Table Club of Fargo led the campaign for a city nurse. The City Commission appointed Miss Grace Robinson, who surveyed the scene and then reported on four conditions which "greatly retarded the cleanliness of Fargoans":

1. Lack of bathing facilities.
2. Lack of privacy.
3. Lack of water.
4. Lack of desire, the latter being the crux of the matter.

According to the Round Table Club minutes,

> The gentle sex considered, resolved on a course of action, descended on the Board of Education and were granted permission to use the Washington School facilities. Miss Robinson personally scrubbed Jewish children on Friday and Gentile juveniles on Saturdays — a number of adults used the tubs by special appointment (Alsop).

Washington School in Fargo was also the site of an educational experiment by Miss Virna Johnson, school principal and Supervisor of Health Education in North Dakota in the 1920s. Miss Johnson's "open-air school" was kept at 60 degrees, windows open at all times, and special mackinaws, with hoods, provided for teachers and pupils. Other less radical, and more lasting educational reforms promoted by the NDFWC include the establishment of kindergartens, parent-teacher associations, mandatory high school education, teacher training standards, teacher pensions, equal education for girls, hot lunch programs, playground equipment, state-paid school tuition, and scholarships for higher education. The NDFWC Pioneer Woman Project, launched to honor women's contributions to North Dakota settlement, included collections of teachers' reminiscences of their daily work lives in the state. A typical reminiscence is that of Susan Stowell Vance, born in Conway, Iowa, in 1879, who moved to Dakota Territory in 1883, completed eighth grade in Barnes County in June 1894, and began teaching with her sister Rachel three years later. Her teaching career lasted from 1897 to 1903, when she married and thus became ineligible for her profession. When the Bismarck Women's Club, founder of the North Dakota Historical Society, collected Pioneer Teacher stories for deposit with the Society, Susan Vance's was among them. Like many others of these stories, this one dramatizes a young teachers' exemplary triumph over physical and psychological adversity:

> One summer I taught the Sibley Trail School and went home every two weeks. After school on Friday I rode my bicycle 25 miles to Valley City, stayed all night in our room there and on Saturday morning rode the 25 miles to our farm home near Lucca. Sunday afternoon I rode back to Valley City, stayed overnight and rode to school by 9 Monday morning. The extra clothing was carried on the handlebars. Ruts of the Sibley Trail were still so deep on the prairie that one could not ride them because of striking pedals. We rode beside the ruts and went over the hills, but did not take the river road, and crossed the Sheyenne River at Ashtabula. Sometimes I was afraid of the cattle that were always near the road in the hill pastures. They were curious about me, whether I was riding or pushing the bicycle up a steep place (North Dakota Federated Women's Club, Miscellaneous File, 1921).

The NDFWC Pioneer Essay Contest entries, also deposited with the North Dakota Historical Society, elicited scores of honorific testimony to the courage, strength, and boldness of women who settled in North Dakota. An unidentified entry from Dickey, sent to the 1926 NDFWC Essay Contest, is typical in its celebratory detail:

> Every home was a little manufacturing plant in those days, where, if one was so fortunate as to have the materials, butter and cheese were made. When we had plenty of sweet milk, mother made large yellow fellows, that tasted as good as any cheese I have ever eaten since. Meat was cured for summer use, stockings and mittens knit. The shell of the men's mittens was made of striped ticking or even good pieces of worn-out overalls. Clothing was practically all homemade, some by hand as not all homes boasted a sewing machine. Mother saved the cracklings from lard rendering and all rinds and scraps of meat to be used in making soap for laundry and cleaning purposes. Tin pans, knives and forks and other utensils were scoured with a piece of old brick, or if anyone did not have a brick, wood ashes -- which make a splendid cleanser. Every rag was saved and rag rugs made, and in the course of time rags were saved for a rag carpet. Strips of goods being torn in thin strips, sewed together, wound in a ball, and finally sent East to be woven into a wonderful rag carpet. As I remember our neighborhood, they were all happy, friendly people where the ladies sometimes exchanged quilt blocks, or silk and plush remnants for a cushion, rags for a rug, and if one had more vegetables than one needed, it might be exchanged for meat or some other necessity, to a neighbor. Hats and such trifles bothered us not at all. I'm sure mother wore hats for three and four seasons, perfectly happy to think she possessed one at all. Mother made me a new sunbonnet for best wear every spring, while I wore my "last year's" best one for play. Mine were stiffly starched, pink or red affairs, while mother's were a black and white pin-check calico, with slats of cardboard for stiffening. Sunbonnets were a nuisance I thought, one could not see well. Possibly one would miss seeing a rabbit, a frog or a bumble bee, so quite often when mother was not around I went without one. And Maude Taylor felt as I did, for did we not as soon as we got to school, hang up our bonnets in the hall, while the rest of the day Maude wore Guy Searle's cap and I wore Earle's. The

Fryar Bros., Ed and Orson, one summer day, drove home from town with a brand new shiny top buggy, the first of its kind in the neighborhood. Some of the neighbors shook their heads and prophesied they would lose their farm, some said Extravagant! Extravagant! while others just hoped they would be asked for a ride. About four years later father purchased a top buggy as did my uncle and we felt prosperous indeed, with a top to keep off sun and rain and to be able to bound over the ground at such a rate of speed. What would people have thought had anyone mentioned such wonders as the telephone, talking machine, horseless carriage, flying machine, or radio (Pioneer Contest Essays).

The writing conventions that govern this essay — past remembrance of simple, honest labor within a real community of caring, selfless neighbors with occasional flashes of minor infractions and mild rebuke or rebellion — are pastoral. The past that this anonymous woman creates is a measure for the present, and it retains its vitality of accumulated detail by the sheer force of the writer's own plenitude. This is history writ by the genteel: pleasant, slightly comic or a mite adventurous, thoroughly self-congratulatory and "progressive." This is history as myth, but not as men might people it, with heroic isolates who prove themselves in lonely battle or by lighting out for the territory. This history is social, domestic, and reaching for the sensual pleasures of everyday use: a hat you can see out of, a magic new buggy which feels at once safe and daring and wonderfully rich.

Another striking feature of the Pioneer Essay Contest entries is that the women writers rarely dwell on themselves or their accomplishments. The "I" — that dark bar that overshadows the pages of men's writing in Virginia Woolf's description — is invisible, offstage, choric. The writers are stage managers of the dramas they create; they orchestrate events as would subtle hostesses or discrete *charges d'affaires*. As we shall see, these genteel props served a crucial function in North Dakota clubwomen's attempts to gain public influence and recognition.

One of the most interesting texts produced by our state's clubwomen is *Prairie Wings*, a little magazine of poetry edited by Grace Brown Putnam, of New Rockford, North Dakota, from 1936-1948. With her associate editor, Anna Ackermann, head of the English Department of Jamestown High School, Putnam published *North Dakota Singing*, an anthology of North Dakota verse (1936). The stated purpose of Putnam's work, evidenced by local newspaper accounts, editorial columns in *Prairie Wings*, and Mrs. Putnam's letters to both contributing poets and her business manager Henry Martinson (of the Non-Partisan League and later the State Commissioner of Labor), was to "illustrate the force of poetry through the narrowing influence of pioneer days, physical disability, and youth." *North Dakota Singing*, said a local newspaper in 1936,

is more than a book. It is the visible turning of a page of state history. It marks a new epoch, the emerging of North Dakota from that period, inevitable to any pioneer state, of complete preoccupation with the hard material facts of existence and entering upon the creative phase of its development marked by keen appreciation of beauty and the urge to express it in some tangible form (*Bismarck Tribune*, 16 October 1936).

A native of Sherman, New York, Grace Brown moved to North Dakota with her parents in territorial days, marrying S. N. Putnam in 1888. Putnam, a lumberyard owner, was the first superintendent of rural schools in Eddy County, North Dakota, and served in the state legislature. He died in 1941. Grace Putnam attended Mayville Normal and the University of North Dakota, graduating in 1904. She was superintendent of schools from 1904 for two terms and again was elected in 1925, serving until retiring after her husband's death in 1941. The description of Grace Putnam as Shakespeare's Portia in the 1904 UND yearbook is an appropriate description of her power strategy: "Her voice is ever soft, gentle and low, an excellent thing in a woman" (UND Special Collections). Discretion and tact served Putnam all of her life. From her editorial "blushes" at mentioning the national scope of her "little mag" to her confidential concern for cultural reform, Putnam struggled to write a place for herself in rural North Dakota. Even her farewell letter to Henry Martinson written shortly after a move to St. Helena, California, in 1946, marks a ladylike exit from North Dakota, taking *Prairie Wings* with her to begin a new life:

> Many picturesque towns and cities are in this area and through the kindness of friends, I have made several delightful excursions to places of great interest. Some of these mountain roads, however, are sufficiently perilous to cause a plainsman like myself to feel a trifle tense and appreciate a strong and skillful hand on the steering wheel.

The "strong hand" on her steering wheel belonged to poet Robert Wallace Smith, whom Putnam met in 1944, when Smith visited North Dakota to do research for a new book of poems. Smith subsequently visited Putnam on at least one occasion, and wrote book reviews for *Prairie Wings*. Smith's description of his friendship with Putnam isn't as physically erotic as is hers, but he makes clear the intensity of their friendship in an undated letter to Martinson, describing her as

> . . . a conversationalist almost *nonpareil* (and sometimes impish at repartee) and we had many lengthy discussions on poets and poetry, literature, life, and the world; it seemed that we might be able to formulate a new Mercatorial system to apply to the universe.

Readers accustomed to thinking of good literature as discourse with no designs on the world find it hard to read *Prairie Wings* poetry as anything but bad verse. Richard Lyons, of North Dakota State University's English Department, voices a typical New Critic's impatience with sentimental poetic diction. He writes as Director of the North Dakota Institute for Regional Studies in 1952 to poet and clubwoman Eva Anglesburg, whose poems he had solicited in hopes of publishing them at the Institute:

> I agree with your daughter that these poems are not so good as you are capable of writing. There is nothing in these poems to distinguish them from multitudes of similar verse. I would hazard the guess that you here have taken to a particular experience or subject a pre-established emotional response and vocabulary. I do not feel that the content has dictated the form. The uniformity of treatment in these poems corresponds with the uniformity of treatment in the typical productions of

women's literary clubs. They have the same anonymity, such that one can change authors and titles without a feeling of discord. You are, at your best, above that level and have an individuality which is worth maintaining. You have, here, fallen back upon a prescribed vocabulary and subject matter, using many words that have lost their precision of meaning through being over-worked. Some of this blurring of meaning results from the effort to write about the "Beautiful," the "True" and the "Good" and confuse these qualities with the words. A "Beautiful" subject does not make a beautiful poem. But a beautiful poem can be made from very mundane subject matter by the artist's handling of his material. The beauty is in the artistic form and meaning given to material, to human experience, not in the material or experience itself. Let me list a few words or phrases picked at random which illustrate this tendency toward worn-out language: "ablaze with red and gold," "pageant" [of autumn], "splendor" [of sunset], "velvety as a night-moth's wing," "harbingers of spring," "boundaries of Infinity." (This is self-contradictory. It does not open imaginative horizons by suggestion, but shuts off imaginative response by diffusing the impact through a lack of precise visual or imaginative image. Can you see the difference between "boundaries of Infinity" and "architecture of Eternity"?), "scourge of war," "fierce" [tornadoes], "flawless textures spun." Are these exact records of your own artist-emotional experience or are they conscious or unconscious echoing of other verse?

Like Professor Lyons, most of us are trained to believe that poetry which makes obvious emotional appeals, poetry ruled by utterly conventional images and hackneyed phrases is the opposite of what good poetry should be, the new expression of an individual voice which forces attention to previously unheeded sensations and ideas. But this romantic dictum misses the point of poetry as a political, collective enterprise, a specifically feminine enterprise, in the case of *Prairie Wings*, by which women wrote somewhere in the spaces between sermons and social theory, codifying and attempting to mold the world women live in. Eva Anglesburg answered Professor Lyon's letter promptly:

> If you had included your poems in the first letter you sent me I would have known that none of my recent poems would have interested you.
> However, if I hadn't sent them I wouldn't have received your fine letter containing so many helpful suggestions. Reader reaction is, I think, always appreciated and constructive criticism, which is so rare, is thankfully received whenever it comes my way.
> You mentioned that you might use my Paul Bunyan poems in your new anthology. If you will agree to certain revisions, you are welcome to use them but not otherwise. Irish Jim, the old lumberjack who told me how they logged North Dakota, used swear words when he related the story but somehow they seemed inoffensive when he used them. He had a gentle, cultured voice (he was the black sheep of a highly respectable family) and had a pleasing personality. I didn't realize how coarse and crude those expressions would seem when they appeared in print. I had the same experience with some of the pioneer poems and child poems which unwisely I recorded too accurately.
> I have been criticized severely for doing so and do not intend to repeat that mistake.

Twenty years earlier, Eva K. Anglesburg made her only public appearance as a poet, at the North Dakota Education Association convention. The *Bismarck Tribune* (1936) noted her reading in the Fibs, Facts, and Fancies Column, under the headline, "Worried Off 4 Pounds":

> Mrs. Eva K. Anglesburg of Thompson, N.D., a native poet, scored a hit on the program of the North Dakota Education Association convention in her first public appearance in 16 years—but she's going back to her kitchen and the care of her four children.
>
> "Never again," said Mrs. Anglesburg when she had completed the reading of a few of her poems. "I had thought I might like the idea, but I just couldn't face a thing like this again. Why I haven't been able to sleep — and I've lost four pounds.
>
> "Not that I don't want to lose weight, but I don't like to do it that way.
>
> "If they liked me I am glad, but no one need ever ask me to appear in public again. I don't do it. I am going back home and take care of my children. I will keep on writing poetry, but if I were to get so wrought up again I would lose all my desire for creative writing. Some one else will have to recite it."
>
> It was that battery of thousands of eyes — or rather the thought of it — which caused Mrs. Anglesburg trepidation.
>
> A tall willowy woman, her face is lighted by an inner glow. The fire which has caused her to write poetry while she has gone through the tribulations of bearing six children and rearing four of them shows in her face. It gives her a charm and dignity which obviously endeared her to her audience, even while they sympathized with her fears.
>
> The way in which this daughter of North Dakota happened to appear on the program, her first and — now she says — her last public appearance, is unusual.
>
> When J.N. Urness got his first job as a school superintendent it was at Thompson where Eva Morris was a teacher. She was dabbling with poetry at that time.
>
> Then came her marriage, the process of building a home and of rearing children, but the urge to write still persisted. Her friends urged her to publish them. Some had appeared in various publications and these, with others, were collected and issued in a small book titled "Of the Level Land." Her fame spread, in a quiet way, and when Urness was arranging the program for the convention he thought of her. Because she was intrigued with the idea and wanted to see how it would go, she accepted. She was grateful to the teachers for their kind reception but unwilling to subject herself to such a strain again.
>
> And for the information of those who wonder what kind of a housewife a female poet makes, it might be mentioned that Mrs. Anglesburg makes her own soap. A lively person, she is not afraid of work. Recently she undertook to remodel an old bedroom by cutting it down to more modern size.
>
> She looks at the world wide-eyed and is obviously in love with it and with life. But she isn't going to recite for it anymore — unless she changes her mind.
>
> And now for a bit of Mrs. Anglesburg's poetry, which she gave *The Tribune* special permission to reprint.

The connections between genteel rhetoric and female "sensitivity" seem especially clear here. The *Tribune* becomes a public platform for Anglesburg's verse, once her private fears are broadcast and her domestic duties are properly recognized. The genteel codes separating private life from public address enable Mrs. Anglesburg's verse to enter the world while the poet, pronouncing herself betrayed by the public, nevertheless comes before it.

Clubwomen often used the codes of gentility to their advantage, as a brief look at just one page of the August 1936 issue of *Prairie Wings* will demonstrate. The chatty tone of "Our Folks," Grace Brown Putnam's editorial column, maternalizes the magazine at the same time that it broadcasts its public innuendo. "I have been standing in a sort of parental capacity to the infant," Putnam wrote poet Stella Lavinia Olson in April 1938, naming her motherly function. The profusion of epithets for "Our Folks" — "Accomplished singer," "Needs no introduction," "Unselfish dreams of social service in the rural school," "charming little book" – sets the stage for the "Laurels" column, where especially talented family members receive awards from professors of literature. The professors, who signify the only center of male power which stands uncritiqued by the ladies, remain ideal objects of reverence, always referred to as "Dr." Notices of awards (often books by clubwomen) and upcoming publications (again by clubwomen) widen and strengthen the circles of uplifting poetic influence.

All three columns, "Our Folks," "Poetry Society," and "Laurels," create the stage of public domesticity, a stage which extends to, but does not exactly include, men. Mr. Reihus, a businessman with ostensibly prosaic concerns, excuses himself for having feelings, too. Mr. Rolfson is one of "Our Folks" since he has a family. Mr. Goozee is introduced to the circle by Mrs. Rudsen. And Mr. MacLeish, who delivered "an inspiring series of lectures" to associate editor Miss Ackermann, "who writes from Columbia [University] where she is doing summer school work," is not allowed exactly to tell us "what modern poetry is, or should be." ("Don't some of us wish we knew!" trills Mrs. Putnam, waving Mr. MacLeish's theories out of the column now that he has served as the excuse for news of Miss Ackermann.)

The irony of Putnam's parenthetical remarks must not be lost on modern readers who might be inclined to entertain themselves with this most telling piece of self-damning evidence which Mrs. Putnam so blithely presents. Since modern American poetry, under the aegis of Archibald MacLeish, fashions alienation, fragmentation, failure of nerve, loss of self, and cosmic precariousness into the exact opposite of the unwavering reassurances of *Prairie Wings* poetry, Mrs. Putnam's attempts to uplift her readers seem lame and ridiculous, even perhaps pathetic. The psychic distance between Olga Tuck's "Hospitals" and the patient etherized on the table in T. S. Eliot's "Lovesong of J. Alfred Prufrock" is immeasurable. But Mrs. Putnam and her clubwomen stand on the periphery of high culture precisely because we have called their work narrow and parochial, beneath notice by literary sophisticates and cultural critics.

But what if this poetry is read with less contempt and more attention to rhetorical strategies women writers use to fashion, out of conventional language, the paradox of being at once watched and invisible? The center of acclaim but reluctantly so? If one characteristic marks many of the 5,000 plus poems in *Prairie Wings* written by women, it is this sense of audience which is more real than the speaking subject. To study *Prairie Wings* as a text made from women's cultural ideals is to reclaim, by sympathetic observation, the validity of women's language and women's experiences. What is so striking about *Prairie Wings* is the obvious attempts made by clubwomen to remake their culture according to norms shaped by genteel values and middle-class ideology. They were determined not to be viewed as "backwoodsy," and set themselves the task of refining the state.

One powerful club which helped North Dakota women think of themselves as professionals was the National League of American Pen Women, a literary club formed in 1897 and still extant in 52 states, with three North Dakota branches in Bismarck, Mandan, and Medora. As the essay in this collection by Cynthia T. Selland testifies, the National League of American Pen Women helped North Dakota women take their work seriously, and it provided a network of contact and support for their efforts. Describing itself as "a professional organization for women artists, composers, and writers," the NLAPW was organized when newspapers and national magazines were expanding their circulations, taking full advantage of the postal act of 1879 which provided for low-cost mailing. The founders of the Pen Women were Easterners (this later galled North Dakota women seeking national offices with no "Eastern" support) Marion Longfellow O'Donahue wrote prose and poetry for the *Boston Transcript*, the *Boston Herald*, and the *Washington Post*; Margaret Sullivan Burke was capitol correspondent for several newspapers throughout the country; and Ann Sanborne Hamilton was a proofreader for the U.S. Government.

Like the Sorosis Club, formed in 1868 when women were barred from the New York Press Club dinner for Charles Dickens, the Pen Women's League was formed after they were refused membership in the Washington, D.C., Press Club. Reaction to years of male exclusivity was only the impetus for club organization, however; female friendship and professional "shop talk" held the club together. The League's motto, "One for All and All for One," and the League's insignia, the owl, symbolizing wisdom, put in a triangle formed by a red pen, a blue pencil, and a white brush, bespeaks the League's collective spirit. Organized "to promote the development of the creative talents of professional women artists, writers, dramatists, lecturers and composers," the League has, from the outset, embodied contradictions between white middle-class women's professional aspirations, their personal experiences of exclusion from the professions, and their ongoing plots for shaping American cultural history.

Unlike other literary circles, culture clubs and historical societies which flourished in nineteenth-century America, the National League of American Pen Women required that its members think of themselves as professionals, whether or not larger society recognized them as such. Proved sales in "creative fields" — prose, poetry, art, musical compositions, and, later, lecturing – were demanded of League members, and the bulk of club records and correspondence documents, in great detail, such proof. Hundreds of letters list, crosslist, and relist Pen Women's "accomplishments," as if proof of enough professional activity were proof of public acclaim. Reports were submitted to regional and national offices, and were checked and rechecked for accuracy. These efforts were extremely time-consuming and complicated; in 1951, for instance, State President Ina Cullom Robertson reported that the three Pen Women branches in North Dakota "turned out a total of 443,995 items, 25,184 in the division of BOOK; and 418,771 in the division of ARTS." Forty Poetry Awards were listed; observation of State Poetry Day was proclaimed, and among "Miscellaneous Activities" were listed

> Critical reading of manuscript for publishers; revision of book for reprinting by publishers; art demonstrators for commercial firm at educational meetings; art workshops; preparation of art exhibits for city and state; writing for trade journals;

written original stories for library children's hour; poetry readings at PTA; organizing record library for children; revival of *Prairie Wings* (NDLAPW Records).

As Selland notes in her essay on the Pen Women, most Pen Women did not earn wages themselves; they were married to middle-class men whose businesses and professions supported their families. As a widow with three children to support, Mrs. Selland was an exception to the Pen Women rule. Since few members nationally, and no members in North Dakota actually earned their livings in ways that would allow them to count themselves as professional according to the Pen Women criteria, these records of sales and publications which **did** count were crucial, as were debates about which women were eligible for membership in the organization. Mrs. Selland is probably using understatement when she notes in her essay "Achievement reports were required every year for both the National and State archives to insure professionalism. This project was what stimulated many to strive for greater success. This also produced some very interesting meetings. The meetings challenged me to do better and to respect my own endeavors more." What appears, at first glance, to be a hopelessly trivial, needlessly wearying, record of sales and possible sales — a poem for twenty-five cents, a song for a dime — is visible proof of Pen Women's attempts to publicly produce culture, and to report accurately, despite societal indifference to their efforts, their work.

Not every Pen Woman soberly counted each word she wrote or each ceramic

---

Pen Women of Fargo

by Cynthia T. Selland

My baby was three months old and the two older children four and five, when my husband died. I was able to secure a position as serial cataloguer and teacher of library sciences at the North Dakota State University library, so I had plenty to do, but nothing creatively stimulating to occupy my mind. Then I was asked to edit a newsletter, the *North Dakota Parent Teacher Bulletin*. I was surprised, but when I was assured that all I would have to do was edit material and manage production of the Bulletin, I accepted the volunteer job for two years.

The *Bulletin* kept my mind occupied, all right: editing, selecting, reporting, researching, composing, rewriting, planning layout, hiring and supervising photographers, pleading for news from PTA units, and usually writing almost everything myself. I shared the *Bulletin* with ironing, canning, sewing, and cleaning, and worked late into the nights after children were in bed. In one of the *Bulletin* issues I printed a poem by Prudence Gearey Sand, president of the Fargo Branch of the National League of American Pen Women, which led eventually to my being introduced to the organization.

Until then, I had resisted trying to join the Pen Women (which had branches in Bismarck and Williston as well as Fargo) because I was too awed by the accomplish-

ashtray she made, however. And several of them wrote very witty applications for membership. Lyla Hoffine's "Thumbnail Biography" is an anti-application:

> I was born on Pumpkin (pronounced pumkin by the natives) Ridge, Iowa County, Wisconsin, several years ago. Like Lincoln I was born in a log house and like him chose the month of February. However, it would be pointless to pursue the Lincoln theme longer since we have absolutely nothing else in common.
>
> Long before I was ready to hand down a decision in the matter I was brought to North Dakota. With no intent toward favoritism among the towns my parents chose Kenmare. I suspect the reason was lack of funds to go farther. In less poetic terms, we were poor, and to date I have succeeded in maintaining the family tradition.
>
> Thanks to the rural and consolidated schools I was able to earn enough money to go to the State Teachers College at Minot and get a degree from the State University.
>
> Having gotten into the habit of eating regularly in my youth, I became enslaved to the habit and continued teaching to indulge it. During all this time I showed no signs of genius. No teacher ever put her hand on my head and said I was destined to become great. As I look back I suspect there were many who said, "Thank goodness I'll soon be rid of that Hoffine kid." Frankly I lacked, and still lack, the artistic temperament completely.
>
> Of course I write but it is not the irresistible urge I have heard about. As far as I can figure it out I have sold myself the idea that I have something to say and the public might be interested in hearing it.
>
> I am interested in children and I write for and about them. Sometimes I'm published, sometimes I'm not. I have sold insurance though most of the time I only

ments of the members, and did not feel my work was up to the professional standards that the organization required. I had edited the *Bulletin* as a volunteer, I felt, without formal training; however, the national organization accepted my application. In the Fargo Branch, I was the only member who supported a family alone; others were homemakers with families, or professional women without children, or women who shared the support of a family with their husbands. All came to appreciate each other's creative efforts and respected each other's endeavors for artistic recognition.

The National League of American Pen Women had been said to consist of "The ladies who pursued culture in bands," these being highly varied, according to the by-laws: "The Fargo Branch shall include professional women authors, dramatists, journalists, librettists, lyric writers, motion picture writers, poets, press and periodical writers, publicists, architects, artists, cartoonists, designers in fine arts and crafts, illuminators, illustrators, painters, sculptors, composers of music, lecturers, compilers, genealogists, collaborators, research workers, and such other crafts as may from time to time be added by the National League."

In accordance with the League's objective "to conduct and promote creative and educational activities in Art, Letters, and Music among its members," branch meetings were filled with sharing of creative work. Members were required to make reports of their achievements every year for both the National and State archives, to ensure professionalism, and these reportings stimulated many to strive for

tried to do so. I have been an editor and liked it. I have attended Kings' College, Columbia University and the Bread Loaf Writers Conference, at Middlebury, Vt. Altogether I think my most enjoyable experience is knowing people and being liked by them (NDLAPW Records, undated).

Miss Hoffine's irreverence endeared her to most Pen Women. But the League is embodied, in all its contradictions, in the person of Edna LaMoore Waldo, a native of Jamestown whose family had pioneered in Dakota Territory. Her brother was western romance writer Louis L'Amour, who changed the spelling of his name to reflect Hollywood aspirations that greatly displeased his family and amused many locals. Born in 1893, Edna LaMoore Waldo graduated from Jamestown College in 1914, with a librarian's certificate, a B.A. in Romance Languages, and a burning interest in history. From 1914-1917 she taught Latin, German, English, and coached debate and declamation teams at Cavalier High School, serving as principal there in 1916-17. "As a principal," Mrs. Waldo wrote me on July 16, 1984, "I had to send boys off to war — but had no vote myself. I applied for war camp library and recreation services for which I was qualified, but was told I was 'too young' — at 25. Men always thought then that we wanted to chase the soldiers. Maybe some did! Not I."

Pageantry, church, and community dramas were very much in vogue then in North Dakota. Edna took great interest in these productions, encouraging her students to take their parts in speech contests and public debate and town dramas. She moved to Grafton for one year, where she taught advanced Latin, 11th-grade English, debate and declamation, taking her students to the University of North

greater success and also produced very interesting meetings. The meetings challenged me to do better and to respect my endeavors. I received a great deal of encouragement from other members and was made to feel that I had something to contribute, and that my efforts were respected. As a widow I needed all the support I could get.

The most prolific author of the Fargo Branch (who corresponded with us but rarely was here to attend meetings) was Vera Kelsey, who wrote *Red River Runs North* about the Red River Valley, an industrial survey of China, histories of Brazil and Guatemala, and murder mysteries set in Central and South America. Sand was a widely published poet, and the League's primary mover in the state: as branch and state president, as organizer of other branches. Thanks to her there was for several years a state-wide day of prayer and junior high school poetry writing contests; a prize for North Dakota Pen Women at a national convention for having the centerpiece most descriptive of the state; publication of chapbooks by the state organization, including a popular volume called *Humbly We Pray* by Stella Halsten Hohncke. Stella Hohncke wrote poetry, children's plays, and religious tracts, and was secretary-treasurer of the Fargo branch, for years being the one who kept it going. She is blind, and still, at age ninety-five performs her poetry, appearing on the stage of the Fargo Theatre in 1987 for a charity event to recite her poems "Love Letter to a Husband," "Why Do I Love Thee," and "Friendship."

Lydia Jackson of Grafton was North Dakota Poet Laureate in 1985. Other especially successful members have included Phyllis Steele Baldwin, society editor for the *Fargo Forum*; Angela Brown

Dakota campus for speech contests. In the summer of 1917, she was hired by the University to grade state examinations given to high school Latin students. But she spent more time exploring the campus than grading examinations. And she discovered history professor Orin G. Libby's pageantry class. "I only audited a few classes, not for credit," she wrote. "But I kept notes and for the first time saw how history could be used. I saw the drama in it. "

In 1918 Edna moved to Mandan, where she headed the high school English Department and continued her work in speech and debate. With her marriage to Frank Waldo of Mandan in 1920, her formal teaching career ended, since married women were barred from such positions. But she hardly stopped teaching, and her dramatics were just beginning. Like many women whose educations and interests had prepared them to produce, rather than to consume, culture, Edna moved her professional efforts out of the classroom and into the women's clubs. Her entry into the General Federation of Women's Clubs was deliberate. She emphasizes, in this retrospective narrative, a fiction of precarious, self-absorbed plan:

> Most of the social-study groups met in homes, which necessarily limited their numbers — most were organized by one or two women with some education (by no means all college women) who wanted "to do" something. There was some study. There were Browning clubs and Shakespeare clubs — but the emphasis was social.
>
> The members were almost always married, the wives of lawyers, doctors, bankers — in short the "ladies" of the community — You had to be invited. Many fine women never were — for instance, as the larger organizations grew and an

---

Bolin, a sculptor whose work is in the collections of the Minneapolis Institute of Art and the Walker Art Center in Minneapolis; Mary Boynton Cowdrey, of Valley City, who edited *The Checkered Years*, the diaries of her grandmother Mary Dodge Woodward; Jessamime Slaughter Burgum, of Arthur, who wrote poetry and fiction and painted scenes of early years in North Dakota; Rose McLaughlin Sackett, writer of books for children, including *Penny Lavender*; Carrie B. Simpson, of Grand Forks, book review writer; May Kelly, art supervisor for the Fargo Public Schools; Ina Cullen Robertson, head of the geography department at Valley City State Teachers College, who wrote about the teaching of geography; Hazel Webster Byrnes, poet and lecturer, responsible for developing bookmobiles in the state; Bertha Palmer, author of *Beauty Spots of North Dakota* and active in WCTU; and Cornelia Adeline Spelletich, author of

Chronicles of Cornelia, much poetry, some historical accounts, and producer of religious sculpture. Along with these artistic accomplishments, many beautiful friendships were developed through membership in the Fargo Branch of the National League of American Pen Women.

Cynthia Selland describes herself as "still an organizational woman." She belongs to the Fine Arts Club, Fargo Retired Teachers' Association (she taught social studies and language arts for 39 years), the Program Coordinating Management Committee of the Hjemkomst Heritage Interpretive Center, and the North Dakota Legislative Committee of the American Association of Retired Persons (AARP).

active member moved away, especially to Florida or California, she could not go on unless and until she was invited again.

In my case, as I'd been head of their high school English department, I was invited at Mandan as soon as I married — a Mandan woman was state president when we moved to Minot and she passed me on to a new club of younger women then forming — she also proposed me for the state press job — and by the time I got to Bismarck in 1927 I was well known for my state work and was invited almost at once.

Many did less well — it took time. The "study" I saw, as a former teacher and librarian, was never impressive — but it did some good, encouraging women "to keep up" and to read. Much was poorly presented. But generally worthwhile. Some clubs bought regular text books. That may have led to their help in starting libraries.

I knew many splendid older women, some of whom had started the North Dakota State Federation — and I believe that most of the things they later did for their communities came about gradually or accidentally. A few clubs may have been formed to "do good" but they were usually outside the Federation.

Somebody would say, "They ought to do — and then it dawned, *We* can." They did parks and playgrounds, libraries. Most of them were well to do, or at least their *husbands* were. I know from my own later experience that people of substance were expected to do some civic work and most men felt that having active *wives* enhanced their prestige. (Until they got *too* active — but that's another story.) (Letter to author)

Waldo's last sentence hastens to cover the more unruly potential of ladies' clubs, but a major source of deviance had already been underscored. The home, it seems, is a site inhabited by those who want "to do" something, not with the gentlemen, really, but with other ladies. Waldo rejects the "unprofessional" nature of ladies' study groups at the same time that she demonstrates their utter necessity to women like herself, women who have been displaced from other sites of formalized consciousness such as the school and the library. The "too active" woman Waldo banishes from her narrative is, of course, herself. She gained entry to the General Federation of Women's Clubs through her position as head of a high school English department, not as a wife. She rose in the ranks on merit of her club work and her contacts with the state club president. Of her husband Frank, she writes nothing substantial. And of her brother Louis, she writes nothing laudatory. Waldo was embarrassed, not sympathetic, by what she called the "bizarre episode" of her family's adopting an orphan boy while she was in college in 1911-1912:

A lot of New York orphans were brought out to Jamestown, presented at the Opera House in a way that now seems incredible. I was not there nor were my parents but young brothers Parker and Yale were. One small boy — John Otto — crosseyed — was left over — How those boys were allowed to bring him home I'll never know and I do not remember the sequence, as I was opposed to the whole idea. Eventually my parents kept him as a playmate for Louis, then about four years old. We certainly did not need a kid at that stage, although he was a cute youngster — my mother's health was none too good. The boys vowed to earn money and help care for him!!! But by 1916 Parker was on the Mexican Border, both he and Yale in France by 1917. I believe (not sure) my parents adopted him later. He went south with them in 1923 but later left on his own in the Los Angeles area — was killed there years ago in a car accident. Louis once heard from his daughter. I was away teaching, married 1920, so I knew little about it and felt it was a serious mistake. But who was I? (Letter to Mary Young, 10 April 1981).

Edna herself got *"too* active" for the General Federation of Women's Clubs. But before leaving the club, she revamped it. From 1924-1927 she was National First Vice President for Press and Publicity, appointed to supervise and encourage membership activity in twelve western states. She had built the *North Dakota Club Bulletin* from a one-page news sheet into a magazine with ads, photographs, and feature stories. But she grew discouraged:

> I got *no* postage money, I was often asked to travel and speak, had no expense allowance. I got myself to the National Convention at Grand Rapids, Michigan, and much enjoyed functioning in the press room. I met many national newswomen and editors, some of them very disillusioned. Finally when I was supposed to attend the next convention in Texas, I began to think it over. I realized that only women of means could afford to go "up" in that organization (Letter to author).

Edna's husband was a district manager for Northwestern Bell Telephone, and his income was modest. But Edna had begun earning her own money, working as a free-lance journalist. She sold several "how-to" articles on club activities to area newspapers, including the *Minneapolis Journal*, which had a large Sunday circulation in North Dakota in the 1920s. Two Minot friends, Kara Dickinson and Huldah Winstad, urged Edna to join the National League of American Pen Women, and though both had left North Dakota (Dickinson remained active in the Seattle branch, sending telegrams and letters of support to the North Dakota Pen Women), before she turned "pro" in 1927, Edna joined the national as a member-at-large (NLAPW Records). In Bismarck now, with small children and little money, Edna was nevertheless determined to join the book world:

> We had *no* bookstores in North Dakota. No chance to browse and pick up things we might want — Libraries were small, under-supported. Some high schools had none at all. Books were my life — I had to have them and in my early married life I could not afford to buy them. Nor did I have any good way to keep up. It was through a tip in a writers' magazine that I found out how publicity departments of large publishers regularly sent out free copies to magazines and newspapers, hoping for mention. Large places got everything, others selected titles (Letter to author).

As editor of the *North Dakota Club Bulletin*, Waldo had received a few books for review. When she took a full-time job as women's editor and feature writer in 1927-28 with the *Bismarck Capitol*, a semi-weekly newspaper owned by old friends, she ordered more books. Her full-time job didn't last long, but she was able to do some legislative reporting, although not under her by-line. ("My husband was with a large utility company Northwestern Bell, then suspect in some quarters," she wrote me.) She also published her book reviews in "Book Chat," the first book column in the state:

> The books came to *me*, and not, as usual, to the paper. I would ask for new

> publishers' catalogues, request titles applicable to our locale. I almost always got them — free! And books were better made and bound in those days — I sold the books for review not only in the *Capital*, but, as time went on, to other papers as well (Letter to author).

Waldo's "Book Chat" columns were romantic histories of the state, popularized stories of cowboys and Indians, the railroads, Theodore Roosevelt. In five years, Waldo built up her personal library, secured books for her children, and filled the papers with news of North Dakota's history as it was being produced by the mythmakers of progress and successful adventure. Located outside the system of school and library, Waldo acted as teacher and librarian for the entire state.

But in 1929 Waldo offended her friends with an article she sold for $150 to the *Pictorial Review*, a large national magazine with a wide circulation. Titled "Why I Am Tired of Being a Professional Club Woman," the article critiqued the shallow programs and mindless busywork of many clubwomen. "It really was not disloyal," Waldo writes of the article,

> but tried to show how hard it was — and I a young woman with children — to spend the time and money to do work that may or may not be valuable — no expense money. My friends were unhappy. My background as a teacher and librarian had made me most interested in program content, how to do reports and papers, and in publicity for the really worthwhile efforts of some clubs (Letter to author).

This article and another written in 1934, "What Club Women Really Want," published in *Real America*, formed the nucleus of Waldo's *Leadership for Today's Clubwoman* (published in 1939). The books's rhetorical structure is animated and practical, filled with examples and instructions for improving club programs and projects. In modern parlance, it is a cross between a self-help book and a freshman composition course. Anna S. Richardson, editor of the *Women's Home Companion*, wrote an introduction to the book, and Waldo gave lectures based on the book to clubs all over the Midwest, especially in Minnesota and Wisconsin.

With this article, Waldo claimed a place as a professional critic of women's clubs, traveling throughout the Midwest to observe and consult with various organizations, serving as a kind of writing and declamation teacher for women's club members. Again, she describes her unprofessional status (no money) as an impetus for her professional efforts. As a member of the Pen Women's League and as a book reviewer in a state that had few book stores, Waldo held no "official" place in the state's formal institutions of consciousness. But she found means to publicize her interest in history and the arts. The *Bismarck Capitol* published her family history, *Yet She Follows*, in 1931, which gave her entree to the large Minnesota Pen Women branch. (This book is a romantic biography of Waldo's grandmother Betty Freeman Dearborn, who came with her parents Jane Cole Freeman and Ambrose Freeman to Minnesota in the 1850s.) Serving with Sibley in 1862 as a captain of the Minnesota Mounted Rangers, Ambrose met A. T. Dearborn, a Union soldier whom Betty married. She followed her husband to Ft. Halleck in Kentucky as a war bride of 1864, later settling in Carrington and Jamestown, Dakota, in the early 1880s. Another popular state history, *Dakota, an Informal History of Territorial Days*, grew from her newspaper column "Way Back When," which was syndicated in many weekly newspapers in the Midwest. In 1936 *Dakota* was revised for use in the public schools. In 1932, Waldo visited and joined the Yankton, South Dakota, Pen Women branch, continuing her book reviews and club news reports for newspaper syndicates.

When the *Bismarck Capital* folded in 1933, Waldo convinced a Bismarck radio station, KFYR, to broadcast her live book reviews. She described her radio shows as "learned lectures," modeled after ones she had heard broadcast from Chicago:

> I knew it was something I could do. But where? How? That took planning. I have always hated to memorize — I was a trained extempore speaker. I began to work out a formula for myself, using the complete book, which I had really studied, clips and small notes, at intervals. I chose dramatic sections to emphasize. These were not short, but a full hour. The book, for the benefit of people who did read or could not. And with the idea also of showing what was going on in the book world — book gossip! (Letter to author)

Again, Waldo writes of her impulse to teach, to illuminate North Dakotans by subjecting them to a "full hour" of enrichment. Situating herself as an insider who even knows about "book gossip," Waldo's pleasure beams out across the plains. Waldo's desires unite various polarized worlds: literate/illiterate; study/gossip; texts/pretexts. And they are variously shaped by her awareness of social conventions which she obeyed in order to make contact with North Dakota women writers who also thought of themselves as professionals. In the 1930s, Waldo created an audience of society ladies who seemed alternately pleased and offended by her "teaching." "Of course" Waldo writes,

> I had to break in socially Sugar Coated! I often gave large teas, as we had many important visitors in Bismarck. So I started with a biography (always best) accompanied by piano music (good friend) at an affair in my own home. Risking, of course, "What's she doing now?" (Letter to author)

The pleasure Waldo takes in recounting the ladies' discontents is one of romantic self-aggrandizement. Waldo constructs a fiction of triumphant penetration and display, most gracefully arranged, as the best affairs are. Her seductions are risky and artful, leaving the ladies delightfully scandalized. As a member of the DAR, Eastern Star, AAUW, the Republican Women's Club, and the author of *Dakota, An Informal History of Territorial Days*, Waldo travelled the state in the early 1930s. "It was routine for conventions to ask me to give talks," she writes, "often to the 'wives,' about our local history and what to see." In the fall of 1935, Waldo got a "big break" when her friend, Mrs. G. Olgeirson, who was trying to start a small tea room and not doing well, took Waldo's offer to do a review occasionally for a percentage of the take:

> Then the Fort Lincoln ladies appeared. Our post has been reoccupied in 1928 and was until the outset of WWII. Women there needed planned recreation and little attention had been paid to them locally. "They don't want to know us," was the story. But they did. They were lively. And most of them had lived all over the world and had much to offer. After that tea room appearance, the Commander's wife,

whom I'd already met at AAUW, asked me to come out twice a month as part of their planned schedule. Paid, of course. They'd usually have a luncheon first, then the review; after there was a tea to which a few town ladies were invited. These were all elegant affairs (Letter to author).

Here Waldo, at the height of her powers, triumphs over the town ladies themselves, entering a world of sophisticates, intelligent and properly uniformed, who are willing to pay for her services. Once again, the desire for love and work locates itself in the same place, or the site of "elegant affairs."

By spring of 1935, Waldo had made enough contacts among North Dakota women artists and writers to form a state branch of the Pen Women in Bismarck. Among her most important contacts was Josephine Hosch, society editor of the *Bismarck Tribune*, who saw to it that Pen Women efforts to interpret the state and to encourage its cultural development were put before the public. "As long as we had Jo, we had the *Tribune*," Waldo wrote to me. The *Tribune's* account of the Pen Women charter dinner shows how the Pen Women combined the societal codes of middle-class convention with the didactic purposes of teaching North Dakotans of their cultural heritage. Besides the 14 charter members of the club, 20 guests gathered at the Rose room in Bismarck's Patterson Hotel, the guests representing various social, study, and women's clubs throughout the state. Representatives from the Current Events club, the North Dakota Poetry Association, the Business and Professional Women's Club, and the Women's Literary Club attended. In her article, Hosch quotes part of an address delivered by Mrs. Esther Selke of Dickinson, who

> summarized a study which she has made of the Pen Women members listed in *Who's Who Among North American Authors* and sketched what she considers the opportunity afforded for creative writing in various locations in North Dakota. She called the formation of the state chapter of Pen Women an epochal step toward development of creative work in the state. Mrs. Putnam of New Rockford, founder of the North Dakota Poetry Society and editor of *Prairie Wings*, a new magazine of North Dakota poetry, spoke briefly of a North Dakota poetry anthology on which she is working at present (*Bismarck Tribune*, 26 April 1935).

For the next fifteen years, the North Dakota Pen Women used society columns in state newspapers, what connections they had with the North Dakota Education Association, and their membership in literary and social clubs to launch their cultural projects. Throughout this period of active campaigns for "arts" issues in the state, the Pen Women linked their work to that of other women. After the Bismarck charter dinner, for instance, Waldo held the first business meeting to honor the memory of Mrs. Linda Slaughter, called the first woman writer in North Dakota. The *Bismarck Tribune's* account of that meeting, again by Pen Woman Josephine Hosch, gives a thumbnail sketch of Slaughter's biography, then notes that Slaughter's daughters and granddaughters attended the Pen Women meeting. Waldo read excerpts from her chapter on Slaughter in *Dakota*, then Hosch spoke of Slaughter's work on the *Bismarck Tribune*, 1879-1893. Finally, Mrs. Burghum, herself a candidate for Pen Women membership, "answered questions concerning her mother's career" (*Bismarck Tribune*, 3 May 1949).

The blend of social and professional themes, staged for the instruction and envy of North Dakota readers, is especially noticeable in Hosch's account of a Writers' Shoptalk Forum held with the Bismarck chapter of AAUW in the municipal golf course club house:

> Covers were laid for thirteen at 6:30 o'clock dinner honoring Miss Clarice Belk, a shop talk forum member, who on June 25 will be married to Leonard E. Nelson of Madison, Wisconsin. Miss Belk found gifts of handkerchiefs enclosed in a large "rejection slip" envelope marking her place at the table. Place cards were roses holding the names on small gold slips. Nut cups and the streamers leading from a bridal picture at one end of the table carried out a color scheme in pastel green, pink and yellow. There were also candy favors.
>
> Miss Marcella Schlasinger, who soon is to leave for a month's vacation in Hollywood, California, brought a box of candy as a treat required from those who have sold material, according to one of the group's traditions. Miss Schlasinger had as her guest Mrs. E. M. Canfield of Williston, who is a woman aviatrix and who writes a column for one of the popular flying magazines (*Bismarck Tribune*, 4 June 1939).

If the bride-to-be has cause to weep, she has means to dry her tears, and inspiration to find her work enveloping. One is tempted to ask, in reading these accounts of brides-to-be and rejection slips, pastel streamers and a woman aviatrix, why such strong social emphases prevail. Waldo herself provides an answer in the *Pen-Gram*, a mimeographed newsletter which Waldo edited and distributed to the Bismarck branch from 1936-1944, when she moved to Minot:

> Our local newspapers and some others in the state are getting increasingly commercial. It is more and more difficult to get space for book or art news. BUT if the new books or the out-of-town member is presented at a large social affair to which the most prominent people in the city are invited, the papers cannot ignore it as NEWS. "More than one way to skin a cat," my dears! (*Pen-Gram* 1937).

What is so striking about Waldo's note is that it gives primary evidence of the pleasure that club women found in finding ways to bring aesthetic issues before the public. Throughout the most active period of North Dakota Pen Women history, 1936-1953, no more than thirty women in the state were active members. Yet the newspapers' society pages, especially in Bismarck and Fargo, were filled with Pen Women news, partly because two North Dakotans, Edna Waldo and Hazel Webster Byrnes, served as National Historians (Waldo 1940-42; Byrnes 1952-54), and they made sure that the state's scrapbooks, sent to national headquarters in Washington, D.C., were full. Byrnes, who was appointed Director of the State Library Commission in Bismarck in 1948, the year Waldo left the state for California, used her office to promote the library work Pen Women had begun. A 1949 social note on Byrnes in the *Bismarck Tribune* observes, "80% of the public libraries in the state are promoted and sponsored by club women, who often provide the libraries, library housing, equipment, and books."

By the early 1940s, the Bismarck branch had grown defunct, but a strong Fargo branch, under the leadership of poet Prudence Geary Sands, helped reorganize western North Dakota into the Medora and Williston branches. Marion Jordan Piper of Bismarck, editor of *North Dakota Outdoors*, led the Pen Women's sponsorship of art and museum exhibits for the Roosevelt Park dedication in 1949. Medora Pen Women President Esther Selke of Dickinson again made links between the newly-formed Medora Pen Women and their historical predecessor, Medora Von Hoffman, the "first eligible Pen Woman in western North Dakota." Writing to Sands on Marion Piper's homemade cattle-brand stationery, Selke created this history:

> The famous Medora Von Hoffman of New York City came to this part of the state in 1883 as the bride of the handsome and spirited French nobleman, the Marquis de Mores. While her husband took care of his vast cattle interests, Medora did lovely paintings and considerable writing. You may be interested to know that the running NP used on this stationery was their brand and, interpreted, means "The Northern Pacific Refrigerator Car Company" (Grace Brown Putnam Collection).

Modern historians of North Dakota will find Selke's romantic narrative of Medora Von Hoffman an entirely inappropriate description of the fruitless designs of the Marquis de Mores. But what they might miss in Selke's text is the attempt, so consciously made, to give North Dakota women artists and writers an intriguing, romantic past, a past now discovered by its female inheritors who can brand themselves with its symbols.

In the 1950s, the North Dakota Pen Women's influence began to fade. A long and sensational court battle over the estate of Prudence Geary Sands' foster mother brought the Pen Women under unwanted public scrutiny (Grace Brown Putnam Collection). Women's professional interests took other directions, and club membership began to wane. Pen Women no longer tried to influence the school curriculum through State Poetry Day, high school writing contests, or intramural art exhibits. *Prairie Wings*, a poetry magazine edited by two prominent Pen Women, Grace Brown Putnam and Anna Ackermann, folded after a twelve-year publishing history. The North Dakota Institute for Regional Studies, the North Dakota Council for Humanities and Public Policy, and the North Dakota Council on the Arts subsequently institutionalized, and eventually displaced the Pen Women as cultural guardians and teachers. One more domestic pleasure, the production of culture, was appropriated by male professionals.

Today, women still fill our creative writing classes, our literary seminars, our art and drama courses. Over sixty percent of the nation's college English majors are women. But only 21% of their teachers are women, and the gap between club women and those with paid careers outside the home has widened. American feminists promoting sexual equality seem blind to the powerful strategies which club women used to link female "identity" — gossip, luncheons, and ritualized conversations — to public and private pleasures.

References

Alsop, Elizabeth. "Role of Women in Early Fargo," Fargo: North Dakota Institute for Regional Studies, North Dakota State University, October 1972.

Bethke, Frances, of Mandan Branch, North Dakota League of American Pen Women, personal interview, September 29, 1983, and Judy Hamelin, Secretary, National Headquarters, NDLAPW, September 30, 1983.

Bismarck Tribune. April 26, 1935; October 16, 1936; May 3, 1949; June 4, 1939; October 9, 1949.

Blair, Karen J. *The Clubwoman as Feminist: True Womanhood Redefined, 1869-1914.* New York and London: Homes and Meier, 1980.

Lerner, Gerda. *The Majority Finds Its Past: Placing Women in History.* New York and London: Oxford University Press, 1979.

Lyons, Richard. Letter to Eva Anglesburg, February 27, 1952, *Prairie Wings* papers. Fargo: North Dakota Institute for Regional Studies, North Dakota State University.

Maxwell, William. *Time Will Darken It.* New York: Praeger, 1948, quoted in Atherton, *Main Street on the Middle Border.* Bloomington: Indiana University Press, 1954.

North Dakota Federated Women's Clubs. Miscellaneous File, 1913-14, 1916. Fargo: North Dakota Institute for Regional Studies, North Dakota State University.

North Dakota League of American Pen Women records. Fargo: North Dakota Institute for Regional Studies, North Dakota State University.

North Dakota League of American Pen Women records. Bismarck: North Dakota State Historical Society.

Pen-Gram, The. September 1937. North Dakota League of American Pen Women Records, A65. Bismarck: North Dakota State Historical Society.

Putnam, Grace Brown. Papers. Fargo: North Dakota Institute for Regional Studies, North Dakota State University.

Schroeder, Patricia. "The Fargo Fortnightly Club: A Study of Club Activities." Master's Thesis. Moorhead, Minn.: Moorhead State University, 1983.

Scott, Ann Firor. "On Seeing and Not Seeing: A Case of Historical Invisibility," *Journal of American History*, 71:1, June 1984.

Scott, Ann Firor and Andrew McKay Scott. *One Half the People: The Fight for Woman Suffrage.* Urbana: University of Illinois Press, 1982.

Waldo, Edna LaMoore. Letters to author, June 11, 1984; July 16, 1984.

Sheryl O'Donnell is Associate Professor of English at the University of North Dakota, where she serves on the Women Studies faculty. She has published studies of British and American women writers, women in popular culture, and the semiotics of gender. She lives on a farm near Red Lake Falls, Minnesota, and raises registered colored sheep.

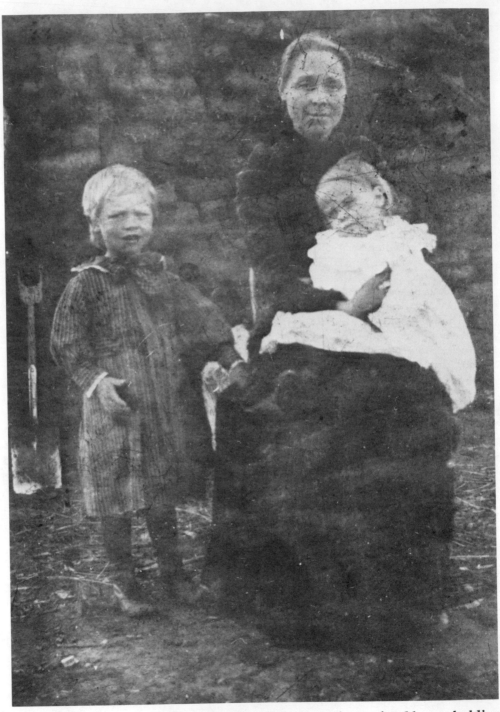

Leonelle Maillard Vollmer in front of sod house holding
Charles F.; Arthur B. at side. Circa 1897. Omemee, N.D.

I

Most people at Turtle Mountain are interrelated somehow or share the same ancestors, so the word "family" might take on different connotations here than elsewhere.

Lise Croonenberghs

St. Ann's Procession of the Altar Society,
St. Ann's Church, Belcourt, N.D., 1956.
Photo courtesy of the *Minot Daily News*.

Metis Women at Turtle Mountain

by Lise Croonenberghs

The Metis, or mixedblood Indian people, emerged in the eighteenth and nine-teenth century as the most numerous population on the Northern Plains and Upper Great Lakes region, the result of Indian-white contact dating back to the seventeenth century. This population has been commonly referred to as "halfbreeds" and "Bois-brules." They were unique among Native peoples in that they alone did not antedate the North American fur trade. Scholarly interest in the Metis is very recent, and written records are sparse. Few Metis-authored materials have survived. For the most part, those records that do exist remark upon exceptional events and colorful people rather than the everyday material, the "canvas" on which history was painted. The following oral-history interviews with women on the Turtle Mountain Indian reservation are an effort to present a different look at North Dakota history. Like canvas, these women were of strong, durable material, holding things together with hard work and inner resolve. They are behind the painting, and they, too, created it.

The word metis is French for "mixed"; most of the original Metis were of French ancestry, but due to the English fur trade, many were of Scottish and other descent also. The word "Michif" is a dialectical variant used at Turtle Mountain. The difference between Michif and Metis and Indian is context-related and can be subtle, non-existent, or obviously marked. Historically, the mixedblood people followed three trails: Indian, white or Metis. Metis is a separate cultural and political unit that evolved in Canada at least one hundred years before the extermination of the bison. This "New Nation" of the Metis was championed by Louis Riel, the Metis founder of Manitoba who was hung for treason and remains a folk hero to many. Some of the Metis fled Canada and joined the fullblood and mixedblood group at Turtle

Moutain, who are federally recognized as Chippewa Indians. This development was never satisfactory to all involved as the land area and resources of the reservation were always too small for such a large sedentary population.

Most people at Turtle Mountain are interrelated somehow or share the same ancestors, so the word "family" might take on different connotations here than elsewhere. Indian people also are used to extended households. I have heard it said that the Turtle Mountain Band is just one big happy family. This is a humorous way of looking at the situation, which is not always joyful and harmonious, but nonetheless constant: these are one's people, and this is their home.

The first interview is with my mother's mother, my grandmother Mary Lefavor Gourneau. She married Patrice Gourneau at Belcourt in 1928, and many of her stories are from his family which traces itself back to a man named Old Wild Rice, a Chippewa mentioned in the fur trade journals of Alexander Henry and Charles Jean-Baptiste Chaboillez. They were connected to the Pembina post between 1797 and 1803. Patrice's grandfather was one of fifteen Indians of the Red Lake and Pembina Bands of Chippewa who signed the treaty at the Old Crossing in 1863 —his name is there as "Joseph Gornon, Warrior of Pembina." His son, Joseph Jr. (who spelled the name Gourneau), was an altar boy to Father Pierre Genin, Missionary Apostolate, North West Territories. His parish was as large as a diocese is today, and Joseph Jr. accompanied him on religious missions and buffalo hunts throughout the territory. As a hunter, trapper, and freighter, Joseph traveled on foot or by horse or dog-sled into Montana, Canada, Minnesota and the Dakotas. Joseph Jr. was called "Mooshum" by the family, meaning grandfather.

My great-grandmother, Eliza McCloud, was born at Pilot Mound, Manitoba, and came to the Turtle Mountains with a hunting party. Several years later the reservation was established and Joseph Jr. came over to stay, from his birthplace at Red Lake, Minnesota. Joseph and Eliza married and farmed as best they could near Belcourt, and had 12 children, 11 surviving infancy. Eliza was said to be a great teller of traditional Indian stories, especially as she was busy with the children while she peeled cranberry bark for "Lydia Pinkham's Vegetable Compound." She was said also to have spoken "Indian" with a Scottish burr in her voice when she was young. This was probably the French-Cree (Michif) fur trade language, as Plains-Cree and Plains Ojibway have no "r". Eliza was multilingual as were many of her people. The lives of Eliza McCloud and her sister, Margaret, are perhaps representative of many of their people as are the three women whose interviews follow.

Mary Lefavor Gourneau

LC: Grandma, tell what you know about Grandpa Pat's family coming here, and what reservation life was like in the early years.

MG: Well, Mooshum. They were staying over there, at Red Lake [Minnesota]. When they came over here they were pretty near starving. It took him *three days* to find a buffalo. They slit its throat and just fell down in the snow and drank the blood, they were so hungry. Everyone was hungry then—but I don't know all that. Maybe somebody around here does. He used to go such a long ways to get things, and he hauled people all over the place with him. One thing I remember, he took a woman and two twin babies all the way back to Red Lake. It was the dead of winter. He just had a horse and one of those things you drag behind, like in the pictures.

LC: He used to drive dog teams too, when he was a freighter hauling supplies and mail for the trading posts and stores in the territory, right? Do you remember any stories about that?

MG: Oh, he would go clear to Montana after he went to the Valley [Red River Valley settlements] and up into Canada. That town is still there, I think, where he had to go get flour that one winter [Wakopa, Manitoba, site of the Bernard LaRivierre trading post]. It was freezing cold. Then he had to go over by Pembina, Mountain City. There was no flour up at that place. He brought back 200 pounds of flour, and he could keep 100. He had to divide that sack up between *so many* families. In the spring he went with horses, turned right around and went back for more. Two trips.

LC: Mooshum did all kinds of things to make a living, before and after he settled on the reservation. He was a hunter for the big hotels and railroad, and hauled the bones of the elk and bison after they were exterminated. What kinds of things did Eliza do to help them make a living?

MG: Well, a long time ago. she told about the bones. The children went running along after the wagon. They were stacked up to the rail road cars, as high as the boxcars. They were piled all along the railroad.

LC: Do you remember when or where this was?

MG: No. That's before my time. They got their land [Joseph and Eliza] from two Indians that were going away, and needed a team and wagon. They traded it for a team of oxen and a wagon. They had to clear it all out, and they grew their own grain. I remember she went in her horse and buggy and she sold berries, five gallons for a dollar, to those farms out there and little towns. She had her chickens. They came in handy, those eggs, when food was scarce in the spring. They would go out and set snares for gophers. Just for a certain time in the spring, when they started to come out of the ground, they were good. There were no deer in those days. They were all hunted out. Even the rabbits were gone a lot of times. Any little thing the boys hunted, she would clean it and cook it for them. She used to help them trap blackbirds with a bedspring, and she would clean them and pick all the feathers — they were little teeny things. Later on, we used to get deer, and for a while there was lots of prairie chickens. The trees around the field were loaded down with them sometimes.

LC: What about wild plants?

MG: Pat's aunt. She was a medicine woman. He used to go with her when she gathered all those plants. That was Shyoosh, Mooshum's sister. She delivered all the babies around here — she was a midwife. She delivered Pat and all his brothers and sisters. When Pat's sister was born she was so tiny. Only 2 or 3 pounds. They put her in a shoebox, and she had tiny clothes just like a doll.

LC: Did Grandpa Pat learn anything about medicine from her?

MG: If we had a cold or a stomach-ache or something he knew what to use. There was some bark he would get for sore throat. He would dig up roots. He would go and get his kinnickinik that he smoked.

LC: How did you and Grandpa Pat get started here truck farming?

MG: Pat learned how from my dad. He got $2,000 from land out West that was sold, that was his share. Then he bought this 120 acres with the old log house first, the rest later, and we moved in. He bought two cows. A team of horses. Harnesses. A sleigh. A winter coat for me. A cookstove. A cream separator. And he had to buy a haystack and feed. His dad gave us a new wagon for a wedding present. My dad gave us twelve skinny pigs. He used to go to all the restaurants around East Grand Forks and get leftovers and fatten them up. People would leave loaves of bread on their tables. But here we had to buy feed for them and it didn't pay. My mother gave us chickens, hens and roosters. But we had to buy feed. If we sold eggs, it barely paid for the feed.

LC: What was it like in the log house?

MG: Oh, it wasn't bad. We mudded it inside and out, and fixed the windows. It had two stories, and a big leanto, so it was bigger than it is now. Pat said he remembered going to dances there long ago, before we came. It was bigger than most log houses around here. Just one room, most of them. But it was nice, I had it fixed all up and whitewashed inside. It had a wood floor. Ask your mom. She lived in there. It was warm, we had a little buck stove — you could hear pop, pop, pop going up the chimney at night, it was like a tin stove — it scared me, boy, and I made a fire in the cookstove. We had a beautiful cookstove, I was sorry to see that go. In the spring, we made extra fence and we started planting.

LC: How did you and grandpa divide the work? Did you work in the fields too, besides all your other work?

MG: I used to pick the stuff up in the fields. The corn. I would peel onions, all that. If there was no one else to help I would go out there. But I had the garden. The cows. I worked in the house in the morning. I did all the canning. If Pat shot a deer, I canned that too. I had to wash the separator, pails, jars, everything after milking. After I didn't have to do that, boy it seemed like it was easy. But no one went hungry around here.

I made cheese on the cookstove and stir in that nice thick cream — better than what you buy in the store now for cottage cheese. The first big row was muskmelons. But the season wasn't long enough so we put them in a box to ripen. Then someone would hide in the corn and eat them. The boys would make a drive every Sunday afternoon, and they'd bring home rabbits. I didn't mind cleaning them. I'd put them in the oven and cook them. They walked in a line and drove the rabbits out in front of them.

But it was hard to make money. One year, it must have been just the right weather and there was too much corn. We only got ten cents a dozen at Rolla. I picked ten gunny sacks and Pat took them to Rolla, and we had to keep doing that. That's the only time that ever happened. Every one was ripe. My dad gave us two pregnant sows, but we had to buy feed. It was only $5 to raise those little pigs all summer. One time we had so many carrots they were piled up in the root cellar going soft. Pat took them and fed them to the cows. But we had enough vegetables during the winter anyway. It wasn't like now, everyone getting commodities and things. If we had

$30, we would buy our supplies for the winter — flour, tea, then coffee when it was in the store and sold so cheap. Sugar, salt, maybe a few little cans and a piece of salt pork. No one is poor anymore. They don't know what poor is!

LC: What do you remember about Eliza McCloud Gourneau?

MG: She would always have a pot of tea boiling. Even if she didn't have much she always invited people in. She always invited anyone in for tea and something to eat if there was anything. Even if it was just galet, just grease even. They would come by because they knew they could always get tea and some kind of snack. Pat had two twin uncles we used to see. Well, she was proud of her Indian blood. She always went to church. All the kids went. Mooshum would walk all the way to St. John to go to Mass, before the church was here. The boys walked to Belcourt and she had a beautiful winter rig that she drove to Mass. She never took a drink, she always prayed, she was always working. But that's the way they used to be.

Mary Jane Davis

Jane Davis was born in 1899; one of Margaret McCloud and Joseph Keplin's 12 children. Margaret McCloud was a sister of my great-grandmother, Eliza McCloud Gourneau. Joseph, Jane's father, was born at Pembina; his parents were Paul Keplin and Margaret Gourneau, who was a sister of Joseph "Sooza" Gourneau Sr., Isabel, and the Pembina-Turtle Mountain hereditary leader called Ka-ish-pah. Jane Davis is active in church and community life, and works nearly every weekday at the Turtle Mountain Counseling Center where she sews clothes and blankets.

LC: What do you remember about your mother, Maggie, and her sister Eliza? My mother remembers that Maggie used to make beautiful beadwork things. She would drive her horse and buggy 60 miles to Rugby where she caught the train that went to Devils Lake and Grand Forks. She would ride it to Grand Forks and back selling her beadwork to people on the trains and in the towns they passed. Eliza, too, sold beadwork for cash income besides all the other work she did.

JD: Oh, yes, she did that. I remember my aunt Eliza. She and my mother lived in Canada, here and there where the animals were. There was no survey, no nothing in those days. It was a free country when they came here. There was no reservation. People would go out by the bunches hunting and everything — they lived with the wild. The bears, the buffaloes, the moose — they went where they went. It was hard times!

LC: How do you think their lives were enhanced or limited by living in North Dakota? What was good or bad?

JD: Oh, when they made the boundaries, when they made the reservation, why then everyone had to try to make a living here. There was nothing for them like they have now. No rations, not even seed to plant. So they had to do the best they could. I'm telling you, people are lucky these days.

LC: In a way, they provided for their descendents by sticking it out all those years so their descendents were able to become eligible for the educational benefits, food programs, etc., that are available today. How else did you see your mother providing for her family? My grandma told me how Eliza would pick berries, snare rabbits, trap birds and grow food for her family. Do you remember anything like that?

LD: I saw that. My grandpa did that. He put a hole in the window with twine through it — then there was a big board, like a door. Your doors were made by hand like everything else. He put a little grain under there, then he'd pull the cord and let it fall down. He'd get a lot of little birds, 8 or 9. Then when we had enough, Grandma made a feast. We snared gophers and put snares out in the woods for rabbits. My ma would boil 3 or 4 of them in water and make a stew first, what you call "La rub a boo" that you could use for the gravy. Then you put them in the oven with some butter and salt and pepper or else salt pork. My ma had a big, big garden. All the canning and drying, she did that. She dried all the chokecherries — oh, we'd grind chokecherries 'till 1:00 in the morning. We pounded them with a stone about this big, and the next morning put them on to dry. Then we had dried chokecherry cakes. "Li gren pelee." Dried juneberries too.

LC: These were for your own use, right? Did you use to have taureaux (too roo) for a treat?

JD: Yes, that was a treat for us. You mixed up the crushed berries with grease, cracklings really, and let it get hard. Brown sugar if you had it. We picked all the berries we could. My ma went out to all these little towns around here just like your

Collaboration
by Sally McBeth

Esther Burnett Horne has been a long-time resident of Wahpeton, North Dakota, where I came to know her, and where she taught fourth grade at the Wahpeton Indian School. This is how she begins to tell about her life:

Well, I was born in 1909, on November 9, and the earliest thing I can remember is being on top of a tall dapple grey horse. It seems to me I still had on a diaper, and so I don't know whether this is truth personified or images remembered from what I've been told. And that would be somewhere in Idaho because my mother and father had to run away to get married. My father was Scotch-Irish and my mother was Indian. Shoshone Indian.

My paternal grandfather was sent with the Shoshones to the Wind River Reservation in Wyoming to teach them agriculture after the big treaty-making in Fort Bridger, Wyoming, in 1871. So that although he liked the Indians very, very much, it was one of those things that was frowned upon. I mean, his son, a young white male marrying an Indian girl, would be called a "squaw man" in those days. And, it was just as much beneath the dignity of my mother as a young Indian woman to be marrying a white man; she would lose status in the eyes of her tribe or family. Be that as it may, they ran away from the reservation and went over into Idaho. And that's where they were married, and that's where I was

great-grandma, in her horse and buggy. She went to Rugby. She went to Rolla, Rollette, Dunseith, Willow City, everywhere. They got 25 cents a gallon — that's a bargain. Nowadays they go for $5 a gallon. She sold cranberries, juneberries, raspberries, plums — we picked those plums green and put 'em in a sack out under the haystack to ripen. There used to be so many wild strawberries out on the prairie you'd squash them when you walked. They're all gone now. Sometimes Ma and Dad would go out in the wagon with all the berries and some eggs. If people out on the farm didn't have money we traded for food. The mothers would get some berries for the children. Dad had two little sheds outside he called the "grainery." He had a big barrel, and my ma would put paper out there and put the cranberries out there. They were better after they froze.

    LC: Your family raised grain and a few animals, mainly for subsistence?

    JD: We never bought anything, hardly. There was nothing to buy around here anyway. There was *nothing, no place*! I'm telling you, people don't know how lucky they are these days. My dad had a good patch of navy beans. We'd pull them off, put 'em in a sack and pound it. He had all the grandchildren knock off the beans, and sold them for $6 a hundred. Anyone in the family helped with that. At Christmas my dad used to butcher. My ma made blood sausage. We had no refrigeration like now. We cut up the meat and kept it frozen in big barrels out in the shed. And some was canned, some dried — "La vyawnd shesh." That was in the hot season if we had meat.

---

born, and that's where I remember sitting on this tall grey horse.

    Both of my parents taught us about our relationship to Sacajawea. My grandfather, Finn Burnett, the frontiersman, the agricultural agent, or "boss farmer" on the Shoshone reservation, worked with her and knew her personally. She was anxious to help teach the Shoshones agriculture because she remembered the Mormon wheat fields and she remembered the Comanche wheat fields and she'd eaten bread and she liked it and she wanted her people to be able to make "T'de Cup" — is the way it is said in Shoshone. So I grew up knowing about our relationship to the "Bird Woman," of her travels with Lewis and Clark, and of her cross-country travels back to her Wyoming home.

    Life histories have been regarded as legitimate approaches to understanding other cultures, for they emphasize the experiences of an individual and provide an insider's view of that life and culture. However, because life histories, as understood in the work of anthropologists, usually are translated, edited, interpreted, re-organized and sometimes even re-written by the "collector" who is non-Native, the result may violate the integrity of the storyteller's words and style, and hence the intrinsic value of the document. In reaction to those criticisms, there is a recent trend among anthropologists toward the production of texts jointly composed by fieldworker and native informant, where jointly told stories recognize and respect the authority of the individual member of the culture better than do traditional life stories more heavily controlled by the field worker. The partnership method allows the individual recounting a life to do so

LC: Tell me what Christmas and New Year's were like. I know Midnight Mass was a big event.

JD: O, my, yes, it was. My ma would put blankets in the sleigh and pack us all under there. She told us, before we went, not to peek out of the blankets or sleep in church. It was 5 miles to church — that seemed like such a long ways back then. I remember my sister and I were under those blankets and peeked out at the stars. It was just black outside, and I looked and saw those bright, bright stars. "Put your head back in. You'll get cold." She caught us.

LC: Did you hang up stockings?

JD: We didn't get much for Christmas, each a little doll for us girls sometimes, dried apples and prunes. We thought those big black prunes were so good. They were really a treat for us children. Oh, it was hard. We were happy with what we got. We didn't use to eat much candy back then, just once or twice. When I was 6 we got oranges. Oh, my ma made pies, and cakes, "lee bang," "lee bullet" (frybread, meatballs) everything like that, galet and light bread, and we had tea with sugar. There was not much coffee at that time, we drank tea. The house would be full around then.

LC: What about New Year's? I believe that's a Michif holiday that lasts two weeks.

---

with less interference or wanton translation, and allows the "informant" a hand in presenting the text in its final form, even to crediting authorship.

In an effort to overcome the difficulties in composing Esther Horne's life history, she and I talked about ways we might avoid the imbalance of power and authority and instead blur the normally sharp separation between "informant" and "ethnographer." We recognized the inherent artifice of a life-as-told, a life history, that it is a narrative influenced by numerous factors including the cultural conventions of the telling, the setting, and the relationship that exists between the teller and the listener. At the same time we recognized that the nature of our projects rests upon dialogue — between us, with the text we jointly produce, and with our intended audience. A life history is not an individual process although it purports to be about an individual's life; it is a collective, public narration designed to be shared.

We saw the advantage of working together, encouraging, questioning, and stimulating each other. While usually informants "speak" and ethnographers "write," the relationship between Esther and me made her more a Native consultant than an informant, and me a learner. We were partners, not object of research and researcher. We continue to seek out fine points of the collaborative process, and the formidable task of jointly editing, organizing and adding detail to the tapes so far transcribed still lies ahead. Transcribing tapes and the initial editing will be my responsibility, but we will arrange the document in its final form together. My contribution is to maintain the structural and cultural integrity of the narrative, while respecting Esther's experiences in the way she chooses to present,

JD: Oh, six days at least, until the 6th of January. That's the Kings' Day (French Holiday). My brother-in-law was born that day so his name is King. But his birth name is Gregory Riel.

LC: So that's why boys are named King sometimes, and I presume Riel was for Louis Riel — I know many boys were named for him, even the little ones now.

JD: That's right. Sometimes people came at 12:00, not always. I remember we had a neighbor who came and shot his gun twice in front of the door, once for my ma, and once for my dad and yelled "La Bon Annee," Happy New Year. But we would get in the sleigh and go on an outing and people were glad to see one another. We had a very good time. Everyone was nice, everyone went. We took care of our own babies. When I was a girl, the big people were polite to us. They would sit us all down to eat and they treated us very well. We didn't have babysitters.

LC: I like to hear about the Bush Dances and New Year dances.

JD: Well, we'd dance until 5 and 6 in the morning. We had a very good time. We didn't get drunk or fight. We had violin music. One would play bass and they didn't have all that racket like they do now. We had waltzes and square dances. I didn't care for that Red River jig. Two of them would each take turns, two or three couples that knew how to do it. We always went to Midnight Mass, every year. We went to Mass every Sunday in our wagon.

---

explain, and interpret them. Horne's sense of personal and cultural worth is entwined with her ancestry, as the great-great-granddaughter of Sacajawea, and she understands much of her life as part of this legacy. For her, telling her life is sharing who she is and what she knows: "When you give, things flow back to you — maybe not materially but in other ways."

Special thanks are due to the Claire Garber Goodman Fund of Dartmouth College for supporting the initial stage of this research.

Sally McBeth is an anthropologist, teaching in Native American Studies and Anthropology at Dartmouth College in Hanover, New Hampshire.

LC: Maybe you can tell me what the Catholic religion has meant to the Michif people. How do you think the Michif people viewed themselves as different from the fullbloods? Is it because of religion, mainly?

JD: We were very religious. It's God's gift to us.

LC: You must believe, as many do, that it is the Catholic faith that has seen the Michifs through so many hard times.

JD: That's right. That was God's help. The fullbloods that didn't go to church, though, they had the rain dance. They could make it rain. We went to them for help back in the Depression when everything was so dry and there was so much heat. The wells even dried up. But the fullbloods did it. They would dance, and they had something powerful and God helped them. He worked through them. They don't go to church, but they have their own way to worship God. I can see that now. I went to their dance one time about three or four years ago, and there was a fullblood lady there. She went to the posts and prayed in her language, thanking God for giving their way of life to them, and I could understand then how we can pray in our own heart and ask for help. I could understand that she said, "I thank you today for all that you are giving to all of our people."

LC: Thank you for explaining this. Many, many people have expressed to me that their religiousness came from their deep spirituality from their Indian heritage, even though they don't participate in the Sun Dance or other Indian worship forms because of their strong Catholic faith.

JD: I know that if you pray then you will have something. That's religion. They have their way. Out here on Davis' land is the Holy Spring. If you are sick, you can come out here and pray by the spring, and then rub yourself with the water. There's no bottom to it. This was our prayers being answered, when God gave us this. There were some that would go and buy something, buy medicine from the fullblood Indians, even if they didn't believe in it. But that can't work when it's the powerful kind, that is their praying that makes it work.

LC: You made a reference to the "Fullblood language." That's Cree or else Plains-Ojibway, and as we have been talking here your daughter Ruth has been speaking "Michif." To me it sounds like she just said something about a story from bow and arrow time.

JD: Well, we have our own language, the Michifs. That's a story my brother used to tell. He went and tried to kill a buffalo. There was *no nothing*! That's what they had to do then. The older men would chase around the buffaloes. There were three boys that went with him. They were supposed to lie down and go to sleep. Through the ground, they could hear the sound of the buffaloes coming. My dad was ready with his gun if they would chase them his way. Well, my oldest brother went out there and got one with his bow and arrows, so when everyone went out and butchered their share he had one. The buffaloes were in good shape yet those days.

LC: That's a good story. I wonder, is there such a thing as a Michif wedding?

JD and Ruth: Sure there is.

JD: I used to make all the wedding cakes for the people around here. Not all of them were Michif weddings. But I would make the cakes, and they were not like the ones you see now, but they were round layer cakes. Sometimes they would bring me everything to make the cake and sometimes I would have to get flour or sugar myself, but they would bring what they could. And it was all homemade, the food and the dresses and everything. We made our own music and had dancing. And I sewed all my children's clothes, and I sewed blankets I gave to the neighbors, and I sewed wedding dresses. We used to make everything, and we helped each other. And I remember when I was little, I would really love it when there was a wedding. Back in those days the young men had to court the girls, and there was no running around together. They had a relative that went with them, and he would have to ask her parents if they could get married.

LC: You mentioned the flu epidemics earlier; did your family get hit?

JD: Our family was quarantined. My ma, my dad, everyone was too sick to get out of bed. Just my brother and I had to take care of everything. I was 16 years old and he was 14. There was a terrible blizzard and we could hardly get out to the sheds to take care of the livestock, to get wood for the fire. I had to take care of everyone inside. It's hard. I used to have 11 children, only 7 lived.

LC: We have a lot to be thankful for nowadays. What do you remember about the happy times, like St. Ann's week?

JD: The Novena would be for nine days, everyone would come from near and far to pray and to worship. They brought their teepees and the tents and camped right on the church ground. Some relatives would come from Montana in their wagon. When they had cars, they camped with their cars. It was a great joy when someone was cured from their suffering. Everyone visited one another again, and had good times together. Every morning and night there was Mass. On St. Ann's Day there was Mass all day, and the big procession. It started at the church and went down the hill. The little girls were all dressed in white and they rode on the hayrack with the statue of St. Ann. They used white horses to pull it. The girls threw flower petals in the path, the wagon was all full of beautiful flowers. When they all got to the altar then they had a special Mass. There was a big picnic down there before the last Mass, music, dancing again. Then the wagon caravans went out again to where they came from, some of them went to Montana. When bunches of people came in their cars, they went off together too. Every year they would come. Now when everyone comes they don't camp at the church, and they are having a party all over town. But, we go to St. Anthony's out here most of the time. Yes, it was very beautiful . . . it was happy times for the people there.

Elma Wilkie

Elma Wilkie teaches social science at Turtle Mountain Community College, and is active with the Aunishinaubag Intercultural Program in Belcourt that promotes and supports traditional Indian culture.

One explanation of the origin of the name of the homemade bread called gallette (pronounced gullet) that she refers to is that it was a voyageur's term for a large smooth mass of rock, a boulder. Boullettes are the traditional Michif meatballs.

My mother didn't really know when she was born. She just told us she was born out on the prairie somewhere. There were not a lot of records back then. The missionaries baptized while they were out where the Indian people were hunting all over the place. These early priests, Fr. Oulette, Fr. Genin, Fr. Belcourt and others, operated out of Winnipeg, St. Boniface actually. That was their home base and a lot of these few records that were there were lost when the old church burned. So a record of my mother's baptism was never found, but she remembered the year and she always thought it was August 18th — her mother told her it was when she was about a month old. This would sound true to me, because that was around the time of the fall hunt when the priests would come to baptize all the newly born babies and to marry people and turn them into Catholics. And she did not remember who baptized her or any of these details, but she talked about a story that had been told to her by her own mother or grandmother

It was said, while I'm thinking of this story, that Fr. Genin was kicked out because he was performing miracles; according to the Church he was supposed to follow guidelines, there were channels to go through. Anyway, she told me about this miracle of the water. At one time, when they were out hunting the buffalo, they were short of water or couldn't find water where they were camped. So this priest then went into a hill where there was a dip, a hollow, in it, and told everyone to pray with him and then they'd find water. Then the water came out of that dip and he told all the women of the camp to hurry up and go get their pails because he didn't know how long it would last. This old man Wilkie, however, would not let his wife go up there. So she was sitting in camp crying and some other women grabbed up her pails and ran up there to fill them.

I assume this was the old halfbreed chief John B. Wilkie because he was the Warden of the Plains at that time. He was in charge of the buffalo hunts. You'll find references to him in the early history that was written by Fr. Belcourt and those early priests. And his mother was a fullblood whose name was sometimes translated as "Rainbow" or "A Light Across the Sky and All Around." Keezhik is sky, and kok signifies it's a woman. Mish-a-Kam-ay-keezhik-kok. My husband Lawrence and I were both descended from her. Since the Fifties we had been doing research for our Treaty and looking for documents to prove the Pembina ancestors to the Turtle Mountain Band, because this anthropologist had come and called us "Bungis" and the government wanted to terminate the Tribe and not pay out the Treaty either. That's "Le Pay" everyone has been waiting for this entire century.

Anyway, we looked around for the records for Sarah and John B. Wilkie, that was your grandfather's aunt Shyoosh and the old halfbreed chief's grandson. We did find them at Neche [N.D.] and they were baptized and married the same day. My idea is that this corresponds to how that old Wilkie was one of those who tried to resist the missionaries as long as they could because he knew that they were bringing in the alcohol, the rum, through the fur trade with the sanction of the Church, and this was going to destroy us. In fact the Indian Liquor Law that was in effect until 1953 was at the request of our own leaders. As far back as 1803 Indian leaders were trying to stop the liquor traffic in order to keep our furs, goods, lands, and way of life from being taken away. As a consequence, then, I could understand how Shyoosh and John, being descended from these leaders, would try to resist being Christianized until they really had to, and finally did as a matter of survival.

They were 28 and 29 years old at that time; they were baptized in the morning and married that same afternoon. They had annuities at White Earth every fall, and the Gourneaus and some others were going over there to get them. Old Wilkie was mad. Stay here, he told them. Only a very few Pembinas were hanging on here; it was like a handful of family clans. In 1874 many finally went to White Earth. My mother remembered going out, picking roots after they were put on the reservation. The best farmland was taken over by the settlers at an early time before the reservation was established. It was just about the same thing as when gold was discovered in the Black Hills, and what happened to the Sioux people. Once those settlers started pouring onto our lands the government had no means to or wouldn't remove them. We were pushed onto a smaller reservation.

At the time of the 1882 negotiations a guy named Beede had come out and reported there were only 27 families here in need of a reservation. Chief Little Shell had wanted a larger reservation, at least 24 by 32 [miles], and he wanted the same price per acre for our lands that were being given up as the Sioux got a little while before, $2.25, for their lands bordering ours. McCumber only offered us 10 cents and so Little Shell walked out of the negotiations. By Executive Order then our reservation was reduced to 6 by 12 miles. Consequently we were left just a small wooded area, hills and sloughs. It didn't take long for the game and the furs to be depleted so there was starvation recorded in 1887.

And this was aggravated by all the Riel refugees coming down from Canada. The agent at Devils Lake withheld rations because only the United States citizens were supposed to get them, and so none were sent to us. And in the winter of 1887 at least 151 people died of starvation. Fr. Genin told about this in his letter: "the deplorable state of affairs and intolerable suffering of the Turtle Mountain Indians." He told how he found a family and buried them, and how there were women who had given birth and had to wait for their husbands to come back from the hunt with just a gopher. And this is documented in the State Historical Society records, where they have his letters. And the way my mother sounded when she'd tell me these things, how they'd go out in these family groups, in caravans, to look for the snakeroot, the senecaroot which was being used as a tonic by the white people, and to gather the millions upon millions of buffalo bones that were scattered all over after the white men promoted their extermination, which was a form of genocide to bring the Indian nations to their knees — then they would go out on the prairie and live more or less the way they used to, free and easy and on their own, picking the buffalo bones that they were buying for some purpose back East, and then at night they'd have their campfire and storytelling the way they used to — to me, then, that was the only bright spot after they were put on the reservation.

While other people in this country were suffering because of the Depression, we hardly noticed it here except that this was the first time many of our people had money, money from the WPA jobs. Before this we had no welfare programs or jobs; people were used to hardship here. And so then there were some good things for the women that came along with this -- these were the cooking, sewing, canning, and gardening projects that enabled the women to make so many improvements for their families. They also built some little two-bedroom houses around this time. Prior to all this the people really were struggling most of the time just to have food on the table.

Because their total way of life had been almost destroyed and in the process the Indian ceremonies, our religion was forbidden until 1934. And it was also during this time that our Indian women became the healers. They were able to incorporate the concepts of Christianity, LaMitasse Rouge that we talked about, that's Red Stocking. Now that's written, but I'm sure my mother must have told me. How she had the cure for cancer. I got a lot of knowledge from my mother, a lot of these stories. That's all oral tradition. And our people never lied.

This is one thing that we have to convince the white people of, that this is the reason we didn't need a written language to sign contracts the way they did. Because when we said something that was our honest word. And that's what made our democracy work, being honest, not lying and not stealing. We trusted each other. You can't have a true democracy if you can't trust each other.

Now the reason Mitasse Rouge had her house right down there by the mission, she could go to church every morning. That way the authorities would leave her alone. The same with old Shyoosh Gourneau. She went to church every day, and then they didn't arrest her for quackery. Because they were suspicious of our Indian medicine since it was associated with our religion, our spirituality. And at the same time the government provided no medical services to us. Now with all this poverty and disease that came, we had no recourse to our spiritual healers as before. My students go out and interview their elders, and there is one story I remember where this woman got caught out somewhere sick. And they went in the vicinity of Cando where there was a white doctor and he wouldn't treat her because she was an Indian so she died. And this is another Federal policy that's a form of genocide.

It's like that old lady in the nursing home told you about how her brothers and sisters died. So then when these plague diseases came, we had no cure for them. Before, you just got up and moved, no one stayed around where there was sickness. But now everyone had to stay on the reservation in these tiny one room log cabins with all the TB, smallpox, everything. Then we had this big flu epidemic. My mother told me her brother went out with the priest and they couldn't even keep up with all the burials, last sacraments, all that. The houses were quarantined, and when a family died they burned down the house and everything in it. They had to. These people you mentioned who went out to the sick who were thought to be immune, I know my uncle and the others drank skunk oil, which as you know comes from skunks and still is used around here sometimes. They sneaked across the border to Canada and got Everclear — it was the only thing that kept them going while they were digging all those graves. And eventually many of these helpers died too.

The years after the reservation was established were the most difficult. It was a very, very sad time for our people, a very bad time in the history. Because of the sheer force of the government and Christianity our people had to adapt in order to survive. We had to become farmers, and of course we had the land that couldn't be farmed. Back in 1863 the mixedbloods were told they could take up homesteads out on the public domain as one of the Treaty provisions, and some of our people were very prosperous around Grafton, but as more and more settlers came they forced those people off of their homesteads. In fact in my line, in my husband's line, some of his relatives had settled in and around St. John. This is oral history again, you won't find it in a book! And there's no documentation, they'll just have to take our word for it.

In the fall they had all their buildings up, their crops in. Then a French missionary came from Canada with a group of settlers and told them that because they were part Indian they were not entitled to stay there, the opposite being true. And they asked them to leave, which they did, because they were at the mercy of the U.S. government and the missionaries. But during the night they came back and set fire to all the crops and all the buildings, and they left and went up to Winnipeg. These people were not enrolled here until 1940 because they were afraid to come back here, afraid of retaliation by the government.

After the reservation was established, one main way our men would make a living was to chop wood. Because we lived in a wooded area here and cut wood for our stoves and to sell to the settlers that were on our lands, in order to take it out we had to have some form of transportation, so we kept horses. And my mother remembered what was used in our family was a Red River cart, and she used this to take the milk and cream to a cheese factory that was south of town somewhere, and then we bought products from the trader; old man Charlebois was one, where we would get our sugar and flour and things that we needed. In order to survive we had to have the cattle and learn to make hay, and our Indian women made huge gardens, and all the children worked in those gardens. Our people always made gardens. That's an area where we don't get credit, because it was the Indian people who made so many contributions from agriculture. Corn, beans, squash, pumpkins, tomatoes — the potato was ours — now they call that the Irish potato. We wouldn't have good things like pizza and spaghetti without the Indian products. Rubber was another, and tobacco, cotton, grapes, pineapple, peanuts, sunflowers, and so on.

But anyway, my childhood days were spent maintaining that garden, pulling the weeds and all that. Remember, I was born in 1923. Because my dad had to work out, putting in the crops and hauling wood and making hay, then it was up to the women and children to maintain those gardens. And this was all done by hand. Regarding your question about the division of labor, the lines were not so marked because the women had to work right alongside the men most of the time. It was a very very harsh life. My mother remembered going out to help make a living, going out in the fall to shock in the white man's fields. She didn't do the threshing but there were some women who went out with their husbands to the white farms and shocked and threshed the grain in order to make a living. Living in a house with no running water or electricity, we used a kerosene lamp and had to chop the wood for our stoves in winter — we children had to get up very early and do our chores before we went to school.

We walked to school, we didn't have buses like they do now. It's a wonder that we survived, really, walking through the snow without warm clothes and boots that they have now. We were lucky to have one pair of shoes a year. Most of the time we went barefoot in the summer so we could save our shoes for winter. We had just one change of clothes because most of the time our mothers had to sew our clothes and if we bought a new pair of overalls it was for the men or the older boys so it could be handed down from kid to kid. I remember my overalls being patched over the patches. But when I look back I think we were very happy, because we were productive, not idle. We did not have to rely on TVs, radios, cars to entertain us. We made our own music, we had dances, played cards and told stories. We made our own toys, and we made games out of our chores because we did not have time to play when there was so much work to do. There was this joke that Santa Claus and his reindeer didn't know how to find the reservation so he passed us by every year.

Looking back on the happy times, we did not celebrate Christmas as much as we did New Year's, and in looking back on this I feel it was because of the Indian influence of paying respects to our elders. On New Year's we would go to visit our elders, our grandparents, and the children of the families would made a game of it. The first one to get there, this was right after midnight New Year's, would be the hero. The first one who got there to greet their parents would be the star of the day, and the last one — we would kill a pig or a heifer or both for the meat for these holidays, and keep the tail. And so the last one who got there, to their parents' house, well they would hang the tail on him sometimes on the sly. He would be carrying this around with him and then people would be laughing at him because they knew this was more or less the lazy one in the family.

To us Christmas was always more or less a fear. To me the Catholic religion was a thing of fear because of the threat of burning in hell, the devil's going to get you, you know. And so on Christmas Eve the older children and our parents would get to go to Midnight Mass, because that was what Christmas was all about — to go to church and worship the child Jesus. So the younger children were left and we usually stayed with our cousins, they were our neighbors, our mothers were sisters and our dads were first cousins, the Davises and the Laverdures. We would play real hard up until midnight, because we were told the devil was chained by only one hair and he would be trying to get loose then, and if he broke that hair, at the stroke of midnight, then all hell would break loose and he would come and destroy us. We would play all night and have a party, have a good time, until just before the stroke of midnight. And I remember we would all be kneeling on our beds, scared out of our wits, and praying as hard as we could that the devil wouldn't break his hair.

These are the childhood memories I have of Christmas. If we were lucky, we hung our stockings up, to get an apple or an orange or a few peanuts or pieces of candy. We didn't get the lavish gifts that they have today that are so costly to buy and are broken or thrown away so soon. If we had a store-bought sled or toy we shared it and took care of it. I would say our New Year's celebrations came most strongly from our Indian heritage. Throughout our history the elders were very much respected. I remember kneeling down in front of my grandpa to receive the blessing, because that's what they would do, when the families and children arrived we'd all kneel down and Grandpa would give us a blessing and later on we could eat. Every house had prepared special boullettes, galette, the best that they had and everyone was invited to eat and you were expected to eat. If you did not eat when you were asked to then that was an affront to them so there was no two ways about it. I remember going from early midnight until the next night eating time and time again and you didn't get full for some reason. Of course those days we were traveling with horses and sleighs and it took quite a while to get from one place to the other. I could understand because of the cold, and a lot of the time we would jump out of the sleigh and run, and that would burn up all that food anyway.

It was at this time that the men would drink too, they would offer a little toast, and this I think came from our white heritage, our French culture because then they'd have to have something "an psi poonce" they would call it, that means a little shot. Since liquor was prohibited for the Indian people they would make their own moonshine and home brew and this is what they would share. Now in those days, up into the 1950s, hardly any of our Metis women drank. My mother would have maybe a little bit of brandy when she was not feeling up to par. On New Year's though, she would have a brandy, but it was mostly for the guests, and wine would be served with the meal. As a whole our Indian and Michif women did not drink until that law was repealed in the 1950s and the bars started here. It was unheard of for a woman in those days to leave her children and go out drinking leaving them without food, warm beds and heat in the house. Those are some of the values that I believe are really being eroded, that have made for very, very unhappy people here on the reservation. Fetal alcohol syndrome is one of the tragic consequences that can be seen on the different reservations now, along with all the other harm the use of liquor is doing to the children.

Back in those days, also, we were honest and really trusted each other. We were so poor, we never locked our houses, we didn't know what a locked door was. When we'd break a window and didn't have the money for a new glass, we'd just put cardboard over it. So what was the reason to lock doors, you see? If anything was lost, any of our goods, cattle, chickens, they were returned promptly or we were told where they were, and there was no stealing. I don't believe there was so much criticism of each other as there is now, or mistrust, distrust among us. We were brought up to respect our elders, and this really went throughout our whole life, to respect all things and to take care of things. Not to be destructive and not to try and break other people's things because we didn't like them. That was unheard of when I was growing up. There was a lot of respect and a lot of trust, there was no fighting like on New Year's. Some one told me about three years ago there was blood running from one bar to the other, from the Legion clear down to the Tomahawk, from the fights that had erupted during their so called celebration. This is the difference between how we observed New Year's in those days and how it is being observed now.

Our traditional St. Ann's Day that we continue to celebrate several days every year was something we looked forward to every summer because we were so attached to the Catholic religion; it was very much a part of our lives just as our Indian spirituality had been. So when we became Christianized we interwove this into our lives also. Every holiday, every Sunday was sacred to us, and we made every effort to go to church, of course, with the threat of burning in hell if we didn't. We had some very very harsh old priests. I hesitate to really come down on the Catholic education or religion that I received through the nuns and priests because I know they were well-meaning people. The early missionaries tried to live according to their knowledge, teaching their beliefs, and because we did not have written languages, or visible formal institutions like churches, schools, or codes of law and order, they thought we didn't have any religion, any educational system, any political system. In their zeal to get souls saved and free access to our lands and resources and to civilize us, they were very very harsh and stern with the Indian people.

My feelings about that are that in the first place our Indian people were very spiritual. Their concept of religion was the world of nature because they lived with it and they could see the hand of the Creator in all that surrounded them, and they had a very deep reverence for all forms of life, both animate and inanimate objects, and they made room for the Europeans when they came over. Because of their spirituality it was easy for the Indian people to understand Christianity because they believed we were all created by the same creator. In fact, talking to some of the elders from this reservation, indicated to me that their early forebears had seen Christ as a Sun Dancer, meaning that he gave up his life to save his people. In our Indian way we have the annual Sun Dance where the young men of the tribe come together and go through fasting, praying and suffering for the renewal of their own people. The difference is that Christ did this over 2,000 years ago to save his people and with us it is an ongoing event which I should point out is coming back very strongly among Indian nations all over this country and in Canada and even here at our reservation. I began to think about other aspects of religion as I became older, more educated and experienced.

One thing I remember when I was taking classes at the University of North Dakota. I had alluded to the fact that our Indian women had been told by the missionaries that they had to bear 12 children in order to gain the key to heaven. And much to my surprise I found out that this wasn't directed to the other — well, to the white women. So there were a lot of discrepancies between what the missionaries expected from the Indian people and what they expected from their own people. Another thing I remember, I did a paper on women's rights, and from my research I came to the conclusion that a lot of the rights the women were fighting for during the late 60s and early 70s our Indian women had had before the Europeans came. They had voting rights, they were very powerful especially as clan mothers, and the heritage was through the mother, as the chiefs were selected through the mother's side. A chief's son did not automatically inherit that title like in European monarchies.

When I was doing research the thought came to me, even in religion there was a difference in the concept of female roles. In the Indian way, Mother Earth was sacred. The mother symbolizes the female of the species. In contrast, we see Eve the mother of mankind, being portrayed as something evil where we have to be baptized in order to be rid of the mark that she left on us. So there was a vast difference in the concept of womanhood. You asked how the women were the keepers of cultural tradition: it has to be that way if the leaders were selected as I mention, and because the mothers were responsible for rearing the children. During the early years the children were with the mothers more than with the men; the mother had to pass on the daily knowledge of how to survive, who they were, the stories, their identity. It was not until later that the men took over, especially in winter time with the education, stories. So it was with everyday living that the culture was passed on, and the women are more or less responsible for that even today.

Now you asked about what kind of educational opportunities were available for me and my mother, what the sacrifices and advantages were, and about the government and mission boarding schools. Very often the children were sent in order that they might have food and shelter, but yes, it could be a hardship too. Because it could be very hard and strict at these places and when the children were away from their families, their language, their history and their Indian culture would be discouraged and they would be punished. And they would be exposed to racism. That's something we would encounter anywhere we went. My mother had a third grade education; she learned to read and write, but had learned all her prayers in French, and her dad did too. He went to the mission at St. Joe, that's where Walhalla is now, and learned there from Fr. Genin.

After the reservation was established she went to school -- St. Mary's or something like that and they called it "le couvent." It was partly a boarding school I think because she talked about going home on weekends and that she had a third grade education. My stepfather went there also, and he said he never learned to read and write because he was too busy working with the cattle and doing the chores to keep the institutions going. My mother was more or less self-educated since the only things they would teach was house and farm work. But anyway she talked about one instance when she had gone home, and her mother had made what they called light bread, that's yeast bread. But our Michif tradition, because they cooked in their encampments, was to make gallette in the coals of the campfire. And that's what they call bannock some places. This kind of bread had no yeast and this is what our people made because they were very adaptable, and they learned to make this when they came in contact with the white flour. We call that gallette in Michif language because it is so interwoven with French, all the nouns and names for things are in French. Well, our people would cook this over the open fire in skillets or bury it down in the ashes when the fire went down. Anyway, my mother had gone home and brought back some light bread. The sisters would check their bags mainly to see if they had brought back any of their Indian articles. Because at that time they didn't want the Indian articles, or foods passed on to the children since they were supposed to become like white people. Anyway, she checked my mother's bag and found this bread and said to her, "Where did you get this bread?" And my mother said, "My mother made it," meaning my grandma. And the sister said, "Well, I didn't know old squaws could make bread like this." My mother hardly ever spoke up but this was one time that she did. She told that old nun, "My mother may be an old squaw but *she* can make bread better than *you* can." At that time, she said they had outdoor ovens that were fired up with wood, and most of the time when they made bread it was burnt on the outside and dough in the inside, and it was thrown away, I presume, because I remember my stepfather saying that the boys would take the bread and make balls and play ball with it. My mother was very upset when the sister said this and so she sassed her back. Later on she had to be very sorry for it and do a lot of penances.

About my own education: my earliest memories were of walking along following my brothers to school because I was curious. Then the teacher let me stay all day because she didn't want me walking home alone. I started at Gourneau Day School, then that closed down after one year. Then a new school was built at Belcourt, but my dad died, leaving my mother with nine children. My brother was going to the Fort Totten school, but he changed his mind and I went in his place. But I came down with a bad case of trauchoma there and lost some years. I was supposed to be in the second grade when a bus came up to Belcourt from the Bismarck Indian school. The second grade teacher asked me if I wanted to go and told me my mother would have to sign the papers. But instead I just went home and packed up. I was ten years old and I forged her name. My mother had to go back and forth to work in her buggy.

She didn't know what had happened to me. She went to the agent to ask where I was. "Oh didn't you know. She went to Bismarck." Someone said she went away in her buggy crying because she didn't know where Bismarck was. At home, she asked my brothers if they had seen me; I had just packed up my little doll's suitcase and went and didn't say anything. I was always curious, always interested in education and wanted to learn. Before I went to Bismarck, I had never seen a bridge, or a river. I thought, that's a big creek. The first night, there were a lot of little lights out there moving by and I kept looking out the window trying to figure out what they were. I had never seen so many cars and things like this. We had to line up for everything. We all wore the same "hickory dress" for everyday. They were like denim but very stiff; they had to be run through the mangle when they were washed.

I worked in the barns, took care of cows, learned cooking, sewing, ironing, house-cleaning, the whole bit. All in all it was a good school for Indian girls; we had good teachers and I had algebra in seventh grade and Shakespeare before high school. We had roast beef, mashed potatoes, all that. There were about 100 girls there from the reservations in North and South Dakota and we kind of stuck together and helped each other out. But still there was this policy not to teach too much U.S. history and no Indian history, no culture or language or any of that, so this was the bad part of it. Because we were from Turtle Mountain we didn't know our Indian traditions like powwows. Most of the girls knew instead about piano music, and jigging. I knew the Michif language; that's not the same as Chippewa.It came to a point where there was some animosity among the girls, and there was one thing that really upset me, that was when they referred to us as "a poor caste of French." So I determined to learn as much as I could about our Indian people and traditions, and I did this on my own. I made many good friends among girls from the other reservations where they still knew of their traditions, and learned from them.

You asked me if I would like to be known as a Metis or as a Native American. Well in my book I was a Native American person first and always will be. It was through intermarriage that we came to be mixed; first of all we were Ojibway. Our treaty documents show this. It was the Pembina Ojibway who were recognized as the land owning entity here at Turtle Mountain. In fact at the time of the treaty negotiations it was one of our full blood relatives who insisted that the Metis be allowed to enter into the treaty rights along with the full bloods. He said that because the mixedblood children had Indian blood, we cannot throw these children away like the white man does to his own blood, and this is how the mixedbloods came into all the treaty agreements and are recipients of the treaty benefits. This is something that hardly any of our mixedblood people here on the reservation know today. This is some-thing that hasn't been pointed out to them, and because of the influence of the French missionaries who said that the fullbloods were inferior people, there were feelings against that throughout our history. "Li savazh" was the Michif derogatory name for the fullbloods, which means savages, from the French.

I would also like to point out that there are a lot of mixedbloods on other reservations and *they* don't call themselves half-breeds. It's only here on the Turtle Mountain reservation where we call ourselves Michifs. And all of these people who go off the reservation and live somewhere, people aren't going to care if they call themselves Michifs or half breeds. To them you're an *Indian*. Our children, when they start to wonder about themselves, spend a lot of time looking in the mirror, searching for their identity. This is about the time they start to believe about dirty Indians and scalping savages, pagans, and shortly after this so many drop out of school, and the rate of dropout is so high no one likes to talk about it. So they have to do something in the schools. If they could see how beautiful their Indian ancestors were, their way of life and their deep spirituality, then they could have something to be proud of. The ancestors we have from Europe came here fleeing from the diseases, war and oppression.

I finished high school in 1942 at Flandreau and then in 1944 I graduated from the State School of Science with my AS in business, and I had to work very hard to get that. The courses I had at Flandreau were no help, arts and crafts and home ec. There were no monies for schooling back then. I was able to take out a small loan just for tuition and books. But to pay my living expenses I had to work downtown at a cafe waiting tables from 4 to 12. A year later I ended up flat on my back at San Haven, because of the work and the exhausting schedule. I came down with TB and had to stay in an entire year. I would not recommend anyone to work and go to school full-time. It was very rough. During war time (1946-1948) I had a job at the Indian Hospital here at Belcourt, our staff was very minimal. Most of our nurses were army "cadets"; this is where they trained. One cadet was in charge of the OB delivering a lot of babies. The old doctor was a Japanese who was relocated from an internment camp in California. He didn't like delivering babies; he was a skin specialist. And so this responsibility fell mostly on the nursing staff. We only called him in in case of really serious complications.

I lived and worked in Minneapolis, Chicago, New York City while I was single, and I liked that—having a lot of things to do, being out on my own, making a living. My husband Lawrence was trained in computers after the war and so we ended up in California where he worked with a big UNIVAC unit. When they started the voice-command programs he got laid off along with a lot of others. We were thinking about moving back here. And one time we took the kids to Disneyland, that sort of decided things for us. There were some Indian dancers there, and my youngest was afraid to go up there with them. We thought, "We're Indian people, we are going back so our kids can see that." Of course there were no jobs in computers in North Dakota at the time, and so we ended up taking different jobs to live on the reservation. Lawrence was a truant officer and I worked for the Neighborhood Youth Corps. Lawrence was an artist. He had had some training at the Minneapolis Institute of Art and Design. So he made up his mind he would go to school, finish a degree, and teach art. I stayed behind with the family, working. In 1974 I joined my husband at UND; we both went back to school. I got a job with INMED [Indians Into Medicine] as a traveling recruiter in the five-state area. Lawrence was killed in a car accident; all he had left was his student teaching. After I got my degree in social work in 1977, I had a daughter who was going to the University of North Dakota and had two children, so I stayed there to help, and worked in the Indian Studies department. Then I was offered a job at the Turtle Mountain Community College when I came back here to the reservation.

Lise Erdrich Croonenberghs lives at Belcourt on the Turtle Mountain Indian Reservation. She is the author of a book on the history of the Turtle Mountain Community College to be published in 1989.

Photo courtesy of Mrs. Mary Folden, Minot, N.D.

That's All They Knew, Was Work

by Niomi Phillips

When I told my daughter Lisa — we were talking about women in the workplace — that "my mother was a feminist," Lisa said, "She was *not*." For this red-sports-car-driving-accountant daughter of mine, *feminist* conjures up bitchy behavior, rabble rousing, bra burning and hairy armpits. Lisa's grandmother was not one of "those." Lisa, and many of her generation, the great-grandchildren of immigrants, only three generations removed from "the Old Country," see few connections between themselves and my mother's life.

I reminded Lisa that it was my mother, Betty Rohn, who had talked to her about increasing opportunities for women in business and told her of the young women she knew in banking. When Lisa herself worked in a bank during high school and college, this grandmother explained interest rates and CDs. To be sure, while Grandma Betty was a fierce defender of women's rights and could argue knowledgeably about "big" issues, her actual influence went to smaller things, like urging men to share Saturday work hours in her office, and seeing to it that women attended state bank meetings and had their fees paid. Hadn't she heard her grandmother rant against men's privileges and discrimination against women? "No matter," Lisa said. "She was no feminist."

I couldn't, then, convince my daughter, and Mother died two years ago, but making connections between the generations of women in my family, and taking account of the changes (and the constants) in our lives from one generation to another has become an important challenge to me. I want my daughter to know how a 1980s great-granddaughter of immigrants got to a desk on the 20th floor of the Radisson Building. A family history such as ours is a familiar one in North Dakota — of great-grandparents who were part of the migration to the Midwest from Russia at the turn of the century, Germans who had lived in Russia for as much as five generations and were leaving to escape increasing government pressures to teach Russian language in their schools, keep local records in Russian, and impress sons into the Russian army — but it is also a history that is being forgotten.

The German immigrants had been used to looking after their own affairs in Russia. Each dorf, or village, was a little Germany, where an authoritarian church (Catholic or Protestant) and strong parental control ran the schools and preserved German language and culture. There was little social contact with other villages; most marriages were arranged, minimizing intermarriage even among German-Russians of different religious faiths. These were traditions German-Russians took with them in their second migration, and unlike most other immigrants, they showed little interest in becoming Americans. The Black Sea German-Russians, my maternal family among them, came to North Dakota "right off the boat," whereas other immigrants had made their way more gradually across the country, sometimes over several generations. For them, the process of assimilation was already underway by the time they settled in North Dakota.

The German-Russians were different from most other immigrants in several respects. They were poorer than most, and plagued by poverty for several generations. By the time many of them arrived in North Dakota (they are the single largest foreign immigrant group in a state that has had the single largest foreign immigrant rural population of any state), only the least fertile land was left for cultivation. Historians think that their settling on poor land in central North Dakota was due not only to the lateness of their arrival, but also to their desire to remain together as much as possible in clan groups as they had in Russia. They came in families, and sent scouts ahead to find enough land for a village group. In Russia, their homes had been clustered together or along a single main street, their farm land lying outside the village, but in the U.S., the Homestead Act required that settlers live individually on the acreage they farmed. Even though the German-Russians were not able to establish their traditional communities (a deprivation that caused hardship to many), they did their best to maintain close ties by holding church services in each other's homes before churches were built, and confining socializing to their own kind. On Sundays they gathered to gossip and play cards. A great-aunt of mine hated most the job of cleaning up the sunflower seeds that were spat on the wood floors during those Sunday afternoon visits. Even the clothes of these latecomers made them look distinctive — dark wool pants and jackets and sheepskin coats on the men, heavy dark dresses and shawls for the women. Such clothing set them apart and drew curiosity and sometimes derision from North Dakotans who had come from other parts of the U.S. and Europe and more readily called themselves "American."

Descriptions in the historical literature of authoritarian, dominating men led me to imagine women wrapped in shawls falling meekly behind their men. Then my grandmother gave me her shawl. She remembered the day it was given to her, on the day her family left Odessa for the United States. But the event itself was incidental, for what mattered to her was that her grandmother had offered three shawls — a gray one, a green, and a black — and my grandmother got the black one because she was the youngest and had the last choice. When I put that shawl on now, I feel the pain of the leave-taking, and think of a woman saying good-bye to daughter and granddaughters forever, the gift the only protection she was able to give them.

The observations I had been making about my family were confirmed for me when I began reading what a few others had written about the German-Russian heritage in North Dakota. A writer in McHenry County, for instance, remarked in 1915 that "their resources are very scanty and their life is a hard one," and that "they engage very little, if at all, in social affairs outside of their narrow horizon of immediate neighbors; their assimilation into the life and customs of America is slow." German-Russians, according to this writer, "maintain an indifferent if not hostile attitude toward education, and believe that school unfits their daughters for the occupation of women's work and child bearing....The women do an immense amount of drudgery. Their position is in striking contrast to the position of American women....The husband is the absolute master; the wife is little more than a servant. The women have a truly hard and monotonous life." Such unequal treatment of women was open to public view:

> The writer is in a position as clerk in a general merchandise store in a small town and notices that the men do all the trading. The wife writes it on a piece of paper and he goes to town. Yet it is she, who with the smallest children does the milking, separating of the milk, churning, and the caring of the poultry flock. Only in the summer do women come in to trade. But when she does come to town, the general store is the only place to which she ventures and there she patiently waits, frequently beguiling the time away with chewing sunflower seeds and spitting the shells on the floor. Is it any wonder then that the wife's inferior status is a great drawback to Americanization? How can she instill in her children the right ideals and customs when she is little more than a slave? (Weber).

Nina Farley Wishek, whose family came from the Midwest, is known for her history of McIntosh County, another south-central region rich in German-Russian settlement. Wishek wrote about a succession of German maids who worked in her family: "One of the strangest ways of the foreigner was the custom of women working in the field....I rather resented it as an insult to my sex. In later years I became accustomed to it and even came to realize that the girls and women preferred working outside. Of course, this outside work was made possible because the home life was so simplified and because children all shared in the work....When the children were very young they were taught to do chores about the house and barn, at an early age began the heaviest work of an adult" (Wishek). The McHenry County writer also spoke of the work of children: "From the time they are able to hold the reins of horses, the children are made to do a man's work....They [the German-Russians] are adverse to allowing the children to go to school when conditions are favorable to work in the fields" (Weber).

Women in my family experienced this collective history. My grandmother is 88 years old, the surviving member of her family who emigrated from Russia in 1909. Her life encompasses five generations of women, from the widowed grandmother she remembers in Russia who managed a winery and farm, to her great-grand-daughters today in college and business. She has lived longer than her husband, her seven brothers and sisters, and her daughters who both died of cancer two years ago. Grandma lives in a low cost housing apartment where a plaque honoring her for 14 years of service as a volunteer for Senior Citizens hangs over the chrome kitchen table. She works two days a week in the kitchen of the Senior Citizen complex, attends mass, takes her turn baking and serving for the Altar Society, and on Wednesdays goes next door to the nursing home to help wheelchair patients get to mass. She is a consummate realist. Soon after her daughter (my mother) died, she bought a casket and arranged for her own burial. She has already distributed the accumulations of her lifetime: some crocheted lace table cloths and doilies, about half a dozen pieces of costume jewelry, and a few pieces of glass.

Grandma is modest but bossy, especially in the kitchen; opinionated but able to keep her opinions to herself when she feels she should. In public, she displays the unassuming manner of a lifetime, accepting men with amused tolerance, smug in the knowledge that it is women who preserve religion, nurture children, protect families, and orchestrate life. Her apron is her armor. Christmas, Easter, the 4th of July, terminal illness, or death: you cover yourself with an apron and get to work. On the endless summer days when Mother was dying, Grandma cleaned the oven, polished the stove, made soup, and never talked about *it*. She came home from the funeral and went to the kitchen.

Later that fall I began visiting her often, to make up for Mother's absence, but being with her made the loss of my mother worse. Our conversations were exhaustive surveys of family doings, and I'd end up weeping. Then I thought of taking a tape recorder with me to start a record of the lives and work of the women in our family for my daughters, but that didn't work either — the machine got in the way. So I began taking notes, which kept me busy and gave us both a framework for the interviews, and our lives. We spent a winter of Sunday afternoons at Grandma's kitchen table, often joined by her sister-in-law, my 85-year-old Great-Aunt Helen. The room became peopled by dozens of women, as bits and pieces of memory, weaving back and forth from Russia to North Dakota, from childhood to girlhood to adulthood began to make a whole. Mothers and daughters and sisters from three generations, living and dead, became one. I found my mother's spirit, her keen wit, her compassion and warmth in grandmothers, aunts and cousins. And telling the story gave Grandma and Aunt Helen a sense that their own lives were purposeful and honorable.

Even my youngest daughter, Laura, got involved. I sent along a list of questions when she went to visit Grandma and Aunt Helen. They entertained her with stories, and she found her feelings changing toward her bossy, quick to criticize great-grandmother. Now this 88-year-old woman who left school at the fourth grade writes to Laura in college. Laura says that Grandma asks her a lot of questions about what she is doing — Laura in turn is serving as Grandma's touchstone with a generation of young women.

Grandma knows she is the last of her generation left to tell the family story, and she was impatient with some of my questions about German-Russian attitudes toward education, or men's domination over women and the status of women. I wanted to know, specifically, whether German-Russians were as different from other North Dakota settlers as I'd been told. ("Did you work in the fields as a child?" "Yes, but everyone did.") I had to be careful not to make questions sound like judgments: Tell me about your mother's work, I learned to ask. What was a typical day like? What was your mother like? Who went to school in your family? What was a day on the farm like? Tell me about your sisters. Didn't one of them die very young? Your sister Julia never learned to speak English very well — why do you think that was? How and when did you learn to speak English? I suspect that some of her answers were restrained, and I thought of how a friend had told me her grandfather's journal ended: "I have written here the things to my best memory and knowledge. It would not be becoming to say the bad things. That we will put in the past memories." Grandma didn't like to dwell on bad things either, which was part of her reason for ending a story with "That's just the way it was," or "That was the style."

Yet she was willing to give details about that style of living, and enjoyed recalling the way things were. Sometimes, after a visit, I'd think of something more I wanted to know, and would call her up. She enjoyed these hour-long conversations; she seemed more intimate on the telephone than face-to-face. Once, thinking of the McHenry County merchant who said that the women and children rarely went to town, I asked her whether her mother and brothers and sisters ever got off the farm. She re-lived Sunday afternoons visiting cousins (dozens of them) and aunts and uncles, going to town for an ice cream cone, going to a small traveling tent show. My question stimulated her, on a cold winter day, to touch again her sisters and brothers.

Grandma worked in the field when she was nine years old. The family was poor, she said, and her older brothers and sisters "worked out," and "they brought home everything that they earned. Every family did it that way." (One time Anton, her brother, spent $7.00 of his wages for the year, and "the folks wanted to know what he had done with it.") Grandma worked with her younger brother and their dad plowing, planting, haying, and harvesting. In between there were chickens to feed, cows to milk, and gardening and canning and washing and ironing — and school, if the crops were in, were out, and the horses could get through the snow. "Schooling was not for girls in those days," she says. "Girls were supposed to be able to cook and sew and keep house." Her older brothers and sisters never attended school; her sister Julia never learned to read English, and until she died in 1983 always preferred to speak German.

Were German-Russian women simply slaves? Grandma says of her mother, Frances Senger, "She took charge. She was stricter than Pa. When she said something, she meant it. He was kind of weak. She would take a fly swatter to us sometimes." Once Grandma's brother hitched a young horse to the threshing machine after being told not to, and then beat the horse when it reared. "Pa was so angry he hit Mike and felt so bad about it, he nearly cried himself. That's the only time I ever seen him hit anybody." Frances Senger "could make a joke out of anything," Grandma said. "She was a happy person. She and Pa talked a lot, but in those days they didn't talk in front of kids about everything like they do now. We listened in sometimes."

What was your mother's life like? I ask. "She was always busy because there were cows to be milked, the separating, pigs to feed, then a big breakfast and the dishes to do, then get ready for dinner which was always a big meal — three big meals a day. Sewing, knitting all the sweaters and the boys' socks, baking the bread twice a week and sometimes buns and *kuchen*." Trips to town were infrequent — "the road was long by team" — but Frances always went "if there were groceries, or sewing things,

In the 1800s there were fewer than ten divorces a year in North Dakota; in 1889 there were 80. In 1970 there were 971, and 2,134 by 1980. North Dakota divorce rates now are about the same as the national average.

I grew up in Crosby, North Dakota, near the Canadian border. Children decorated mud pies with yellow mustard blossoms and red berries; I played croquet with the boy next door. We cruised "Main" in '55 Chevys and threw water balloons at other cars. We camped out at Crosby Dam with the Girl Scout troop and danced the jitterbug at the Community Hall Canteen after high school football games under the lights. I met friends at the Crystal Cafe, went to Saturday matinees at the movie theater and marched with the high school band. I saw myself finishing high school and going to college to be a teacher, getting married, having six children with brown hair and brown eyes, returning to teaching at age 50 when the children had grown, and teaching until retirement. I did finish high school, graduated from college with a teaching degree, married, and began teaching long before age 50. But reality did not quite match my hopes and dreams, for I was divorced after 16 years of marriage.

In the idealized small town atmosphere that I knew, people were shocked by divorce. In the 1950s the word wasn't mentioned, even though there were 600 divorces that year in North Dakota. Marriages were expected to end with death — being widowed was painful, but a natural course of events. In a small town, what seem to be private issues become the topic of discussion at social functions and are disguised as concern. You are given advice from people who may feel unsure of their own marriages. In farm families, divorce may mean that the farm is auctioned off after the divorce settlement.

In my own divorce I have experienced not only the personal pain, and the stress of re-structuring my life on my own, but a realization of how fragile is the idealized image of small-town America. Of course Crosby depends on farming and on the oil and gas industries for its existence, but it also depends on a pre-1950s version of two-parent families for a view of itself that my generation did not sustain.

Suellen Schultz Steinke
Crookston, Minnesota

or like that, to pick up, that wasn't a man's job." If it wasn't a busy time, the kids got to go, "to get an ice cream cone, or go to a show. A travelling show, sometimes two wagons, monkeys and magic, just a show — not much, but for us it was."

Her family settled in North Dakota around 1910, and soon after Frances became a midwife for neighbors. Roads were bad, the climate severe, and people too poor to go to doctors. Midwifery was a common occupation for prairie women; it was one that drew respect even among the most tradition-bound. My German-Russian Mennonite grandfather kept a journal, and in it the only mention he makes of women's work is about midwifery:

> Ma used to be a nurse and midwife. When we landed on these prairies it was hard to get a doctor in case of sickness so it came in handy. There were no phones and very poor roads so they would come for her. She was out a lot especially on confinement cases. I wish I had the record she kept of the infants she brought into the world. They would come after her on cold stormy nights. Fortunately she had a Russian wolfskin coat that we brought with us from Russia. Then we also had a large sheepskin fur robe that she would wrap herself into. With a hot soapstone at her feet to keep them warm and her coat and robe she would be quite comfortable.

Frances Senger charged $5 a delivery when people could pay, and she was in not so friendly competition with a Mrs. Usseldorf. Her mother "loved babies," Grandma says; once when a new mother was too ill to nurse her newborn, Frances brought it home and fed it from a spoon until it was strong enough to nurse. Frances was probably more frank in informing her daughters about childbirth than most parents of her time. She talked to Grandma and her two sisters about difficult births "when we were old enough and she knew we were going to be women someday and needed to know." But Great-Aunt Helen tells me that she was nearly 12 years old before she learned where babies came from. Grandma thought her mother was too sympathetic with another sister who "had trouble every month, so she was spoiled. 'Go do this because Julia is sick,' Ma would say to me. That gets into somebody. She was spoiled from young on. Then she worked out for an aunt who was a complainer too so they made a pair."

Frances read the German newspapers , and after Church instead of talking only with the women, she'd join in the thick of discussions, spitting sunflower seeds "with the best of the men." Grandma says, "My mother didn't take a back seat to any man. I mean as far as work or to know things, as far as talking about business, government, what was going on. She read German newspapers. When the men were talking about things, she knew what it was about. A lot of the men didn't like it when women spoke up. She said what she had to say and didn't care. Pa never argued with her if she'd read it and knew what she was talking about." (There were as many as 29 German-language newspapers printed in North Dakota at the turn of the century, the most popular including the *Das Nordlicht* [1885-1927], printed in Bismarck; the *Mercer County Republican* [1889-1913]; *Der Volksfreund* [1890-1924], Richardton; *Nord-Dakota Herold* [1907-1954]; Dickinson; and *Der Staats-Anzeiger* [1906-1945], Rugby and later Bismarck (Sherman *et al*).)

Great Aunt Helen implied that Frances was not popular with the other women: "She was a tough one, she'd tell the men off. Once Mother said when dinner was ready, 'Go get the men,' and someone asked where Mrs. Senger was, and our mother said, 'You know where she is, with the men.'" In contrast, Aunt Helen says that her own mother was "a sweet person. She wouldn't open her mouth. My dad thought that because she was a woman, she didn't know anything." "My mother wouldn't sit still for that," Grandma says. "If you could read, you were respected unless your husband made a fool of you." When Grandma's two oldest brothers were married and ready to take over the farm, her parents bought a butcher shop in town. Frances cut meat, made sausage, and waited on customers along with her husband. "She was good with figures," Grandma says.

Frances also saw to it that her grandchildren got a proper Catholic indoctrination even if they lived among "the heathen" Scandinavians, who, she told my mother, "had bedbugs." A parade of grandchildren spent part of each summer with her in order to go to catechism class. "She was strict and severe," one of them remembers. "I don't think anyone ever got close to her. She wouldn't answer if we spoke English." But my mother said, "Grandma told me all kinds of things that surprised me even then. She talked about her daughters-in-law. I don't think that she liked any of them. None were good enough for her sons. She told me about her quarrels with Mrs. Usseldorf...I think Grandma Senger was a gossip, maybe a troublemaker, interfered in her sons' lives. She arranged a marriage for one of them and then the woman was ill most of her life and she felt guilty." Frances also told my mother that she had to deal with the neighbor who came to discuss the inopportune marriage of one of his sons to one of her daughters. She referred to him as a "blackbearded devil."

A grandson describes Frances and her husband as "devoted" to each other: "They worked side by side all of their lives." "They really loved each other," another grandson says. How did he know that, I ask. "They went to mass together every morning. They sat at the kitchen table and played cards. He died only two weeks after she did. He didn't care to live without her."

Grandma expected her life to be much like her mother's. "That's what we knew. That's the way it was," she says. Not so Aunt Helen, who had no intention of being a farmer's wife. Her views about women's lives were not so temperate. The babies who "came in blankets" from Mrs. Usseldorf, for example, were not always welcome. One Sunday afternoon when Helen was about ten, her mother complained of a backache. Her dad hitched up the wagon, left, and returned with Mrs. Usseldorf who carried something in a blanket. A couple of hours later her father came out of the house to tell her and her brothers and sisters to "come in and see." "Another kid," Helen says disgustedly. "There were always women walking around pregnant. I told my mother I was never going to have kids." (She had one child.) "Women were slaves. They had to get up early in the morning, carry in the water, then carry out the water, raise the kids. Work like a man. All the old German ladies have arthritis in their arms now. Sure. The Norwegians don't. My neighbor doesn't have an ache in her body."

Helen has strong opinions on the German-Russian attitude toward education: "The Norwegians seen to it that their kids got an education. My sister [the oldest girl] didn't get to go to school at all. The boys did, when the weather was good and there was no work. Your grandpa got the most. He finished 8th grade. (He also taught in that school one winter when they needed a teacher.) I had to milk three cows before I went to school. The Norwegian girls didn't have to work outside. Pa wouldn't even let us speak English at home." Her dad didn't like her, Helen thinks, and she didn't like his temper. "He'd come in and pound on the table when things went wrong outside. You had to know your place and if you walked in on the men's talking, he would tell you to 'get in the kitchen and mind your own business.' Let's run away, I told my mother one time. Girls could get jobs in town, at the cafes and hotels. People were anxious to hire the German girls. They could earn $4 a week, plus room and board. You had to sleep three in a bed sometimes, but it was better than the farm."

"My mother was a kind person, sweet. She cried a lot. My brother Joe helped her — cooked, helped her in the kitchen." Helen's recollections of her parents support general observations of German-Russians. "My dad was a real son-of-a-bitch," she says matter-of-factly. "I was so glad to get away. I was never so happy as when I got married — lots of girls got married to get away, to have it easier." Getting married and having your own home was expected, Grandma says. She was 18 when she married a neighbor, a worldly young man by her standards. He had ventured to Grand Forks where he had worked on the railroad, and as Grandma says, "mixed with all kinds and learned English." For two years they lived down the street from her parents in the Catholic German-Russian milieu in which they had grown up. Then Grandpa got a job with the Soo Line, and they moved to Harlow, "where there were Americans," and later to Alsen, in Cavalier County, a community of German-Russian Mennonites and Lutherans.

Grandma had lived in North Dakota for nine years before she learned English. "I went a lot of times to the store to get things and couldn't ask for it." How had she learned? "You can learn things by yourself. You can study with your kids. You get different ideas too when you are with different people. Like where we came to from the Old Country, it was nearly all family, all one group, you didn't mix." A steady income and not more than two children made life easier for Grandma than it was for her sisters and brothers on the farm. They were trying to make a living on infertile, rented land. Grandma took care of her sister Julia's two little boys so Julia could help her husband harvest. Another sister, Katy, took her babies with her to the field where a young relative watched them. "There was no one else to do it. Everyone had their own work, and there was no money to hire anyone."

Grandma can recite a litany of deaths: babies at birth, sisters-in-law in childbirth. Sister Julia had two miscarriages and then her third baby died of convulsions at eight months. Sister Katy died of a ruptured appendix two weeks after her sixth baby was born. Her oldest daughter, 15, went to work at the School for the Deaf in Devils Lake where room and board were furnished. The other children were parcelled out in the family. Grandma's third child, a boy, died at birth. Brother Anton's wife Helen died leaving four children, the oldest age seven; Grandma took the baby, but it had jaundice and lived only three weeks.

How had she endured all these losses? "You had children to care for, work to do. You had to be strong. Women had to stick together. The men were more to themselves. You had to keep going. You had friends to come and help, to talk to you, share their problems with you. You prayed. Women came through better than the men. When a woman died, the husband depended on other people. When my sister Katy knew she was dying, she asked her sisters to take care of the children. You have to keep going, that's the idea you have to have if you are going to survive. You just have to do it. You need the love and support of family. You have to have your own confidence that you can do it." Her change here from past to present tense tells me she is expressing her philosophy of life.

"Norwegians had big families too," Grandma would say if I asked whether they talked about family planning. And with a smile, "What good would talking do?" Women expected to have large families and accepted that fertility was not a private matter. A great-aunt told me that brothers teased her husband, told him they must be "sinning" because they had only two children. A man's masculinity was the object of speculation and ridicule if there were few children. Dictates of the Catholic Church were taken seriously. Another aunt confided to my mother that she was so concerned she had confessed to the priest that she and her husband were using withdrawal because the doctor had told her it was dangerous for her to have another child. The priest told her to say more penance. Babies were a mixed blessing. Mother remembered a cousin crying when she found out her mother was pregnant again — more work.

And that leads to the story of the next generation, my mother's, the first generation born in the U.S. From Mother's cousins I have a picture of a life of work. Grueling, unrelenting physical labor dominates every conversation about the past. One of the girls "escaped" to town to work as a hired girl, but her father came to town to collect her paycheck. She turned it over to him, as he had turned his over to his father when he came from Russia as a boy. Cousin Jennie said, "While growing up

---

Growing Up At Standing Rock
by Dorothy Lukens

My father was the first settler to purchase land on the Standing Rock Indian Reservation in 1915 when Sioux County was organized. Just across the river, Mark Afraid-of-Hawk and his family lived in a two-room house during the winter and in tents during the warmer months. Dad called him his Indian father, because Mark taught Dad the Sioux Dakota language and many things about wild life and the Indian way of doing things.

In October of 1917 Dad brought his bride to the two-story house he had built. Mark and his family welcomed Mother, but she was a bit apprehensive at meeting Indians for the first time. One day, Mark, dressed in his buckskins, came to see Dad. Mother retreated to the dining room, leaving the men to converse in Sioux. She heard the pitch of Mark's voice rise and glanced into the kitchen just as Mark grabbed from the table a long butcher knife and began waving it about. Mother emitted a half muffled cry, and Dad, turning to her, explained that Mark was demonstrating a fight that had occurred at the Indian agency sub-station.

The road to our house went down a steep incline, and the Indians liked to come down at high speed, although I am not sure the women riding in the wagons enjoyed the thrill as much as the men. When I came to ride my pony down that hill, it was scary but thrilling. As the years passed the road wore down and is now overgrown with vegetation.

Mark Afraid-of-Hawk and the other Indians were generous in their gift giving.

we had to work out and earn money to care for ourselves. And I was glad to leave home. As we were so hard up then, so many kids to feed and dress. But Elizabeth and Frances had it a lot better, at least I thought they did. They lived in town and graduated from high school. None of us ever got to go to high school. I didn't even dream of it. Women worked so hard, that's all they knew, was work." Another cousin, Tom, reminding me that the times were "the Dirty Thirties," said, "I quit school in the second year of high school thinking that was the thing to do, get work of some kind and try to make a few dollars. Everybody back then seemed to learn how to work and work hard. I guess the folks seemed to think that learning how to work was more important than school. I remember that my mother washed clothes by hand on a scrub board. I think it was in 1935 we got our first Maytag washing machine. I remember that she never failed to come out and help us kids milk the cows twice a day." Another cousin told me that when her mother died and she went to live with her Aunt Julia, she didn't get to school very often. Julia, who had not gone to school herself, thought school was unnecessary for girls. Girls needed to learn housework, so on washdays and canning days and during the harvest, Frances had to stay home. It was 1930 and she was thirteen years old.

My own mother's life was somewhat different, possibly, one cousin thinks, because she lived in town. But also important may have been the fact that the town was of mixed ethnic groups, including "Americans." Mother saw differences and sympathized with cousins who were trapped by repressive attitudes and lack of opportunities. She told me, the year before she died (and I wrote it down because

Mark made Mother a beautiful diamond willow cane with her initials carved in it, and when my brother Don was born, he gave him beaded moccasins, a pair every year for several years. Other gifts included beaded bags and jackets and several necklaces.

Our family felt the Indians were protective of us. One day my wandering three-year-old brother, with his wagon, was brought back by the Indian women. They had seen him start down the road toward their house on one of his imaginary trips to get hay or some other farm supplies. Mother was relieved to see the women leading him back home.

Another time Mother had taken Don and me with her to pick berries along the riverbank. I was a roly-poly toddler and managed to roll myself down a bank of poison ivy. Mother rescued me, but had to leave without many berries, although luckily I did not develop poison ivy rash. All of this was not unnoticed by the Indian women. From then on, Mother never had to pick berries. Pails full of washed, leaf-free berries would arrive as soon as they ripened, to be exchanged for Mother's bread, sweet butter or cream. Mother baked huge batches of bread twice a week, but during the berry season it was even more often.

I was about twelve when we learned that Mark Afraid-of-Hawk was sick. Dad went to see him, but there were rituals that he did not attend. One evening I heard loud wailing, and Dad explained that Mark was dead and the family was putting ashes over their bodies and the wailing would continue throughout the night vigil. Later a funeral was held in the Catholic church of the Porcupine station.

Dorothy Lukens lives in Wilton, N.D.

she was so impassioned) that German-Russian men were totally without compassion for their wives. "The women had babies every nine months and ten minutes. They worked in the house and in the barnyard. The men worked in the fields, but the horses needed rest, so they'd have to stop. The men came in from the fields, unharnessed the horses, and were done for the day. They cared more about their horses than their wives. The women cooked three large meals a day for as many as 14 people, baked bread, planted gardens, canned vegetables and meat, sewed everything but overalls, and pregnant or not, did the milking and took care of the pigs and chickens. Life was hell for women. At a meal a woman would have a baby in her lap, one in a high chair on one side, another on a stool at the other side. No man would so much as give the babies a cup of milk or a piece of bread — woman's work."

She said that the women made the best of it because they had no alternatives. "If you were married, you at least had a home of your own." There was a "spinster" who lived with successive brothers, pushed from one house to another to work and was "treated horribly by their wives, always a maid in someone else's kitchen." She said also that the German-Russians didn't value education, though her own father expected good grades and high school graduation. Mother graduated from high school at the head of her class. But it was 1937, and there were no jobs for women and no money for college. She worked as a hired girl and married the next fall.

As a young married woman, Mother lived in a community much like the one her parents had come to as children from Russia, a community of Black Sea German-Russian Catholics. Even so, Mother tried to make a less restricted life for herself. She helped organize women's clubs and 4-H clubs because the only existing social gatherings for women or children were church related. She served as clerk of the school board; she took the civil service examination and got the highest score in the county, although the postmaster job went to a World War II veteran. She belonged to the Book-of-the-Month club, helped a neighbor girl with algebra night after night one winter, and led me through the forest of English grammar.

We moved, and mother went to work at a variety of jobs — picking potatoes, selling Stanley Home Products, managing a Dairy Queen — and saved enough money for me to begin college at the University of North Dakota. In her early 40s she began working as a bank teller and in twenty years became an officer of the bank.

Tracing Mother's life, I felt always that the place where we lived between 1944 and 1953, where German was spoken in school and on the street, was "different." I found a writer who thought so too: Joseph Voeller, Superintendent of Schools of Pierce County and a German-Russian descendent, who wrote a thesis in 1940 about German-Russians, calling them "the problem people in North Dakota." He wanted them "to appreciate education," and described them as "backward, socially and emotionally retarded." He denigrated their clannishness and their absorption with farming at the expense of their children's education — observations not much different from the McHenry County storekeeper in 1917.

Voeller found that in rural areas there were some of the first-generation born in the U.S. still speaking German exclusively in their homes. In Pierce County and in other counties where German-Russians predominated, it was difficult to get them to send their children to school and keep them there (Voeller). At some schools four years of high school were not available until the late 1930s; by comparison, communities with predominantly Norwegian populations had four-year high schools ten years earlier, and more Norwegian than German-Russian students entered high school (Handy-Marchello). In my town it was still common to hear people speaking German in the mid-50s; the priest gave one sermon in German and another in English. Women and girls (with the nuns behind us to ensure good behavior) sat on the left side of the church, the men on the right. Some of Mother's contemporaries sat with their husbands, to the disapproval of the black shawled women at the back of the church.

A woman I'll call Teresa Schmidt confirms this reluctance to change among German-Russian communities. When she left for college, in 1970, German still was spoken in her home. Her older sisters, in the late 50s, had not been allowed to attend high school because they would have had "to board out," and there was no money for that. One of them cried and begged, futilely. Once country schools were consolidated and buses provided, the other children in the family of 12 did attend school and were expected to graduate from high school. Her father, born in the U.S., was not particularly concerned about "schooling," but he read the newspaper every day, ordered the World Book encyclopedia from Sears & Roebuck, and read, it seemed to his children, everything in it including the dictionary. He took an active interest in politics, and always voted. He went with his wife into the voting booth, and when that no longer was permitted, he marked a ballot at home for her before they went to the polls.

One of Teresa's sisters is still angry. She resents the fact that their mother never

---

I am an American Chippewa Indian. Life has not been exactly easy for me or for my children, but the four of us are here, and doing all right. My oldest daughter has been in the gifted program at her school for two years. She is a bright child who I feel is well adjusted. My four-year-old is in day care and a natural born leader. She has a unique personality and is so full of life. My baby is also very special, so even tempered, so content, and such a talker. They have each brought such joy to my life, and that is what keeps me going.

Nancy Pierce
Devils Lake, N.D.

had any money but what came from selling cream, that she had to wait on their dad, who told her she was "dumb," and that they all were deprived of so much when there seemed to be money for the farm and land. They battled mice because the house couldn't be fixed, although the barn always got painted. But Teresa says "Why be angry. It's not constructive. Actually I worked hard to please my dad all my life." She says he was a fairly quiet person who played ball with them on Sundays after church, and checkers and marbles on a board that he made. He loved flowers and fruit trees and did most of the gardening. Her parents went everywhere together. Her father never went to town without taking her mother along, although the kids, twelve of them, had to take turns, and got to Minot or Devils Lake "maybe once a year." Often they went for a Sunday afternoon ride just to look at the crops. Her father was an intelligent man, Teresa says. "The land was poor. You can barely eke out a living on it, and the only reason he did was that he was smart enough to raise sheep and pigs and cattle." He was an authoritative, dominating man as were most of the men she knew at church and school, all German-Russian Catholics.

Teresa came along when there were already three girls to do housework, so she worked with her father and brothers outside, and liked it. What she didn't like was that after spending the day in the field, she was expected to help milk the cows, make dinner, and then wait on the boys at the table. Their work was done when they left the field. Both boys and girls in the family milked the cows before they left for school in the morning, and then the girls helped with the breakfast and made all the beds, including the boys'. "It wasn't fair," Teresa says. "Early in life I knew that education was the key to getting out. No one told me, I just knew. I was never going to live like that. I was not going to marry someone from that area and live that way." But her dad insisted that she spend summers at home working on the farm, and she obeyed. Nevertheless, she worked her way to a B.A. and after marrying and raising a family, to a Master of Business Administration.

It took some families several generations to change attitudes about education and the role of women. Those who remained in rural areas remained the most conservative, clinging to the ways of "the old country," preferring the company of German speaking families of their own religion, and resisting outside influences. They disregarded and were suspicious of education. Historians note that only a handful of us, the second generation born in the U.S., graduated from college in the 1950s and 60s. Others, like my cousin Kay, chose to be farm wives and homemakers like our great-grandmother, and her grandmother, and mother before her.

When I first met Kay a year ago, I asked her about her life on the farm, because it seemed a good example of the changes in rural women's lives; I wanted to compare the work she did to the work of our immigrant great-grandmother. I had learned by then that women paint their work and their lives with broad strokes. What we do seems trivial, not important enough to be part of the historical record. My paternal grandfather, for example, wrote pages of minute details of breaking sod, making bricks for the sod house, planting, harvesting, and the like. He never mentioned any women's work except midwifery. So I suggested that Kay keep a journal for two weeks and write down everything she did. Give me a picture of your life, I asked. And she did. While her life has changed, some of her values are not different from those of previous generations.

Like great-grandma from Russia, Kay goes to mass regularly, but she is a partner on the farm, not a servant. She doesn't shock grain or work in the barn because she and her husband hire someone to help with farm work, but she moves machinery from field to field when they need her, takes lunches to the field during harvest, keeps up the yard around the house, and keeps books. She plants a garden and cans vegetables and fruits. One fall day she canned 22 pints of tomatos, 9 pints of beet jelly, and 14 pints of beets. Kay hops into the car at a moment's notice to take a son to Catechism class, or to a 4-H meeting or baseball or play practice. She crossed one whole week off her calendar when the 4-H club she leads was involved in exhibiting. She was appointed judge for the first time and was excited and proud. She organized, delegated responsibility, and transported animals — rabbits, kittens, a goat — snatched snacks with her 4-H'ers at Hardee's, helped them prepare for the parade, and shared in what she calls "the joys and the tears" of the winners and losers.

In her ten pages of recorded activities, I find a woman with what we might describe today as a full life. She has a sense of humor and a natural warmth as well as the positive attitude that our great-grandmother had, that I see in my grandmother, and knew in my deceased mother. She concludes: "This is typical of my life. Soon it'll be boys basketball and James will have practice after school, and Brian will practice after that. We will go to all the out-of-town games." The McHenry County American who despaired that the German-Russian women in 1915 never got off the farm should hitch a ride with Kay Senger. She drives to town to "get a part," to pick up the Sunday paper, to go to church, to 4-H, to chauffeur kids, her own and others. She speeds off to Webster, Starkweather, or Devils Lake to visit her parents, to Grand Forks to shop and visit her daughter at the university.

Like the women before her, who Grandma says depended on each other, Kay is a caregiver. She helps a neighbor whose husband is an amputee, and does errands for an elderly neighbor couple who can't get out in the winter. She takes her mother-in-law 90 miles to the doctor and cooks and bakes for her church.

This is a long way from the steppes of Russia, but only a memory away for my grandmother and other immigrant women who came to the U.S. in the 1900s. Change has been slow. Tradition and culture contributed, but "we were poor" echoes in the reminiscence of three generations. That poverty and the attitude toward education were powerful influences. From the perspective of my grandmother, and all the women of her generation, the changes in women's lives in her lifetime are dramatic: from a 4th grade education to college, from the field and barn to the Radisson.

Grandma grew up in an authoritarian society isolated from and resistant to change in values, but her husband "cared about schooling" as she says, and their moves to culturally diverse communities created a different environment for their daughters. Mother lived among the Scandinavians and German Mennonites and made comparisons. She went to high school. She sympathized with her cousins who were trapped on the farm by poverty and repressive attitudes, and chaffed at the place she had to occupy because she was female. Later, when it was necessary for her to work outside her home, the inequality and discrimination in the workplace stimulated her early feminism. She and others of the first generation born in the U.S. were the catalysts for change, but it wasn't until my generation that change was possible. Like Teresa Schmidt, I grew up knowing that education was a way to escape poverty. It made you free.

Our daughters, the third generation born in the U.S. and in North Dakota, accept education as part of the fabric from which choices are made, the myriad of choices that they assume simply a right. The plaintive "we never went to high school, we didn't even dream of it" has no place in their consciousness. The stories of the women who preceded us are important though for my Lisa and her generation. I want them to be aware of the strength of spirit they've inherited, to realize their debt, and to feel a bond to the black shawled mother in Russia, the field hand on the prairie, the midwife, *and* the feminist bank officer.

References

Handy-Marchello, B. *Heritage Review*, May 1987.

Sherman, W.C., P.V. Thorson, W. Henke, T. Kloberdanz, T. Pedeliski, and R.P. Wilkins. *Plains Folk: North Dakota's Ethnic History*. Fargo: North Dakota Institute for Regional Studies, 1988.

Voeller, J. "The Origin of the German-Russian People and Their Role in North Dakota," Master's Thesis. Grand Forks: University of North Dakota, 1940.

Weber, N. "The Russian German Settlements in McHenry County, North Dakota." Ms. #497. Grand Forks: University of North Dakota Special Collections, Chester Fritz Library, 1927.

Wishek, Nina Farley. *Along the Trails of Yesteryear*. Ashley, North Dakota: Ashley Tribune, 1941.

Niomi Phillips has served on the Grand Forks School Board and Library Board, taught English, and is now Assistant to the Dean of the Graduate School at the University of North Dakota. She is married and the mother of three daughters.

Hazel Miner, Angel of the Prairies

by Lucille Gullickson

Because of the way the land lies around Center, North Dakota, where I live, the 15 miles between the consolidated school and the place where the highway turns south is known to locals as the "blizzard belt." This is where Hazel Miner died on March 16, 1920.

I

Under the headline "Lost in Blizzard: The Children of William Miner Lost in Storm on Way From School," the *Center Republican* for March 18, 1920, began its account of the story:

Hazel Miner, the 16-year-old daughter of Mr. and Mrs. William Miner, perished in the blizzard which swept this part of the state Monday and Tuesday, while attempting to make it home from school.

Monday afternoon Mr. Miner, who lives about two and a half miles north of the Consolidated School started out on horseback to escort his children home from school.

The three children: Hazel, aged 16; Emmett, aged 11; and Myrdith, not quite nine years old, were accustomed to driving back and forth from school in a light covered sleigh. Upon arriving at the school house Mr. Miner hitched up the horse to the cutter, and told the children to wait until he could get his own saddle horse from the school barn only a few rods away. When he returned he found the children had already started for home. Passing through the north gate of the school yard they disappeared in the storm, and for 25 hours were exposed to the bitter elements of a March blizzard. The father, hoping to overtake his children, hurried on, but soon realized that they had lost their way. He then went home, notified his wife what had happened, and started out in search of the lost ones.

II

Although only four and a half years old at the time, Anna Starck Benjamin still lives in Center and when I talked to her she remembered the day the Miner children were found. They had been brought to the farm home of her parents, the William Starcks, after their upset sleigh and horse standing nearby were discovered in a deep coulee. According to Anna Benjamin, "The weather had been beautiful, melting snow and running creeks. Bright March sunshine. It looked like Spring was really here. Then one evening it started raining, got colder, and turned to snow by morning. Anna remembered her mother's younger sister and her brother, Herman, had been staying with them. "My grandparents had come to take them home." Anna said they apparently had come before the storm, then had to wait it out before going back to Sweet Briar where they lived. She recalls that the storm had cleared, and too young to be part of the searching party, Herman had ridden out in the afternoon of the 16th. With the dog, he had come upon the scene about the same time the searchers arrived. Emmett had seen the dog running across the field and thought it might be a coyote.

Anna described the scene in her family's house:

> Children were protected in those days, but I recall sitting in the east window with my grandfather when they brought the children to the house, and I suppose they wanted me out of the way, but I remember to this day the sound of Hazel's outstretched arms as they brushed against the furniture as they brought her into the house, and took her into my parents' bedroom. The crackling sound as that of frozen laundry brought in off the clothes line in winter. Then I remember the crying, so much crying.

As we go about the work of organizing our "Hazel Miner Circle," may the realization of what this heroic girl — Hazel Miner — suffered and endured in that terrible snow storm of March 15-16, 1920, cause us to imbibe her spirit.

By the same spirit of self-denial and sacrifice, shall not we, too, help to erect a building that shall be the means of saving untold hundreds of needy children from the ravages of hunger, cold and homelessness, and place them in Christian homes, where they may be safe?

E. E. Saunders
The North Dakota Children's Home Finder
15 January 1921

It wasn't clear whether Hazel was dead when they brought her in, or whether she died later, as some reports tell. At any rate, Anna is sure now that Hazel never regained consciousness, although they worked over her for many hours. "The pain of their frozen limbs, when they got into the warm house, must have been terrible," Anna said, speaking of Emmett and Myrdith. After the children were found, Mrs. Miner was brought to the Starck farm. "I suppose neighbors stayed with her during that long, long vigil. She had stayed up all night, but must have at some time dozed off, because she later said that Hazel had come to her in a dream and said, 'I was cold, Mama, but I'm not any more.'" Mrs. Miner sat in a rocking chair, and just rocked and rocked while others worked over her children to bring feeling back into their frozen bodies. Anna had been once, in a sleigh, to visit the Miners, and played with Hazel's big doll: "I thought that was the prettiest doll I had ever seen."

III

The *Center Republican* account of 1920 continues:

The alarm was quickly given over the telephones, several searching parties were soon out on the prairies where they remained until it became so dark and perilous that the search had to be given up until daylight Tuesday morning.

At nine o'clock Tuesday morning word came to Center that no trace had yet been found of the missing ones, and a request was sent in for more help. A party of 14 men volunteered for service. After some delay in securing a team, C. S. Sorensen agreed to make the attempt.

The others in the party were Reverend C. B. Madsen, W. H. Rappuhn, Ernest Wick, Henry Cordes, Jr., L. D. Monson, Jimmie Maher, Roy Light, Paul Wolff, Myron Simon, Harry Potter, Harry Clark, Gus Mantz, and E. F. Mutchler. [Neighbors also joined in the search, but the account names only people living in Center.]

Teams were changed at the W. H. Herrington farm, and the party pushed on to the school house. After a light lunch the south half of section fifteen was gone over without result. This land lies north and east of the school house. A conference was then held at the Tom McCrea buildings a mile or more east. While this conference was being held, with numerous parties, most of whom had been out since daylight, Gus Mantz, and a few men who had been with him, came in and reported that they believed they had struck a trail a short distance to the northeast. Investigation proved the trail to have been made by a single horse and sled. This track led to the west line of Ted Starck's pasture, where it turned south on the section line and again east where all signs were obliterated. Immediately about 30 men, some on horseback and others on foot or in bobsleds stretched out for a distance of half a mile or more, started east and south, where in a coulee a mile south of Ted Starck's the upset sled with horse still attached was found.

"With breathless haste we hurried to the rig and will never forget the sight that met our eyes."

Hazel, the oldest child had placed two blankets underneath the smaller ones, one over them, and had lain down to her last sleep without covering of any kind except the clothing she had on.

Lifting the cover, Emmett and his little sister were found to be still alive. They

Hazel Miner (Brave Dakota Daughter)

Tell it again, the story
  How Hazel Miner died,
How she won a martyr's glory
  In that blizzard grim and hoary—
Broad the storm gods' icy legions
Bombarded our open regions,
  With the impulse of a blast,
Then we sense the power that fought her
  Our brave Dakota daughter,
And she battled to the last.
  Not alone for wartime glory
Are deeds of valor done;
  Peace too often tells the story
Of the greatest laurels won.

Give her a place in history,
  Give her a place in song,
Let the children hear her story,
  And give her the fame and glory
That to such deeds belong.
  No praise could over-rate her,
No fight was ever greater
  Than her battle with the cold.
Then she soothed her brother's crying
  When she knew that she was dying—
What braver things are told
  By the fear of death undaunted,
In that raging blizzard blast;
  By no human terror haunted
She was faithful till the last.

Give her a martyr's wages
  And a tribute carved in stone—
By the lore of slab and page
  Speak the past to future ages
That she may still be known.
  Her coat around the others
She saved her sister's life, and brother's,
  From death in the ice and snow;
With her scanty garb around her,
  In the morning, first they found her,
Yes, let the future know!
  Let her name and fame live ever
With her monument in view
  In our human, weak endeavor
To give our great her due.

**by John Howard Ladd
Reprinted with permission
from the Center Republican.**

Photo courtesy of Lucille Gullickson.

The Story of Hazel Miner

Wings on snow
 a fate not chose
morning finds
 a dove so froze
who too soon thought
 the spring arrived
In warmth below
 her love survived

Up in Oliver County
 on the West Dakota plain
lived a farmer's daughter
 Hazel Miner was her name.
She was soon to come in bloom
 a prairie rose of spring.
She'd never seen the young girl dreams
 her sixteenth year would bring.

Hush a-bye
 don't you cry
Cold is like
 a sorrow
Sing a song
 it won't be long
You'll be warm tomorrow

A nineteen-twenty mid-March storm
 caused school to let out early
So each child could reach their farm
 before the blizzard's fury.
Her brother sister bundled tight,
 Hazel hitched the sleigh
But in the night of blinding white
 she somehow lost her way
For half a day they plodded on
 then darkness - desperation
Hazel put the young ones down
 and lay her body o'er them

Hush a-bye
 don't you cry
Cold is like
 a sorrow
Sing a song
 it won't be long
You'll be warm
 tomorrow

Silent song
 paling wind
Storm at end
 again begin
Not all to soar
 the winds aloft
Stiffened wings
 feathers soft

The next day the searchers came
 and found the horse still standin'
Its eyes and nose frozen closed
 no duty more demandin'
They lifted Hazel from the snow
 only limp her hair
With sadness joy the girl and boy
 alive beneath her there

Hush a-bye
 don't you cry
Cold is like
 a sorrow
Sing a song
 it won't be long
You'll be warm
 tomorrow

Wings on snow
 a fate not chose
Morning finds
 a dove so froze
who too soon thought
 the spring arrived
In warmth below
 her love survived

Hush a-bye
 don't you cry
You'll be warm
 tomorrow

by Chuck Suchy, copyright 1986
(from the album "Much to
Share"). Reprinted with permission.

were lifted carefully into the waiting sleds, taken to Mr. Starck's home, and tenderly cared for.

Whether the children did not understand their father's instructions to wait for him, or whether the horse started off by herself, is not known. The horse was a very gentle one and was driven without a bridle and had not stirred after the tip-over. She had remained in her tracks evidently since early Monday morning until two o'clock Tuesday afternoon. Any movement would have spilled the precious human freight in the snow.

From the position of her body, holding down the cover over the little brother and sister, to keep them from freezing, and from the story told by little Emmett, it is known that Hazel died a heroine, sacrificing her life to save the lives of Emmett and Myrdith.

IV

Emmett's version of the story, told in the *Center Republican*, as well as in a recounting of the event in the *Bismarck Tribune* (16 March 1963) is as follows:

Papa told us to wait for him, but Old Maude started off and we could not hold her. After a while we got into an awful place, the tugs came unhooked. Hazel got out and hooked them up, she got in the water. She said, "Oh my! I am wet clear to the waist and my shoes are full of water." [This coulee was north of a farm owned by J. O. Wilson, and the children had passed within 200 feet of the house, but could not see it.]

When Hazel got the horse hitched up, she led the horse until she was tired out, then I helped her. When we tipped over Hazel was thrown out over the dash board. Hazel then fastened the robe over the back of the sled to keep out the wind. The robe kept blowing down and Hazel kept putting it up until she got so she couldn't put it up any more. Then she covered us up with the robe and lay down on top of it. I told Hazel to get under the covers too, but she said she had to keep us children warm, and she wouldn't do it.

She kept talking to us, telling us not to go to sleep, and told us to keep moving our feet so they wouldn't freeze—she kept punching us and told us to punch each other to keep awake. I tried to get out to put the cover over Hazel, but I could not move because she was lying on the cover.

The snow would get in around our feet so we couldn't move them, then Hazel would break the crust for us. After awhile she could not break the crust any more, she just lay still and groaned. After awhile she stopped groaning, I thought she must be dead, then I kept talking to Myrdith so she wouldn't go to sleep.

The obituary carried in the *Center Republican* remembered Hazel Dulcie Miner as having had a quiet, loving disposition. She liked children, who found her a helpful and sympathizing friend. She would have finished the eighth grade and hoped to enroll in the Bismarck high school in the fall. The Reverend Madsen preached a funeral sermon on the text "Greater love hath no man that he lay down his life for his friend," and said, "Here and there are occasionally people who by their acts and lives endeavor to imitate Him."

V

According to the *Center Republican* for April 15, 1920: "It is within the possibilities that the heroic death of Hazel Miner, who gave her life to save a younger brother and sister in the storm of March 16th, will be commemorated by the erection of a beautiful hospital in Center in the near future." Articles appeared weekly telling of donations given as memorials to Hazel Miner. Then on October 14 the paper reported that the idea of building a hospital had been abandoned when Mr. and Mrs. Miner notified the memorial committee that they wanted a monument erected instead.

The *North Dakota Children's Home Finder* (15 January 1921) tells of how the Children's Home Society hoped to use the growing interest in the Hazel Miner story ("this guardian angel of the prairies, covered with a thick sheet of ice, gave up her own life to save her brother and sister") to raise money toward building a home for children: "The making of this Home a memorial to pioneer days dovetails in nicely with the plan of organizing Hazel Miner Circles over the state as auxiliary to the Children's Home Society; thus interesting a large number of people in our work of saving children in danger of perishing." The newsletter account continues:

> School children all over the state have contributed to erect a suitable monument
> . . . at the grave of Hazel Miner. This is highly proper and as it should be, but her
> action in giving up her own life for others deserves a fitting memorial that shall daily
> be in use in the saving of lost children to lives of usefulness, and her actions are so
> in keeping with the purposes of the Children's Home Society, that our Building
> Fund Solicitor, Rev. E. E. Saunders — himself a pioneer pastor of 32 years in the state
> — has launched the plan of organizing everywhere groups of friends of the Home
> and its work, to be known as "Hazel Miner Circles." They are to assist in gaining
> additional members and contributors to the building fund for the new Home. The
> idea is taking readily, and we hope will spread to every corner of the state, so that
> the memory of Hazel Miner may be perpetuated in our new main building, one wing
> of which will be known as the "Hazel Miner Corner." Should there be sufficient
> support from this source, the building itself may be known as the "Hazel Miner
> Memorial Home."

A six-foot memorial on the courthouse lawn was finally dedicated on July 19, 1936, after Governor L. B. Hanna's family donated a granite monument. The inscription reads:

In Memory of Hazel Miner
April 18, 1904-March 16, 1920
To the dead a tribute, To the living a memory, To posterity an inspiration.
The story of her life and of her heroic death is recorded in the archives of Oliver
County on pages 130-131, Book of Miscellaneous Records
STRANGER READ IT

Lucille Gullickson is a reporter-photographer for the *Center Republican* and farms near Center, North Dakota, with her husband. She is the mother of five grown children.

Sherida's Story

by Edna L. Uecker

Three percent of the population, or 18,000 to 19,000 in North Dakota, is estimated to have some form of mental retardation. The state constitution provides that "there shall be located at or near the City of Grafton an institution for the feeble minded." In 1904 the State School at Grafton began operation, and because of overcrowding and staffing problems, in 1966 San Haven, originally a tuberculosis sanitarium, was opened to the severely retarded.

By the late 1970s, North Dakota had institutionalized more persons per capita and spent less on institutional services than any other state. Today (1988) North Dakota ranks among the highest in expenditures for services to the mentally impaired. This dramatic turn-around was spurred by a complaint filed by the Association for Retarded Citizens of North Dakota in the U.S. Federal District Court, which led to passage by the 47th legislative assembly of a comprehensive program for deinstitutionalization and development of community services.

Although the handicapped haven't yet achieved full acceptance in society, services in the state have improved, and now include support groups, group homes and supported living arrangements; day activities; and training in day service centers leading to gainful employment. In 1971 the federal government mandated that special education be available through the public school for children from three through 21 years of age in the "least restrictive" setting. In North Dakota there is a home-based infant development program for children under age three. Other services in North Dakota include respite care (caretakers come into a home to stay with the disabled person so the family may be free for short periods of time); and family subsidies, which give limited financial support toward the cost of care for disabled persons. Over 60 professionals are employed in 36 human service agencies throughout the state to monitor services to the mentally handicapped and ensure their legal rights.

Our story spans much of the history of the treatment of the mentally and physically disabled in North Dakota. On June 29, 1958, we were a typical "all-American family" on our way to church when a drunk driver collided with us. Korliss, our two-year-old daughter, my husband and I received only minor bruises and scratches. But our five-year-old daughter Sherida, who was lying on the back seat reading a book, had her head turned toward the side of the car that was hit.

When a doctor arrived and examined Sherida, he found that she had a severe head injury. He drove us to Richardton where doctors determined that she had received multiple skull fractures. She was then air-lifted to St. John's Hospital in Fargo. In addition to the trauma caused by the blow to Sherida's head, a temperature of 107.2 contributed to extensive brain damage. Exploratory surgery removed clots from her brain, but there was little else to be done except wait, and the agony was almost unbearable. She remained in a coma for nearly three months.

About three weeks after the accident, my husband Charles returned to his veterinary practice, which he had just established. Korliss went to live with relatives. I moved into an efficiency apartment near the hospital, but stayed with Sherida nearly all the time, waiting. Finally, because Korliss was suffering too, we moved Sherida to the hospital in Dickinson, so we could be closer together.

Though Sherida's vital signs leveled off, there was no evidence of consciousness. The weeks passed slowly. Anxiety, depression and continued separation of our family caused additional stress. Finally, the week before Thanksgiving of 1958, we moved Sherida home. At that time there were no government programs to assist parents of a handicapped child, and no Association for Retarded Citizens available for support. Even domestic help was difficult to obtain in a small town. After she came out of the coma, our daughter was unable to speak or move. We knew she could hear, but because her eyes were permanently dilated and somewhat fixed, we didn't think she could see. Her hair had been shaved during surgery, and the left side of her face and body were paralyzed — this little girl looked nothing like our Sherida, and we weren't even certain she knew who we were. She was spoon-fed a soft diet, and needed six to eight glasses of liquid every twenty-four hours. Sherida also had to be turned and re-positioned in bed every two hours to prevent bedsores and pneumonia. She was given passive exercises twice a day. Her schedule plus household chores left little time for Korliss, my husband, or myself.

Each person experiences feelings of being alone during a lifetime; I felt very much alone in the care of our daughter. And so I began my endless search for help. I read as many books as I could on mental retardation, made phone calls and searched for other parents of handicapped children — parents who had learned to cope with the anxiety and pain. Time and again we were advised by doctors, friends, and family members to institutionalize Sherida, but I could not let go of this child. Often when I held Sherida and spoke to her, I felt we were "plugged into" each other.

Sherida passed from crisis to crisis. What progress she made was very slow, although she did begin to say words, which encouraged us. As I became more immersed in her care, I also became overly protective of her, and did not trust sitters with her demanding routine of feedings, positioning, and so on. Even when Charles and I went out for an evening my thoughts stayed with Sherida. Our marriage bonds were stretched. Often Charles became very depressed and withdrew from me and the children, most especially Sherida. It was his way of dealing with painful emotions he, too, was experiencing. Sherida had been his companion on so many country visits. Now it seemed she had become a source of pain between us. At this time, Charles felt the only way to solve the problem was to get away from it by institutionalizing Sherida. Certainly I was fatigued and anxious much of the time, yet I was not able to let go of our daughter.

A year after her accident, we took her to the Sister Kenny Institute in Minneapolis for evaluation. I traveled back and forth on weekends. Again our family was torn apart. Korliss once more was moved from relative to relative, from friend to friend. After three months, we were told there was nothing more that could be done for Sherida. We brought her home, and the next fall tried again to seek treatment by taking her to Hot Springs, South Dakota. Although her speech and sight had improved, rather than being helped by the staff at Hot Springs, she became very withdrawn after only a few days, cried a lot, and was afraid to be left alone. After two months we were told she had regressed and that nothing more could be done for her.

Again we brought her home, and this time we settled into a daily routine. Sherida seemed more content, and began enjoying music, stories and family activities. Then in July 1960, just when we felt our life was stabilizing, I discovered I was pregnant. I was anxious that the continuous lifting would harm the fetus, and worried about how I'd manage with the added care of a new baby. But the pregnancy went well, and I gave birth to a healthy baby boy on March 1, 1961. Jonathan was happy and content and caring for him was a joy.

But feeding, bathing and caring for both an infant and Sherida became a grueling routine for me. I was tired most of the time, and there was little communication between Charles and me. Our problems again appeared insurmountable and irreparable.

It would be wrong to blame all discord on the accident, but it was so very traumatic for all of us, and like many couples who married and started families in their twenties, we'd had little time to develop a solid foundation for working through differences before the accident; too much had come too fast. Our main goal was to stay on top of the anxiety and pain caused by the accident. All else was secondary.

And so the next time Charles brought up the subject of institutionalization, I was ready to listen. It seemed to be the only solution. In the summer of 1963 we made an appointment at the Grafton State School. We toured the institution, and then were told Sherida would have to be placed at San Haven where the most severely handicapped patients were kept. That same day we drove to San Haven, in silence and with heavy hearts. There an orderly offered to show us the grounds. He said nothing about placing our daughter.

We entered the building where bedridden patients lay. Outside of an occasional rattle of a bedrail, there was total silence. I heard no music, no radio or television, no laughter.

"It's so quiet in here," I said to the orderly.

He agreed that it was, but seemed used to it. He said the patients weren't very active.

Charles asked him what he meant. "Do they do anything for activities?" he inquired.

No, most of them are heavily sedated, and most of them are waiting to die, the orderly said. Our decision was made. Both my husband and I knew we wanted more than this kind of existence for Sherida. On the way home, we agreed San Haven could never be a permanent home for her. We knew if she was ever going to develop her potential, it would have to be in a normal environment of love, life and acceptance.

We stood alone in our decision, but now I had Charles' support. And so we settled into a near-normal life. Since we had always been an outdoor family, we continued our winter sports and summer camping trips, though they were shorter and closer to home. Sherida enjoyed both when her health and the North Dakota weather permitted. She enjoyed roasting marshmallows around the campfire. In winter, we would bundle her, tie her on a sled and take her skating or tobogganing.

There is no doubt that keeping our handicapped daughter at home affected our other children. Whenever there is a seriously ill child in a family, much is sacrificed for the sake of that child's care. Since we were told that Sherida's life span would be short, we always felt stress whenever she was ill, but it was a kind of stress that made us lean on one another for support.

Korliss had to make the greatest adjustment, for she had experienced long periods of absence from her family at a crucial age. She was forced into a role reversal by going from little sister to big sister, and the birth of a new baby meant less attention for her. Our son Jonathan seemed to adjust easily, since he had never known any other way of life. There was a junior-high period when he had difficulty having his friends see Sherida, but that passed. Both of the children's friends were very accepting of Sherida, and many learned to know and care for her.

There have certainly been periods of guilt for me, times when I was too burdened and fatigued to read between the lines of my children's lives. I did not always listen with my heart. The children tend to shield us from the bad parts of their lives, perhaps sensing that often their father and I were already over-stressed.

But Korliss and Jon are compassionate adults, with a great deal of perseverance. Korliss received her BS in nursing and a BA in music at the University of North Dakota, and a Masters in opera from the Julliard School of Music. Currently she is nursing and singing professionally in New York City. After completing a degree in archeology, Jonathan graduated from the UND School of Medicine in 1988.

Sherida, now 35, is still at home. She is completely handicapped physically but she is able to communicate by speaking slowly and in short sentences, and loves to tease and be teased. The other day when I lifted her into her wheelchair, I groaned and said, "Sherida, if you get much heavier, your old mother won't be able to lift you." She grinned and started to sing, "The old gray mare ain't what she used to be."

Her physical condition continues to deteriorate, which is to be expected after a 30-year disability. Often she has been near death. Last year she became malnourished because her weakened muscles were unable to push food through her esophagus. On December 26, 1987, a gastrostomy was performed; Jonathan stayed with Sherida during surgery and Korliss helped with the nursing care.

The decision we made over 25 years ago to keep Sherida at home may not be acceptable for all families with a handicapped child, although I believe we would make the same decision today. Certainly our family was not immune to other problems. These might have occurred even without our daughter's handicap and her presence in our home, but we've known no other way of life.

Even though Sherida continues to have many health problems, she is content most of the time. Her days are spent watching television, listening to tapes and records, doing therapy and pleasing those she loves. Time and again, our family has been drawn together because she has taught us so much about love.

Edna Uecker lives in Hettinger, North Dakota, where she writes for such magazines as *Lutheran Digest, North Dakota REC/RTC, Dakota Farmer* and *North Dakota Horizons*, paints with oils and watercolors, and markets a line of her notecards.

Aunt Lena and Uncle Joe

by Virginia Remington

My freshman year of high school, I was elected cheerleader. I was elated to be that well accepted in my new school, and dashed into the house to tell Aunt Lena. "Ach, never!" she said. "You would have to ride on the bus with the boys to go to games, and who knows what hanky-panky goes on there." There were only two families in Regent "stained" by divorce, and, according to Aunt Lena, because I was the daughter of divorced parents, and because I was my mother's daughter, I had to be a model of virtue. I could wear little or no makeup, dress very modestly, speak very little to boys, and above all, "no flirting or hanky-panky." Although she allowed me to be in school plays, I never saw a basketball game until I was out of high school. Whenever I did anything Aunt Lena disapproved of, I was "just like the Funks" (my mother's family).

Uncle Joe was given to practical jokes; one of his favorites was mopping up a puddle. He'd set one of us on the floor, pour water between our legs, then give his victim forks to wipe up the water. He'd feign wiping, and then suddenly pull the child through the puddle. Another joke, he thought, was a "seeing stars" routine. He'd make one of us lie on the floor and look up through a coat sleeve to see stars. Uncle Joe then poured water down the sleeve, laughing boisterously.

Life with Aunt Lena and Uncle Joe began on Columbus Day, 1943, when he appeared at our school in Taylor, North Dakota, collected the six of us — my older brother, myself, and our four younger brothers and sisters — and crammed us and our belongings into the small car he'd borrowed. He then drove us to his and Aunt Lena's farm at Regent.

For us, it was just another uprooting. My parents had gone to Ohio at the beginning of World War II to work in the war plants, had separated, and sent us back to North Dakota. Nobody wanted six children, and we were to be parcelled out, in lots of two, when Aunt Lena, my father's sister, and her husband, Joe Dolezal, intervened. They had no children. Aunt Lena said, with some asperity, "Those children have suffered enough, they didn't have to be separated, too!" She and Uncle Joe meant well, and my brothers, sisters and I were grateful to be taken in, especially during difficult war years, but their benevolence was tinged with cruelty whether they were aware of it or not.

In some ways my years on the farm were good ones. Although I will never forget their harsh, authoritarian child-rearing methods which left me with such bitter memories of my high school years, I did realize that such attitudes came partly from the rural, European culture in which they were raised. Eventually Aunt Lena and I developed a close relationship. I never forgot that she and Uncle Joe gave us a home when we had nowhere else to go.

From city life to life in the country was a difficult transition for us. Aunt Lena started our education as soon as we arrived by taking the boys out to the barn to learn how to milk cows, while I was assigned to kitchen duty to finish preparing the evening meal. It didn't matter to Aunt Lena that at 12 years old I knew little about the rudiments of cooking. "Don't worry," she said. "I will make of you a good cook."

From then on, the boys worked in the barns and the fields, the girls in the house. Even though Aunt Lena herself had always worked side by side with Uncle Joe, putting in long hours in the fields, she never had me work outside, except for such minor chores (she felt) as gardening or feeding the chickens. "A woman's place is in the home," she said firmly. Before World War II, she had been milking ten cows (by hand); after Pearl Harbor she increased her milk herd to 20. Every dollar from her cream checks went into war bonds.

She considered herself a true patriot, but had a difficult time justifying the large hoard of sugar cached in her attic, stored when sugar rationing became imminent. "Those town people, they don't need as much sugar as farm people do, because they don't can as much as we do," she said. It was the only infraction of her otherwise 100% effort to support the war. Even coffee drinking, one of their main indulgences, fell by the wayside when coffee was rationed, and they started drinking Postum (made out of wheat).

Farm food, especially during wartime rationing, was also different. In town, bologna had been our main meat. Aunt Lena and Uncle Joe butchered a beef and a hog every fall. Most of the meat was stored in lockers in Regent, but the cured hams and bacon were hung in the granary. They made their own sausage and Aunt Lena made head cheese, which she canned, and blood sausage. The thick soup derived from cooking these meats was stored in a large kettle in the cold sun porch, with some heated up each day until it was all gone. Aunt Lena and Uncle Joe filled the root cellar each fall with the vegetables they'd grown, and also kept there the root beer she'd made.

Life on a farm also introduced me to a close family life I'd never had before. In the evening we'd all sit around the kitchen table (the front room and dining room were only used when we had company), do our homework, read (as a former schoolteacher, Aunt Lena had an extensive library), and listen to "Amos 'n' Andy" and "Fibber M'Gee & Molly" on the radio. Sometimes we'd play "Red Dog," a Bohemian card game, with Uncle Joe. Sometimes Aunt Lena would tell us stories about her childhood, about the "Old Country," as she called it, or about our family, or life as it used to be. A gifted storyteller, with a flair for mimicry, she was often called on to give a German monologue at neighborhood parties. Her stories made me aware of my German-Hungarian heritage, and proud of it. Aunt Lena played the piano, and when we showed an interest in music, purchased secondhand musical instruments for us. Uncle Joe drove us to New England on Saturdays to take lessons from the nuns at St. Mary's.

Farm life, of course, introduced us to working, but when working together it didn't seem like drudgery. All of us would walk behind the potato digger, Uncle Joe manning the machine, and we'd pick up potatoes and bag them. We'd hoe in the garden together. Culling out good potatoes from rotten ones in the root cellar was a loathsome job, though sometimes Aunt Lena would start us singing while we worked. Aunt Lena loved music. Uncle Joe, although tone deaf, did too, and sometimes favored us with a tuneless, but hearty rendition of "Bevo Chervene" (Bohemian for "Red Beer").

Aunt Lena and Uncle Joe's home was built in a crook of Coalbank Creek, just before it poured into the Cannonball River (actually, their house was the old cook shack from Coalbank itself, remodeled). The waters of the creek, especially during spring freshet time, would hold a particular fascination for me. The rushing torrent washed out the mud crossing and, inexorably crept forward across the plateau in front of the house, while in back the waters slowly inched higher and higher. Each year we faced the possibility of evacuation to a nearby bluff, but eventually the waters would recede. In order to get us safely across when the crossing was out, Uncle Joe, on the first school day we were there, winched a plank across the creek, just behind the house. I could never walk across as the others did. Instead, I'd crawl across on my hands and knees.

As I learned to love nature, I also learned to respect it. Hailstorms were to be feared. Aunt Lena once woke us all up in the middle of the night. The sky was exploding with thunderclaps, wild streaks of lightning, and a deluge of water and hailstones. Stumbling down the steps, we were herded into the living room where we knelt with rosaries in our hands. In the midst of pans and buckets, with the rain pinging into them, and Aunt Lena crying and leading us in our prayers, exhorting God to save the crops, we sleepily mumbled the responses by rote.

Aunt Lena could be cruel in her idea of discipline. If she caught two of us in a fight, she stopped it, then handed each of the combatants a stick, keeping a third with which she belabored whichever fighter was striking the weakest blows. Soon both children, tears pouring down their faces, were hitting each other viciously while she struck them indiscriminately. Her stratagem against one of my brothers who persisted in wetting his bed was to make him drape the wet sheet around his shoulder and stand on the front steps until the school bus came. Then he had to remove the sheet, climb on the bus, and go to school. My own worst infraction was voting for Roosevelt in a mock school election. When she heard about it, she slapped my face.

When she was angry, Aunt Lena spoke German. She'd call me a "shyster," but

I was sure she wasn't calling me a "crooked lawyer," but something more vulgar in German. When angry, Aunt Lena didn't mince words. "Ach!" she would say when especially exasperated, throwing her hands dramatically in the air and rolling her eyes skyward. "Today I have earned another star in my crown of heaven!" "Schwenzel" was another of her favorite words, a German derivative, I thought. If she found me spending too much time "primping," she'd accuse me of "schwenzeling," and demonstrate by putting her hands on her hips, twitching her plump bottom from side to side, and taking mincing steps. Later, when I found out the word referred to the movement of a dog's tail, I could remember her mimicry with some amusement. But at the time, I thought her mean, especially when she'd mimic the "town girls," as she called them. Instead of wearing a neighbor's cast-off, outdated dresses and dark brown lisle stockings, I would have given anything to have been like them — to be accepted, to dress like them in swirling, pleated skirts and soft pastel sweaters, nylon stockings and bobby sox.

Virginia Remington lives in Grand Forks, North Dakota.

Gertie

by Hazel Retzlaff

It may be easy to forget that immigration to America was just one event in the lives of people who came; they were people with continuing lives, not just "Immigrants." My aunt Gertie was older than most single women who left Sweden for reasons perhaps only she knew. By the time she arrived, and met a suitable Swedish-American man, my Uncle Solomon, she was past normal child-bearing age. This shy couple became unlikely participants in the American Dream, and for a while it worked for them. By 1916, Solomon was enough involved in land speculation for his more conservative father to warn him that he'd lose his shirt if he weren't careful. Solomon's younger brother Gust entrusted him with some of his small reserves for land investment, and Solomon came to own several farms in North Dakota. He did lose everything, even his own farm in the rich Red River Valley, whereupon his brother made the long trip to see what remained of his investment, and found a quarter of swampy land, almost worthless for farming. Perhaps if the American Dream hadn't failed for Solomon, Gertie might have become a more secure American.

After the loss of the land, Gertie and Solomon lived in the small farm house south of Fargo that I remember. There, on the few acres left them, they raised chickens and cows. She churned butter, which he sold, along with the cream and eggs, to customers in Fargo. My sisters, brother, and I remember the shades drawn in that tiny house when we made infrequent visits. Because they had no children, their home seemed strange to me; so different from ours, crowded with the eight of us. Their home seemed quiet and dark, but Gertie was happy to see us when we visited, and my brother remembers how she laughed when one of us showed appreciation for the canned peach or pear sauce and raspberry jam she served with the perfect krumkake and rosettes. She spoke English to us, but said little, and spoke Swedish to Solomon and his brother, my father. Once she gave us small American flags to play with and take home. They were special to us, I remember, perhaps because they were bright and new.

Gertie's sisters-in-law, Jennie and Tillie, born here and very American, wrote to her in Fargo from Washington and California where they had active lives, and their comments about her to each other in the old letters seem to me a little smug. Jennie writes to Tillie that she "wishes Gertie wouldn't fret so about the rosettes" she's baking for Jennie's Grange meeting. Gertie apparently worried that they'd break in the mail to Washington. Her rosettes seem to me to have been small transmitters of Swedish culture from the Red River Valley to the more diverse and sophisticated western states.

Gertie's contacts with people outside her small house were limited to members of the Free Church she belonged to in Fargo. No one in my family remembers why she didn't belong to the Swedish Lutheran Church, but all of my father's family were religiously very conservative. At any rate, she found some friendship there.

After several years of what seems to have been a good marriage, Solomon died, in 1949, of cancer. Within the year, Gertie took the action that most separates her from our idea of typical immigrant women. She took the little money she had and returned to Sweden, not to visit, but to stay. Her return made me think more than ever that she was someone who felt throughout her life here that she was a stranger in a foreign land.

When I remember the small American flags she gave us, I wonder why she had them, what they meant to her, and why she gave them to us. Was she trying to establish her loyalty, or ours, to this new country? One of the members of her Free Church who maintained contact with her in Sweden told my Uncle Gust that Gertie regretted her decision to return to Sweden, but that she lacked the money to come back here.

Gertie seems to me now so individual, a woman who, as one of the events in her life immigrated to America, and as another, returned to Sweden, and found both countries difficult, not because she was hard to please, but because of changes in America, in Sweden, and in herself at different times in her life.

Hazel Retzlaff writes: "I grew up in a house where my father and uncle spoke Swedish. My father was the youngest of nine surviving children, five of them born here." She teaches English at Moorhead State University, Moorhead, Minnesota.

II

It was not an easy life to be a pastor's wife and at mother's time it was indeed hard. The parsonage was a free hotel to all the travelling ministers, teachers and laymen, and it was not unusual to have three or four extra adults. I remember once there were six ministers, their wives and some had one or more children along. Mother took this as a matter of fact and enjoyed the fellowship it gave.

I remember one yearly Ladies Aid project was to gather enough money to buy up a lot of flannel, calico and bolts of other staple material. Then in the spring, a committee would meet and cut this up into different garments, label each garment and give some packages to each woman in the congregation to be sewn. In the fall they would meet at a home for the "Ladies Aid Auction." Whole families would come in wagons, surreys, single buggies, carts or horseback to this place. Then the sale began. We children really did have fun. Of course, the money went into the church fund.

Tulia Skjei Christensen
(Contributed by Doreen Christensen Bakke
Larimore, N.D.)

Lace made by Hankinson Franciscan sisters.

Catholic Sisterhoods in North Dakota

by Mary Ewens, O.P.

The first Catholic sisterhood to be established in what became North Dakota was founded in Pembina around 1853, the creation of Father George Belcourt, a French-Canadian Indian missionary. Belcourt felt that Indian women were the key to the Christianization of their tribes, but found them very shy in the presence of white male missionaries. He conceived the idea of founding a native sisterhood whose members would teach the women and children of their tribes the tenets of Catholicism. Many of his flock were Metis, descendants of French-Canadian traders and Indian mothers. It was among them that he would recruit the first members of the community later called the Sisters of the Propagation of the Faith.

Encouraged in his plan by other missionaries with whom he spoke, he gathered a small band of young women from the Pembina area to form the nucleus of the new group. One of them, Isabelle Gladu, he appointed superior, and gave her the name of Sister St. Francis Xavier. Madeleine Ploufe became Sister Madeleine, Catherine Lacerte took the name of Sister Philomena, and a fourth recruit became Sister Gertrude (Cline). Belcourt sent Sister St. Francis Xavier and two others to the Grey Nuns in Montreal for training in the religious life. They were ready to teach in his school at St. Joseph (now Walhalla) in 1854.

These women arranged both living quarters for themselves and schoolrooms for their pupils in the basement of the church. The windows were thick and arrowproof for protection from the Sioux, who had killed Protestant missionaries in the area in 1852. This school was a popular one, which soon filled up with two hundred pupils and became widely known. Father Belcourt obtained some government support for it, but the sisters were very poor. Regular students paid nothing; boarders were charged $30 for six months. The people of the area brought food to the sisters — a custom that would see many North Dakota sisterhoods through their times of need.

Belcourt wrote to a friend, Charles Cazeau, on November 5, 1855, that interpreters in Chippewa, Cree, Sioux, Assiniboine, French, Italian and German could be found at the school. English is conspicuously absent from this list. But the sisters found that there was a great demand for the teaching of English, even among people who spoke only French themselves, so Sister St. Francis Xavier and Father Belcourt began a search for young women whose mother-tongue was English who might wish to join the group.

Other missionaries who heard of the good accomplished in Pembina asked for sisters to open schools on their missions, but the community had to grow before that would be possible. The outlook for this first North Dakota sisterhood seemed promising, but one evening while Father Belcourt was away, some of the sisters — they may have been postulants who were still deciding whether they wanted to join the community — attended a local dance. The people were shocked, and so was Father Belcourt upon his return. He dismissed the young women from the sisterhood. To cover up their own disgrace, they spread innuendoes about Father Belcourt, which were reported to his superiors. Even though an investigation upheld his innocence, he was ordered back to Canada, and the sisterhood was disbanded. Most members of the group later married; many continued to teach their people. It is said that a descendant of Isabelle Gladu Dease, who had been the superior, joined the contemporary Indian sisterhood, the Oblate Sisters of the Blessed Sacrament, based in Marty, South Dakota.

The Bismarck Benedictines

When the federal government declared Dakota Territory "open" to settlement in the 1870s, Benedictine priests came to serve the needs of the widespread Catholic population. Even before Martin Marty was appointed bishop of the new vicariate of Dakota Territory in 1879, Benedictine Sisters had come to the settlement at Bismarck to start a school. St. Mary's School was the only one in the area, and these sisters from St. Joseph, Minnesota, were able to attract a large clientele, despite the complaints of some non-Catholics. Sister Magdalen Walker arrived to take charge of this school in 1892; her fifty-year term as principal was marked by educational achievement and growth.

In 1885 five more of these sisters arrived in Bismarck, this time to administer St. Alexius Hospital. Under the direction of Sister Boniface Timmins, its chief administrator from 1892 to 1934, St. Alexius brought the latest in medical techniques to western North Dakota. St. Alexius attracted an interesting clientele in its early days, including riverboatmen, outlaws of all sorts, wounded prisoners, and railroad men. The government paid 90 cents per day for the care of riverboatmen, and the city gave $1 per day for the care of the poor. Begging trips by handcar to railroad work camps and army agencies supplemented this meagre income.

These sisters continue to serve the area in educational and medical ventures. They currently sponsor The University of Mary, the only Catholic institution of higher education in North Dakota.

The Irish Presentations

Catholics poured into the Dakota Territory in the 1870s, and Bishop Marty sought help in coping with his widely spread flock. Presentation Sisters from Ireland had already been negotiating for an American mission when Bishop Marty approached them. They came to the southern part of Dakota Territory in 1880 and settled in Fargo in 1882. The founders, Mother St. John Hughes and her sister, Mother Agnes, were imbued with the strength that marks women of their Celtic heritage. Hasia Diner, in her study *Erin's Daughters in America*, points out that Irish women in the last half of the nineteenth century were strong, assertive, boisterous, and very much in control of family finances. They lived in a world separate from that of men even in marriage, amid an ethos of gender hostility. Males were often weak, drunken failures. Those who expected Irish women to exhibit the passive, subservient qualities prescribed for "true womanhood" in nineteenth-century America soon found that other values ruled their lives.

Such was the case with the Hughes sisters. Contemporary accounts of priests and Bishop John Shanley, first bishop of the Fargo diocese, tell us that they dominated Bishop Marty, carried on "a constant warfare with the priests in charge of the parish," and influenced their appointment and removal. The fact that Bishop Marty, desperate for help in serving Catholic needs in the vast Dakota Territory, welcomed priests who had been dismissed from other dioceses for alcoholism or worse, may have had something to do with this warfare. These sisters were astute business-women who rightly resented attempts of others to interfere in their affairs, particularly "incompetent men." Bishop Shanley explained that fear of the Presentation Sisters was one of the reasons Bishop Marty chose Jamestown rather than Fargo as the seat for the new North Dakota diocese that was created in 1889. In a confidential document intended for his successor, Shanley advised him to stay as far away from convents as possible. Bishop James O'Reilly did not heed this advice, however. He became a close friend of Mother Joseph Cregan, who led the Presentation Sisters from 1920 to 1937. He would take her out riding in his touring car, and together they would make many of the most important decisions of the diocese — or so it seemed to the clergy. Priests of that period interviewed by Father William Sherman, sociologist at North Dakota State University in Fargo, attest that "Ma Joe," as they called her, had more influence with Bishop O'Reilly than anyone else in the diocese. Many of them recall the tongue-lashings she gave them when she thought they were out of line. Oral tradition in Mother Joseph's community also affirms her influence over the bishop, according to Presentation archivist Sister Mary Jo Hasey. Some also thought that Bishop O'Reilly exerted undue influence over the sisters' internal affairs, including the re-election of Mother Joseph.

The Presentation Sisters opened a school in Fargo in 1882. The rule of their order stipulated that they could only teach the children of the poor, without accepting any recompense, but these sisters like all others in America had to adapt to the American economic and social situation by teaching children of all classes and accepting tuition from those who could afford it. They built a fence around the St. Joseph Academy and convent in keeping with European ideas of demarcating "the cloister" from "the world," but parents used to the open prairies objected to this constraint on their children, and the sisters made a second concession to Dakota mores. They moved the school to a new location with spacious grounds and no fence, and changed its name to Sacred Heart Academy. This school offered a high quality education and prepared its graduates for the teaching profession, thus providing an invaluable resource for the state. These sisters opened St. John's Orphanage in 1887, and added health care to their work in 1939.

The American Congregation

A second native sisterhood was founded in North Dakota in 1891, under the auspices of another missionary priest, Father Francis M. Craft. Like Father Belcourt, Father Craft thought there was no substitute for native missionaries, sharing the same culture, customs and language, working among their own people. His observations of the Benedictines at Standing Rock may have impelled him to write the following paragraph in an undated document found in the archives of the Bureau of Catholic Indian Missions:

> Missionaries must do their work in the Indian homes and families. . . .If they *cannot* or *will not*, they must provide a *native clergy* who *can* and *will*. . . .If we cannot at once have native clergy, *we can have native catechists*. . . .The only thing in the way of this is the vile and unCatholic *race prejudice* that has hitherto been the cause of nearly all (and perhaps *all*) our mission troubles and failures.

Sister Boniface Timmins

by Barbara A. Gehrki, O. S. B.

Sister Boniface Timmins was Superintendent of St. Alexius Hospital in Bismarck, North Dakota, from 1892 until 1934; she died in 1937 at age 83. In addition to setting the stage for a modern hospital, her long and successful career as a hospital administrator illustrates a woman's life in public service in the early days of statehood. She was energetic and forward-looking in her profession: she emphasized the need for a well built and equipped facility; she had high regard for the education of nurses and other personnel; she recognized the need to keep current with trends in health care. She was politically astute: she kept close associations with members of the civic community; she was successful in fund raising and adept at promotion and public relations. Sister Boniface was willing to take risks and willing to be both collaborative and innovative. How Sister Boniface negotiated among the numerous demands made upon her — by her Order, and by hospital staff, doctors, and the general public -- is a story of her time, and also of the many women who at any time have undertaken administration in their professions.

Sister Boniface, Mary Ann Timmins, was born September 7, 1854, in Benton, Wiscon-

Craft pointed out in an article in the June 1897 *Catholic World* that the rapid establishment of a native clergy had always been the practice among Catholic missionaries, but this had stopped abruptly when the natives were *Indian*. Craft believed in the intellectual and spiritual capabilities of the Indians, and praised the many positive values he saw in their culture. He encouraged a number of young Indian women to enter the Benedictine novitiate in South Dakota. However, he felt they were the victims of prejudice there. That, coupled with his disgust at contemporary missionary methods, and eagerness to prove the truth of his theories about the Indians' abilities, impelled him to establish a new native sisterhood, the Congregation of American Sisters, or the Red Sisters for short. He arranged with Bishop Shanley to transfer the Indian sisters' membership from the Benedictine group to his new one on November 1, 1891.

The first prioress-general (superior) was Josephine Crowfeather, daughter of Chief Crowfeather, who had entered the Benedictine novitiate on Easter Sunday 1889. and she was given the religious name Sister Catharine. Craft added her Indian name to that, and called her Mother Catharine Sacred White Buffalo. Alice White Deer was known as Mother Liguori Sound-of-the-Flying-Lance, and became prioress when Mother Catharine died from tuberculosis in 1893. Susie Bordeaux took the name Sister Anthony Cloud Robe. Nellie Dubray became Sister Gertrude Brings Forth Holiness. Other names were more usual: Bridget, Theresa, Margarita,

---

sin. Her parents were Irish, and not long after her birth moved to St. Paul, Minnesota. When she was seventeen, Mary Ann entered St. Gertrude's, the newly-founded Benedictine Community in Shakopee, Minnesota, and received Boniface as her religious name. She completed the initial training required to become a professed member of the Order during the beginning years of the Shakopee Community, where there were twenty earnest members who experienced hardship, poverty, mistrust from Church officials, and intrigue.

Women religious in the nineteenth century enjoyed little freedom in governing their own communities; sometimes they were not allowed to conduct financial affairs or to elect their own superiors. Instead, canon law gave the bishop jurisdiction over all institutions in his diocese, so that he or a church official appointed by him often directed the internal affairs of women's communities. Not surprisingly, such arrangements led to serious problems for the young community at St. Gertrude's, most of which could be attributed to outside governance: by the clergy who interfered with the leadership within the community; by Sister Mechtildis Richter's lack of loyalty toward the administrators; and by excessive financial obligations. There were differences of opinion over the ownership of some properties. A local pastor accused the nuns of not being able to teach German and they were dismissed from the parish school. These events are recounted in a history of St. Gertrude's, a book titled *The Leaven*, by Claire Lynch (1980).

Yet in spite of such obstacles, community members remained steadfast in their determination to work through their trials. However they were not prepared for what

Cecilia, Francis White Eagle, Joseph Two Bears.

These sisters opened a school and hospital, both at Elbowoods and at the Armstrong sub-agency, on the Fort Berthold reservation. Father Craft, who had had medical training, guided their care of the sick. In 1894 they visited schools and hospitals in St. Paul, Minnesota, to observe methods that might be useful in their own institutions. The number of pupils in the schools (which taught English and citizenship) ranged between 15 and 25. Their hospitals had 28 patients in 1895. They also helped the destitute and nursed and taught in the Indians' homes. In 1896, the Indian agent reported that "The Sisters are efficient in their care of the sick, either at their homes or when brought to the mission, and their kindly ministrations have a beneficial effect." The Catholic Directory for that year lists nine sisters at the two locations, and three novices.

Bishop Shanley provided some financial support for Father Craft and the sisters. Though Craft apparently forbade the eating of meat, there are stories of trapping rabbits and eating cat, and of the sisters fishing for their supper. In reminiscences published in the *Minot Daily News* in 1951, Father Conrad Lotter, who became pastor at Elbowoods in 1910, said that Father Craft marched them to a different Indian dwelling each day for food.

Gossip again touched the lives of native sisters in April 1897, when charges of improper conduct between the sisters and various people at the Indian agency were alleged. Craft protested, and asked the support of Church leaders, but this was

they considered a great injustice: the joining of their community with that of St. Benedict's Convent in St. Joseph, Minnesota. This change was brought about by a former member of St. Gertrude's community, Sister Scholastica Kerst, who in 1880 had been appointed superior of St. Benedict's. She remembered that the sisters of St. Gertrude's were better educated and more talented than those of St. Benedict's, and that they represented more varied nationalities in contrast to the predominantly German community at St. Benedict's. Sister Scholastica arranged with the bishop for the amalgamation. When the sisters of the Shakopee community voted against the plan, they were given the choice to amalgamate or disband. Sister Boniface, who was teaching in the parish school in Belle Plaine, Minnesota, was among the sisters forced to join St. Benedict's.

During her years in the community of St. Benedict's, Sister Boniface taught in schools in Duluth, Melrose, and Stillwater, Minnesota, and in 1892 was named superior and superintendent of a combined hospital and school in Bismarck. The hospital had been bought by Abbot Alexius Edelbrock of St. John's Abbey in Minnesota. It was a partially-constructed, and financially crippled four-story building, planned originally as a hotel. The Abbot had been searching for a site for a men's college but became aware of the greater need in this frontier region for a hospital, and proceeded quickly to have the hotel converted. And, because he had been given jurisdiction over the sisters at St. Benedict's Convent, he arranged for them to administer the institution. Thus, in May 1885 they opened the first hospital in Dakota Territory — the only one between St. Paul and Portland, Oregon.

The *Bismarck Tribune* (12 February 1922) remembered the opening enthusiastically,

apparently not forthcoming. He and the sisters fought a constant battle against racial prejudice, and Mother Catharine wrote to a friend as early as March 17, 1892, "I don't know if we will be allowed to go on. Every one seems to want to stop us because we are Indians."

The appointment of a new agent and the removal of some of the corrupt employees seem to have brought peace to the reservation, but Craft and the sisters, tired of reservation politics, left Fort Berthold in the summer of 1897. They spent time with the Sioux in various camps at Standing Rock, Cheyenne River, and Fort Pierre. Several of the sisters left the community at that time and returned to their families. Many continued to perform works of charity among their own people for the rest of their lives.

Four of the sisters remained with Father Craft. When the Spanish-American War broke out, many sisterhoods volunteered their help, including the Josephites working in North Dakota. The remaining members of the American Congregation wired the War Department, pointing out that their frontier experience would fit them better than others "to attend on either white or colored soldiers, as we are accustomed to attending the sick under conditions much harder and more trying to health and strength than any existing in military camps. We thought we might be of service where others would break down." Their offer was accepted, and Craft, Mother Bridget Pleets (prioress), Sisters Joseph Two Bears, Anthony Bordeaux and Gertrude Clark went to Camp Cuba Libre, Florida. Later they served in Savannah,

---

describing the building as having had "room and to spare, to attempt the care of the sick in the county and the town." Quotations from Sister Boniface were more skeptical. What she had found on her arrival, she said, was "a bare, unfurnished building, heated by the inadequate device of stoves in some of the rooms." It was "more of a boarding school than a hospital, although the institution had taken care of patients." She was faced with no telephones, no electricity, and no elevators to carry patients from the first to the fourth floors. Water had to be transported from the river at 25 cents a barrel, and drinking water was pumped from a well across the street. She arranged for the school to be housed in another building near the Catholic Church.

These and other details appeared in the newspaper on the occasion of the celebration of the 50th anniversary of St. Alexius

Hospital in 1935 (*Tribune*, 12 September 1935). Sister Boniface recounted how, during the first two weeks of her administration, she took steps to replace the small sheet-iron stoves, used in some of the rooms, with a central heating plant. She had no funds, but a woman encouraged her to appeal to the business men of Bismarck, and together they raised $800 in two hours, along with the promise of more money if it were needed.

It was the hospital's policy to accept all patients who needed care — "as Christ Himself" — and there was a wide variety of clients: residents of the County Poor Farm, river boatmen, prisoners from the local jail and penitentiary, Native Americans, and blacks. When the Poor Farm burned, Sister Boniface said, "the men were taken in by our hospital at the request of the Commissioner, at a rate of 45 cents per day." Sitting Bull's son was a patient for four months.

Georgia, and Havana, Cuba, where they resigned on February 27, 1899, to open the first orphange in Pinar del Rio, Cuba.

Craft wrote that though the sisters were "much fatigued by their long service in military hospitals," they "have gained honor and fame here, and among the many hundred patients who passed through their hands there were but two deaths — both cases of incurable tuberculosis." U.S. Surgeon-General Sternberg wrote to thank them, and Congressman Fitzgerald praised them in Congress, saying they would "live forever in the hearts of American soldiers."

On July 19, 1899, Craft wrote to a friend,

> Mother M. Anthony, the granddaughter of Chief Spotted Tail and grandniece of Chief Red Cloud is slowly dying of a disease of the lungs contracted in the military hospitals by hard work and exposure. She will be buried with military honors.

Then the government ended the subsidy supporting the orphanage, and Craft realized that no new recruits would join the group in Cuba. With only himself to support the sisters, Craft felt that the wisest course would be to disband the community and see that the remaining three women got safely back to their own homes. The taps over Mother Anthony's grave would be "the last salute to her order as well." What he wrote of Mother Catharine Sacred White Buffalo at the time of her death sums up his assessment of this bold experiment:

> When the story of Mother Catharine's life is told, the Church will know how to

---

He was "a great singer who sang so loud" he had to be asked to be quieter. Theodore Roosevelt was hospitalized there with pneumonia during his years in the Badlands, and in 1903, during the third year of his presidency, he returned for a visit.

St. Alexius Hospital did not remain long in its rugged and improvised state. In 1899 Dr. E. P. Quain joined the staff. He was a graduate of the University of Minnesota medical school, a young man responding to the opportunities offered by an ambitious frontier town, and he was welcomed for bringing the promise of modern medicine to the new hospital. One of his first innovations was to introduce asepsis to hospital practice, so far unheard of in Bismarck (although Pasteur had described the role of bacteria in spreading infection in the early 1860s, his "germ theory" took a long time to be widely applied). In his book *Just Memories* (1951), Quain described his first day,

when a ball player was brought in with a broken nose. He asked the sister in charge of the operating room for sterile gauze, only to learn that neither sterile gauze nor a sterilizer was available. When he proposed instituting "modern surgical methods to the hospital personnel," he was surprised to learn that the "Sister Superior did not take readily to my new-fangled — and costly — ideas," although before long "she saw the light and became very enthusiastic over my endeavors. Her real conversion came one day when she discovered that boiling the needles and the tap water used in giving hypodermic injections put a stop to sore arms and abscesses." Until a sterilizer was purchased, (out of an operating budget, in 1899, of $312.17), surgical instruments were carried down four flights of stairs to the basement kitchen to be cleansed in boiling water.

With the coming of Dr. Quain, and the

appreciate her work, and will understand how deeply both Church and Indians are indebted to her. By the successful establishment of her Indian congregation under trials and difficulties more than usually cruel and severe, she has removed . . . her church's and her people's reproach of four centuries' standing, and triumphantly vindicated the Catholicity of her Church and the spiritual and mental abilities of her race.

Mother Anthony died in October 1899, and by early 1900 two of the three remaining sisters had returned home, where they would marry, bear children and eventually die. The last remaining sister returned home in 1901. When Anna DuBray, the former Mother Bridget Pleets, died at Fort Yates in1948, she was given a military funeral, but her grave there is unmarked. In an unidentified newspaper clipping regarding Ella Clark Philbrick, the former Sister Gertrude, the headline announces "'Red Sister Sole Nurse Survivor of Spanish War." She spent her last several years at the Old Soldiers Home in Hot Springs, South Dakota. The remains of the first two sisters to die at Elbowoods, Mother Catharine Sacred White Buffalo and her sister Claudia (Sister Theresa), were moved to the Queen of Peace Cemetery near Raub as part of the Garrison Dam project. Their graves give no indication that they are the daughters of Chief Crowfeather or pioneers in a Native American religious congregation. The Corps of Engineers' markers merely identify them as Sister Catherine and Sister Theresa, and incorrectly call them "Gray Nuns."

---

full support of Sister Boniface, the hospital seemed to move quickly to the latest medical and surgical practices, performing appendectomies, installing a surgical table covered with rubber and supplied with drains, and welcoming other innovations. In 1901 Dr. N. O. Ramstad joined the staff.

But there were set-backs as well that Sister Boniface had to contend with as hospital administrator. In 1899 there was a fire that "broke out in the depot and for a while threatened to sweep the town. A shift of wind at the last moment saved the hospital." In 1909 a cloudburst struck Bismarck. Although "twenty-five men worked through the night to keep out the flood, their efforts were ineffectual." Water in the basement damaged equipment and a month's food supply, and wooden sidewalks were washed down the hill and landed "in a pile all about the hospital," according to the retrospective *Tribune*

article. Epidemics of typhoid and diphtheria were severe in Bismarck because of unsanitary housing and bad drinking water.

The success of the hospital, and the rapid growth of the town of Bismarck, meant a need for expanded facilities. With permission from her superiors at St. Benedict's Convent, Sister Boniface saw to the construction, for $9,000 (according to the *Tribune* for 23 January 1906) or $12,000 (according to later articles), of a three-story wing that included operating rooms and a separate sterilizing room, a dressing room for the treatment of wounds, a number of patient rooms and bath rooms, and a dormitory for the eighteen sisters. The *Tribune* again enthusiastically described the dedication on January 23, 1906. The hospital was "a grand institution. It is doing a great work for the sick. Its patrons come from a wide radius surrounding Bismarck and with the able corps of physicians is

French Presentation Sisters

A second strongly ethnic sisterhood established its roots in North Dakota in 1903, when the Sisters of St. Mary of the Presentation arrived from Brittany, France, via Canada. They had had to leave their native land because of the persecution from an anti-clerical government which had expelled them from the public schools. Little did they dream that they would encounter similar prejudice in the land that promised them religious freedom. Upon their arrival they were warmly welcomed by the Fargo Presentation Sisters, who helped them to pass the teacher certification examinations and qualify for teaching credentials. After an initial residence in Wild Rice, where the French-Canadians appreciated the French culture they imparted to their students, these sisters moved their headquarters first to Oakwood, and then to Valley City, where they established schools and hospitals. These sisters remain affiliated with their French motherhouse and, until after the Second World War, broadened the perspective of their North Dakota recruits with a two-year training period in France. The young women from North Dakota were objects of amazement to their French colleagues. Not only did they know how to pitch hay, they also extended their friendship to the lay sisters, thus helping to democratize the class culture which pervaded this Breton convent.

---

making the city favorably known to the afflicted in all parts of the state." Doctors Quain and Ramstad continued to head the staff, even though they disagreed with one of the governing principles of the hospital, that it should be open to all qualified medical staff. Quain and Ramstad wanted a closed medical staff, that is, one limited to doctors selected by the administrative staff. Then in 1909 a second hospital opened, Bismarck Hospital, which acceded to the doctors' wishes for a closed staff. Sister Boniface continued to administer an open medical staff. Quain and Ramstad headed the medical staff at Bismarck Hospital, but continued on the staff at St. Alexius, and, according to two women who had worked under Sister Boniface — Sisters Maximine Firner and Ernee Nester — Sister Boniface always had "a private surgical suite maintained for Dr. Quain."

While internal hospital politics with doctors demanded Sister Boniface's tact and diplomacy, the same was true of her relationships with her Order, 400 miles away. At the time of the expansion of St. Alexius, she had wanted to construct an entirely new hospital but had been denied that request. However, within five years, the new wing was not enough to accommodate the numbers of patients coming from all over the region, thanks to expanded branch railroad lines and better roads. To learn about the latest improvements in hospital construction, Sister Boniface traveled to a number of hospitals in the eastern states. This time, the Order voted to approve the construction of a new hospital, and by May 1914, construction began in Bismarck, a few blocks from the original hospital. The building was completed early in 1915.

Again the *Tribune* waxed enthusiastically over the five-story building that could accommodate 125 patients: "Thousands

The Richardton Benedictines

After the death of Bishop Shanley in 1909, a second North Dakota diocese was created, with Bismarck as its center. Benedictine Abbot Vincent Wehrle was appointed its first bishop in 1910. He immediately looked for others to help in the work among his mostly German-speaking parishioners and the Indians on the Fort Berthold reservation. For the latter group, who had been without sisters since the departure of the American Congregation in 1897, he recruited Benedictine sisters from St. Mary's, Pennsylvania. They established their motherhouse at Elbowoods in 1910 in the same buildings used by Father Craft's group. The distance from civilization prompted them to move their headquarters to Garrison in 1921. Ever in search of the best location for their motherhouse, they moved it to Minot in 1942 and finally to Richardton — where collaboration with the Benedictine monks of Assumption Abbey was a special attraction — in 1967.

The endurance of extreme hardship and poverty have marked this community's ministrations to the Indians and immigrants of the state. They lost their savings, along with many others, during the depression when banks failed in Garrison and Underwood. The struggle to obtain teaching credentials for the young farm women who joined their ranks drained them of energy and resources.

The holiness and kindness of their first superior, Mother Pia Tegler, who came out of a comfortable retirement to lead the pioneer sisters to Fort Berthold, are still recalled by Indians whom she taught. The sisters shared with the Indians a

---

inspected the new institution which stands unsurpassed in anything but size in the country" (16 February 1915). The hospital was the first in the state awarded a Class A rating by the American College of Surgeons. In April 1915, Sister Boniface realized another dream, the opening of a school of nursing.

Sister Boniface's trips to look at modern hospitals were typical of one of the ways her career was different from that of most nuns in her Order — she traveled a good deal, to meetings to learn about new medical developments, to see new medical technology, and generally to educate herself in the administration of a hospital. She also saw to it that her sister nurses acquired whatever extra training they needed in such emerging specialties as anaesthesia, medical technology, X-ray, and school directorship. She joined national health associations and attended their meetings. The National

Catholic Hospital Association honored her by chosing her "as the most fitting sister at the convention to unveil the tablet on Spruce Street, which will mark the site of the first hospital in St. Louis and the first west of the Mississippi river" (*Tribune* June 1933).

Sister Boniface received wide recognition for her long and successful career, no doubt owed in part to the pains she took to cultivate good relationships with the business community. Each week she spent a day making the rounds of the main business establishments. According to Sister Joan Brun and Sister Harlindis Fischer, two sisters who often accompanied her, "No matter what the manager was doing when Sister Boniface entered, he left his work and came to greet and visit with her — often it was to ask advice on one or other matter." She benefited, in turn, from respect, and appreciation in the community. Her re-

profound sense of loss in 1953 when the new Garrison Dam flooded the fertile bottomland along the Missouri River including Elbowoods, headquarters of the Fort Berthold Agency and the site of the sisters' beginnings.

Holy Cross Sisters

Unable to find any American sisters to staff a hospital in Dickinson, Bishop Wehrle visited the motherhouse of his old friends, the Sisters of Mercy of the Holy Cross, in Ingenbohl, Switzerland, and refused to leave until they had promised to send him sisters. His tactic worked, and they opened St. Joseph Hospital in Dickinson in 1912, and later opened schools as well. They moved their motherhouse to Wisconsin in 1931, but continued to provide health care in western North Dakota. Community historians tell us that these German-speaking sisters experienced bigotry during and after the First World War. Some doctors expressed anti-German sentiments in front of them, complained about their inability to speak English, and tried to put a lay nurse in charge of the hospital and relegate the sisters to the menial tasks. Sister Lauda, the administrator, pointed out that they were not German, but Swiss, and that the sisters who were born in Germany were not responsible for the hostilities of the war. If the doctors would show them how they wanted things done, she said, instead of simply criticizing, everyone would benefit. She also told them that if they wanted the sisters to speak English, they should provide a way for

sponse to accolades and to the suggestion that she should retire was "There will be time for rest in heaven."

On the occasion of her fiftieth anniversary as a Benedictine sister, the town of Bismarck turned out to celebrate with receptions and other festive events. A *Tribune* editorial (8 February 1922) paid tribute to her "unselfish Christian spirit," her desire to make "Bismarck and the entire Slope a better place to live in," her "executive ability of a high order, combined with a tact and kindness that drew people of all creeds" and concluded that "The fiftieth anniversary of Sister Boniface accentuates the place the hospital occupies in this city as well as in the entire Northwest."

Her work went on. She saw to the building of a residence for nurses that included both classrooms and residential facilities, completed to the east of the hospital in 1927. The golden anniversary celebration of St. Alexius Hospital came in 1935, an occasion to celebrate its importance to medical services in the northwest and her role as administrator. Although she never learned to drive, she was presented an automobile by grateful business and professional people of Bismarck.

But Sister Boniface was not only a professional and civic leader; she was also the religious superior for the sisters living with her. I have spoken with some of the sisters who were at St. Alexius during Sister Boniface's administration about their views of her as superior. All agreed that she insisted on regular attendance at daily religious exercise. Boniface herself often arrived for the five a.m. prayer with her high-topped shoes still unlaced. Sister Angele spoke of her as an organist who "loved to trill up and down the keys" even though the choir was "not always together." Sister Gwendolyn described Boniface's

them to learn the language.

Domestic violence struck in 1926 when the sister cook, maddened by the repeated tardiness of sisters whose duties kept them working long hours, poisoned the peas (or was it the soup?), killing five of them.

The Hankinson Franciscans

The oldest Franciscan sisterhood in the world, which traces its origins to Dillingen, Bavaria, in 1241, established a provincial house, that is a regional headquarters, in Hankinson in 1928. Teaching sisters who had prepared themselves for the American education system opened a grade school in 1929, and a high school in 1930. A vestment department was also begun, with so many orders that the seamstresses rose at 3 a.m. to work on them. Hospital work was begun in 1947, and homes for the elderly in 1945. These are the works which still engage their members in the state.

The Belcourt Benedictines

Five Benedictine sisters from Ferdinand, Indiana, came to Belcourt in 1933 to work among the Chippewa and Cree Indians on the Turtle Mountain Reservation. They established St. Ann Mission School there in 1936 and taught released time religion classes in four government schools as well. Difficulties in communication

---

"spiritual life" as her top priority. She said, "Even though she was insistent about being at community prayer, she was always compassionate if someone were unable to come." To this Sister Wanda agreed and recalled how "she stood by justice — even if she had to give a correction she did it kindly and never referred to it again." Each of the sisters spoke of how they loved her, of her wonderful sense of humor, of her business ability and leadership, and the high regard the doctors had for her. These sisters said that no one ever was in doubt as to who was in charge of either the religious community or the hospital.

St. Alexius Medical Center continues under the sponsorship of the Benedictine Sisters now based at the Annunciation Priory in Bismarck and functions with its own Board of Directors, a majority of whom are Sisters of the Order. Only a major change in the hospital's purpose, its dissolu-tion, or some other highly significant change, such as relocation, would require approval of the entire order.

Barbara Ann Gehrki, a Sister of St. Benedict of Annunciation Priory, teaches English at the University of Mary in Bismarck, North Dakota.

with the motherhouse 1300 miles away, and the need for a corps of sisters especially dedicated to work among the Indians led Father Hildebrand Elliott to establish a Benedictine motherhouse there. His efforts met with success and Queen of Peace Priory was established in 1956. It became independent in 1963. Its members work among the Indians and also carry on various types of parish ministry.

Carmelites

Members of the strictly cloistered Carmelite Order established a monastery in Wahpeton in 1954, and moved to a new building on the Wild Rice River a few miles from Wahpeton in 1964. Mother Rose of the Sacred Heart led the original group of sisters on their trek (actually a plane ride, the first for several of them) from Allentown, Pennsylvania. They were soon joined by new recruits from North Dakota and elsewhere, making larger quarters necessary. These sisters lead lives of prayer and meditation on the word of God. Protestant ministers have been particularly drawn to this center of prayer and spirituality.

Strategies for Survival

The geography and climate of North Dakota had a profound effect on all who came to live in this last remnant of the American frontier. Farmers found it more profitable to cultivate farms and ranches with a large acreage. The vast distances and sparse population made electrification difficult. Severe winters, dust storms and grasshoppers, when added to the depressions that affected the whole country, meant periods of great poverty and hardship. The Catholic sisterhoods that settled in North Dakota had to adapt to the environment along with everyone else.

The sisters' schools and hospitals were often located in small towns, and the climate and great distances made it difficult for their clients to get to them. When times were hard, those who valued their services were unable to pay for them. Only the hardy and the resourceful survived in North Dakota, and sisters were as ingenious as any in adapting to the hardships in order to survive.

The basic need for human survival is to have one's share of daily bread. The Lord's Prayer voices the first petition of pioneer sisters, for sustenance for themselves and for those whom they served. If they had food for themselves, their students and their patients, they could manage whatever misfortunes might befall them. The generosity shown to the sisters by neighbors who brought them food has continued through all of the intervening generations. People have appreciated the sisters' labors for others and have responded to their needs in whatever way they could. Nuns in their turn have devised interesting ways in which to continue to serve others even in times of hardship.

In the small rural schools which served farming communities, where distances were great and the roads often impassable, the sisters' solution was to establish boarding schools where their pupils could stay overnight during the week, and return to their homes for the weekends. Former pupils report that there was a healthy mix of study, recreation and chores in these schools, and a warm feeling of family. In other parts of the country the boarding school was an elitist institution, and those run by sisters were strictly limited to a female clientele. Not so in North Dakota, where boys as well as girls had their dormitories in the sisters' schools, and even the poorest child could attend.

And what could be more logical in an agricultural economy, than to accept food in lieu of payment in cash? This is what the sisters did, with interesting variations in the different communities. Sister Imelda of the Richardton Benedictines has described the practice at the school in Fallon in the 1930s. The children were given a list, when they went home on Friday, of the foods they should bring back with them on Monday. The food brought to the school was combined, and shared with all. Live chickens, geese and ducks were brought in gunny sacks. On Monday nights there was a "chicken party," at which the students helped to butcher the poultry that would grace their tables during the week. Milk was boiled so that it would keep until Friday.

At St. Catherine's School in Valley City, the Presentation Sisters kept each child's food separate, and the poor cook had to prepare individual servings, being sure she used the right portion for every student. Notre Dame Academy, Willow City, was perhaps the only school that actually advertised the fact that it accepted payment in kind. This attracted Sister Agnes' parents to send her there, even though there were other boarding schools much closer to their farm. Her father butchered pigs and cows for payment, and also brought potatoes. Conditions were such that he couldn't sell this food anyway, he said, so he was happy to be able to receive good value for it. Sometimes he would exchange potatoes for apples, or wheat for flour, to provide some variety.

It is interesting to read the Hankinson Franciscans' account books for the early 1930s and find, for example, that John Birnbaum paid part of the bill for his son Lorenz with:

25 bbl. wheat @ 55 cents = $13.75
85 lb. veal @ 6 1\2 cents = $5.38
28 lb. honey @ 8 cents = $2.24
6 ducks @ 35 cents = $2.10
3 lb. butter @ 32 cents = $.96
20 lb. of wax @ 15 cents = $3.00

Twenty dozen eggs were worth $1.40, and six bushels of potatoes yielded $1.50 — the same amount as five pounds of feathers. Mr. Scheller's 85 pounds of beef were valued at 8 cents each, for a total of $6.60. Mr. Henepha, the father of another student, however, received $46 credit for 46 photographs!

Account books for St. Aloysius Academy, Oakwood, for the later 1940s and early 50s show that these practices continued. One can find there families whose bills were paid almost entirely through deliveries of produce and some work done by the students. In 1948, 150 pounds of pork were assessed at 35 cents per pound. Fifteen dozen eggs were valued at 45 cents each on November 13, but at 50 cents each on December 7 and 31 cents on January 13, so market prices must have prevailed. Beef was 36 cents a pound in December 1949.

A notation in the Oakwood accounts for September 1952 reveals an episode that must have been repeated many times in the sisters' schools. A couple came to thank the sisters for all they had done for their daughter, and to promise that they would pay their bill when they could. The daughter would soon be earning a salary, and the parents hoped to have money when the crop came in. The $361.65 debt was marked "due if and when possible" on the books. It was finally paid off in two installments in October 1961.

From the earliest days of their history, American sisters have also supported themselves by growing their own food, and this tradition was carried on in North Dakota as well. The Hankinson Franciscans have been particularly active in this endeavor. Their account books for 1930 show that they raised tomatoes, cucumbers, kohlrabi, peas, beans, beets, cabbage, carrots, sweet corn, watermelon, sugar, squash, pumpkins, onions, and potatoes. In 1941, the value of farm and garden products supplied to their motherhouse and boarding school was $6,283.80. Canning, pickling, and preserving were as much a part of the sisters' lives as they were of other pioneer women's.

Sister Imelda recalls that at Elbowoods, Father Reinhard had a large vegetable garden, and the produce was used by the sisters, the boarding school and Father Reinhard. 1937 was a very difficult year, she said. They had no meat all year long. Father Reinhard shot a goose for them to eat at Thanksgiving, and Sister Imelda cleaned it. They had eggs and milk from this farm, as well as vegetables. When food was scarce, sisters went to bed hungry; when there was food, monotony marked the menu. One sister confessed to another that she didn't think she could live that way —she thought she'd starve. Her companion replied, "I used to feel that way too, but I'm still here, and so will you be." Another younger sister who didn't think she could stand it was saved by the discovery that bread with syrup was always available for a snack, just as it had been at home.

The pupils helped the sisters pick vegetables at the farm after school, and even Bishop Wehrle, when he came upon the sisters and priests picking produce, took off his coat, pushed his pectoral cross to the side, and started harvesting with them. The Carmelite Sisters at Wahpeton still produce much of what they eat.

Class and Financial Arrangements

This whole question of finance is of great interest where Catholic sisterhoods are concerned, and one in which enormous adaptations have been made to fit into the American economy. In Europe it was common for benefactors to donate a large sum of money or a piece of property for the foundation of a convent. The income supported the nuns living there, and they could pursue their lives of prayer and good works without worrying about finances. In addition, women from wealthy families brought dowries with them when they entered the convent. The dowry was part of a class system which characterized the Old World for centuries. Wealthy young women became "choir sisters," chanted the official prayer of the Church, and perhaps taught in convent schools. Sometimes they brought their servants with them, to take care of the more menial tasks. Young women from poor families chose to enter monasteries as "lay sisters."

European communities which established daughter houses in America often brought these customs with them, but gradually realized that these habits had to be discarded. In the United States, few Catholics could afford to endow convents, and dowries, where they existed at all, were minimal. Bishop Martin Marty, and others, hoped to import the European method of supporting convents, and so Bishop Marty invited the Irish Presentation Sisters to come to the Dakotas, according to Father Emil Perrig's diary for July 8, 1891. However, the custom never became established in the Dakotas and when the Presentation Sisters returned to Ireland to recruit more members, one of the inducements was that those who joined the American group would not have to bring a dowry.

In North Dakota we see remnants of the European traditions. The marvelous French cooking that is a hallmark of the Valley City Presentation convent is a benefit from a French family that could not afford the 4,000-franc dowry that would entitle their daughter to choir sister status. Instead, she became a lay sister and an expert cook and brought with her the traditions of French cuisine. German lay sisters who came originally to run the food service at St. John's University, Collegeville, Minnesota, are responsible for the "johnny-bread" and other special German confections that fattened generations of students and faculty members at that college. Part of that European class system is the custom whereby the superior and other officials sat at a special table for meals, with fine china and food that was better than that of the rank-and-file. One test of the Americanization of an immigrant community is the date this custom was abolished.

Sources of Income

If sisters of North Dakota had to find other, more "American" ways of supporting themselves, how did they do it? The usual American way was through "select" schools or academies, in which the wealthy paid a fee that actually provided for their own school and also a free school for poor children. By the time North Dakota was settled, this practice was dying out, and the more democratic parish school was providing for all the Catholics in a given area. In North Dakota, except in Fargo, where the children at St. John's Orphanage had a separate "free" school for a time, there was only one school in a region. The sparse population and scarce financial resources made this a necessity. Those who could pay did, and those who couldn't made other arrangements — for labor or other gifts in kind. Income from boarding schools supported sisters at the motherhouse or elsewhere who received little or no remuneration for their work.

Another important source of income for motherhouses throughout the country and also in North Dakota was music lessons. Americans had an insatiable taste for piano lessons, it seems, and sisters were able to support their new and also their aging members by meeting that demand. Sisters who could teach piano were kept busy six days a week. Often they taught school music, directed the parish choirs, and sang for weddings, funerals, and high masses as well. When the French Presentation Sisters took over St. Catherine's School in Valley City, for example, they built St. Cecilia Music Conservatory there for Sister St. John, who had an excellent reputation as a music teacher. She soon had a hundred pupils.

Sister Teresa Fitzgerald recalls the day she amazed the audience at a grade school concert in Minot by adding high school choir members for the grand finale, a four-part rendition of "White Christmas." Sister Patricia made the Hague public high school the envy of the surrounding towns by directing not only a glee club, but a band that could play for athletic events. To have both a band and a glee club in such a small high school in North Dakota in the 1940s was thought quite remarkable.

The income from music lessons and boarding schools was necessary because very often the schools in which the sisters taught paid little or nothing to support them. Only gradually did sisterhoods come to realize the full significance of the American economic situation and insist that their teachers had to be paid regularly if the community was to survive. They needed not only food and clothing, but money for education, medical expenses, retirement, the upkeep of the mother-house, and the support of community officials. When the sisterhoods realized the actual cost of supporting a sister for a year, they then had to convince bishops and pastors to pay adequate salaries.

The sisters at Elbowoods in 1938 were provided with food but were not paid a salary; the only contribution to motherhouse expenses was one load of potatoes. That year the sisters at St. Nicholas School in Garrison were paid $30 each per month for nine months. In 1941 the total salary for the year for four teachers at St. Philip's School in Hankinson was $900. In 1955 Mother Edana told Bishop Lambert Hoch of Bismarck that the nine months' salary of $50 per month paid to teaching sisters was not adequate. The Bismarck diocese had standardized sisters' salaries at $700 per year in 1963, but the actual amount needed was $1,043. When some sisters were relieved of teaching duties so as to study for college degrees, the sisters were expected to help pay the cost of lay replacements.

Hospitals, in which patients or their insurance companies paid fairly fixed rates, were a chief means of support for the communities that owned them. In 1957 various regulating bodies insisted that the sisters working in hospitals must be paid the same salaries as other employees, thus providing income for education, motherhouse expenses, and works for the poor. Bishop Leo Dworschak of Fargo realized that the sponsorship of hospitals could help to stabilize the finances of communities that had little income from their schools, and encouraged them to take up this work. The availability of Hill-Burton funds granted to the states by the federal government for building and expanding hospitals made this easier than it might have been.

Some communities, like American sisterhoods before them, turned to particular projects that would help support their works for the poor. Thus did the Hankinson Franciscans begin a vestment department, and the Carmelites the making of altar breads. Through their vestment department the Franciscans brought to North Dakota skills and crafts that have enriched the life of the state. One of these is the art of making bobbin lace, which Sister Rosalia Haberl, at the age of 90, continues to practice and to pass on to others. She learned these skills at the Royal Bobbin Lace School in her native Bavaria, from which she graduated at the age of fourteen. The Fargo Presentation Sisters had some income from painting on china.

One way in which sisters supported their works was by begging. This was particularly common among the Fargo Presentation Sisters. St. John's Orphanage in Fargo was supported almost entirely by this means for many years, until an annual diocesan collection and government payments for wards of the state came to take its place. Sisters Cecilia and Bernard regularly went on begging trips. Sister

M. Camillus Galvin has described their work in *From Acorn to Oak*:

> Every Fall, for many years, these two highly cultured women set out on their
> travels ... [which] covered North Dakota, other midwestern states, and occasionally
> the east and west coasts. Farmers, lumberjacks, railroad workers, and combine
> crews knew them well; barns, open fields, and the back of a buggy were often their
> only resting places.

A friend recalled an annual trip with Sister Bernard to a camp in northern Minnesota
where ice was cut and shipped. They rode fifty miles in a bob sled over the frozen
river for the last lap of their journey.

The practice of begging continues into the present, but with modern methods
such as bazaars, fairs, raffles and benefits of all kinds. All of the Fargo Presentation
sisters sold Mason's chocolates in 1959 to pay for the pews of their new motherhouse. Few find it as difficult to ask for money as did a pioneer Fargo sister who
decided, after a tour as far west as Mandan to sell $1 tickets to a fair in 1883, that she
could not stay with that community. She later joined a Presentation Convent in New
York. Many of the first recruits who entered the North Dakota sisterhoods were
unable to withstand the hardships and returned home. None of the young women
who joined the Benedictine community at Elbowoods in the first four years
remained with the group.

The sisterhoods of North Dakota were blessed with astute businesswomen, who
were able, by skimping and saving, managing and planning, to complete massive
building programs for schools, hospitals, orphanages, and motherhouses, and to
pay off the large loans that these projects often required. Sisters Jane, Andriette,
Boniface, and Magdalen of the Bismarck Benedictines; Mothers Benedict and Anita
from the Richardton group; Mother Joseph, Sister St. Kevin, and Sister Mary
Margaret of the Fargo Presentations are some of the many who had this ability. The
church required that permission be obtained from Rome before taking out large
loans. Bishops who had experience with poor financial management in some male
institutions were sometimes frightened by the sisters' bold ventures, unlike the
priest who said, "I never worry about the sisters; they always seem to manage
somehow."

We have looked at ways in which sisters adapted to the North Dakota environment in order to survive financially. Let us look at other aspects of their life and
work that were also affected by their location. North Dakota is dominated by areas
of distinctive ethnic settlement, and often a particular religion is a part of that ethnic
culture. This too, has influenced the sisterhoods.

Public Schools

In the days when one- and two-room schoolhouses dotted the landscape, local
economies could not support both a Catholic and a public school. If the sisters
operated a school in a German Catholic area, for example, there might be few, if any,
students left to attend a public school. In addition, it was often difficult for a local
public school board to find teachers who were willing to settle in isolated areas and
teach in buildings without indoor plumbing and electricity. Therefore Catholic

school buildings often were used as public schools and vice-versa. Sometimes religion was taught in public school buildings during the noon hour or after school; there were no religious symbols on the walls, but the teachers were nuns in their religious habits. Local school boards usually paid them a salary that was less than the going rate for public school teachers but more than the Catholic schools could pay.

There were few objections to these arrangements, even among non-Catholics. Most seemed to feel that they were lucky to have found sisters willing to take on this work. In Karlsruhe, where grades 1-6 were taught in the Catholic school building and 7-12 in the public, one of the two non-Catholic families did object — to use of the Catholic school building. Thereafter their children went to the public school building each day, and the sister who taught seventh grade gave them their lessons for grades three and five on the side.

A suit was brought against the Gladstone school board in 1935 for hiring nuns in religious garb to teach in its public school. The Supreme Court of North Dakota ruled in 1936 that there was nothing unconstitutional about sisters in religious garb teaching in public schools. In 1948 a movement to ban the wearing of religious garb by teachers in public schools prompted a referendum on this question. Catholics saw it as the opening wedge of a Communist plot to take over America. Anti-Catholic groups used the occasion to spread vitriol. When the referendum passed by a slim margin, it was thought that the 75 nuns teaching in 19 public school districts would have to leave their positions.

To the amazement of all, particularly the sisters, the Catholic bishops of North Dakota called a press conference and announced that the sisters would continue to teach in any public school that wanted them, in lay dress. In Europe Bishop Aloisius Muench, the pope's representative in post-war Germany, carried on some high-level diplomacy, getting permission from Vatican officials for this unusual step, and pressuring the head of the Hankinson Franciscans at their Dillingen motherhouse to allow it. The bishops stressed that it was important for the Catholic Church in the whole country for the sisters to remain in the public schools and insist on their rights as Americans to do so.

Among the sisters involved there was, as the Hankinson sisters' chronicles state, "a putting off and trying to forget about the issue. But to forget about it was as hard as to forget about eating when starving." As the time for fall assignments approached, the tension mounted. Finally the names of the eight who would have to don lay garb to teach in public schools in Selz, Karlsruhe, and Mt. Carmel were announced. The chronicle continued:

> I only can talk with admiration how bravely they shouldered this cross and how bravely they went to work in getting ready. We purchased clothes, modest, yet according to current style. It's providential that the style is quite decent.

The stories of the experiences and emotions of individual sisters whose hair and legs had to be uncovered after being swathed in yards of serge for years are tragicomic. They either put off until the last minute their first appearance in public in their new clothes, or did a "dry run" across the playground. Children playing there later reported to their parents that two women who talked like their teachers but didn't look like them had been on the playground. One sister who had cut her hair very short for the summer, having been assured she would not have to remove her habit, had to buy a wig. When she later taught about the Tories and the Whigs, the latter term caused great merriment among the students. A pastor, in talking to students in church, picked out a bright-looking eighth-grade girl for a question, and belatedly realized that she was the teacher.

For the most part the sisters found only sympathy for their predicament. Benedictine Sister Patricia Fitzgerald recalls that at Hague the people wept when the sisters had to remove their habits. High school girls embraced them and said "I feel so sorry for you." Many confessed that they had been confused in the voting, and thought a "yes" meant the sisters would stay in the schools. The names of those who petitioned for the inclusion of the referendum on the ballot were a matter of public record, and bitter hostilities divided neighbors and harmed businesses when the names of those who favored the measure became known.

The school supply business felt the effects, for example. Walter L. Stockwell, president of the Northern School Supply Company of Fargo, and Grand Secretary of the Grand Lodge of the Masons of North Dakota, was one of the promotors of the anti-garb measure. His name figured prominently in letters and articles publicizing it and containing anti-Catholic sentiments. Those who opposed his ideas and resented his efforts chose to buy their school supplies elsewhere. Six directors of the company tried to dissociate themselves and the company from its president's activities, and begged the bishops to do something about the situation!

Recent Developments

The Second Vatican Council asked the sisters to study the special gifts of their foundresses and the gospel in the light of contemporary culture. There was an emphasis on lay ministry and vowed religious life as one way of living the Christian vocation. No longer was it seen as superior to the vocation of marriage. Sisters who studied for undergraduate and graduate degrees returned to their communities with new ideas about theology, interpersonal relationships, organizational structures, social action, adaptation to American culture, etc. Older sisters who had not been exposed to these ideas felt that they threatened traditional modes of religious life and resisted their implementation. Discussions of the renewal of religious life according to the directives of the council were painful for all concerned. Many concluded — or were told — that they could best live out their vocations as Christians by leaving the sisterhoods. The Franciscans, according to Sister Patricia Forrest, their historian, lost one-third of their members between 1963 and 1970. Fewer young women have chosen to join these groups in recent decades. Some who have left their communities but still wish to dedicate their lives in a special way to the work of the Lord have made vows of poverty, chastity and obedience before the bishop, as His visible representative, and live them out on their own, rather than as members of traditional sisterhoods.

Those who remained in the sisterhoods saw many needs around them that were outside of the schools and hospitals they had traditionally sponsored. They diversified their ministries to meet these needs. In the 1970s and '80s North Dakota nuns have gone as missionaries to Africa and Latin America; worked in pastoral positions in parishes and hospitals; taught and nursed in a variety of settings; directed justice and peace centers; worked among the poor in Appalachia and with public agencies and ecumenical groups; done research in medicine and other areas; directed retreats. The list could go on and on. Communities themselves have taken stands on peace and justice issues (and allocated money to groups promoting their solutions), such as nuclear weapons and women's rights. They have opened up their buildings to community groups of all kinds. Though there are fewer sisters today, their impact reaches into many more areas.

Typical of the kinds of individual ministry that now attract sisters looking for the best use of their talents is that of Sister Mary Beauclair, who represented District 14 of Wells and Foster Counties. In 1976 she became the second sister to run for a seat in the state legislature, and the first to win. She saw work in the legislature "as a worthwhile form of service to people just as nursing is." She wanted to represent the poor and powerless, and was particularly interested in environmental issues, land use, corporate farming, and projects that affected hospitals, pharmacies, and North Dakota's rural communities.

Conclusion

It is difficult to gather accurate statistics regarding the works sponsored by sisters in North Dakota, or the numbers of sisters who engaged in them. The statistics we do have tell us something about the scope of the sisters' work, though they cannot tell us about lives touched and changed, or what the state's development would have been without their contribution.

Up to the time of the Second Vatican Council, most sisters were involved in schools or hospitals, while a few ran retirement and nursing homes, catechetical centers, or orphanages. Figures from Sister Borgia Sondag's manuscript history of the Fargo diocese and Father Terrence Kardong's history of the Bismarck diocese, show that North Dakota sisters worked in the following institutions up to the 1960s: 31 high schools, 68 grade and junior high schools, 40 health care centers, eight nursing and retirement homes, three seminaries and colleges, two catechetical centers, two industrial schools and one orphanage. These figures do not include part-time ministries such as teaching religion on weekends and in the summer to children who could not go to Catholic schools, or working among the migrant workers who come into the state every summer.

The *Official Catholic Directory*, which annually issues a massive volume of information about the American Catholic Church, has been notoriously blind to the contributions of women and did not begin listing total numbers of sisters for each diocese until 1945 (though about eight different categories of male church workers, the number of converts, etc. were tallied). More recent editions do give some useful information about the number of sisters who worked in North Dakota, however, as can be seen from the following graph.

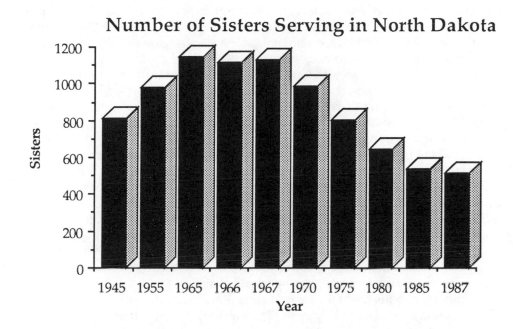

Number of Sisters Serving in North Dakota

The graph indicates the numbers of sisters from all communities, not just those with motherhouses in the state, for specific years. This table yields some interesting information. 1965 was the peak year for numbers of sisters serving in the state. Only half as many live in North Dakota in 1988. This is due in part to the fact that the number of sisters teaching in schools has declined sharply and a higher percentage of the sisters are retired now. It is also one of the unexpected results of the Second Vatican Council.

In any given year there have been many more sisters than priests working in the state. If we assume that a sister who worked with her students or patients every day had at least as much influence as a priest — who usually saw his congregation once a week — upon the Catholic and non-Catholic people of North Dakota, we can form some judgment about the contribution made by sisters. Yet most histories give much more space to churchmen than to churchwomen. Without the sisters, many North Dakotans would have lacked up-to-date health care, a high level of education, professional instruction in the tenets of Catholicism, and the alleviation of many social ills. Both natives and immigrants would also have been denied the personal and moral support and example of these women as they faced the hardships of living on the prairies.

Church historians are just beginning to contemplate the implications of Vatican II's definition of the Church — all of the people of God, not just bishops and priests

— for the practice of their profession. Practitioners of women's history, social history, immigrant history, labor history, oral history, and state and local history know the importance of looking at and listening to the stories of those who have been left out of the official institutional histories.

This work is only beginning. While histories of some of the sisterhoods have been published, much more needs to be done. The Benedictines of North Dakota have only manuscript histories of their communities, and the French Presentations have studies of their French roots but not their American experience. Almost all of the communities mentioned here have archives that are open to the public by appointment. Individuals such as foundresses, administrators, community "characters," and ordinary members could be studied further. The sisters themselves, in every convent in North Dakota, are the greatest resource for historians, especially when their recollections can be supported by documentation. The histories of individual schools, hospitals, and other institutions need to be written. How did people experience the controversy and tension associated with the anti-garb law? What were the sisters' experiences in the public schools, and how did the local communities view them? What ethnic tensions did the immigrants experience? How do the European recruits of the Fargo Presentations or the German Franciscans view their transplantation? How were hardships on the frontier survived; what of the sisters' boarding schools? What else do the account books tell about gifts-in-kind and the financing of large-scale operations with little money? What was the experience of the North Dakota members of the French Presentations at their French motherhouse, or in internment during World War II?

Architecture buffs could look into Marcel Breuer's creation of the buildings for the Annunciation Priory in Bismarck. The musician might collect songs that have been important in these sisters' lives, beginning with that sung by the Richardton Benedictines upon their triumphal entry into the city of Minot. A recipe book would have to include all the favorites from the Hankinson motherhouse. The Franciscans would have much to tell about farming and about the folk arts practiced in their vestment department. What experiences did sisters have in Africa, Latin America, and with migrant workers? The list could go on and on.

Many more details of the sisterhoods are available in their archives and community histories. They were profoundly influenced by the state's geography, climate and economy, and they in turn have affected the health care, education and social services of the state. They have been willing to go to areas of extreme hardship, and to endure hunger, loneliness, isolation, primitive living conditions, and long hours of work in carrying out their vocation of living the Christian gospel through lives of prayer and service to others.

Some have said that the women who settled the plains came west reluctantly, and played only passive roles in the settlement of the new states. This cannot be said of the Catholic sisterhoods, whose members were instrumental in building the institutions that are essential for the well-being of all citizens. Perhaps we can best appreciate their contribution by reflecting on what would have been missing in communities throughout the state had they not been here.

References

Bantin, Philip C. with Mark G. Thiel. *Guide to Catholic Indian Mission and School Records in Midwest Repositories*. Milwaukee: Maquette University, 1984.

Carmel of Mary. *All Her Paths are Peace*. Wahpeton, N.D.: Carmel, 1979.

Craft , Francis. "Native Indian Vocations," *Catholic World*, LXV, June 1897.

Diner, Hasia. *Erin's Daughters in America*. Baltimore: Johns Hopkins, 1983.

Duratschek, Sister Mary Claudia, O.S.B. *Crusading Along Sioux Trails*. Yankton, S.D.: Sacred Heart Convent, 1947.

_____. *Under the Shadow of His Wings*. Yankton, S.D.: Sacred Heart Convent, 1971.

Ewens, Mary. *The Role of the Nun in Nineteenth-Century America*. Salem, N.H.: Ayer, 1978.

Forrest, Sister M. Patricia, O.S.F. *Prairie Praise*. Fargo, N.D.: Pierce Printing, 1978.

Galvin, Sister M. Camillus. *From Acorn to Oak*. Fargo, N.D.: The Presentation Sisters, 1969.

Kardong, Terrence G. *Beyond Red River*. Fargo, N.D.: Diocese of Fargo, 1988.

_____. *Prairie Church: The Diocese of Bismarck 1910-1985*. Fargo, N.D.: Diocese of Bismarck, 1985.

Lackey, Sister Marie de St. Jean. "History of the Congregation of the Sisters of St. Mary of the Presentation of Broons," Vol. III. Valley City, N.D.: Sisters of St. Mary of the Presentation, 1948.

Mooney, Sister Mary Margaret, P.B.V.M. *A Centennial History*. Fargo, N.D.: Sisters of the Presentation, 1982.

The Official Catholic Directory. Wilmette , Ill.: P.J. Kennedy & Sons, various years.

Peterson, Susan and Vaughan, Courtney Ann. *Women with Vision: The Presentation Sisters of South Dakota, 1880-1985*. Champaign: University of Illinois Press, 1988.

Reardon, James Michael. *George Anthony Belcourt*. St. Paul, Minn.: North Central Publishing Co., 1955.

Sherman, William and Lamb, Jerry. *Scattered Steeples*. Fargo, N.D.: Burtch, Lonergan and Lynch, 1988.

Thomas, Evangeline , ed. *Women Religious History Sources: A Guide to Repositories in the United States*. New York: Bowker, 1983.

Mary Ewens, O.P., is Associate Director of the Cushwa Center for the Study of American Catholicism and Adjunct Professor at the University of Notre Dame in Indiana. She has published many studies on the history of the American nun.

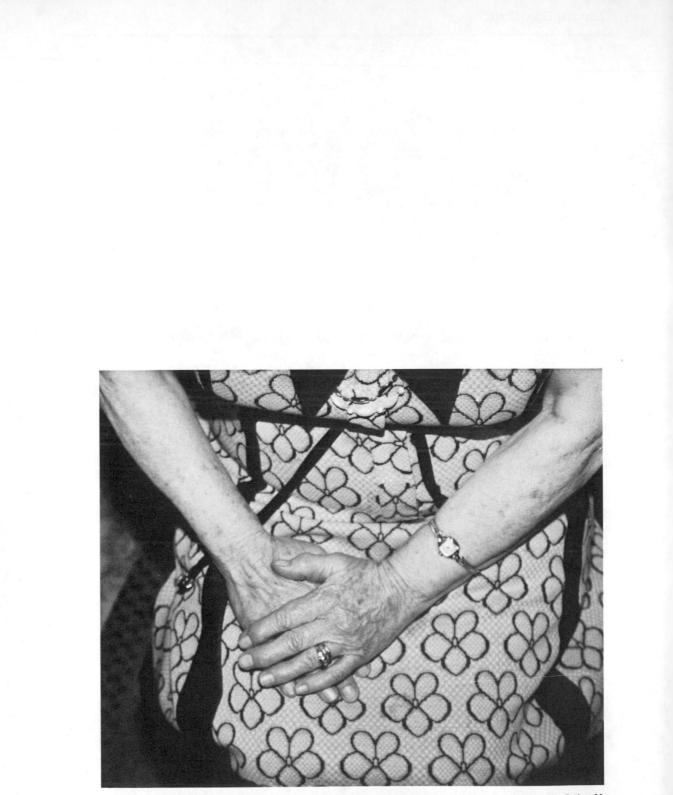

Katherine's "miracle hands," Spring 1987. Photograph by Lony B. Schaff.

Belief in Tender Hands:
Three German-Russian Faith Healers

by Timothy J. Kloberdanz and Nadine Engbrecht-Schaff

It's the belief. You have to have a lot of faith in the Lord and know that He's going to do it. The Bible tells us too that He will. All we have to do is have a strong belief.

Katherine, folk healer

For generations, folk healing and folk medicine practice have been integral aspects of health care in North Dakota. The rural, isolated nature of many communities in the state made it possible — perhaps necessary — for various types of traditional medicine to persist and flourish. Even today, with the increased availability of physicians, registered nurses, and modern medical facilities, present-day North Dakotans of many ethnic and economic backgrounds occasionally take advantage of folk medical knowledge and traditional healing techniques.

Generally, women have been key figures in the transmission and perpetuation of folk medical traditions. This is particularly true when one considers the roles of Euro-American ethnic women. The focus of this study is on three German-Russian female folk healers who learned how to diagnose and treat clients without the benefit of official training or formal education. All three women were born and raised in North Dakota and continue to make their home in the state.

German-Russian Folk Medicine

The Germans from Russia brought with them a rich and diverse body of folk medicine. German-Russian folk healing takes one of several forms: midwifery or folk obstetrics; herbal "doctoring"; therapeutic massage; bone-setting; blood-letting; folk psychiatry; and Brauche (magico-religious folk medicine or faith healing). Most German-Russian folk healers tend to be rather eclectic in their approach, as they often choose to focus on one or more of the above varieties, depending on the situation and the nature of the problem.

Generally, folk medicine can be divided into two main categories: 1) natural or herbal, and 2) magico-religious (Yoder 1972). In many cases, however, distinctions are not easily drawn and the two varieties are used simultaneously. At times, materials gathered for herbal medicine are obtained in conjunction with magical ritual. The herbal category includes most "home remedies," in which herbs and household ingredients are made into teas, poultices, salves, and other mixtures. Among the most common of these ingredients are onions, garlic, chamomile, wormwood, willow, dill, honey, lard, vinegar, soda, lemon, salt, sugar, alum, camphor, sulphur, and various alcohols. Minerals and animal substances also are used, including such things as mud, clay, bones, animal organs, and human urine. Popular also among the German-Russians were commercial tonics and salves that could be bought in drugstores or ordered in bulk through the mail. These included: Dr. Forni's famous "Alpen-Kraeuter," Dr. Forni's "Heil-Gel" Liniment, Knorr's "Genuine Hein Fong Essence or Green Drops," Jean's "Family Salve," and Smith's "Rosebud Salve."

The magico-religious category includes a variety of supernaturally-based practices. One of these is the magical transference of disease. Sympathetic magic is the basis for this practice, which involves the transference of a disease or affliction "to another person, to animals, plants, and to various kinds of objects. . . by direct or indirect contact" (Hand 1980). This magical transference is evident in various German-Russian "wart" cures, in which a wart is transferred to a piece of string or a dishcloth and then buried in a Misthaufe (manure pile), and in the practice of plugging, wedging, or nailing, in which the disease is transferred to trees or shrubs.

Magico-religious healing may also focus on the use of "words, charms, amulets, and physical manipulations in the attempt to heal the ills of [human] and beast" (Yoder 1972). This form is found in the German-Russian magico-religious healing practices of Brauche. These practices generally involve the recitation, in German, of prayer-like verses, concluded with an invocation in the "three highest names" of the Christian Trinity. Brauche charms or rhymes often were written in notebooks, or preserved on loose sheets of paper in recipe books or in the family Bible in many German-Russian households.

Women as Folk Healers

In German-Russian culture folk healing existed primarily among women. While men occasionally did serve as bone-setters and magico-religious practitioners, it was far more common for women to adopt such roles. Midwifery was a phenomenon particularly dominated by German-Russian women and it was rare for male villagers to engage in this specialized activity. The healing arts practiced by certain women were assumed as a responsibility in addition to numerous other activities — childrearing, cooking, baking, milking, hauling water, washing, weaving, sewing, gardening, and agricultural work.

The following profiles focus on three North Dakota women who are representative of German-Russian female folk healers: 1) "Katherine," a farm woman in the west-central part of the state, whose folk medical knowledge and techniques include massage, bone-setting, reflexology, accupressure, herbalism, Brauche, and folk psychiatry; 2) "Lis-Bas," an elderly farm woman in south-central North Dakota who specializes in the magico-religious treatment of three disorders; and 3) "Veronica," a retired farm woman in southwest North Dakota who confines her folk healing skills to members of her immediate family. These women also represent three major types of female folk healers: generalized folk practitioners, specialized folk practitioners, and familial folk practitioners.

Most of the information regarding these healers was obtained in directed and non-directed interview sessions. Katherine was interviewed on several occasions from 1984-1987. Lis-Bas and Veronica (as well as a number of other German-Russian healers and their clients) were interviewed during the period 1979-1987. First-name pseudonyms for all three informants are used here to protect their identity, as well as the privacy of family members.

The three women were not as resistant to questions about their lives or certain healing techniques as one might expect. All three seemed appreciative of the fact that academic investigators found their lives and skills worthy of study and serious attention. (Such research was made easier perhaps because both investigators are themselves of German-Russian descent and thus are familiar with various facets of German-Russian culture and interpersonal relations.) Initially, Katherine even hoped to train Nadine Engbrecht-Schaff to assume the position of community healer. When Engbrecht-Schaff told her that her motives for learning about German-Russian folk healing were different, Katherine decided that at least she could pass on valuable information for posterity via the processes of in-depth interview and scholarly documentation.

Katherine, A Generalized Folk Healer

Katherine's grandparents were Protestants from the Black Sea region in Russia; they came to America from the Glueckstal settlement northwest of Odessa. Katherine's parents were born in South Russia and were young children when the families first settled in Nebraska. They soon moved near Eureka, South Dakota, where her parents married and began their family. When they had the opportunity to homestead in North Dakota, Katherine's parents moved to the western part of the state, where Katherine was born in 1908. When she turned 21, she married her "school sweetheart," Henry, and joined him in farming.

Katherine's mother was a healer, as were her grandparents. She was chosen by her mother to continue the tradition and began her training at age fifteen. Katherine recalled:

> I kept saying to her, "Mother, I don't think I can take this; this is hard work."
> "Well," she said, "we'll do just like my mother did with me. We'll take our time on this and get your muscles built up."

Katherine's mother taught her various massage and "bone-setting" techniques. She also kept a number of small black notebooks with remedies and Brauche charms carefully written in German; Katherine was instructed to add any information given to her during her training period. Katherine's mother performed midwifery duties as well and although Katherine didn't continue this tradition, she accompanied her mother on some of those visits. When Katherine was first married, she would treat an average of one client each day, because she was busy farming. Gradually, her mother was unable to continue her healing duties and Katherine was expected to assume them. At times, her workload was overwhelming, but her mother and husband encouraged her to continue. She was told she had been given the talent and must not waste it. Katherine said:

> Sometimes they'd stop, come driving out to the field, and I'd say, "[Henry], I can't go. We'll have to tell these people off, because that doesn't work." And he'd say, "No, you can't tell a sick person to go. You just go home with them and give them the treatment and when you're through you shall soon be back. They'll bring you back out to the field." And that's what they did. In the wintertime then, when it wasn't snowbound, I was busy then. I took more on. And usually in the evening, after chores and everything was done, I had a patient yet. Sometimes I thought, "It's impossible," but I slowly hung on to it because my mother wouldn't let me quit; she just pressured me all the time. She said her mother did that to her; she wouldn't let her quit. She said the time to come is going to pay for itself and if the Lord gave you those talented hands, you have to use them.

Doc Wink
by Jacqueline K. Dohn

A folk hero's fame is generally created by and remains in the community which sees the hero's lifestyle or actions as out of the ordinary. The stories and memories put Dr. Helena Knauf Wink, a female physician in Jamestown, North Dakota, at the turn of the century, in that category. Dr. Alec Bond, professor of English at Jamestown College between 1972-79, recognized "Doc" Wink as a folk hero in his article "Folk Biography in Dakota Territory," *Journal of the Folklore Institute* (1980). In this article, Bond says that Wink did not fit into the Western female roles of refined lady, helpmate or "bad woman." Instead, she became legendary because she was the "best and most humane doctor around."

Wink's medical skill and her concern for her patients are well illustrated in the anecdote told in *Memories of Yesteryears: A Story of Dakota Territorial Days* (1976) when she performed the first appendectomy in the upper Midwest on her dining room table. The Jamestown hospital had not been built, and Wink called in a local doctor and two doctors from the state hospital to assist her at home. Most patients at that time would

Katherine and Henry never had children because of his sterility, a fact Katherine knew before their marriage. The couple farmed through the Depression, gradually buying the land they rented. After Henry had been retired for a year, doctors found he had a heart condition. Katherine applied her knowledge of massage and reflexology (compressing specific areas of the feet).

> I massaged his arms, his left arm. I worked in the inside of his left hand, where what we would call the reflex to the heart, and then I worked the bottom of his left foot, by the two smallest toes — that's also the reflex of the heart. And usually when I did that, then he could breathe again.

Despite Katherine's efforts and attention, Henry died in 1973, and she moved into town, where she resumed her work and continues today, although on a limited scale. At this writing, Katherine is 79 years old.

Katherine's mainstay is massage, supplemented by the practices of reflexology and accupressure. A typical "session" will consist of one or two hours of massage. When Katherine does massage, she applies pressure to the area until "it walks away." She will find a "lump" of knotted muscle and slowly massage, gradually applying more pressure. It will feel as if it's "melting." During these sessions, Katherine assumes the role of therapist, treating the mental as well as physical aspects of illness. "[The people who come to me] have so much faith in my work, that they'll walk out with help, regardless. They leave everything here. They

---

have died from the "inflammation of the bowels," but nine-year-old Lizzie Stuff survived. Wink stayed up for three days and three nights after the surgery to care for her patient.

Wink was born into a large family on May 26, 1854, in Jackson County, Michigan, near Waterloo. Her drive for an advanced education began early. With a first grade teaching certificate, she taught preschool through eighth grade and started to save money for college. Her $13 monthly salary did not allow for many expenses so she boarded with students' parents. After graduation from the University of Michigan medical school at Ann Arbor in 1883, Helena followed ten of her brothers and sisters to Jamestown. There she began a career that spanned 53 years, more than 5,000 births and 25 years as state medical examiner. At the time of her death she was local medical examiner, a position that many people would have deemed unladylike in anyone else. But then, little of Wink's behavior conformed to expectations either for a physician or for a woman.

As a physician she more often cared for her patients in ways expected of female behavior than in ways expected of doctors. When she made her rounds, she always brought along some of her homemade Boston brown bread. Occasionally she brought groceries for her needy patients and would stay with a new mother for a few days, cooking and cleaning until the mother was up again, something few male doctors would have done. Wink never refused to see a patient, regardless of his or her financial condition. Sometimes she refused payment. Jamestown native Bill Mason remembers his mother asking Doc Wink for a bill. Wink told his mother that when she wore a better dress than the

complain to me and tell me what's wrong and they leave all their things with me."

Katherine possesses a wealth of herbal and household remedies which she has gathered from many sources, including the notebooks kept by her mother. She makes limited use of Brauche, something she claims was more popular years ago in west-central North Dakota. However, she says there are some illnesses that cannot be treated by medical doctors, such as "colic" and "St. Anthony's fire" (shingles). She uses Brauche in conjunction with some massage and supplemented by herbal remedies. For example, in the treatment of "colic," Katherine will apply lotion to an infant's stomach and massage the stomach, while exercising the infant's limbs and reciting a "prayer." She will then feed the infant chamomile tea. In the treatment of a sty, Katherine uses a boric acid rinse and blows in the infected eye three times while saying:

> *Schussblotter geh' raus!*
> *Oder ich rab dich*
> *Mit mein'm rechten Daume' raus.* +++

[+++ = name of the Holy Trinity]

> Sty blister, go away!
> Or I rub you out
> With my right thumb. +++

doctor, then she'd send one.

Because she was a woman, no one would have thought twice if Wink had had her own driver to take her on her rounds. But not Wink, who broke her team of sorrels and later used Hambletonian horses to pull her carriage. She drove like a madwoman, so local sources report. When the Model-T came to town, her vehicle changed, but not her driving. People had to jump out of the way or be hit when she was on the move. Once she had to take the Galloping Goose, a single motorized passenger coach train on the northwest Pingree-Woolton line to visit a patient. The only transportation back to Jamestown that night was a freight train, but regulations did not allow a woman to ride in the caboose. Doc Wink just threw her medical bag on a flat car and rode home.

Part of the reason that stories about Wink are still so oft repeated and vivid in the minds of the tellers is that she brought many of these tellers into this world. Quite a few of the silver spoons she distributed each year at high school commencement to the "Doc Wink Babies" still grace Jamestown homes, and their owners swap tales about Wink when they gather. Each one has a different story to share or even a different version of an old favorite, including how she prescribed her own little brown pills for every ailment from toothaches to pregnancy.

Even in death Doc Wink remained legendary. According to the *Stutsman County Record*, on the Sunday morning of Feb. 16, 1936, while dry-cleaning her clothes with naphtha gas, she caught fire and burned her entire body. Legend tells how the imprint of her body remained on the wall she fell against and that, in her last few hours of consciousness, she directed others in the treatment of her pain.

The most important element of success in Brauche lies in the belief of the patient. Katherine's reliance on faith as an integral part of healing is reaffirmed by numerous stories about seemingly unbelievable cures. For example, she vividly recalls how her mother once cured Anna, a younger sister, of a bothersome case of warts. Their mother instructed Anna to walk over a certain hill in the pasture and do exactly as she was told:

> Mother told her, "The first bone [you see], pick up that bone and then . . . rub it on all those warts and you lay that bone down again just like you picked it up." And she did that for one whole week, every morning at sunup. . . .But she wasn't allowed to tell us and we wondered, "Why is that little girl running over that hill every morning so early?" So we said, "Mother, what's going on with Anna?" And she said, "You just let that Anna alone; she knows what she's doing." But, see, it was Mother and Anna that put this up together and Anna believed it so strong that whatever Mother told her is gonna happen, and her hands were full, her whole forehead was full, thick full of warts. And she didn't like that; she was about five years old. And so [Mother] took care of her. And [the warts] went away. It took awhile, all at once, and we wouldn't say anything because we forgot it kinda and she didn't either and pretty soon she comes up and says, "Did you look at my face; did you see how I haven't got any more warts?" [Laughter] And [she] was real happy about it. It's just how you believed, I guess, and it's that same thing today yet. If you say, "I'm gonna do this, but I just don't believe it's gonna help," well, then it's not gonna help.

In a speech to the Tabernacle Society of the St. James Catholic Church, Eva Plunkett, Jamestown newspaper woman, quoted what Dr. W.A. Gerrish said at the time of Wink's death: "Never did our beloved Dr. Wink ask any quarter because of her womanhood; she stood shoulder to shoulder with the masculine members of the profession all these long years." The male doctors may have respected her medical skill, but as Mary Young, a Jamestown historian, points out, they never asked her to combine her practice with theirs.

Jacqueline K. Dohn lives in Jamestown, N.D.

Katherine, like many folk healers, considers her ability to heal a "gift from God." She speaks constantly of her "miracle hands".

> One lady said to me, "All you have to do, [Katherine], is talk to me and I right away feel the healing power." But, a very tender hand it takes, though....Who gives you those miracle hands? It's the Lord. You only have certain people that have those.

Katherine's strong religious faith is matched by a warm concern for fellow human beings, two special qualities often commented upon by her clients. Along with such diverse healing skills as massage, bone-setting, reflexology, acupressure, herbalism, and Brauche, Katherine also practices a form of folk psychiatry in dealing with "her people," encouraging them to think positively and trust in the ways of the Almighty.

> You have to keep going. Life never stops till the very end comes and that we don't know when it will be or what it will be like. The good Lord only knows that. Have your soul prepared; when the Lord calls, you're ready to go. That's the main thing; I tell my people that all the time.
> I always say, "Make sure that your soul is safe." Especially when I know I got some very sick ones and the time will come when they won't make it very long. Then I stress it; I say, "Get your soul prepared for when the Lord calls, then you're ready to go." I always say a prayer for my people.

Lis-Bas, a Specialized Folk Healer

Elizabeth is known to many as "Lis-Bas" (Aunt Liz). "Bas" is an old country term of respect and affection that she deeply appreciates, for it underscores the closeness of her relationship to a large number of relatives, friends, and clients. Lis-Bas was born in an *"alte Semlank"* (old earthen house) on the rocky prairies of south-central North Dakota in the late 1890s. The home of her early childhood was typical of other German-Russian dwellings of that period, with the thick walls of *Batse* (sun-dried clay brick), low ceilings, and dirt floor. The paternal ancestors of Lis-Bas were Black Sea German colonists from a village in the Beresan region of South Russia (located northwest of the present-day Soviet city of Nikolajev). Her mother's people came from the Glueckstal area of South Russia, an area of Black Sea German settlement known for its many folk healers, midwives, and bone-setters.

Lis-Bas worked hard as a youngster and took pride in the fact that she could outdo the older, male members of her family. Lis-Bas seldom expressed bitterness about the hard work she constantly did, for it helped make her a "strong woman":

> I worked hard all my life, boy oh boy! When I was young and at home yet, I even beat my older brother when we had to use the pitchfork. I always did more than him. And I worked fast! Then after I got married, I worked even harder. I milked all the cows, I carried two big pails of milk, I carried the coal to the house, I separated the milk, I fed the calves, I did all kinds of work. When my husband cut with the binder, I shocked right behind him. By the time he was finished, I had the last row done, too.

Hard work didn't hurt me. It made me strong, really it did!

In the early 1920s, Lis-Bas married, and she and her husband farmed in south-central North Dakota. Their household eventually included eight children, two of whom died as infants. Lis-Bas was familiar with German-Russian folk medicine by way of her mother and other female relatives. She never actively practiced folk healing, however, until she was well into adulthood. Lis-Bas learned Brauche from "an old woman" even though she realized that this magico-religious tradition was supposed to be passed on to a member of the opposite sex. "Women often learned it from other women," Lis-Bas explained. "There just weren't enough men who were interested and so the women tended to do it a lot more."

While Lis-Bas collected a large number of handwritten herbal remedies and even became familiar with reflexology, it was the tradition of Brauche with which she developed the most expertise. Lis-Bas learned how to diagnose and treat three ailments with magico-religious folk medicine: A'wache (Angewachsen, "Grown-On" or "Liver-Grown"); eye irritations caused by cold spring winds; and bleeding (especially nosebleeds, superficial wounds, and hemorrhage). The first ailment, A'wachs, is a culturally-defined illness not unlike susto among Mexican-Americans or "ghost sickness" among many Plains Indians. Because A'wachs is not recognized by non-German-Russian medical practitioners, its treatment by competent folk healers is all the more critical.

Lis-Bas claims that A'wachs, a problem that affects mainly newborn and young children, results when a child is suddenly bumped, jolted, or frightened. "It is not colic," Lis-Bas contends. "Colic is in the intestines, but A'wachs is a swelling higher up, inside the stomach." In diagnosing the malady, Lis-Bas would place a child on its back and then draw the child's left knee up to the right elbow and repeat this action with the right knee and left elbow. If the limbs could not be drawn together easily or the child cried, Lis-Bas suspected A'wachs. In treating this condition, she lightly massaged the child's abdomen and limbs and recited a Brauche verse three times to effect a cure. An example of one such text for A'wachs (not used by Lis-Bas but that appears in a small booklet in her folk medicine collection) is the following:

Schlag aus dieses Kindes rippen;
Jesus lag in der Krippe! +++

Depart from this child's ribs;
[For] Jesus lay in the crib! +++

Following the treatment, Lis-Bas advised mothers to keep the child warm and feed it no milk for several hours. "If the child gets hungry," Lis-Bas advised, "give it a little warm Kamille (chamomile) tea but no milk."

One of the reasons Lis-Bas learned how to treat A'wachs was so that she could doctor her own children. Her late husband also was afflicted with eye problems that resulted from wind exposure. Lis-Bas said her husband was a farmer who "always had to go outside every spring and look up at the clouds and see what was going on." Whenever he did this in the spring, he invariably "hurt his eyes." Lis-Bas diagnosed this condition (in her husband and in other clients) by carefully studying the inflamed eye. If a tiny, white-looking blister was discovered, she recited a special Brauche verse. For reasons of ritual secrecy, the verse used by Lis-Bas is not provided here but the following text is an example of a Brauche "prayer" for eye problems:

Nichts ist fuer die augen gut,
Als das warme Christi Blut.
Der christliche Glaube vertreibet
Alles Fallen und Nebel,
Und Zugleich fuer geschossene Blatter. +++

Nothing is as good for the eyes,
As the warm blood of Christ.
Christian faith drives out
All danger and everything unclear,
As well as festering blisters. +++

The third malady treated by Lis-Bas is bleeding, ranging from serious nosebleeds to life-threatening hemorrhages. When Lis-Bas learned how to "stop blood" with Brauche, she was somewhat uncertain of her own ability. She believed in the power of Brauche but feared that she might, in a state of excitement, get the sacred words of the blood-stopping Brauche verse "all mixed up." Lis-Bas vividly recalled the first time she used the powerful charm:

> I went over to visit my neighbor one day and saw that she had a real bad nosebleed. She was bleeding a lot and asked me to do something. . . . So I took a clean white handkerchief and put it under the woman's nose and said the prayer as I placed my other hand on her. I said the prayer three times to myself, making sure I didn't skip a word. This woman believed in Brauche and a short while later the bleeding stopped. She was so thankful for what I did. Not long after, my house was filled with people who came from all directions. They all wanted me to help them.
> But I could Brauche for only a few things. Still they came. I had to turn many away.

While Lis-Bas had expertise in the magico-religious treatment of *A'wache*, eye problems, and bleeding, these three disorders remained her only specialties. When clients asked for help she always asked if they believed in the power of Brauche. If they expressed any doubt, Lis-Bas declined to treat them. Individuals who sought her help only as a last resort might be cured if they had complete faith and had not undergone surgery for the condition already. Lis-Bas explained that such surgery interfered with God's will and the normal healing process within the body:

> When it [the afflicted area] is cut once, it [Brauche] doesn't help any more. My uncle didn't believe. They [his family] told him he should go and have [his skin cancer] tended to. "Ach," he said, "zu dene alte weiber dort gehe — was wolle die wisse? ["Oh, go over to those old women — what do they know?"] So he went to the doctor in Bismarck for his skin cancer. . . . He had the surgery and it was okay for a couple of months. But then here it [the cancer] came back again. And then Brauche couldn't help him. And he died. He didn't believe in Brauche.

The strong belief in Brauche that Lis-Bas professes is matched by her equally strong faith in Protestant Christianity. Lis-Bas sees no problem in reconciling official religion and folk religion. "After all," she contends, "Jesus was the first bloodstopper" (a reference to the Biblical passage in which Jesus heals the woman "with a hemorrhage of twelve years duration," Luke 8:42-43). To Lis-Bas, both Protestant Christianity and the German-Russian tradition of Brauche demand the same thing of all adherents: faith.

> If you take a person that doesn't believe on this Brauche and you do something for them, it won't help. The one who suffers has to believe just as much as the one who heals.
> Now if you're working on a little baby the parents have to believe for that baby. If it's an animal, then you have to believe for it.
> My husband was dehorning calves [one time] and all of a sudden he came running and asked me to help him with a calf. The poor thing was losing an awful lot of blood. By the time I got to [the calf], it was lying on its side. The blood spurted up just like a fountain. I took a white handkerchief and put it on the wound. I said the prayer three times and the bleeding stopped. Pretty soon, that calf was jumping around with all the others. The Heavenly Father takes care of everything, if you believe in Him.

Veronica, A Familial Folk Healer

Unlike Katherine and Lis-Bas, Veronica never identified herself as a folk healer to the other members of her larger German-Russian community. Nonetheless, she is familiar with numerous "home remedies" and herbal medicines, as well as the magico-religious tradition of Brauche. Veronica's healing skills and knowledge are confined entirely to the sphere of her immediate family. In this respect, Veronica actually typifies most German-Russian women in North Dakota, past and present.

Veronica was born in an earthen house in southwestern North Dakota in 1912. Her parents were Catholic Black Sea Germans who traced their ancestry to the Kutschurgan area of South Russia. Veronica was one of ten children and "learned nearly everything" from her mother. Veronica's mother was intimately familiar with a wide range of folk medical traditions and was said to possess "healing hands." She also was known as a very devout Catholic who believed in frequent church attendance and the power of prayer.

Although Veronica's mother knew how to cure a variety of ailments, it was an ordinary blood blister that led to the woman's death. According to Veronica:

> My mother got blood poisoning from a blue blister on her hand. It came from helping in the field during the harvest. She had heard that to cure blood poisoning one should take a big squashy toad — not a frog -- and tie it right over the wound. This was supposed to draw out the poison. It would even kill the toad. But Mother said "I'll die before I ever tie one of those things on me." And so she died.

Veronica grew up at a time when there were few doctors in southwestern North Dakota. "I was eighteen years old until I saw my first real doctor," she says. "Before

that, you could have told me a doctor had horns — I'd have believed it!" During the
Depression years, Veronica married a German-Russian tradesman who later tried
his hand at prairie farming. Veronica described their life together as "Good but
poor. If you get married poor, you stay poor." While living on the farm, Veronica
and her husband faced innumerable challenges that also plagued earlier generations of Great Plains settlers: drought, hailstorms, incessant wind, and even an
occasional prairie fire. Despite such hardships, Veronica and her husband "made
the best of it" and raised eight children.

Veronica feels that the folk medical knowledge passed on to her by her mother
proved helpful on many occasions. Once, during a bad blizzard, two of Veronica's
small children became ill with pneumonia. Since this was a serious illness that often
claimed young lives, a doctor was summoned but he was unable to come, due to the
severity of the storm. Veronica described what she did in an effort to care for her
children:

> I doctored for that pneumonia with scrambled eggs and goose fat. I mixed these
> up real good and then heated them up until they were kind of slimy. After that, I put
> all of this on a flannel cloth along with some 190-proof alcohol. Then I put it on the
> kids' chests. One hour later they could both breathe.
>
> When the doctor was finally able to come out and see them he told me I cured
> them. He asked what I did and then he wrote it all down. He just couldn't believe
> it.

In treating the illnesses of her children and other close relatives, Veronica
followed a number of home remedies well-known to many of North Dakota's
German-Russians. Her chamomile tea was considered one of the most effective
herbal remedies and it was used for a variety of disorders. Veronica often served
it with lemon for family members suffering from bad colds or indigestion. She grew
chamomile near her home, along with numerous other varieties of herbs and
flowers. When the chamomile blossoms were ready for harvesting, Veronica
carefully picked and washed them, then dried the herbs by hanging them from the
wash line in clean cloth bags.

Instead of cough syrup, Veronica fried sugar and onions together and then
extracted the juice. "Raw onion and pepper sandwiches" also were prescribed for
family members who were badly congested. Chicken soup was a cure-all and
although Veronica admits she does not know why, it is the "best thing there is for
sickness." A cold remedy still used by Veronica and members of her family calls for
a tablespoon of honey and a tablespoon of apple cider vinegar mixed in a glass of
boiling water. "It works better for me than anything you buy in a store," she says.

Like her mother, Veronica believes in the miraculous power of prayer and the
mysterious power of Brauche. Her mother knew the ways and words of Brauche
but these were carefully guarded. Veronica offered few details about Brauche, but
she did tell the following story:

> Ja, my mother could do that [Brauche]. She taught me how to do it. Once, I did
> it for a daughter of mine who cut her head real bad while playing outside. I was in
> bed with a new baby. My sister-in-law was there and she brought in my daughter

who was hurt and bleeding. Her little coat was soaked with blood, all the way to her belt. What a sight!

My sister-in-law was real scared and made me get out of bed to help her. I told her, "Just get me a slice of white bread." My sister-in-law said, "For God's sake, what do you want with white bread at a time like this?" I said, "Just do what I ask."

Well, she got me the bread and I placed it on my daughter's head and I said something. But I can't tell you what I said! The blood, it just oozed through the bread and then it suddenly stopped. When I took the bread away, my daughter's hair was clean where th bread had been and there was a white crust on her cut. My sister-in-law said, "That won't last — it'll open again and start bleeding." I said, "No, it won't."

That wound never did open. You have to believe, you have to have faith. My kids don't believe [in Brauche]. So I've never told them what my mother taught me.

While Veronica steadfastly refrains from describing herself as a "healer," she possesses the knowledge to cure a variety of ailments. In making use of the German-Russian healing traditions available to her, Veronica was (and remains) both practical and selective. She has attempted to pass on certain folk beliefs to her family members (such as cold remedies), despite occasional resistance and skepticism. Other traditions, such as Brauche, perhaps will be taken with her to the grave. Veronica feels that no matter how efficacious they may be, some of the old healing traditions of her people are better "unused than abused."

My mother had ten children. She was a German-Russian immigrant who came to the United States with my father in 1912. They brought with them three small children. Three headstones marked the graves of three older children who had died in the Volga village they left behind. After seven years in the Minnesota beet fields (and three more children), they bought land near Cavalier, North Dakota. Mother was pregnant with her tenth child the fall they arrived in the state.

Mary Guenther
Cavalier, N.D.

Conclusions

These women represent three major types of German-Russian folk healers. Katherine is an example of a generalized folk practitioner, a healer who is competent in the areas of massage, bone-setting, reflexology, acupressure, herbalism, Brauche, and folk psychiatry. She is acknowledged as an effective healer within and beyond her own North Dakota community. Lis-Bas, while familiar with many types of folk medicine, focuses only on three maladies that could be treated with Brauche. In this respect, Lis-Bas epitomizes the specialized folk practitioner whose expertise is limited to only certain illnesses and a particular form of traditional German-Russian folk medicine. Also, Lis-Bas's reputation as a healer is not as widespread as that of a generalized folk practitioner such as Katherine. Veronica, on the other hand, represents the familial folk practitioner whose knowledge of folk medicine was learned within a family setting. Veronica's healing skills are confined to the members of her immediate family as well. Thus, she represents the familial folk healer whose power to cure is reserved for close relatives alone.

Anthropologists and other scholars have provided researchers with a number of provocative hypotheses and theories regarding folk healers and the phenomenon of folk healing. Judith Hoch-Smith and Anita Spring in their book *Women in Ritual and Symbolic Roles*, for example, argue that those "women whose reproductive capacities are limited . . . often symbolically rechannel their reproductive energies into helping other women bear children by becoming midwives or healers." This hypothesis may help explain the existence of so many more German-Russian female folk healers than male folk healers. Yet, it is possible that this anomaly may be related to a whole host of economic, social, cultural, and historical factors other than merely limited female reproductive capacities.

Although compensation for childlessness does not apply to cases of Lis-Bas and Veronica (both of whom had eight children), there is some basis for the hypothesis in Katherine's case. Katherine never had any children due to her husband's sterility. Yet is is important to remember that Katherine, "chosen" by her mother, began her training as a folk healer when she was only fifteen years old. She had no way of knowing then that she would always be childless. Additional counter-evidence to the "barren woman as healer" compensation hypothesis is the fact that of twenty-seven German-Russian midwives and healers studied in North Dakota, Kansas, and Saskatchewan, only four women had given birth to fewer than three children. Indeed, the average number of offspring for the twenty-seven female healers was 7.5 children.

While the profiles of Katherine, Lis-Bas, and Veronica exhibit a number of differences, it is most interesting to note how much the three women share. Despite such obvious differences as age, religious background, and place of residence within North Dakota, all three healers were rural German-Russian women whose lives were dominated by hard work. The outstanding similarity that draws them together is their insistence on faith as an integral part of the healing process. "You have to have a lot of faith," Katherine repeatedly tells her clients. In a similar vein, Lis-Bas claims that "the one who suffers has to believe just as much as the one who heals." Veronica echoes the sentiments of both women with her statement: "You have to believe, you have to have faith."

Medical scholars who study the popularity and efficacy of folk healing techniques among the world's peoples invariably single out the importance of faith as a prerequisite to successful healing and recovery. Bruno Gebhard, a physician and medical historian, argues that folk medicine has one indisputable advantage over scientific medicine: folk medicine "has no doubt, it believes. Scientific medicine moves from truth to error to truth — it must search and re-search" (Gebhard 1976).

Katherine, Lis-Bas, and Veronica do not claim to be scientific in their approach to healing. Each folk practitioner emphasizes different traditional techniques and tries with all the skill, energy, and faith she can muster to combat illness and its physical manifestations. During North Dakota's early settlement period, folk healers served a vital need in the absence of professionally-trained doctors, licensed nurses, and modern medical facilities. Today, German-Russian folk healers like Katherine, Lis-Bas, and Veronica continue to fill a need that remains particularly important among those of their people who believe "You have to have a lot of faith."

References

Gebhard, Bruno. "The Interrelationship of Scientific and Folk Medicine in the United States of America Since 1850," *American Folk Medicine*, Wayland D. Hand, ed. Berkeley: University of California Press, 1976.

Hand, Wayland D. *Magical Medicine*. Berkeley: University of California Press, 1980.

Hoch-Smith, Judith and Anita Spring, eds. "Introduction" to *Women in Ritual and Symbolic Roles*. New York: Plenum Press, 1978.

Kloberdanz, Timothy J. "The Tradition of Brauche: Facts vs. Fallacies," *Heritage Review*, vol. 15, September 1985.

_____. "The Daughters of Shiphrah: Folk Healers and Midwives of the Great Plains." Paper presented at the 11th Annual Great Plains Symposium, University of Nebraska, March 1987.

Yoder, Don. "Folk Medicine," *Folklore and Folklife*. Richard M. Dorson, ed. Chicago: University of Chicago Press, 1972.

Timothy J. Kloberdanz is Associate Professor of Anthropology at North Dakota State University, Fargo.

Nadine Engbrecht-Schaff lives in Inver Grove Heights, Minnesota. She is a native of western North Dakota and has a Masters Degree in Anthropology from North Dakota State University, Fargo.

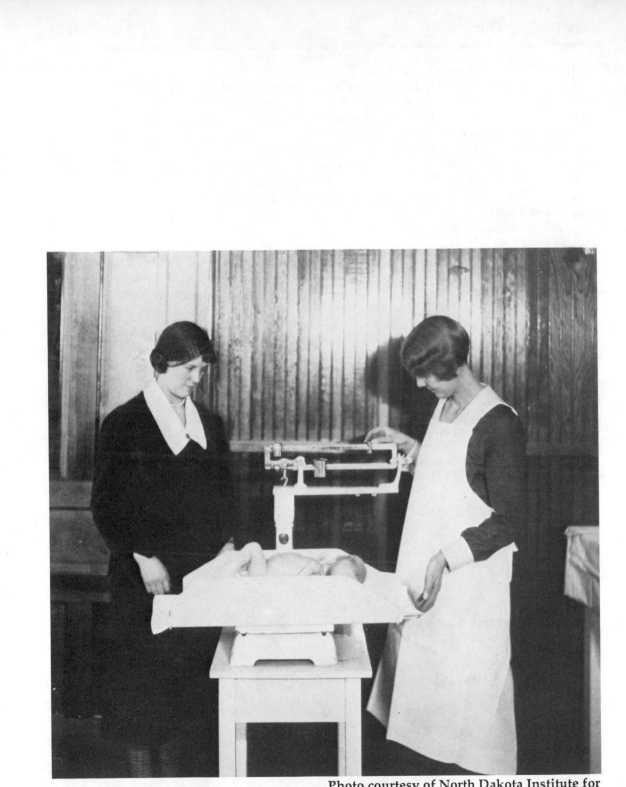

Photo courtesy of North Dakota Institute for Regional Studies, North Dakota State University.

Nursing in North Dakota

by Bonnie Clark

My mother is having her seventieth birthday. She grew up at a time when hard work was everything, and she impressed on me the value of work, much of which I resisted. Or rather, it was not so much the work itself I resisted as drudgery, work that was endless and not valued. I learned to work *too* hard. Like most young women, I did not want to work as hard as my mother had, and yet now I can begin to see how that hard work was necessary to her and her family if they were to survive in the harsh farming ventures they undertook.

Mother tells a story that captures for me a great deal about how she saw her life. She went to school during the Depression in a one-room dug-out school. At Christmas time there were oranges; (fresh fruit was a special treat). Children would pick up orange rinds in the school yard that others had dropped and eat the pulp on the inside of the rind. To this day Mother still eats the pulp on the inside of orange rinds. I watch her, and realize why she does it. (I'm not even sure she knows she's doing it.) But her habit reminds me of that tradition of poverty and hard work, how it meant survival for so many people, women especially. It carries me on, also, in my own work in the field of nursing, in spite of changes.

My personal expectations and hopes have changed as well. I've achieved a measure of success, from being a nurse to teaching nursing. What hasn't changed as much is the popular images of nurses which treats them as handmaidens, sex objects, dingy blondes or battleaxes, in spite of the hard work, knowledge, and training which contradicts such connotations. Nurses seem to gain greatest respect and admiration during emergencies, when there is no one else to do the work — in war time, and in periods of major dislocation, as during the years of western settlement, when there were few doctors and communities were trying to found hospitals in response to a sudden swelling of rural populations. Although salaries and working conditions of nurses now (in 1988) are improving, doctors, (usually males), continue to receive the highest status in health care professions. As in many professions dominated by women, nursing is undervalued. There seems to be a correlation between low status and the honors "good" nurses can achieve — in North Dakota a nurse can be named to the North Dakota Nursing Hall of Fame, a title that sounds damning with faint praise. To write of nursing in North Dakota thus combines a history of prejudice against nurses (and women generally) with a history of developing communities that desperately needed care for the sick and injured.

The settlement period here, in the late nineteenth and early twentieth centuries, coincided with a period when women in more urban areas in the U.S. and Europe were increasingly engaging in good works — such as charities, settlement houses, and orphanages. Middle and upper class women were founding libraries and schools; they were enthusiastic about dress reform, "purity crusades," public health, the cemetery movement. Such projects were seen as extensions of women's accepted occupations as mother and homemaker; they could be described as care-giving and housekeeping on a public scale. The larger towns in North Dakota eventually experienced similar efforts by women's clubs and public-spirited individual women, but during the earlier days of settlement, the idea of women's special "mission" as we might call it, of doing good, found expression in the most immediate and necessary skills, such as nursing, teaching, and religious instruction. It was women's special mission to do good. What Florence Nightingale, "The Lady

---

Ruby Bishop Maurer, of Mandan, North Dakota, sums up those early experiences in nursing:

I entered St. Mary's Hospital School of Nursing, in Minneapolis, Minnesota, in January 1933, and was graduated and awarded a diploma in January 1936. During my career I worked in public health, obstetrical (care of mothers, delivery room and nursery), clinic nursing, and industrial nursing (construction sites).

How things have changed over a period of 50-some years. No automatic-controlled beds — all were hand-cranked, if we should be so lucky. Many of them had backrests that were entirely pulled by hand. Shock blocks were pyramid shaped blocks of wood with a "grooved out" depression on the top for the casters to rest in. One nurse would grab the foot of the bed and lift it up while the other nurse would shove the 8-inch blocks under the bed's legs. Oh, my aching back! In the delivery room and in surgery all soiled linen was washed out by hand before being sent to the laundry. Air conditioning was unheard of; we almost cooked under the hot lights in surgery, and in the delivery room also. All the *vernex caseosa* [a substance that looks like cheese and covers a baby's skin at birth] was scrubbed off the

With The Lamp," had done to bring comfort and clean bandages to soldiers dying in the Crimea, settler women and their daughters did among the farms and growing towns of early North Dakota. Working conditions, pay and the amount of respect they received weren't often discussed.

For young women growing up at a time, in North Dakota, when work and survival were about all our mothers had expected to accomplish, the profession of nursing (rather than only home-care nursing) presented to us an avenue both to escape that dedication to drudgery and at the same time continue a devotion to human betterment. Nursing promised change in some aspects of life that so far had appeared unattainable. Nursing also offered young women a way to move beyond family to more public experiences.

I received my first instruction in what a history of nursing could mean from Lucille Paulson, who was recently inducted into the North Dakota Nursing Hall of Fame. She graduated from high school in New Rockford, North Dakota, in 1917, and began nurses training at St. John's Hospital School of Nursing in Redwing, Minnesota, in 1919, when she was twenty years old. But her aspirations were somewhat checked. This was the time of World War I and she had wanted to go to an Army school of nursing, but because her mother feared she might be sent too far away, Lucille chose the nursing school in Redwing, where her grandparents lived. An aunt who was a nurse inspired Lucille to follow that career. For Lucille Paulson and many others, nursing began as a way away from family, yet a career that was suggested and bound by family ties as well.

---

babies immediately after birth before they were admitted to the nursery. This, of course, opened a perfect field on which to gain a good case of impetigo, and that is exactly what happened.

Fathers were not allowed in the delivery room and no one was allowed in mother's room while the babies were out-to-breast [feed]. Siblings were not allowed in maternity. Mothers were not allowed out of bed for 10, 12, or 14 days. Can you imagine all the bed baths, bedpans carried and the like? All wore breast binders which were closed down the front with about five large safety pins. Abdominal binders were closed the same way. One nurse, or if we were lucky, two, would care for as many as 30 newborns in the nursery. Pampers and the like were unheard of. All diapers were cloth, which, by the way, had to be washed out by hand before going to the laundry. All packings used in the delivery room were made by

hand at the chart desk when we weren't busy. Most of my pediatrics training was at the Minneapolis General Hospital. Keeping in mind that we were still in the Depression years, our supplies were very limited. Instead of ice coolers, we used pig bladders which were purchased from one of the packing companies in the Twin Cities. They were filled with ice and secured shut with a rubber band, then twisted in the middle which formed two balls, one going in either side of the throat. The pneumonia patients were put on porches.

In my "home" hospital, when taking care of patients with infected wounds, we applied maggots to eat up the dead tissue. We used cages of a sort to keep them (the maggots) where they belonged. They didn't bother the living tissue. They had to be removed frequently, before they hatched into something else,

That career advanced steadily. In her first two years after graduation she worked as a private and general duty nurse in Rochester, Minnesota, and at the Henry Ford Hospital in Detroit, Michigan. For four years after that she taught nursing at Lutheran Hospital in Sioux City, Iowa. Then, for 28 years she was nursing instructor and then director of the nursing program at Deaconess Hospital in Grand Forks, North Dakota. Lucille returned to the University of Minnesota for a BSN degree, which took nineteen years of summer school. She began in 1931, was interrupted by World War II, and finished in 1950, then completed a Masters Degree in education at University of Minnesota in 1959. Her essay, "A 75-Year History of Nursing Education in North Dakota, 1903-1978," (published in 1979 as a special edition of *The Prairie Rose* by the state Nurses Association), shows that nursing in North Dakota has tried to conform to national trends in appropriate clinical experience. A "primary objective," she wrote, was "to provide educational rather than service needs of the hospital." Lucille Paulson was a member of the North Dakota Board of Nursing for ten years, and from 1959-1970 was its executive director. Altogether, she spent 58 years in North Dakota as a nurse educator and administrator.

When she became a nurse, training consisted of a three-year program that included two to five students caring for fifty patients, and twice-a-week lectures from a physician. On the floor, doctors didn't distinguish between students and trained nurses, and Lucille worried that she would be given orders that she would not know how to carry out. (She avoided the problem by cleaning bathrooms while the doctor made his rounds.) In their junior year students were allowed to give

the regular housefly. Psychologically, this treatment was very hard on the patient. No intensive care units were in use at the time. We took care of those critically ill patients in the same units with our regular medical and surgical patients.

When a patient died, it was up to the nurse to give the body a complete bath, put dentures in the mouth; if it was a surgical patient, apply clean dressings to the wound but first get all the old adhesive marks off with acetone — as we all know, acetone is not available for general use any more. The last thing done was to put packing in the rectum and vagina. The body was then taken to the hospital morgue and placed in storage until the mortician could pick it up. This was a rather "spookish" job at night. Of course the morgue was located in the hospital basement in the most out-of-the-way and darkest corner. I can still almost feel goose pimples going up and down my spine.

In a way, nurses were like a bunch of "zombies." We were always pressed for time and very much so at the chart desk. Along would come a doctor to check his patients' charts and we would have to jump up and stand at attention until he left and this would be repeated every time a doctor showed up. It is a miracle we ever got to class on time or off duty. In our nurses training, I swear we lived by the bells. They gonged us out of bed in the morning, gonged us to bed at night, even in the dining room we ate by the bell. The eating time was very short. If we were held up in surgery or the delivery room or because we were standing at attention at the chart desk, not getting our charting done, by the time we made it to the dining room we maybe had five minutes to go

medications, usually dispensed only by older nurses. Students were put on duty almost as soon as they entered training, and beginning students were instructed by seniors in an apprenticeship system that did not always work well.

Lucille told me about the first time she saw sulpha used for an infection. She was caring for a young girl with a streptococcus infection that had set into her jaw. Often such an infection could only be stopped by removing the bone surgically. The girl's face was swollen, her temperature rose to 105-106, and she was not expected to live through the night. But one evening, as Lucille was leaving work, the girl was given sulpha, and the next morning her temperature was normal. That cure seemed a miracle. Such advances in drug therapy changed also the profession of nursing. No longer were nurses barred even from taking temperatures. As drugs became more widely used, nurses extended their involvement from care-giving — keeping patients clean and comfortable — to greater responsibility in medical duties.

As health care grew increasingly to depend on nursing staffs, work loads became oppressive, and nurses realized they needed to organize for better working conditions. During the Depression, the American Nurses Association promoted the eight-hour work shift for nurses as a way of providing more people with employment. Before then, a nurse in private duty could be on the case twenty-four hours a day until her services were no longer needed. Nurses taking care of patients in a hospital were provided a cot to sleep on, and were only allowed to leave for a couple of hours in the afternoon to sleep or clean up, while the floor nurse was responsible for the patient. Usually, Lucille said, she spent that free time worrying about her

through the cafeteria line and eat. Then the superintendent of nurses would strike the bell and we had to get up and leave. You can well believe every dime we could get our hands on went to the corner drug for candy. We also found how to manipulate the locked lids of the icecream cans in the freezers in the storage room. This was our advantage only if we were on the 3 to 11 shift or nights.

Public health nursing meant shoveling myself out of snow banks in the winter while traveling from school to school or to the country homes for follow-up visits. We had no doctor in our county and I was the only RN at that time. I was in the county to promote public health — to teach the residents how to keep well. I was called out all hours of the night by people with sick children or other family members. I even delivered two babies, one of which was named after me. These were

jobs I shouldn't have been doing, but so far from medical help I had to.

In the country schools some of the teachers were having hot lunch programs of their own. The teachers and families took turns bringing a hotdish which was put on the large heater and by noon the kids had a nice hot dish along with their sandwiches, cookies, cake or whatever else they might have in the lunch pail. Quite a clever idea. After each rural school visit, follow-up visits were made in the farm homes of the children. This visit was to encourage parents to have their children's hearing, eyes and teeth checked by doctors or dentists. I was amazed to learn that the majority of parents did not realize the six-year molar is permanent, so naturally the six-year molar showed a great deal of neglect. Seven-year itch and headlice were prevalent. These home visits were also to explain the benefits of a well balanced diet plus the benefits of milk and fruit juices. In

patients because she knew the floor nurse was too busy to give them much attention, and she felt she might as well have stayed. A private duty nurse had no time for a private life. During training, nurses were not allowed to marry, and many who married were expelled from training programs. Pregnant nurses had to resign in their seventh month. Many nurses worked as private duty nurses in order to earn enough money to leave for larger cities and better jobs. "You could feel their sense of adventure," Lucille said, as they left to work in larger hospitals, see the world, and have new experiences.

To change the twenty-four hour scheduling, nurses knew they would meet opposition from physicians. In Grand Forks, nurses organized a dinner at which to present their proposal for the shorter work shifts, and invited physicians and prominent members of women's clubs. Doctors argued that shorter shifts would result in inferior care, but nurses said that difficult cases were wearing them out. The dinner party was not a success in persuading the physicians to the nurses' cause, but they won their argument anyway, for the hospital alumnae association and the District Nurses Association began making out cards for nurses that announced their availability for private duty on eight-hour shifts. The hospital helped to organize a registry, and soon the eight-hour shift became customary practice at hospitals across the state.

The first training school for nurses opened in 1901 at St. John's in Fargo, and by 1929 there were twenty in the state. The Nurse Practice Act of 1915 resulted in regulations of the practice of nursing and guidelines for the curriculum; it provided

---

one of these home visits, I asked the mother if she were giving her nine month old baby fruit juice daily. Her reply was, "Oh my yes, two or three bottles of nectar-water (Kool Aid) daily." So you see there was lots of room for explanations and education.

On another occasion, while still doing public health nursing, I visited a home in the summer or early fall. No screens on windows and no screen doors. The family was at the table, the flies were so thick I could scarcely see the food on the plates. I glanced around the kitchen and noticed about two dozen quart jars of what appeared to be home-canned candied peaches with plenty of raisins in each jar. This family, at the time, were complete welfare, so I went into my little talk about how much less sugar it would take for just plain canned peaches rather than making candied peaches and how

much better it would be for the kids. I mentioned that adding the raisins was fine. Well, much to my surprise and chagrin, the mother said, "Oh nurse, there aren't raisins, them's flies." I almost flipped my lid. My industrial nursing was at a construction site on an electric generating plant. My clinic nursing was very interesting also. Both these were in more recent years and modern equipment and measures were in use — so would be of less interest. I'm sure some things I've written of nursing in yesteryears seem impossible, but that is the way it was. I hope you have enjoyed this trip through the past.

Ruby Bishop Maurer was interviewed by Bonnie Clark.

for a Board of Nursing to inspect hospitals claiming to have "training schools." Yet several smaller schools could not meet minimal standards, and closed. Students provided most of the patient care, working 10-12 hours shifts with little or no supervision. Class size varied from 1 to 10 students, and each student cared for 6 to 25 patients a day. Class records were inadequate or absent. Students were paid $5 to $10 a month and lived in inadequate quarters.

While the demand for nurses during the First World War was crucial in professionalizing nursing and standardizing nursing care and training, home health care continued on a fairly informal basis in rural areas like North Dakota, into the 1930s and 1940s because hospitals and physicians were still not widely available. Berniece Holm, now an administrator at United Hospital in Grand Forks, tells how her mother, Gilma Carlsbraaten, of Esmond, North Dakota, used a brown leather-bound reference book in her home care nursing practice to treat any number of ailments from frostbite to broken bones. She gave hospice care to the dying.

Interviews conducted in 1987 by the State Nurses Association for their 75th anniversary give further insight into the every-day life of nurses. Responses, from 200 women who had been in nursing for 40 years or more show that they had a sense of humor, as well as a definite sense of self identity and pride. Many nurses talk about their long-standing friendships with colleagues. The most constant theme is that despite the hard work they would do it all over again. Their work brought great satisfaction and they treasured the people they met along the way. Responses also reflected on improvements in medical care, such as sulfa drugs, penicillin, polio vaccine, as well as modern equipment that gradually became available to treat conditions that earlier patients would have died from.

As we know, women became midwives to their neighbors because neighbor women needed help in childbirth when doctors were unavailable. When doctors and hospitals were distant, women took care of the sick and injured in their own families as best they could, and moved out to help among their neighbors. Daughters of these initial settlers who improvised, in the early decades of the twentieth century, continued their mother's tradition of healing, but on a more professional level. The daughters, like me, went to nursing school, and then became hospital nurses, public health nurses, teachers and administrators of nursing programs. They were continuing, they thought, a highly respected and valued tradition; they were doing "good" as women were supposed to do.

But something happened to the value placed on that tradition. As long as modern medical care was scarce, nurses in North Dakota were well regarded, whether "helping" as neighbors, or more formally trained. The pay was low, working conditions difficult, and their knowledge of medicine almost as limited as the equipment and medicines they had to work with. Nevertheless, neither the nurses nor their public doubted that theirs was a worthy profession. By the 1950s, after World War II, medical services improved rapidly in rural areas. Better roads, better communication, as well as medical advances and the building of more hospitals and schools of nursing brought the level of health care closer to the quality available in urban areas.

However, in the very years of such social and technological improvements, there came a changed ideology about women's work. The old idea that women gained value partly because they sacrificed themselves in hard work and low pay — which helped to define the idea of doing "good" — gave way to women's desires to advance in all professions, including nursing. Women should no longer sacrifice — since what was first a tradition of sacrifice was now considered exploitation. Women should set their goals the same way men did, toward self-advancement, higher salaries, and positions of actual power in administration. Health care is a more firmly sex-separated profession than most: most physicians are men and acquire the greatest amount of education and training and receive the highest pay, power, and prestige, whereas the seemingly secondary profession of nursing is largely held by women. Women as well as men have tended in the last thirty years or so to think poorly of nurses and of women who enter the profession. Nurses deserve to be secondary, if not inferior to doctors, according to such thinking, and women who become nurses probably deserve their inferior status for not aspiring to more ambitious professions.

These historical movements have been discouraging to women who have wanted to follow what they had thought was a useful, exciting, and even somewhat romantic line of work. Many have grown discouraged partly, I think, because they have been cut off from knowledge about their own history. While subjected to that

---

My grandmother, Ethel, and my grandfather, William Atkinson, were stricken at the same time with the 'flu on their isolated homestead on December 28, 1918. My grandmother was expecting their second child, and the first night she was ill with the 'flu the baby was born. Grandfather Atkinson was deathly ill but he managed to help deliver the baby. The little girl was born with the 'flu and died in my grandmother's arms two hours later.

When daylight came two strangers came riding up to the door through the snow to ask directions to a ranch some miles away. My grandfather managed to get to the door, and he asked them to go to the next homestead, about two miles away, and tell the neighbors who lived there what had happened so they could come and help. The riders said they would, but they never stopped anywhere at any of the neighboring places.

Miraculously, the neighbors, Mr. and Mrs. John Nester, arrived anyway that morning to check on them. When they discovered what had happened they went to work to do what they could for Ethel and Bill. Mary Nester bathed the little baby and dressed her in her white christen-ing gown and took her into Ethel so she could have a last look. John Nester went for another neighbor and together they made a little casket for the baby. Mary Nester lined it with white satin that she happened somehow to have. The men dug a grave and they laid the baby who was named Rachel Ann to rest on the hillside behind the house between two pine trees that Ethel and Bill had planted the year before.

Ann Berquist
Rhame, N. D.

history, they have been unaware of it; it is not mentioned in school courses, on the news, in ordinary conversation. My own growing realizations of this history has changed the way I see my work as a nurse and an instructor of nurses. My awareness has given me a way to connect myself to the past of women's experience with a feeling of continuity rather than tension and alienation. Understanding these changes gives all of us not only a connection to our past and firmer grounding in our present, but a vision of where we should be going as well.

References

Bower, Sister Carista. "The Women in White March Across the North Dakota Prairies," Master's Thesis. Grand Forks: University of North Dakota, 1950.

Cory, Margaret Heyse. *Nurse: A Changing Word in a Changing World: The History of the University of North Dakota College of Nursing, 1909-1982.* Grand Forks: University of North Dakota Centennial Committee, 1982.

Bonnie Clark grew up on a farm near Hazen, North Dakota. She teaches at the University of North Dakota College of Nursing, and is especially interested in women's health.

Kathleen Besse, Starkweather, N.D.
Photo courtesy *Minot Daily News.*

Hoping for Better Days

by Marjorie Flegel

I was born in 1934, in the middle of the drought and dust storms. As I grew up, I heard bits and pieces of stories about those times. Having since married and raised four children, and knowing the effort involved, I began to wonder how the women, most now in their seventies and eighties, coped during those years of drought and dust storms.

I interviewed five of these women in the Kulm, North Dakota area. These women were the daughters, in some cases the granddaughters of immigrants who came here to find a better life. And they did. Life was very good, compared to what they had previously. There was no reason to think things would change.

Christine Goehner remembers the dirt blowing into the entry and kitchen area of her house 10 miles southeast of Kulm. "That part of the house was older," she said, "and the windows were in bad shape, but we had no money to fix them. I used a coal shovel and broom to clean the dust from the window sills and floor every day. And before I could set the table for a meal, I would have to wash the table."

Christine and Fred, her husband, had a well and so could water a garden. She fed her ducks and chickens unsalable grain, screenings, table scraps and peelings. "Even the crumbs from the bread went to the chickens."

She sewed her own clothes, from new material when affordable, but mostly re-made. "I remade my wedding dress so I could have a Sunday dress for church." Christine also re-made clothing for the children from adult clothes. Each family member had one set of clothing for church, which was saved and taken care of. Everything else was much mended.

The government gave them potatoes to feed to their cows, and they bought straw and hay. "The potatoes were dyed blue so people wouldn't eat them, but once in

Carrie Kloebec Brandes came to LaMoure county in 1904; became post-master in 1945 after the death of her husband; then was head of the county's Selective Service. I interviewed her before she died (in 1981).

We came to Dakota from Iowa the 16th of March, 1904, and started school the next Monday. It had gone out over the telephone, "The newcomers are here, the newcomers are here. And they have five kids." We were very much welcomed. It was a tight community. When my sister Bessie turned 16 a month after we moved here, they came and had a surprise party on us. Somebody brought a violin and somebody chorded the piano. We danced and danced. We weren't prepared for 25 people dancing in two rooms. Everything went out that possibly could.

There was no corn raised here when we came. I believe it was too harsh a country. But there were all kinds of grain, like flax and wheat and rye and barley. But no corn for years. My mother planted sweet corn and it froze. She thought she'd be smart and plant peanuts and sent to a seed house in Iowa. And everything froze the 18th of August — cucumbers, squash, everything froze. But it seemed like as the country got more settled and trees were planted, we didn't have those early frosts. They raised vast quantities. I still plant a few hills of potatoes just to prove I can.

A bachelor in the neighborhood went to Minnesota to get his bride and we decided to surprise them with a chivaree. It was in April, already dark, the chores had to be done first. They had gone to bed. They brought their pie tins and dish pans and pails and rattled them outside the window. They brought music with them, one had a fiddle and one an accordion. Oh, we did have fun. We took down the bed and danced in two rooms. It was so wonderful that Bessie and I could dance.

And hair. We put it up as soon as we could. I got myself a switch. A switch is a hairpiece. You could twist it up any way. We'd snarl our hair up just terrible and use kind of a filler called a rat. We had curls in front and bangs. Bessie had long hair, long braids, and for Christmas she would let it hang down. Mother would braid it up wet so it would be wavy. I'd be so jealous, but then I'd get curls with a curling iron, got my ears burned.

Bessie got married when she was 19 and I was left behind. I never went to high school and neither did she. I went to summer school one summer and taught in a country school. I went to Valley City for summer school and thought I'd die of homesickness. I couldn't come home and my mother wasn't much of a letter writer, but I got my certificate. I taught at a school over west about four miles. They could never get a teacher to teach over there because no one would board her. I only taught there one year and then I came to town to work for Porter and Crum. I was 21 years old. That's the year I met my husband, Carl.

How foolish I talk of the past, but that's the way it was. We came here when Bessie was 15, Edwin and Bill were older and George was younger. I'm the only one left.

Gayle Schuck
Bismarck, N.D.

a while there were some not dyed, and those we did eat."

One of Christine's happier memories is baking bread. "I want to say, even if I have to say it myself, I baked very good bread during those years. There isn't bread anywhere that tastes as good as it did then."

What Esther Miller remembers, her grandchildren don't believe. "To them it sounds like fiction. Like dust storms that completely shut out the sun. It was like a blizzard, only instead of snow it was dirt."

She also remembers not having enough money for a stamp. "We took wheat to the Kulm Mill and exchanged it for ground flour," she said. "We took eggs to town and traded them for a few groceries. I made sure I didn't buy more groceries than there was egg money." The money from the sale of cream paid for gasoline for the car and tractor. Flour sacks were bleached and used for dish towels, slips and underwear. The sacks that the chick feed came in were used for aprons or dresses for herself or her daughter.

Miller's well went dry during this time. "We dug a well by hand by a spring, put a hand pump on it, and were able to provide water for the livestock and house. There was no water for the garden. In 1936 I planted potatoes and other garden seeds and nothing came up. The ground stayed black."

Taking care of their two children, worrying about food and clothing was stressful, she said. "Sometimes we wondered if we would ever have a crop again," she said. "We lived from day to day, hoping for better days to come."

The women all worried about lack of rain for crops and gardens, but there were other problems as well. Margaret Herman remembers planting a garden in 1935 just over a rise from her house. "One day I went over to check it, and the grasshoppers had eaten it all," she recalls. "There wasn't a thing left."

Herman's farm had no well, and Richard, Margaret's husband, dug many holes by hand "all over the farm" looking for water. He finally found it close to a small creek, and covered the well with boards. A team of horses lent to them by his father moved the boards, and one horse fell into the well head first and drowned.

They lived in an old schoolhouse. "I swept dirt out every morning. We also had bees in the wall, and got five gallons of honey, which was really lucky. We had cows, chicken, flour and sugar to live through the winter. The winters were very cold during those years. One year we had six weeks of minus 15 degrees or colder. My husband went to town with the neighbor, on a stone boat pulled by horses, to get kerosene and sugar. I made cookies and candy for Christmas presents. I had no money to buy anything."

They sold cream, and grain, when they had any to sell, and sometimes had to charge groceries. Paying the bills later kept them back "like elastic." They got government commodities of a quarter of beef, beans and prunes. They also bought a pressure cooker from the government for six dollars. Some cattle starved from lack of feed and grass. The government killed excess cattle, allowing farmers to have only the number they could feed. The farmers had no say about this, and were paid for each cow or calf that was shot.

The dirt in the yard blew back and forth like sand dunes and swirled around the buildings, Margaret remembers. "We burned cow chips for cooking and baking, and for warmth. We would get a wagon load and put them in the granary, because there was no grain in it. We cut buck brush (a woody type of weed) for burning."

Margaret picked plums by Edgeley for $1 per bushel and made jelly. "Sometimes all we had was bread, butter and jelly," she said. "I made my own soap, washed on a washboard." They got a government check "maybe twice" for having no grain.

Rose Steinmetz was still at her parents' home 14 miles southwest of Kulm during the drought and dust storms. Her mother had 11 children to feed. "I know my mother spent many sleepless nights worrying about what to feed her children, but she never complained, and took those years quite well, considering everything. When we went to church Sunday mornings we had to have the lights on, in order to see the road, and sometimes we had trouble seeing it even then. The ditches were full; the fences had caught rolling thistles and filled up with dirt. Even the cemetery was filled in — just the tops of the tombstones showed."

Rose's father had a lot of oats and corn left in granaries, and they used that to feed a few geese and chickens. They also kept cows to milk. Some of the cows died and her father cut open one to find the cause. He found its intestines and stomachs filled with dirt.

Some of the older children occasionally worked for neighbors for board and room and one or two dollars a month. They gave the money to their mother. They always had a well, but all the sloughs were dry. The buildings were gray because the dirt and wind blasted off the paint. "It always seemed gloomy. It was miserable getting the cows in the barn, the eyes got full of dirt."

Before Nora Gackle married she worked as a store clerk. She and her husband, John, moved back to Kulm when they married in 1932. Nora worked at a lunch counter in the Farmer's Store, and John was a barber, each making $20 per month. Living in a rented room, they managed to put aside enough to buy a house for $800 in 1933. They continued to live in the room and rented out the house. They became managers of a cafe in Kulm about 1934.

"People just seemed to need an outlet," Nora said. "They would come into our cafe and buy themselves a treat. One woman came in and had a strawberry sundae whenever she had the money." Pie (made by Nora) was 10¢. "Meals were about 35¢, ice cream, 10¢. We had one girl to wait tables, full time. She made $2.50-$3 per week. There was little charging, and no families, only individuals." The cafe bought milk from local farmers and purchased meat from the meat market in town. When farmers came to town on business, they brought their lunches into the cafe to eat it. "We didn't mind, because we knew times were hard."

These women improvised and made do. They used every scrap for something — bread crumbs for the chickens, feed sacks for items of clothing — and were creative in the face of adversity. If they were lucky enough to have a goose to butcher, the skin was cut into pieces and rendered. The pieces of fried skin, or cracklings, were reheated for breakfast, and the goose lard was spread on bread and sprinkled with salt for a sandwich. They and their families did not have a varied diet during those years, and there were few luxuries. Even after the drought and dust storms were gone, they lived carefully in order to pay off debts, which held them back, like "elastic," for years.

Majorie Flegel has lived on a farm all of her life near Kulm, North Dakota.

The 1940s

by Edna M. Boardman

I lived my teens during the forties on a farm near Benedict, a small town in north central North Dakota. My summer chores began with hand milking at 4:00, as soon as it was light, and often ended with helping unload hay in the dark. In the winter I shivered through the icy morning darkness to feed the chickens, then ran out to gather newlaid eggs before they froze and cracked. At night I turned the hand crank on the machine that separated the cream, washed the milk pails, then ran to the house in the moonlit shadows. The rhythm of work was much as it had been when my mother and grandmother were young. My parents, first generation Germans from Russia, revered hard work. But changes swept through our lives in the decade of the forties, and we welcomed many of them as a great bettering of our lot, especially in the lives of women.

We could see this change taking place in the ways we cared for clothing. When the 1940s began, my mother, Ella Berg, and her mother, Margaret Faul, did laundry always on Monday — with a tub, washboard, and bar soap they'd made from lye and fat rendered during butchering. They wrung the wet clothes by twisting them with their hands, and starched everything that would be ironed with a product that had to be boiled (even that was an improvement over an earlier starch made from potatoes). They carried water from the well or slough with pails, heated the water on a stove for which they had gathered the fuel, then carried the pails to the slop-pile outdoors when the washing was done. They boiled white cottons, often with lye added to the water, and hung each item early in the morning sun both to enhance the pristine whiteness of their linens, and to impress neighbors with their house-wifely efficiency. If the weather turned stormy, they might have to take the clothes in and hang them out a second time. The women hand sprinkled those that needed ironing, using a dish of water. On Tuesday, they ironed with heavy sadirons heated on a hot cookstove. The iron stayed hot about five minutes before it had to be exchanged for another. To heat the stove, they carried fuel from the coalbin or gathered and chopped wood. They usually baked bread on ironing day to take full advantage of the fuel, so ironing day began with the mixing and kneading of dough, and ended with carrying out ashes from the stove. The perfect stiffness, whiteness, and smoothness of their husbands' shirts marked them as excellent wives.

Then along came a wooden washing machine powered with a handle that worked back and forth while you stood upright. No more bending over the washboard. Commercially made bar soaps were available, but still had to be shaved with a knife into the wash water. Liquid bluing, added to the rinse water, made white appear whiter. Spring clothespins replaced the one-piece wooden ones. A sprinkler head that could be fitted onto the top of a glass bottle made it easier to sprinkle clothes evenly.

With the invention of the small gasoline motor, the motor-driven washing machine with the roller wringer meant cleaner clothes with far less work. A hand-worked pump, which was a small version of the pump at the outside well, drew the water from a cistern. Water still had to be heated on the stovetop, carried to the machine, and then carried outdoors after the last load was done. Soon, the water was drawn from the cistern, with a special pump, activated by demand, which brought the water into the kitchen as needed. This water was acceptable for washing, but water for drinking was still hand-carried from a well. The washline and sprinkler bottle remained, but the carbide iron and the electric iron powered by a low voltage on-farm power plant made it all easier.

When full-voltage rural electricity finally came, near the end of the decade, a quiet-running electric motor replaced the noisy, smelly, problem-ridden gasoline motor. Powdered, commercially-made soaps were used at least part of the time. My aunt Gertrude Berg remembers Hi-lex as a fine innovation, because clothes could be whitened with a relatively mild chemical, without boiling. A clothing starch appeared on the market that could simply be mixed with cool water. The water system on most farms was now more sophisticated, tapping directly into a clear well and draining into a scientifically-designed septic tank. Electricity quickly heated the iron and kept it at a uniform temperature even in a cool house. Standards for our family's clothing remained high, with the whiteness of the husband's all-cotton shirts in church on Sunday still especially important. But now making it happen was easier.

Finally, in the late forties (or the early fifties in some homes) the modern washing machine arrived, with a spinning action to wring clothes. An electric or gas water heater warmed the water, and plumbing brought the water into the machine and drained it away automatically. We used powdered detergents, some containing bluing crystals, milder bleaches, and spray starch. With the electric dryer the source of neighbors' knowledge about the state of our clothing disappeared, and with it the social significance of when washing was being done and how white the white clothing and linen was. Wash and wear meant that many articles did not have to be ironed at all. The steam iron eliminated the sprinkling, making it possible to skip the step of sprinkling and rolling each garment and waiting for the moisture to absorb evenly. An attendant social and economic difference was that with laundry made easier, we all changed clothes more often. The emphasis moved from smooth and white and starched, to style. But the work never again got to be as hard as it had been.

Meat preparation had been, by long tradition, the result of arduous labor involving all available hands. Both men and women in our family worked hard to feed and care for cattle, hogs, and poultry. The cool days of fall brought butchering, with the slaughter of these animals, cutting and grinding the meat for sausage, and preserving by curing, smoking, and canning. By the end of the forties, almost none of this work except raising the animals was still done by us. The abattoir in Minot made its slaughtering services available to farmers. Public locker plants were erected where we could rent lockers to store the meat. When this proved inconvenient, what with thefts of meat and the long distance to town, people bought home freezers. Home economists hired by the Home Extension agencies of the Department of Agriculture came to teach farm women how to use their freezers. When my mother put flash-frozen packages of meat from town into her freezer, she had hundreds of hours less work to do than she'd done the year before. As the work disappeared, so did long-familiar food items such as smoked sausage, liver sausage, and head cheese. Gone was the need for family and neighbor hands to help with the work and the camaraderie we associated with butchering time.

It became increasingly clear to us that electricity was the key to making our work easier. This was certainly not a repudiation of the work ethic because we tended to raise expectations and there always remained more than enough to do. As we yearned for full-power electricity, we clutched at all sorts of make-do precursors. My grandfather installed a carbide plant that produced a gas that heated our iron and lit the house with an eerie harsh glow. This was followed by six-volt batteries charged first with a wind charger mounted on the barn, then with a tall free-standing charger. The batteries gave us light and powered the radio so we could listen to "Fibber McGee and Molly" and a popular Minot preacher who read endless song dedications. But it was hard to keep the batteries charged, for summer storms often blew down the chargers. Then my father installed a 32-volt system powered by a gasoline motor, and we got special appliances — a toaster and a motor for the washing machine — that would work with this voltage.

Then it seemed that the government discovered us and developed a philosophy that we deserved help in making our lives better. The most spectacular thing it did for us was rural electrification, because when we finally got electricity in 1947, all the mechanical helpers we'd dreamed of became ours.

We bought appliances, sometimes going to the "slightly damaged" outlets, as fast as we could scrape up the money for them. The lights, to begin with, were bare bulbs, but these were soon replaced with fixtures. In just two or three years, we had a toaster, an iron, a waffle iron, a vacuum cleaner, an electric mixer, a radio, a record player (and about a dozen 78 rpm religious records we played over and over), a hot water heater, a refrigerator, an electric range, a freezer, a pump to bring water into the house, another motor for the washing machine, and a fan to cool the house during hot summer nights.

My father and grandfather learned to do their own electrical work, and in our farmyard, motors hummed everywhere. Electricity replaced the windmill that pumped water for the cattle. It ran an electrical milking machine to milk 20 cows and the separator that produced cream we sold to buy groceries. We soon had a heat lamp to warm the young chicks in the spring and a tank of pressurized air to fill flat tires quickly. Electricity powered an auger to take the work out of shoveling grain from the truck into the bin. It ran the grain cleaner, the feed grinder, and the welder that saved my dad long trips to the blacksmith's shop in town. The home extension agents I mentioned earlier visited homemakers' clubs and taught cooking, canning, and sewing. County agents gave advice on grains and animals. 4-H clubs helped young people develop independence by encouraging them to raise their own animals. I was never a part of these clubs, because of their distance from us and because of my family's German-Russian philosophy that kept us from associating with other ethnic and religious groups. But on the radio and occasionally in the county newspaper, I heard and read about these opportunities. I saw that there was a wonderful world out there, and thought that surely others didn't have to work as hard as I did, or at least did more interesting things.

Enter the automobile. How we loved cars. My grandfather William Faul, the family story went, had one of the first in the community. He got someone to take him to Minot, bought a car, nodded as the salesman explained how it worked, and drove it home by himself, learning to drive along the way. The men of my family figured out how the mechanics worked and tinkered constantly. In the early forties, a complete overhaul job was still necessary before we undertook a trip to visit relatives in Harvey, less than a hundred miles away. My father Emil Berg spread pieces of car motor over a quarter acre of ground, with the firmest instructions to my sister Vivian and me not to touch anything. Part by part he washed and examined everything, replacing gaskets and anything else that was worn. The roads were rough gravel, and we could count on at least one flat tire on the way. In the late fall, the car was put up on blocks to ease the pressure on the tires, and wasn't used until spring.

By the end of the forties, we could use the car year 'round. The roads were still gravel and given to drifting shut in the winter, but we never retired the car entirely. The heater warmed slowly. We were never really warm until we were near our destination, so we always took plenty of blankets along. The men still knew the mechanical workings of our vehicles and did their own routine servicing, but overhauling was no longer needed so often. How the cars expanded our horizons! They took us often to Minot, thirty miles away, for shopping, for piano lessons, and for occasional eating out. It became easy to run to town for parts for the machines, to the neighbors for socializing, to the fair, to the doctor (formerly done only in the most extreme emergency), and to church. My parents went to Yellowstone park, bringing back a big chunk of obsidian, as everyone did), and dreamed of one day going to California. My parents and grandfather traded for a new car every year or two, and we always found the new models bigger and more smooth-riding and fancier in style.

The extent and rapidity of other changes can best be appreciated in retrospect.

My mother gradually stopped sewing our clothing and began buying it, even as the available fabrics, patterns and machines improved. Many new labor-saving food products appeared: Crisco, Jello, Sure-Jel, canned fruits and vegetables, sliced bakery bread, cake and pudding mixes. We moved out our wood-coal range, switched to a kerosene stove, then to a propane stove, and finally to the clean, convenient electric stove. Cooking utensils began with iron pots to be replaced with aluminum, copper-clad aluminum, and finally stainless steel. Other farms not too far from us got the telephone, but we did not get it until the fifties. Birth control became socially acceptable and available. Childbirth moved from the home to the hospital, as did the care of medical emergencies. Tetanus shots and penicillin appeared. Permanents began as complicated beauty shop operations I associated with scalp burns from electric heating equipment. They quickly became available to the home when the chemicals were perfected.

Innovations in chicken raising (each summer we raised about 300 chickens for our own use and for sale) began with the home incubator and the brooder house. Gone were the brooding hens we called clucks. A coal-burning stove, used to warm the chicks, was replaced with one burning oil or kerosene, which was replaced in turn with an electric heat lamp. Soon factories incubated the chicks and we bought them live. By the end of the forties, the raising and slaughter of chickens for food and eggs gradually moved production away from our farm, and we simply bought packages in the grocery store.

Almost everything, in this sharply telescoped period of time, whether high or low-tech, showed this kind of change. Even then we wondered at its accessibility to us. The makeup of our community changed as well. Neighbors sold their land and went to work in Minot or Oregon or California. We missed them. Photographers several decades later saw the decaying farmsteads as romantic, but they did not seem romantic to us.

Farming changed significantly for those of us who managed to stay. Rubber tires replaced metal lugs on tractors at the beginning of the decade, and the big green John Deere tractors my dad bought were always bigger and more powerful and had more features as the years went along. The disks and drills, always larger than before, made it possible for him to cover ever more land alone. Bales replaced loose hay. Most of the money earned on the farm, it seemed, went into new machinery.

No machine helped us as much as the combine. It had been in existence since the twenties, but was troublesome and expensive. It was not perfected until the forties, when the departure of young farm men for the war made it essential to find a way to accomplish the harvest with fewer hands. (The need to maintain a very high level of food production was ever-present because of the war.) The harvest season became shorter as each farmer in our community had only his own land to attend to. The combine was advertised to women as well as to men. In one advertisement, the farm family that used the combine was shown in its car leaving for a vacation. The neighbors, who used traditional threshing methods (the binder and threshing machine), were shown still laboring in the fields.

We women learned that it was easier to drive a grain truck and to use the hoist and auger to unload the grain than it was to produce the huge high-quality meals necessary to feed a threshing crew. My aunt Emma Berg tells of an incredibly demanding day of doing it all alone, cooking three large meals plus three snacks. She also had the normal animal-care chores to do without help. Mavis Vix, a neighbor who still farms with her husband Wesley near Sawyer, says, "When I was a girl, I thought I'd never be able to get married because I'd never be able to cook for threshers. Grandmother wished something could be invented to do away with threshing, but couldn't imagine what." The popularity of the threshing show in the eighties in many small towns near my home reveals that threshing fulfilled social needs as it got the work done. Farmers and townspeople drift about in nostalgia for a day at the threshing shows. But few women who carried the burden of producing good food (or had a negative reputation for not living up to the community's standards) mourn the passing of Cooking for Threshers.

Education was not valued very highly in my German-Russian family. My mother barely finished the sixth grade; my father the eighth grade. Neighbors who spent time reading were held in some contempt. "There he sits and reads while the tractor sits in the field and the summer fallow turns green." The term "educated fool" was applied to anyone with as much as a few months of college. Somehow an educated person's farming errors stood out above everyone else's. Allowances were made for the minister, the banker, the doctor, and the teacher, who obviously had to know things other people didn't, but learning for its own sake was the province of our Scandinavian neighbors, and we didn't know or understand them very well.

What education there was, through our rural school, was as available to girls as to boys, though there was an idea that education for women especially was a waste. When my sister and I persisted through high school, people in church would cluck with disapproval and say, "Are you girls *still* going to school?" Yet when I finally knew someone who went to college, it was a woman. She wanted to be a teacher or missionary, which was all right, and after all, the comments went, she probably wouldn't be the one to take over the family farm anyway. Not until the fifties did young people from our social group generally go to high school and then to college.

Our church was an extremely important part of our lives. It shaped our values and the faith we learned there served as our "invisible means of support" as we went about our tasks. The church provided a center through which we got to know others in our community. How terribly isolated I would have been without Sunday school. The emphasis in our Mennonite faith revolved around personal piety and morality and knowledge of the scriptures. Old animosities brought from Europe persisted as the issues in our ministers' sermons, and we were taught to fear and distrust neighbors who went to other churches. Marriage outside my narrowly-defined faith was depicted to me as a family disaster and a sure route to hell. Birth control within marriage was tacitly accepted as it became available, and families of four or fewer were becoming the norm in our group. In my community, youth meetings, Bible school and camp, songfests, harvest festivals, Sunday evening and midweek worship, and revival meetings became major social events. Whether one was "saved" or not was an important social marker. We were not allowed to go to movies or dances or sports events of any kind. I never knew anyone who drank or played cards. My relatives tell me that these were attitudes stricter than in previous decades, and it represented an effort to control young people that couldn't be maintained when television, youth ownership of cars, and universal attendance at high school, came along.

Saturday night at Benedict or Velva was an institution in our community. My mother, sister, and I washed and set our hair, wrapped scarves around our heads, and we all headed for town for two or three hours. Clusters of older people sat on benches and visited in German or Russian or Norwegian. Sometimes Youth for Christ held meetings lest we be tempted to wanton entertainments like roller skating to popular music. There was also the interest in saving our souls if we had not made the commitment elsewhere. Clusters of us young people would link up and walk up and down the streets, spend our tiny allowances (none of us was paid for our work on the farm), and go home.

The languages of the immigrants were gradually relinquished in our community during the forties. I understood the German dialect my parents and grandparents spoke, but never learned to speak it. I was often amused as I listened to the adults visit on a Sunday afternoon. Their sentence structure would be German, but the operative words were English. The men would say "Ein combine," or "Ein tractor." They used so many English words I wondered why they bothered with the German. They seemed to need an interim language between the old and the new. My church continued to seek ministers who could preach in German one Sunday a month. The German language was greatly revered by my grandparents William and Margaret Faul and Sam and Kathryn Keller, and they spoke with pain of its passing into disuse. I wanted to dissassociate myself from it, and today remember only a smattering.

Our work as women on the farm was extremely valuable. I never felt that we occupied some kind of pedestal or had a second class status. We were expected to produce to perfection and without complaining within the home among the animals, in the field, and in the church and community. Our surroundings were to be clean; we were to cook and can and sew and be available to help in the yard and in the fields. "Good worker" was our ultimate accolade. Our efforts had the solid economic value that city women later found in paid jobs.

In all this, I believe, we lost significant traditional independence and self-sufficiency. We became more dependent on money and materials, including especially electricity, from the outside. But for the most part, we saw our lives getting better and better during the forties. So much in the hard old days was behind us. We did not foresee that we would do anything but continue a positive move forward.

Edna Boardman grew up on a farm near Benedict, North Dakota. She is library media specialist at Minot High School and historian of the History and Archives Committee of the United Methodist Church in North Dakota. She lives in Minot.

Mission School, Fort Totten Indian Agency
(Devils Lake), 1881. Photo courtesy of the Haynes Foundation Collection, Montana Historical Society, Helena.

Grey Nuns

by Eleanor Merrow

Devils Lake Reservation is situated in a pocket of fertile rolling hills and woodlands in northeast North Dakota. Game and bird-life were abundant in the nineteenth century, and the variety of wild berries attracted many pickers. Small lakes dot the region. Devils Lake, stretching fifty miles east to west, comprises the northern border of the reservation, with the Sheyenne River forming the southern border.

In 1867 the Sisseton, Wahpeton and Yanktonnai Sioux signed a treaty that established the reservation. The Yanktonnai Sioux came from the western plains; they were followed by the Sisseton and Wahpeton Sioux from the Minnesota woodlands after they were driven away following the 1862 uprising there. The 1867 treaty required that before an agency could be established, 500 Sioux would have to settle on the reservation, and it was not until 1871 that an agent was appointed. Although the Devils Lake Sioux received some help from the military, many perished from hardship in the four intervening years of the reservation.

The Roman Catholic Church became involved in the Devils Lake Reservation through what was known as President Grant's peace policy, whereby, in the 1870s, a single Christian denomination supervised each reservation, and replaced the generally corrupt political appointees. Supervising churches had the right to nominate all agency employees, and accepted an unstated obligation to set up a mission school. The government hoped that installing the churches in such a position would hasten Indian assimilation into white society.

The Grey Nuns who arrived at the Devils Lake Sioux Indian Reservation in 1874 brought with them a history of frontier mission work across Canada. Founded in 1738 in Montreal, their name is said to have originated in an early attempt to discredit them as *les soeurs grises*, a double entendre meaning both the grey nuns and the drunken nuns. They countered the pun with the adoption of their gray habits.

Although individuals were considered subordinate to mission work, a few facts about the four founding sisters can be gleaned from their papers in the Archives Soeurs Grises de Montreal in St. Boniface (now within Winnipeg), Manitoba. Sister Rose Clapin had had fifteen years experience in St. Boniface (she was the local superior), and was noted as a gardener. The other three began work in the motherhouse in Montreal. Sister Lajemmerais-Chenier was trained in medicine, and at Devils Lake worked nearly to exhaustion in health care. Sister Philomene Drapeau had charge of the school boys; she took them on camping trips and engaged in their games. Of the four founders she lived the longest on the reservation. Sister Celine Allard was in charge of the school girls, and she chronicled the early mission life (her writings are referred to as the Fort Totten Chronicles). Their number increased to eleven by the turn of the century.

The Grey Nuns' primary activity on the Devils Lake reservation was to run the vocational boarding school for the Sioux children. Their contract with the United States government allowed them food rations from the government store. The Sisters opened the school within a few weeks of their arrival on the reservation, as soon as they could get the schoolhouse cleaned, woodstoves installed, and clothing made for the first pupils. Sisters and students communicated entirely through an interpreter, with the children speaking in Dakota, the Sisters in French, and all working to learn English.

According to the Fort Totten Chronicles, the diet was poor that first year: residents existed on salt-pork, lake fish, flour, lard and water. The sisters and students had no coal oil to light lamps, using candles at supper and the light from the stovefires to dress for bed. They provided school supplies and material for clothing to the students, who constructed most of their own garments under the Sisters' instruction. The Sisters accomplished a good deal of the training and teaching of their students by involving the children in sewing, cooking, husbandry, and cleaning. At timesthe work must have been difficult and tedious for the children, but there were occasional rewards which came with achievement, as when one student won a blue ribbon at the regional fair for a pair of knit stockings (Report of the Commissioner of Indian Affairs 1888).

Besides the vocational work and the usual school subjects, the Sisters also taught the students to play the piano, sing, and act in plays, and often provided opportunities for the students to display their skills before gatherings of agency personnel, military officers, or other Sioux.

Relations between students and Sisters were difficult, especially at the outset. In order to obtain an enrollment at the school, the Sisters traveled to Sioux homes to recruit children. In August 1875 Sister Allard wrote to the motherhouse, "It is no small task to tear them away from their parents and their prairies." During the first few years, students frequently ran away from school, and so the recruiting of children was an ongoing task. Although many parents had been glad to have the Sisters, and to send their children to the school, it was another thing to expect the children to adjust readily to the school routines and the organization of a boarding school. Thus there was a good deal of talk against the school. It could not win acceptance without some adaptation on the part of the Sisters as well. They were careful to comply with the children's and parents' wishes in matters of dress, allowing those who asked to wear long hair and traditional Sioux attire. Early in the school year, many afternoons were spent in the woods gathering nuts and berries. "With this improvement in the class schedule," Sister Allard wrote in 1882, "it costs the children less to leave their homes: they find here what kept them away." In spring and summer students and sisters picnicked or went camping. The Sisters were not averse to strong incentives, however, such as depriving students of vegetables until they did their share of gardening.

The Sisters and a few Sioux women worked up a garden plot by the school that first spring. Their journal for that year reports a yield of 175 bushels of potatoes, nine bushels of turnips, five bushels of onions, and 150 bushels of cabbages. The harvest increased over the years; new varieties were added, as were flowers, trees and animals. In 1879, Sisters Clapin and Lajemmerais homesteaded some land on Stump Lake, just east of the reservation boundary. They made the claim in Grand Forks the next summer, after having a cabin built and some land plowed. Although they never lived on the land, the Sisters used it for retreats or day-trips with the students.

The Sisters leased the farm operation to a Catholic family in exchange for a certain amount of butter, chickens, grain, half the income from marketed livestock, and half the wool produced. In this way, the Sisters assured themselves of a varied diet and defended themselves against shortages in government rations, which plagued the school from the beginning.

The Sisters' food production also improved their status on the reservation. They helped the hungry and the sick with gifts of food, and served food to visitors on

Marion Russ Whitman and her brother and sister were raised by their father on the farm he homesteaded in 1903 in Kidder County. In order for the children to go to school they lived away from home during the few months of the school, but according to Marion, "Papa always saw to it that we boarded with good Christian families." Marion became a teacher and taught at Lake Williams Township until she was married in 1913, in her father's home, to an ambitious bachelor named Frank Whitman. After two years a chubby son joined them, and every two years or so they were joined by another, until there were six healthy boys.

Hilda Carlson
Bismarck, N.D.

special holidays. Each year, for example, the journals report that their parlors were filled with Sioux, singing, chatting and eating on New Year's day. Thus, in small ways, the Sisters' efforts at gardening improved the quality of life on the reservation, and especially at the boarding school.

The Grey Nuns had been recruited by the Devils Lake agent because he antici-pated that they would become involved in health care in addition to teaching school; that obligation increased when the agency physician left his post shortly before the Sisters arrived, and the agent turned over medical responsibilities to Sister Lajemmerais. It was through the care of the sick that the Sisters had the most contact, and ironically the most conflict, with the Sioux. The Sisters held the conviction that health care should be a gift shared with all — Catholic or not, Indian or white; at the same time their skill in medicine was a part of the Euro-American culture that challenged Indian practices such as the medicine dance.

Sisters Clapin and Lajemmerais, accompanied by an interpreter, visited the sick, by horse and wagon when available, more often on foot. If they had a wagon, they often went up to twenty miles to make a call. In addition to treatment of common illnesses, they tried to teach the Sioux how to care for themselves and how to contain epidemics, according to Bureau of Catholic Indian Missions papers.

In spite of their dedication, the Sisters were unhappy about accepting the responsibilities of agency physician because that involved treating all of the Sioux and agency workers' illnesses, making out monthly government reports, and housing the pharmacy. Sister Lajemmerais was often called away, sometimes for

**Indian tree burial.
Denver Public Library,
Western History Department.
Courtesy of UND Special Collections.**

days, and her absences increased the workload for the Sisters at the school. Nor were the Sisters paid for the physician's work, those responsibilities having simply been added onto their school contract. In all the Sisters received $2,000 in 1878-79. The same year, the military physician received $400 for his part-time services attending to cases which the Sisters were forbidden by their constitution to handle, such as venereal disease, childbirth and surgery. In spite of these obstacles, Sister Lajemmerais continued for many years as agency physician, an arrangement that ensured a close working relationship with the agent, which was essential to the mission. By 1883, Sister Lajemmerais, exhausted by medical responsibilities, relinquished her official duties.

Caring for the sick was, nevertheless, a duty to which the four Sisters were faithful both before accepting the physician's responsibilities, and after relinquishing them. One Sister wrote in 1884, "It goes without saying that this [visiting the Indian sick] does them good; they have much confidence in the Sisters, and in this way, we win many of them to our holy religion" (Fort Totten Chronicles 1884). The Sisters noted two instances when Sioux leaders came to the mission for baptism with their medicine sacs ready to hand over, to symbolize the abandonment of that part of their lives.

One of the hardest things for Sioux parents to do was to leave a very sick child with the Sisters. At times, these situations led to tremendous arguments between Sisters and parents. The Sisters' journal tells of an instance in 1874 when they locked a sick child in the dormitory away from its mother while "reasoning with her for an hour"; another in 1898 when a mother dragged her sick boy out of bed while he clung to the Sister's habit and everybody argued over him.

From the beginning of the Sisters' tenure on the reservation, Indians who were sick occasionally came to stay with them or called the Sisters to their homes. When the school received an addition in 1878, a hospital was established in one wing. The Sisters had hoped the hospital would serve to isolate the diseased both from the healthy and from their traditional medicine. However, as Sister Allard wrote to the motherhouse in July 1879, "the hospital is occupied from time to time, the sick who come never stay long, they are so unaccustomed to a sedentary life." In time the Sisters realized that a hospital was unsuited to the Sioux culture. Late in 1882, in spite of the agent's wishes to the contrary, the Sisters closed the hospital.

The Sioux and the sisters also were at odds over the essential rites of death. The Sioux tradition of mourning the dead involved immediate disrobing, embracing the corpse, dancing, and loud lamentations, practices that contrasted with the more reserved Catholic use of music and prayer, and their treatment of the body. From the Sisters' point of view, the Sioux's nudity was intolerable. The lamentations, however, drew varied reactions. At times, the Sisters were genuinely moved by them; at other times, they considered them only clamorous. Another point of conflict was over interment of the dead, which the Sioux abhorred, preferring to suspend the body horizontally eight or ten feet in the air.

After the Sisters' arrival on the reservation, the Sioux held more frequent medicine dances out of fear, it was said, that the Sisters' medicine might be stronger than theirs. After receiving a visit from a group of Sioux dressed for a dance, Sister Allard wrote, "I found they had the air of devils rather than of human beings.

However, upon observing them closely, one discovers something likable" (Fort Totten Chronicles 1874). Soon the Sioux avoided the Sisters when they were dressed for the dance.

The overall conditions the Sisters found when they arrived at the reservation were dismal. Indian morale was very low. Shortages of supplies were frequent due to the remote location of the reservation. These were only a few of the many troubles to be overcome, but the Sisters tackled them pragmatically: helping with food shortages by raising huge gardens; teaching the Sioux to combat some of the whites' diseases such as whooping cough, and caring for their sick; even drawing the military officers into their circle of supporters.

The Grey Nuns' tradition of community life, which proved appropriate to frontier living, can be credited with giving them a good deal of their strength and versatility. Community life prepared them well for the inevitable necessity of sharing and pitching in; it helped them understand the politics of living in the insular community of the reservation; and community life allowed the Sisters to easily enlarge their workforce as their mission grew.

While the Sisters were dedicated to their religion, they had their feet firmly planted in the temporal world. In their ministry to the Sioux, the Sisters were realistic enough to address material and physical needs at hand before spiritual needs. Baptism was not a price to be exacted for health care, or schooling, or other aid. These Grey Nuns were not single-minded, prudish women with little knowledge of the world at large. Rather, their realistic assessment of the situation at Devils Lake Reservation, their willingness to work long and hard, their versatility, and their generosity all contributed to improving the quality of reservation life in its early years.

References

Archives Soeurs Grises de Montreal, St. Boniface, Manitoba:

  Annales, vol. 17, 1921.

  Constitutions des Soeurs de la Charities. Montreal: L'Hopital-General de Montreal, 1880.

  Ecole de St. Michel Photographs, vol. 1

  Fort Totten Chronicles, 1874-1900. Journal of Sisters Celine Allard, S.G.M. and others, translated by Sister Irene Borowski, S.G.M., Sister Marie-Therese LeClair, S.G.M., and Sister Lise Turcotte, S.G.M., 1966-67, St. Michael's box.

  Fort Totten Correspondence, 1883-1900 (actually 1874-1881, letters to the Motherhouse), Fort Totten Correspondence box.

  Fort Totten Lettres, 1874-1883; Fort Totten Lettres II, 1883-1921, St. Michael's box.

  Ledger-book of hand-copied letters, 1887-1901, Fort Totten Correspondence box.

Brennan, Mary R. "The First School at Fort Totten." Collections of the State Historical Society of North Dakota, 1910.

Bureau of Catholic Indian Missions Papers. Milwaukee, Wisconsin: Marquette University Memorial Library Archives.

Fritz, Henry E. *The Movement for Indian Assimilation, 1860-1890.* Philadelphia: University of Pennsylvania Press, 1963.

Kappler, Charles J., comp. & ed. *Indian Affairs: Laws and Treaties II.* Washington, D.C.: Government Printing Office, 1904.

Meyer, Roy W. *History of the Santee Sioux: United States Indian Policy on Trial.* Lincoln: University of Nebraska Press, 1967.

Prucha, Francis P. *American Indian Policy in Crisis: Christian Reformers and the Indian, 1865-1900.* Norman: University of Oklahoma Press, 1976.

United States Department of Interior. Office of Indian Affairs. Letters Received by the Office of Indian Affairs 1824-1881, Devils Lake Agency, 1871-1880. Washington, D.C.: National Archives and Records Service, 1958.

United States Department of Interior. Office of Indian Affairs. Letters Sent by the Office of Indian Affairs 1824-1881, vol. 151. Washington, D.C.: National Archives and Records Service, 1963.

United States Department of the Interior. Office of Indian Affairs. Annual Report of the Commissioner of Indian Affairs to Secretary of the Department of the Interior. Fiscal year 1883: House Executive Document No. 1, part 5, vol. II, 48 Congress, 1 session, serial 2191. Fiscal year 1888: House Executive Document No. 1, part 5, vol. II, 50 Congress, 2 session, serial 2637.

Eleanor Merrow lives with her husband and two children in Grand Forks, where she is active in the Food Co-op, Habitat and other community organizations.

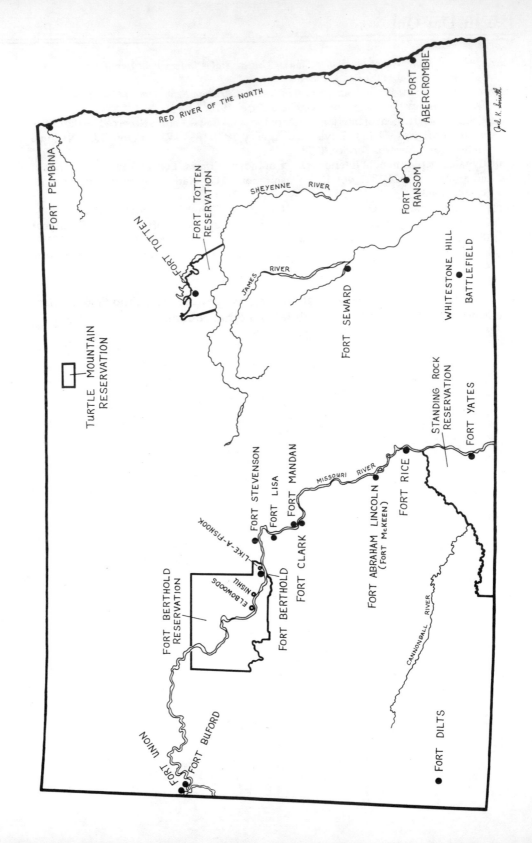

FORT PEMBINA

FORT ABERCROMBIE

RED RIVER OF THE NORTH

FORT TOTTEN

FORT TOTTEN RESERVATION

SHEYENNE RIVER

FORT RANSOM

JAMES RIVER

FORT SEWARD

WHITESTONE HILL BATTLEFIELD

TURTLE MOUNTAIN RESERVATION

STANDING ROCK RESERVATION

FORT YATES

FORT STEVENSON

FORT LISA

FORT MANDAN

LIKE-A-FISHOOK

FORT BERTHOLD RESERVATION

NISHU

ELBOWOODS

FORT BERTHOLD

FORT CLARK

MISSOURI RIVER

FORT RICE

FORT ABRAHAM LINCOLN (FORT McKEEN)

CANNONBALL RIVER

FORT UNION

FORT BUFORD

FORT DILTS

Carl R. Smith

The Garrison Life, the Delightful Rides

by Jane Coleman

At the twelve forts established between 1857 and 1872 in what is now North Dakota, the army gave little thought to personal comfort, particularly to the comfort of women, even though from the beginning, laundresses, camp followers and the wives of traders, as well as the soldiers, lived in the forts. Their presence was both a luxury for those men who could have their wives with them, and important to morale. Women also did much of the necessary labor of the camps, like washing, and there were obvious class distinctions. Although the wives of officers rated no mention in the regulation manuals except under the general heading of "camp followers" (a term with derogatory implications, as it included prostitutes), servants and laundresses did rate a "mention" in Army regulations as washerwomen who were entitled to quarters, a daily food ration, and medical attention. The wives of officers tended to view post assignments from a different perspective than the women working at the forts. Moves to the forts were made out of a sense of duty, rather than economic necessity. When Elizabeth Custer and her husband, General George Custer, were sent to Fort Abraham Lincoln three miles south of Bismarck in 1873, she recorded the fact that, to her, it seemed as if they "were going to Lapland." Later, after having spent several winters at that fort she wrote, "There was never a station to equal those frozen-up regions." *Following the Guidon* (1890) and her other book from those years, *Boots and Saddles* (1885) as well as similar journal accounts by other army wives, were very popular, and attest to one kind of "work" that army wives performed -- publicizing, in a favorable light, the army's staffing of Indian forts. They made national policy appear a brave adventure.

Elizabeth Custer's book also reflects the attitudes and experiences of some of the settlers, army and railway personnel, and other newcomers to the region: that it was vast and unpopulated, little explored, hot and dry in summer, frigid in winter, and cut off from the rest of the country by blizzards that stopped all travel. On the march between Yankton and Fort Rice, Elizabeth Custer counted more rattlesnakes than she had seen in five years in Texas, and reported that the soldiers killed forty in one evening. Her first week in Dakota was marked by a sudden and severe April blizzard that resulted in death and frostbite for many of the men and illness for General Custer. She and her husband and their servant took refuge in a cabin on the plains "somewhere" outside of Yankton, keeping warm and nursing the sick as best they could (Custer 1885).

Men and women alike felt they were vulnerable to attack from Indians, and to death from exposure or from poisonous snakes and insects. Indians, like the weather and distances, were what one had to contend with, and in the years following the Civil War, when many veterans moved west to fight "Indian wars" and to staff forts, the non-native population accepted as fact that it was the mission of the army to enforce white settlement on Indian lands, and to "protect," in this instance, emigrants, railroad workers, and those traveling on the Missouri River from attack by Indians. Many forts served in the dual capacity of Indian Agency and army fortification, but almost no one among the non-Indian populations gave much thought to the Indians' cultural history in a landscape that to them was not at all vacant.

Katherine Gibson Fougera, who came to Fort Lincoln and married Lieutenant Francis M. Gibson of Custer's Seventh Cavalry, described in her memoir, *With Custer's Cavalry* (1940), the birth of a Ponca Indian child one "sizzling hot day," a story that reflects the ambivalent, and contradictory results of Anglo-American Indian policies. Her husband was among a group of soldiers who were marching some Indian families that Fougera termed "lawbreakers" to the fort. A woman dropped out of the line and went behind a bush, returning in a short while with a baby. Fougera's husband helped the woman into one of the wagons and gave her water to drink while "her man, trudging along behind the wagon, looked on in sullen silence."

In addition to the dangers they described, officers' wives and their families complained of being crowded into living quarters that consisted of one room — whether of adobe, planks or canvas. Wives of enlisted men and the laundresses, on whom so much domestic comfort at the forts depended, were faced with even greater domestic difficulties. If unmarried, the laundresses were quartered in hovels, old stables, or whatever shelters were available, and when the regiment moved, they were required to move with it, cramming themselves, children, washtubs and household goods into whatever conveyance could be found. Many enlisted mens' wives supplemented their husbands' pay by working as cooks, servants or laundresses. Pay for the services of a laundress was set by the Council of Administration in 1866 at five dollars per month for officers, and two dollars per month for enlisted men (Stallard 1978). By the 1870's there was usually one laundress for every 19 men, but the army kept scanty records and we can't be certain how many women were in a fort at any given time. (Depending on necessity, U.S. army posts had between 250 to 1,000 men stationed in them. For example, sometimes the entire Seventh Cavalry — about 950 men — was stationed at Fort Abraham Lincoln.)

The situation for women following the army — in whatever capacity — is well summed up (from the army's point of view) in what Lieutenant Jack Summerhayes said to his bride Martha in 1874. "You are pampered and spoiled. You will have to learn to do as other army women do. . .Cook in cans. . .Be inventive and learn to do with nothing" (Summerhayes 1978). After a year abroad, Martha Summerhayes had returned to America, married her "old friend Jack," and, as she wrote in her memoirs *Vanished Arizona* (1908), "joined the army herself." Although at the time she spoke lightheartedly, when she and her husband arrived at his regiment at Fort Russell, Cheyenne, Wyoming Territory, in April 1874, she labeled it, "The wildest sort of place."

Elizabeth Custer and Martha Summerhayes were representative of nineteenth century officers' wives in their upper-middle class backgrounds. Some wives had traveled abroad, but most had never camped out, or cooked meals in the open, if they had cooked at all. Whatever their social class, nothing had prepared women who were wives of either officers or of enlisted men for the difficulties of army life on the frontier.

Yet in spite of such strains, most of these women followed their husbands gladly. Fougera described how her husband had officiated at the birth of a baby on the Kansas prairie. He was traveling with an enlisted man's wife who suddenly turned to him and said, "I'm sorry, sir, but you'll have to stop the ambulance. I'm going to have a child." With "water, a few handkerchiefs, and a penknife" serving as surgical instruments, Gibson and the driver delivered a four-and-a-half pound premature infant. Shortly afterwards, the infant, wrapped in Gibson's jacket and wearing his forage cap to keep out the sun, and his mother were laid on the floor of the vehicle in which they had been traveling, and the journey continued. Both mother and child survived.

Child-bearing in the nineteenth century was, in the best of conditions, a risky experience, but for women on the frontier those risks were multiplied. Army wives as well as immigrant women bore children often without the help of midwife or doctor; in the case of army women, the doctor was likely to be a surgeon more qualified to deal with gunshot wounds than obstetrics. Yet nearly all these women survived, and their children too. In fact, it was often noted in memoirs that army children, once over the usual childhood diseases, were not only healthier but more self-reliant and happier than their city counterparts.

Providing variety of diet was a problem that harassed all army wives, many of whom moved often and so could not harvest a garden. Gardening was usually difficult due to lack of water or the location of gardens. Milk, butter, eggs, and fresh vegetables were luxuries — overpriced and usually unavailable. Elizabeth Custer wrote that she bought a cabbage in Bismarck, paid $1.50 for it and considered herself fortunate, and she rejoiced when her small garden at Fort Abraham Lincoln produced a few radishes. Frances Roe in her letters describes at length the snow-white hens she kept at Fort Shaw, Montana, Dakota Territory. She found the hens at various ranches and went to great lengths to keep them warm and laying in winter, roofing a pen and cutting up strips of carpet for their roost. Eggs, she stated, cost upwards of $1.50 per dozen.

Elizabeth Burt, wife of Major Andrew Burt of the 18th Infantry, moved from Fort Bridger to Fort Kearney to Fort Laramie with a coop "containing our big buff

Brahmah rooster and his family" tied to the wagon. She also had purchased a cow, "a wise investment, giving our baby boy his good fresh milk three times a day during that long journey." Not all wives were so fortunate, however. Most were limited on the march to what could be contained in three chests (Mattes 1960).

There was no lack of game to vary the steady issue of army beef and salt pork, and hunting and fishing became popular with both men and women. There was also plenty of native fruit — wild plums, chokecherries, raspberries, and wild strawberries — preserved to spark the winter diet. The lack of such basics as eggs and butter, however, drove army cooks and wives to inventive heights, one of which was vinegar pie, the pioneer women's substitute for apple pie in a region where apples were hard to come by. Katherine Fougera writes in her reminiscences of a farmer's gift of two sacks of onions to the Seventh Cavalry. They were received with delight, proclaimed "nectar of the gods," and eaten raw, like apples, on the spot. In short, what these officers' wives learned to do without was everything they had been brought up to expect: adequate housing, clothing, food, medical attention, books, music, religion, and simple comforts. In exchange they received independence, physical and intellectual freedom, and in most cases, a degree of good health they might not have had at home as Victorian gentlewomen. They were proud of their achievements, of their abilities to make the frontier "homelike." As Frances Roe wrote, "We will see that the tents are made comfortable and cheerful at every camp, that the little dinner after the weary march, the early breakfast and the cold luncheon. . . are as dainty as camp cooking will permit" (Roe 1909).

To this end, these women labored to make bare walls and dirt floors pleasing, using whitewash for paint, army blankets sewed together for floor coverings. They cherished even the smallest photographs as wall decorations, and went to great lengths to provide entertainment, not only for their families, but for entire regiments. Balls, musicals, charades, amateur theatrical productions, and card games were popular, and Elizabeth Custer mentions that all the old hymns were sung.

The American lifestyle from which white middle-class women are fighting to free themselves has not taken hold in Indian communities to any large extent. Tribal and communal values have survived after four hundred years of colonial oppression.

Kate Vangen
Ann Arbor, Michigan
From "Thoughts on Indian Feminism," *Plainswoman,* **December 1983.**

Most new cavalry wives learned to ride and shoot, as much out of necessity as for entertainment. Elizabeth Custer was an exception on shooting. Although she was a good horsewoman, she never "ventured" near her husband's firearms. Katherine Gibson Fougera reported that upon her arrival at Fort Lincoln to visit her sister Mollie, who was married to Lieutenant Donald McIntosh of Custer's cavalry, she was asked, "Do you ride? Shoot?" so often that the questions got on her nerves. After she had learned to do both under the tutelage of Custer, she answered a newcomer with, "Yes, but I don't chew yet."

Frances Roe became an accomplished rider and hunter. Most of her letters deal in some part with her excitement at riding spirited horses over desert and plains. In one she says that her "hands and arms are unusually strong from riding hard-mouthed horses." Indeed, with her, the harder the better. She loved the challenge, and challenge it must have been in most cases, since she rode sidesaddle, as was the custom for women. When she and her husband left the frontier, she boasted, "I have ridden twenty-two horses that had never been ridden by a woman before — unbroken as some were, I was never unseated. Not once!"

Among the officers, cooks and servants were customary. They helped make the lives of the wives easier, except that female servants never stayed at their jobs long. Army posts served as marriage bureaus for servants and for the unattached female relatives of the officers and their wives. In the West women were scarce, and at the forts, serving girls came and departed in matrimony, often within months of their arrival. Fougera comments that after a time the desperate army wives specified to eastern employment bureaus that only the old or the ugly be sent out to them. This seemed to make no difference. Even these soon "began to paint and powder," then married, leaving the housewives distraught and frustrated. There are interesting class observations to be made here. It would appear that for working class women, employment on an army post gave the possibility of mobility and marriage, but for the wives of officers it could mean a more restricted life by comparison to their servants. They lacked steady domestic help and social and cultural amenities of urban women, but many spoke also of the "freedom" of garrison life — the horseback riding and other outdoor activities that they enjoyed.

Katherine Fougera became engaged shortly after her arrival at Fort Lincoln and the marriage was planned soon after. "What will Mother and Sally say?" she asked her sister Mollie, who answered. "Who cares? They have led shallow, sheltered lives, so you can't expect them to understand. . .But they will after I've finished with them" (Fougera 1980). In *Boots and Saddles* Elizabeth Custer wrote: "The question of servants was a very serious one. . . Servants were almost certain to marry after the trains were taken off [the trains did not run during the cold months], and no new ones could reach us." She went on to say that, except for the soldiers who were especially fond of children, some wives might not have endured their domestic difficulties; the lonely soldiers sat and played with the children giving their mothers some respite. Some of the soldiers, she said, "regretted that they could not sew when they saw an overtaxed lady wearily moving her needle."

Much of the clothing was sewn by hand out of whatever material was available at the quartermaster's store. The silk for Katherine Gibson Fougera's wedding dress was sent to her by her mother, and the pattern cut and fit by women at the fort. A common occurrence was the arrival of one of a pair of shoes in the always uncertain mail — with no guarantee that the mate would ever arrive. Emily FitzGerald's letters home contain long lists of items needed for her children, shoes and diapers being the scarcest (FitzGerald 1986).

Indian women often were engaged as nurses, and Indian men and women worked as servants in army households. Martha Summerhayes had an Indian servant, Charley, and a Mexican nurse when she and her husband were stationed at Ehrenburg, Arizona. A young Apache woman, Pattee, was nurse for the children of Evelina Alexander at Fort McDowell, and Martha Gray Wales, in her memoir published in *North Dakota History* (Spring 1983) mentions Tonka Mary, her Indian nurse at Fort Stevenson. Elizabeth Custer was one of the more fortunate wives in regard to servants staying, for the general brought with him two black servants, Henry and Eliza, who had been with him since the Civil War. Both stayed until nearly the end of his career. Life for black servants was a lonely one. Chances for the social life they had enjoyed at home were small unless they were attached to a black regiment. "You got the general," Elizabeth Custer quotes Eliza as saying. "But I aint got nobody and there aint no picnics nor church sociables nor no buryings out here."

Officers' wives and their servants were not the only women living on army posts. There were also the wives of the Indian scouts, the women of the Indian tribes, the wives of enlisted men, and those who fell under the category of laundress. Some laundresses were the wives of enlisted men and others were, in truth, "camp followers," and supplemented their income with prostitution. Of course the wives of the enlisted men faced even greater domestic difficulties than the officers' wives in regard to quarters and economics. Often they lived in adobe hovels or tents, or in one large, partitioned room where they cooked, ate, slept, and reared children. Married enlisted men ate at home rather than in the company mess, and their wives were issued army rations: beans, beef, hardtack, and salt pork, with little or no variation. Laundresses who also worked as prostitutes elicited ambivalent reactions from army officials. At least two commanding officers supported their presence on the army posts including those in North Dakota. General George Sykes was one; he commented that the presence of women in general had a good influence on the soldiers. The other, General J. C. Kelton, stated in his report to the Banning Committee (a Congressional Committee headed by Henry B. Banning which held public hearings in 1876 on the army) that, "no community of men can prosper where there are no wives and children." There were also regular prostitutes who followed the army, sometimes living on the post and sometimes on "hog ranches" (or brothels) nearby. There were several such establishments across the Missouri River from Fort Abraham Lincoln. During the spring flood of 1875, Elizabeth Custer wrote that the officers' wives, watching through field glasses, saw at least one woman from one of these "ranches" swept away in the waters.

No account of post laundresses is complete without the mention of "Mrs. Nash," the Mexican wife of one of the enlisted men at Fort Lincoln. Mrs. Nash was large with a deep voice and had retained the Mexican custom of wearing a veil over her face. She was a fine laundress and a capable and gentle midwife to many a newborn. The story she told about herself was tragic. She had been married several times, she said, to men who had stolen her hard-earned funds and left her destitute. After she died of what was probably appendicitis, "Mrs. Nash" was discovered to have been a man. The reasons for her disguises, and what her husband thought of them, haven't been recorded.

The record is incomplete for women connected to army posts on the frontier after the Civil War. We know most about a few officers wives, because they were the ones who wrote and found publishers eager to satisfy a public hungry for such books of female adventure that writers like Elizabeth Custer or Martha Summerhayes could provide. But from laundresses, or wives of enlisted men, or "camp followers," or even Indian women, we hear much less. The portrait is skewed in favor of those women married to officers who for the most part could say they enjoyed their years in camps, and described them in the spirit of adventure. Certainly they compared themselves favorably with their contemporaries who lived in cities. Elizabeth Custer wrote, for instance, "We are the pioneer army women, and proud of it." Frances Roe was more overcome by the desolation of cities she had been visiting than the reputed loneliness of mountain and desert: "It is the feeling of loneliness [in the cities] I mind — of being lost and no one to search for me. I miss the garrison life, the delightful rides." On her return to the mountains and prairies, she wrote, "It really is delightful to be in a tent again."

References

Custer, Elizabeth. *Following the Guidon*. New York: Harper & Brothers, 1890. Reprint. Norman: University of Oklahoma Press, 1961.

_____. *Boots and Saddles*. New York: Harper & Brothers, 1885. Reprint. Norman: University of Oklahoma Press, 1986.

FitzGerald, Emily. *An Army Doctor's Wife on the Frontier*. Abe Laufe, ed. Lincoln: University of Nebraska Press, 1986.

Fougera, Katherine Gibson. *With Custer's Army*. Caldwell, Id.: Caxton Printers, 1940. Reprint. Lincoln: University of Nebraska Press, 1986.

Mattes, Merrill J. *Indians, Infants, and Infantry: Andrew and Elizabeth Burt on the Frontier*. Denver: Old West Publishing Co., 1960.

Myers, Sandra L., ed. "The Colonel's Lady at McDowell," *Montana: The Magazine of Western History*, Vol. 24, #3, 1974.

Report to the Banning Committee. House Report #354, February 1876.

Roe, Frances M.A. *Army Letters from an Officer's Wife*. Lincoln: University of Nebraska Press, 1981.

Stallard, Patricia. *Glittering Misery*. San Rafael, California: Presidio Press, 1978.

Summerhayes, Martha. *Vanished Arizona*. New York: J.B. Lipincott Co., 1908. Reprint. Lincoln: University of Nebraska Press, 1979.

Wales, Martha Gray. "When I was a Little Girl: Things I Remember From Living at Frontier Military Posts," Willard B. Pope, ed. *North Dakota History: Journal of the Northern Plains*, Vol. 50, #2, Spring 1983.

Jane Coleman lives on a ranch in Rodeo, New Mexico, and is the author of *No Roof But Sky* (poetry forthcoming), *The Voices of Doves* (fiction 1986), and *Shadows in my Hands* (essays on the southwest).

Governor Lynn Frazier signing the Women Suffrage Bill, 1919.
From the picture collection of the State Historical Society of North Dakota.

The Pull of Tradition:
The North Dakota Association
Opposed to Woman Suffrage

by Paul A. Hefti

The obituary in the *Fargo Forum* for December 5, 1950, of Mrs. Newton C. Young, a North Dakota resident since territorial days, ended: "Politically she was also active and was a very ardent opponent of women's suffrage, serving as president of the state Anti-Suffrage League." An article by Ann Watkins in the weekly *Outlook* magazine for May 4, 1912, is representative of the anti-suffragist viewpoint. Entitled "For the Twenty-Two Million: Why Most Women Do Not Want to Vote," it argues that men and women are inherently different and thus, properly intended to serve separate roles and functions at all levels of society. Women's natural attributes, Watkins claimed, are better applied to other than political pursuits and responsibilities, for which they were physically and temperamentally unsuited.

Moreover, the antis (as they were called) firmly believed that in general women were politically well-represented by the men of their social group. Women did not need the extra, unnecessary burden of having to decide about candidates and cast ballots. Exempted from political obligations, the antis insisted, women were free to devote themselves to their primary duty – to care for and train children for adulthood – and to engage in various volunteer and philanthropic endeavors of benefit to everyone. Collectively, the antis viewed themselves as "conservationists": "Our aim is to conserve the home, to conserve motherhood, to conserve womanhood" (*New York Times*, 14 August 1913) – not unlike the opponents of such measures as the Equal Rights Amendment, subsidized day care, and pay equity for women.

Confronted by threatening change, the antis of 1912 recognized that like the suffragists, they needed to organize if suffrage was to be prevented. Burgeoning suffrage movements in New York, Illinois, and Massachusetts prompted the creation of a rival association, the National Association Opposed to the Extension of Suffrage to Women. Mrs. Arthur M. Dodge, of New York City, a prominent social and civic leader was chosen as the association's first president. (Her insistence upon being identified by her husband's name captured another important aspect of the anti-suffrage attitude. She, and Mrs. Young, and other antis preferred that to using their own first names.)

The antis hoped to persuade the public to their view and in that way to block any vital reform. They did not intend to hold public rallies and demonstrations, which they thought unseemly, but to circulate pamphlets and distribute newspaper materials, eventually through a central clearing house. Otherwise the antis limited their activities to what they considered to be traditionally acceptable forms, such as social functions, club meetings and booths at county fairs. Actually, the antis rarely gathered in public at all. Even in North Dakota, it took a suffragist rally or parade or a scheduled referendum vote for them to show their strength openly. Platform appeals and street marches seem never to have formed any part of the antis' campaign.

These genteel tactics succeeded for more than 30 years. The antis, comprised for the most part of well-respected, well-positioned, and socially prominent women and their followers and admirers, convinced legislators everywhere that women did not want the vote. However silent, they explained, theirs was the real majority. Sincere and thoughtful women, the antis suggested, should not have to demean themselves in popular and public gestures to protect their interests.

So too was the case in North Dakota, according to Mrs. Newton C. Young. She was born Ida B. Clarke in Iowa City, Iowa, on March 16, 1867. Ida, like her two sisters, attended Iowa State University, where she received a bachelor of philosophy and, in 1887, a master of arts degree. She was elected to Phi Beta Kappa, the national scholarship honor society, and there she met her husband, Newton Clarence Young. He graduated from the law school at Iowa State University on June 22, 1887, and they were married the following day.

They moved to Dakota Territory, settling initially in Bathgate, where Newton Young opened a law practice. He held the position of Pembina county attorney from 1892 to 1896. In 1908 he was elected the youngest justice of the state supreme court, winning re-election several terms before resigning and returning to private practice in Fargo. Politically a Republican, JudgeYoung served on many of the party's committees. He was a member of the University of North Dakota board of regents from 1906 to 1914 and during World War I chaired the state Red Cross. He helped organize and retained an interest in the Bathgate National Bank, and served as president and vice-president, respectively, of the Citizens National Bank of Streeter and First National Bank of Napoleon. Judge and Mrs. Young had three children: Laura, Horace, and Dorthea.

Newspaper accounts of Mrs. Young's civic concerns and involvement appear as early as 1904. A speech presented before the Federation of North Dakota Woman's Clubs, of which she was elected president four consecutive terms, underscored her dedication to certain ideals long before the creation of a local anti-suffrage movement. Entitled "Problem of the Western Boy" (reprinted in the *Bismarck Daily Tribune*, 25 October 1904), Mrs. Young compared a mother's role to that of an educator. A woman's education, she maintained, was meant to prepare her for fulfilling the "office of mother." She advised women to "be good mothers to our own boys, and train our daughters to be more intelligent and wise than we have been. . . Give them first this broad education and then if their talents specialize, well and good."

Initially, there seemed little need in North Dakota for an anti-suffrage organization. Foreign born, unassimilated settlers were also thought to harbor traditionally conservative views of the role of women, and wished to frustrate woman suffrage. The German-Russian immigrant population, newly arrived and predominant in the western counties, stood solidly behind those who opposed prohibition of alcohol, prohibition being generally considered a parallel reform movement supported by the women suffrage cause. The antis were thought to include a combination of political interests, the liquor industry and the railroad. Whatever the nature and composition of the antagonists, they held power through the first decade of the century. Suffrage had been blocked at every turn except for the right to vote for school board members and superintendents at separate and specially designated ballot boxes. A heightened revival of the suffrage movement, evident by 1912, brought about the first serious thoughts of renewed dedication to woman suffrage in North Dakota. The antis' coalition, correctly gauging the renewal, reacted. Perhaps this explains why Mrs. Young, after four consecutive terms, relinquished her presidency of the Federation of Women's Clubs, as if to ready herself for the upcoming contest.

The story, as told in day-to-day accounts in the daily press, suggests a forgotten drama whose players received, at the time, equal coverage with their rivals. On May 30, 1914, Miss Carrie E. Markeson appeared in North Dakota, fresh from anti-suffrage work in Montana. She was the personal representative of Mrs. Dodge, president of the newly revised National Anti-Woman Suffrage association. Miss Markeson "visited a number of the local newspaper offices," according to the *Fargo Forum*, April 2, and "made general inquiries about the suffrage sentiment." She declined to reveal her identity, it was reported, while "at the same time admitting she was working in the interests of the anti-woman suffrage cause."

She was soon joined in Fargo by Miss Minnie Bronson of New York, secretary of the national association, whose arrival marked the organizational start of the antis' North Dakota chapter. By 1914, Mrs. Young was a prime fixture in both Fargo and North Dakota society, so it was fitting that she should host Miss Bronson's arrival to promote the anti-suffrage cause before a select group of locally influential women. The *Forum* in reporting her lecture at the Stone auditorium on April 22, said the "meeting . . . was a model for quietness and decorum. No opportunity was given for discussion and, as the audience was made up mostly of suffrage sympathizers, there was no great applause, but, neither was there any sign of disapproval." Judge E. B. Goss of the state supreme court introduced Miss Bronson at her speech in Bismarck some days later. Her presentation, which the *Bismarck Daily Tribune* billed as "Women Do More Without Votes is Argument," claimed that "the laws for the protection of women today, whether property owning or wage earning women, are better than the laws for men." Then, in a curious digression, she called the woman suffrage a small part of the larger socialist movement in national affairs. During a recent gathering in Washington D.C., she noted, the antis had proposed that "1,000,000 Socialists are working and voting for woman suffrage." Miss Bronson's appearance stirred some suffragists into action. They followed a woman as she posted advertisements around town, destroying them behind her. Some days later the Reverend F. L. Watkins of the North Dakota Enforcement League, WCTU, sent a letter to the *Forum* demanding the names of the officers of the state Association Opposed to Woman Suffrage and a disclosure of its funding. Miss Bronson, by then in Helena, Montana, telegraphed: "The North Dakota women who are opposed to woman suffrage are now organizing and the officers will be announced as soon as the state wide organization is complete." She returned to the state in late May and claimed the national association had a active membership of 125,000 women. Obviously, she said, her most recent efforts in assisting with the establishment of additional state associations should further add to that total.

Organizational activities for North Dakota began in Fargo on June 3. Mrs. Young and Miss Marjorie Dorman officiated. Miss Dorman, a New Yorker, was a well known journalist and the secretary of the National Woman Wage Earners' League Opposed to Suffrage, a closely allied group. She had come to the state to help outline the publicity campaign. The antis aimed specifically to defeat the suffrage amendment at the referendum scheduled for November.

The North Dakota Association Opposed to Woman Suffrage formally introduced itself to the public on June 6, 1914. Mrs. Young was its president. A statement of its belief and principles followed, reinforced thereafter by a series of semi-regular newspaper columns under the heading "Anti-Suffrage Notes." Usually these columns featured crisp, often pungent comments and short editorials on the passing scene. All of these were intended to demonstrate, of course, that woman suffrage was hardly a foregone conclusion. It was also clear that many notable North Dakota women had become directly involved in anti-suffrage campaigning. Long lists of names began appearing in local newspapers, implying that the majority of North Dakota women stood in opposition to suffrage. Women in the eastern part of the state predominated, many among the wealthy, yet many were women of average rank who resided in rural settings. The lists were too long and too exact to dismiss as false.

Now the contest began in earnest. Three anonymous editorials appeared in the state press over the next few days, all of them inferring that financial ties existed between the anti-suffrage people and the liquor interests. Mrs. Young and her organization, they declared, were supported as well by "the Personal Liberty League of the German American Alliance, which has a candidate for governor, with two planks in his platform, one for re-submission of the prohibition question and the other against woman's suffrage." Anti-prohibition and anti-suffrage, it was charged, "are political Siamese twins." The issues had been joined, and the antis never mastered the problem of how to separate them. Undaunted, Mrs. Young countered on June 13, denying all allegations. "I have lived in the territory and state of North Dakota for twenty-seven years," she said, "and have always been, and still am, a prohibitionist and an abstainer. . . .So that you may know I am sincere in my belief," she volunteered, practically all expenses to date had been paid from "personal funds."

On July 11 Mrs. Irma Poppler, local suffragist and social worker, challenged a Miss Dorman to a public debate. After much discussion, the debate was scheduled to take place on July 25 at the Sons of Norway Hall in Fargo, using the format agreed to for the Lincoln-Douglas debates in 1859. Judge Charles A. Pollock presided and the rules stipulated that there be no irregular interruptions, and that the suffrage league defray the hall rental and other costs.

Nearly 1,500 persons, five times the number expected, came to hear the debate. The *Fargo Forum* called the occasion a "tremendous success." Mrs. Poppler had spoke first. She detailed the "inexorable" advances of feminism and equal rights, alluded to financial backing of liquor interests and closed with the pointed inquiry, "Mind it is not a question as to who is helping you, but who are you helping?" Miss Dorman emphasized women's role in child-bearing and rearing, and her association's utter lack of interest in voting. There had been a primary election on June 24, she noted, in which women were at liberty to vote for both county and state school superintendents. "The great majority of the women of Fargo, of Cass county, of North Dakota, do not want to vote," she concluded. "Their absence from the polls was proof." At the close of the evening, Mrs. Young presented Miss Dorman with a bouquet of roses.

A second debate challenge followed within a week, emanating this time from Mrs. Alice Nelson Page, president of the Votes for Women League of Grand Forks. She proposed that Miss Dorman debate Miss Jane Thompson, national secretary of the suffrage organizational committee, who was visiting the city. Both parties accepted, agreeing to the same rules and conditions as before. They met on July 31 at the Grand Forks Auditorium. The topic of the evening was "A Woman Should Be Given Full Franchise." Miss Thompson labelled the antis enemies of the people and charged that their stand worked to the profitable advantage of commercial and liquor interests. Miss Dorman reminded the crowd that her purpose was to provide a better understanding of the antis' beliefs. The members of her organization were content to leave political issues in the competent and experienced hands of men. "There have been more girls led astray," she asserted, "owing to the neglect of their mothers who were too busy talking politics to care for their children and see that they had the right start in life, than there were in the years preceding the franchise."

The *Grand Forks Herald* interviewed Mrs. Young. The state Federation of Women's Clubs, she said, existed solely for the purpose of "bettering the social and moral conditions of the women of the state." The suffrage issue had no place in its proceedings and, for that matter, would violate its constitution if imposed upon the agenda. Suffrage had been "pushed simply to advance the ideas of some politicians of various [branch] clubs," she believed, but most members recognized it as "entirely foreign" and potentially dangerous.

The antis' leadership became more enthusiastic. Plans developed for a large meeting, tentatively set for October 17, with personal visits expected from Mrs. Dodge and Mrs. A. J. George, a noted Boston lecturer. Miss Dorman prepared the press release which again emphasized protection of the home and womanhood. Financial support, she promised, came from the voluntary contributions of friends and members. Public enlightenment, or education, remained the chief goal, as before, in behalf of the "sisters who are in the vast majority."

But spirits ran high in the pro-suffrage camp, too. Dr. Anna Howard Shaw, president of the National American Woman Suffrage Association, arrived on the scene even as Mrs. Young and Mrs. Oliphant were on tour. The antis disgusted her, she implied, while offering several allegations connecting them again to big-business selfishness and manipulation. Mrs. Oliphant, in Bismarck, maintained her composure. In Dickinson on September 13, she reiterated the now familiar tenets of anti-suffrage, without ignoring Dr. Shaw's attack on her private life in New Jersey. Implicitly, both sides were anticipating an unheralded confrontation during the annual convention of the Federation of Women's Clubs in Jamestown on October 14. Pro-suffrage forces had invited Mrs. Robert M. LaFollette, wife of Wisconsin's liberal Senator, a veteran of the Chautauqua circuit, and a pro-suffrage advocate, to appear as near to the event as possible. On the news, Miss Dorman issued a challenge to debate. Mrs. Young approved, despite her apprehensions of mixing politics and club affairs. Although Mrs. LaFollette spoke in Fargo, there was no debate, for unexplained reasons. Yet the antis may have misread the mood of the convention. For, despite the antis' plea that the Federation was too venerable for all women to yield to a fleeting political passion, the organization soon showed itself ready for a major departure. Later that same day, to the surprise of the antis, the convention adopted a resolution in support of woman suffrage by a vote of 118 to 35. The antis' procedural protest got nowhere. Miss Minnie Nielsen, superintendent of Barnes County public schools (Valley City) and an acknowledged suffragist, was elected to a second presidential term.

Now certainly, if not before, it became clear that pro-suffrage sentiment had taken control of perhaps the single most important women's group in North Dakota. Despite this setback, the general meeting of the North Dakota Association Opposed to Woman's Suffrage took place as scheduled on October 17. Mrs. Dodge, the national president, was unable to attend. Mrs. George, active in the national Red Cross and several other altruistic organizations, spoke about women's family obligations and the fallacies of militant suffragism. "Suffrage would produce social revolution," she predicted. "The doctrine rests on the basis of economic independence, and economic independence is impossible without social independence and domestic independence and sexual independence." Yet, on November 1, Mrs. Young felt compelled once again to deny allegations that the antis' depended on liquor interests for their financial backing. "Not a penny has come from liquor or vice interests or from outside the state," she insisted. "It has all been contributed by our members and by men and women who believe as we do that woman suffrage is a menace to the home." To prove it, she had appointed a special investigating committee consisting of Judge Pollock and two other distinguished men. They had unrestricted access to her organization's accounts, she stated, "including bank books, checks, vouchers, receipts, and contracts of printing."

At the invitation of Mrs. J. B. Gilnilan, president of the Minnesota anti-suffrage chapter, antis leaders from four neighboring states met in Minneapolis in early December to coordinate plans preliminary to a national conference of Democratic women in Washington, D.C. President Woodrow Wilson welcomed their delegation at the White House on January 6, 1915. He spoke encouragingly. "Ladies," he said, "I am tied to a conviction . . . that changes of this sort ought to be brought about state by state." His constitutional principles, he said, prevented him from supporting a suffrage amendment.

In November, there had been a referendum in North Dakota for woman suffrage. By mid-December, the results had been tallied and analyzed. Unquestionably the antis had achieved a triumph. Woman suffrage had been soundly defeated by a vote of 49,410 to 40,011. Pro-suffrage did not dispute the count. Thirty-five of the state's 50 counties had turned suffrage down, with the eastern, more populated parts levying the heaviest blow. Previously, it had been expected that western sections would provide the greatest obstacle to the reform.

Undeterred, the suffragists regrouped and shifted their strategies from educational persuasion to political activism and legislative pressure. They caused a suffrage bill to be introduced in the lower house of the state legislature in January 1915. Press reports, like that in the *Forum* of February 14, treated the matter skeptically. After all, the paper noted, suffrage "was defeated by a much larger majority than prohibition was carried by [in 1890] and that has stood for 25 years as the will of the people."

The bill passed, nonetheless, by a two to one margin. Their motto, "Back to the Home," sought to neutralize the signs reading "Out of the House," the suffragists' slogan. Mrs. Young's role in this effort is unclear. Victory for the suffragists seemed imminent, if not for the presence of Senator H. P. Jacobson of Adams and Hettinger counties, a staunch opponent of woman suffrage. He managed to isolate the bill in committee for the balance of the session. Although Mrs. Young's stature continued to grow, the antis' began to decline. The organization had grown static. Evidence of its activities by the end of the year declined to brief and intermittent mentions on the society pages. The members' convictions worked against them. Their object had been to spare women from involvement in popular politics, yet their new battle invited the very tactics they shunned.

Mrs. Young gave the main address at the antis' Minnesota convention in Minneapolis on December 6, 1915. Pre-convention publicity, especially in the *Minneapolis Journal,* credited her for having developed woman's clubs and activities throughout rural North Dakota while president of the Federation. Her loyal support of religious, social, cultural and philanthropic endeavors in Fargo, including her directorship of the Florence Crittenton home for "fallen" women, deserved attention, her supporters claimed. Her address, titled "Why We Are Anti-Suffragists," spoke to the awkward position the antis now faced.

> The nature of the suffrage campaign has forced us into a negative position, but we are a positive, not a negative force in society. We are constructive in our work, not obstructionists. We do not seek to destroy. Ours is a God given vision as we believe. We see as the first goal the perfect home, the prime foundation of social order. We see a new respect of women for womanhood, a true conception of woman's place in the creation; no longer depreciation of her own labor, no more vain striving to be other than herself, no more yielding to vain temptation.

Yet, beyond keeping the faith and holding fast to tradition, Mrs. Young could offer no solution to the antis' predicament. Organized anti-suffrage efforts stalled well before antagonists could point to victory. There was no concerted opposition to the suffrage bill introduced in the state legislature that convened in January 1917. What legislative opposition did emerge again was headed by Senator Jacobson, but this time it was defeated in the Senate by a 37 to 11 margin with one abstaining vote, and it was defeated in the House 89 to 19. This bill, modeled after the Illinois bill, allowed for only partial suffrage. North Dakota never adopted complete suffrage by locally sponsored legislation. Rather, the state approved the nineteenth, or Susan

B. Anthony Amendment, in December 1919, which was ratified in August 1920.

Mrs. Young did not abandon her dedication to anti-suffrage. By March 1918, she had become one of seven vice-presidents of the National Association Opposed to Woman Suffrage, headed now by Mrs. James W. Wadsworth Jr., wife of a New York senator. Reduced in numbers, narrowed in branch chapters, and disturbed by leadership turnovers, the antis ceased to be a coherent force and lacked credibility outside certain Eastern states and urban centers. One of their last remonstrances, filed among President Wilson's private papers, had them still standing for "home and national defense against Woman Suffrage, feminism and Socialism." The contradiction had become complete. To prevent that which they fervently opposed, required political judgment and action. But to emulate the suffragists also meant to compromise the ideals they most wanted to preserve.

Although 30 more years remained to her, little is known of Mrs. Young's later life. She left Fargo in 1940 to live with a daughter in Waseca, Minnesota, where she died on December 3, 1950. She is buried at Riverside Cemetery in Fargo.

References

Buhle, Mary Jo and Paul, eds. *The Concise History of Woman Suffrage: Selections from the Classic Work of Stanton, Anthony, Gage and Harper.* Urbana: University of Illinois Press, 1978.

Flexner, Eleanor. *Century of Struggle: The Woman's Rights Movement in the United States.* Cambridge: The Belknap Press of Harvard University Press, 1959. Revised, 1975.

Hennessy, W.B., comp. *History of North Dakota.* Bismarck, N.D.: Bismarck Tribune Co., 1910.

Howes, Durward. *American Women: The Standard Biographical Dictionary of Notable Women.* New Jersey: Zephryus Press Inc., 1974.

Kraditor, Aileen S. *The Ideas of the Woman Suffrage Movement, 1890-1920.* New York: Columbia University Press, 1965.

Mambretti, Catherine Cole. "The Burden of the Ballot." *American Heritage.* December 1978.

Outlook Magazine, May 4, 1912.

Reid, Bill G. "Elizabeth Preston Anderson," in *The North Dakota Political Tradition.* Ames: Iowa State University Press, 1981.

Tucker, Jeanne F. "The History of Woman's Suffrage Movement in North Dakota." Seminar paper. Grand Forks: University of North Dakota Special Collections, Chester Fritz Library, 1951.

Paul Hefti received a Master's Degree in European History from the University of North Dakota. He is a music specialist at Dartmouth College and lives in West Lebanon, New Hampshire, with his wife, Kathryn.

Women and North Dakota Politics

by Lynn Severson

Since time immemorial, women have been drafted to fill low-paying jobs; consequently, it's surprising that there haven't been more women involved in North Dakota politics....Oh, we have provided more than our share of workers in the field.

Representative Aloha Eagles, Fargo.

The first women "workers" in North Dakota politics were reformists, interested in such causes as suffrage (both for and against) and temperance. These causes were undertaken without pay, and when the cause was won (or lost), they usually withdrew from the political process. More recently, women have tended to enter politics for the same reasons men do. While reform issues are still likely to be important to them, politics is thought of as a profession, or as a means of career enhancement through service in the legislature, for example, rather than an extension of volunteer service. Those in politics are likely to persist in efforts at re-election regardless of the outcome of specific issues.

In the late nineteenth and early twentieth centuries, women introduced bills in the legislature and ran for office usually as a way of extending into the public sphere their private convictions and their club programs. In North Dakota, as elsewhere, the suffrage movement was largely carried out by women who belonged to the WCTU (Women's Christian Temperance Union). Many women worked for suffrage as a volunteer cause connected to their opposition to alcoholism, which they could see was causing family violence and poverty, and having the vote was crucial to carrying out other reform movements. The motivation of volunteerism lasted until the 1920s; more career-minded ventures into politics began with the resurgence of the women's movement in the 1960s, the intervening years showing less political activity by women in the state.

In the early years of statehood, it looked as though women might jump ahead of their contemporaries in other states when North Dakota almost wrote women suffrage into its constitution twenty-five years before the Nineteenth Amendment. A Dakota Territory law of 1863 allowed women the vote in school elections, in elections for state superintendent of public instruction, and for county school superintendents, but the State Constitutional Convention of 1889 not only defeated a woman suffrage bill, it made future passage nearly impossible by saying that any amendment for suffrage would have to receive a majority of all votes cast in the election, rather than a simple majority for the particular admendment, as was the requirement for other amendments. Even so, at the legislative session of 1893, a suffrage bill passed in the legislature on the last day, only to disappear mysteriously from the record. (According to Elizabeth Anderson, the leader of the opposition had said that if the bill became law, "every Norwegian woman in the state will vote, and there won't be a white woman in the state that'll vote, and the result will be that in a few years not a man can be elected by the Legislature unless he's a Scandinavian" (Anderson, papers, N. D. Institute for Regional Studies).

Women have made progress in joining the political process, although one hundred years after statehood, no woman has yet joined the North Dakota congressional delegation, or been governor. As of 1988 only nine women have held statewide office. The two offices that most favor women candidates at both the state and county levels have been superintendent of public instruction and auditor. The

---

Kate Richards O'Hare was arrested for sedition at Bowman, North Dakota, in the fall of 1917, then convicted and sentenced to five years imprisonment in Fort Leavenworth, Kansas. She was born into a Kansas farm family that lost their land to drought and foreclosure, sending them, as she described, into the "sordid, grinding, pinching poverty of the workless workers." But Kate became a machinist and turned to "fight the cause and not the effects" of poverty by joining the Socialist Party in 1901. In 1902 she married the writer Frank O'Hare, and, along with people like Eugene Debs and Mother Mary Harris Jones ("Mother Jones"), Kate O'Hare became a prominent Socialist propagandist. In 1916 her name was placed in nomination for the Socialist Party's candidate for vice-president.

At the time of her arrest Kate O'Hare was on a Midwest speaking tour trying to stop farm support for the war. She described World War I as a foreign war of no concern to Americans, but one that was depleting two of North Dakota's main resources, men and wheat. She appealed to the mothers of North Dakota not to send their sons off to the war run by eastern imperialists. Mothers were being asked to be "brood sows" for death, she said. Her talk in Bowman gave the federal government the excuse it wanted to arrest her for sedition.

Sharon Neet
Valley City, N.D.

two current state office holders — State Supreme Court Justice Beryl Levine and Tax Commissioner Heidi Heitkamp — were appointed. Others who have run (Alice Olson, for example) have faced opposition from their own party. The history of women's participation in politics in North Dakota might be seen as a continuing history of small results that are out of proportion to the high degree of energy and talent that a few dedicated women have invested in one effort after another — whether to a particular issue, like suffrage, peace, and environmental concerns, or toward seeking office.

Other patterns may be emerging in the 1980s. Women with political careers tend to be highly educated, and many are lawyers (as are the men). In the last ten years women have been elected from both major parties. Until the Democratic-NPL began to succeed in winning some of the major offices and even occasional majorities in the legislature, women tended to run as Republicans even though sometimes their liberal views on social, environmental and other issues might better make them resemble candidates of the Democratic party. In the years when the Republican party was significantly stronger than the Democratic, women knew that winning support from the Republican party made winning an election significantly more likely. In the 1980s women are running in both parties, and, indeed, show some propensity toward being the better at both political extremes. When viewed as a block, women legislators in the state are arguably from a reformist (progressive) philosophy, even though in the 1972 session, Senator Shirley W. Lee is remembered for having introduced the resolution asking for a Constitutional amendment to ban abortion.

Politics is still a male dominated activity, best suited, in North Dakota, to farmers, lawyers, and other professions that can allow time off during the bi-annual winter legislative sesssions. Some women have remarked that women, more than men, need a male mentor in order to achieve state-wide office, or any office beyond the state legislature. Sheila Christensen, of Fargo, who ran twice for the legislature, believes that it is more difficult for women to raise money for campaigns. "Men generally see the advantage of donating, and they generally contribute to other men."

Women have held state wide office since 1892, when Laura J. Eisenhuth was elected Superintendent of Public Instruction and served one term. Others state wide positions have been filled by Emma B. Bates, who succeeded her (1894-95), and Minnie J. Nielson in the same office (1919-1926) who stirred up controversy by opposing state aid to education. She was succeeded by Bertha R. Palmer (1927-1932); since then the office has been held by men. Berta E. Baker served as State Treasurer (1929-1933), then as State Auditor (1933-1957); Bernice Askbridge was State Treasurer (1968-1972). Ruth Meiers was elected Lieutenant Governor in 1984; In 1988 Heidi Heitkamp was elected Tax Commissioiner, Sarah Vogel Agriculture Commissioner (the first woman elected to that position in any state), and Beryl Levine won re-election to the State Supreme Court.

The legislature that met in 1973 marked a water shed for North Dakota's election of women to political office; thirteen women joined the Legislature that year, two of them in the Senate. Before 1972, not more than five women had served at any one time, and since then their number has twice reached 20, in 1979 and 1987.

Between 1923 and 1986, 41 Republican and 24 Democratic women have been elected to the North Dakota State Legislature — 10 of them to the Senate and 57 to the House of Representatives. Their names, chamber, post office, political affiliation, and terms served are as follows (legislative publication F10914, December 1986):

Levina Ansberry, House, Wheelock, Republican, 1929.
LuGale Becklin, House, Bismarck, Republican, 1973
Sister Mary Beauclair, House, Carrington, Democrat, 1977.
Pauline Benedict, House, Berthold, Democrat, 1977, 79.
Florenz Bjornson, House, West Fargo, Republican, 1979.
Rosie Black, House, Grand Forks, Republican, 1977, 79, 81, 83.
Kay Cann, House, Fargo, Democrat, 1975.
Connie Cleveland, House, Grand Forks, Republican, 1985, 87.
Minnie Craig, House, Esmond, Republican, 1923, 25, 27, 29, 31, 33.
Judy DeMers, House, Grand Forks, Democrat, 1983, 85, 87.
Patricia DeMers, House, Dunseith, Democrat, 1987.
Dayle Dietz, House, Minot, Democrat, 1923.
Aloha Eagles, House, Fargo, Republican, 1967, 69, 71, 73, 75, 77, 79, 81, 83.
Nettie Ellingson, House, Rugby, Republican, 1947.
June Enget, House, Powers Lake, Democrat, 1985, 87.

Growing up with the Farmers Union

by Jeanette Ross

One of my memories as a child of five or six is walking to the Lutheran Church for Sunday school, holding the hand of whichever younger sibling was old enough to make the trek with me. I enjoyed classes, in a mild sort of way — the friendly women who taught us stories about heroic folk from another time, and the pictures we colored while we ate graham crackers.

But Farmers Union — now that was *important*. Our entire family sat proudly and listened to my father and other organizers speak at monthly meetings. We learned the words to Union songs before we started school. I still feel the surge of joy in belonging to something large and important which came from singing "Organize, Oh Organize" with a thousand others at state conventions.

At school I studied history; in summer Farmers Union camps I learned the meaning of history. My school teachers spoke of people and motives distant from me. Lesson books at camp provided the rest. We studied how to rotate crops and how to find world peace, all in booklets written by Gladys Talbott Edwards, the woman who created the

Helen Claire Ferguson, House, Rugby, Republican, 1967.

Stella Fritzell, Senate, Grand Forks, Republican, 1973, 75, 77, 79, 81, 83.

Frances Froeschle, House, Fargo, Republican, 1965.

Agnes Geelan, Senate, Enderlin, Democrat, 1951, 53.

Brynhild Haugland, House, Minot, Republican, 1939, 41, 43, 45, 47, 49, 51, 53, 55, 57, 59, 61, 63, 65, 67, 69, 71, 73, 75, 77, 79, 81, 83, 85, 87.

Bonnie Heinrich, Senate, Bismarck, Democrat, 1977, 79, 81, 83, 85.

Elynor Hendrickson, House, Grand Forks, Republican, 1973.

Jean Herman, House, Fargo, Republican, 1977, 79.

Julie Hill, House, Roseglen, Democrat, 1983, 85, 87.

Pam Holand, Senate, Fargo, Democrat, 1975.

Carolyn Houmann, House, Westhope, Republican, 1979, 81.

Terry Irving, House, Grand Forks, Democrat, 1973, 75.

Susie Jane Ista, House, Walcott, Republican, 1939.

Patricia "Tish" Kelly, House, Fargo, Democrat, 1975, 77, 79, 81, 83, 85, 87.

Sybil Kelly, House, Devils Lake, Republican, 1959, 61, 63.

Marjorie Kermott, House, Minot, Republican, 1973, 75, 77, 79.

Vi LaGrave, House, Mandan, Republican, 1973.

Fern Lee, House, Towner, Republican, 1967, 71, 73, 75, 77, 79.

Shirley Lee, Senate, Turtle Lake, Republican, 1973, 75, 77, 79, 81, 83.

Mabel Lindgren, House, Minot, Republican, 1929.

---

camps and developed the leadership training institute which inspired my father and taught him how to organize. Her father, Charles Talbott, was the first president of the North Dakota Farmers Union. While other farm organizations such as the Grange and Farm Bureau had separate, nonpolitical auxiliaries for women, or assigned them to kitchen duty, the Farmers Union was structured as a cooperative, with all participants sharing work and costs equally. Although few achieved positions of leadership, Farmers Union women were involved in classes on public speaking, parliamentary procedure and the history of economic systems. The women trained in these classes went on to work in the organization as education directors and fieldworkers who directed classes, camps for children, and more leadership training institutes.

Gladys Talbott Edwards began her active public career when she was living in North Dakota. She taught in a rural North Dakota school before she began traveling with her father as he organized farmers. She wrote and distributed mimeographed information on the history of the cooperative movement and the need for organization. Soon she had a column in the *Farmers Union Herald*, a St. Paul newspaper. By 1933 her columns were syndicated in 50 newspapers. In 1936, three years before I was born, she organized the first Farmers Union summer camp for young people. By the time I was eight they were yearly events in 31 states. She organized essay contests for youth and served on planning committees for the first White House conference on problems of rural youth, the fourth conference on children, and on President Franklin Roosevelt's advisory committee to the War Manpower commission. National headquarters of Farmers Union based their edu-

Joann McCaffrey, House, Grand Forks, Democrat, 1977.
Mary McGinnis, House, Jamestown, Republican, 1927.
Ruth Meiers, House, Ross, Democrat, 1975, 77, 79, 81, 83.
Jerry Meyer, Senate, Berthold, Democrat, 1983, 85, 87.
Dorothy Moum, House, Ayr, Republican, 1981.
Corliss Mushik, House, Mandan, Democrat, 1971, 75, 77, 79, 81, 83; Senate, 1985, 87.
Rosemarie Myrdal, House, Edinburg, Republican, 1985, 87.
Donna Nalewaja, House, Fargo, Republican, 1983, 85; S 1987.
Carolyn C. Nelson, House, Fargo, Democrat, 1987.
Rosamund O'Brien, Senate, Park River, Democrat, 1953, 55, 57, 59.
Dagne Olsen, House, Manvel, Republican, 1981, 83, 85, 87.
Nellie Olson, House, Wilton, Republican, 1937.
Anna Powers, House, Leonard, Democrat, 1961, 63, 65, 75, 77.
Jean Rayl, House, West Fargo, Democrat, 1983.
Mary Rathbun, House, Crystal, Democrat, 1933.
Burness Reed, House, Grand Forks, Republican, 1981.
Catherine Rydell, House, Bismarck, Republican, 1985, 87.
Laura Sanderson, House, LaMoure, Republican, 1925.
Mary Kay Sauter, House, Grand Forks, Democrat, 1985.
Catherine "Kitt" Scherber, House, Fargo, Democrat, 1987.
Beth Smette, House, Newburg, Republican, 1985, 87.

---

cational program of study units, camps and institutes upon her work, and, in 1942, she was appointed national Farmers Union educational director.

By the time I was in high school, I was attending monthly Farmers Union classes in the basement of the state office building while my parents attended meetings upstairs. My textbook was titled *United We Stand*, by Gladys Talbot Edwards. She wrote, "There is no place for competition in an age of abundance. . . .Work for achievement." The discussion questions sound like consciousness-raising issues brought up 20 years later. "Do you like best the feeling of playing a good game — of skill in the game — or of winning? List the things which give you most happiness. Which ones are competitive?" Other lessons brought me into community with the

adults in the organization. One suggested, "Discuss with your parents or other people who have lived in your community a number of years the changes they have seen in the ownership of the land there." And others were action oriented. Edwards' book asks, "Do you need any more cooperative enterprises in your county? Could you use a health cooperative? A recreation cooperative?" I took the questions seriously.

And as I got older, I became involved in the civil rights movement, the women's movement and Vietnam war protests. Later I went back to school in northern Idaho and organized a graduate student's association and a town peace group. While others my age were alienated from their families, I knew the only way I could have embarrassed my parents was by remaining silent. My causes are different now, but looking back I see their beginnings in those monthly Farm-

Grace Stone, House, Grand Forks, Republican, 1967, 69, 71, 73.
Marie Tierney, Senate, Bismarck, Republican, 1981.
Elaine Vig, House, Grand Forks, Republican, 1979, 81.
Cheryl Watkins, House, Fargo, Republican, 1973, 75.
Janet Wentz, House, Minot, Republican, 1975, 77, 79, 81, 83, 85, 87.
Adella Williams, House, Lidgerwood, Democrat, 1983, 85, 87.

Lynn Severson lives in Bismarck, N.D., where she teaches English and journalism at Bismarck State College. She is the editor of *The Women of Plum Creek*, a collection of writings about women in Minot, North Dakota.

ers Union meetings and Gladys Talbott Edwards'
influence. I was told, and I believed, that I had
the right to choose my own direction and the
power to make necessary changes, as long as I
found others who believed as I did.

Jeanette Ross lives in Boise, Idaho.

Picketing the Sweet Shop Cafe in Bismarck, N.D., about 1950. North Dakota State Historical Society, Bismarck.

III

In 1907, my aunt, Josephine Danielson, staked a claim in western North Dakota, near Tioga and Ray, which became the scene of an exciting event when, in the 1950s, oil was discovered in Williams county, including some on her land. About ten years before that she had decided to quit paying taxes on the land and was going to let it be redeemed by the state. My father (her brother) decided to pay the back taxes and keep the land in the family. Little did they think that it might prove profitable. For a few years, the number of wells increased and soon the countryside was dotted with derricks. But then oil prices fell, and many promising wells have had to be shut down.

I take a special interest in this claim of Josephine's, because after she died, and my father and mother as well, the land was passed on to my two brothers and two sisters and me. So now I own 1/5 of 1/2 of the land which was homesteaded by Josephine Danielson so long ago, and I have a share in the oil found there. The 1/5 of 1/2 sounds strange, but it happened because her older brother bought the land with my father, so he is entitled to 1/2 plus 1/5 while the rest of us get 1/5 of our father's share.

Orva Bridgeford
Hillsboro, N.D.

Ev Miller's play "Little Casino" was produced in Wilton and Bismarck, N.D., in 1988. Susan Kambeitz is pictured here in the title role. *Bismarck Tribune* photo.

Little Casino

by Frances Wold

She received mail under two names — Ida Lewis, and Elizabeth McClellan — but it was as Little Casino, "the madam of the toniest bawdy house in town," that she is remembered in North Dakota's capital city. She used the deuce of spades (little casino) as her calling card, presenting it to Bismarck merchants who honored it with instant credit. Emblazoned above the door of her house in the red-light district, the black deuce burned itself into the consciousness of residents of the frontier village, as did the mysterious woman with whom it was identified.

People said she came from Brainerd, Minnesota, but left after authorities there informed her she had worn out her welcome in their city. Bismarck was a perfect location for Casino's line of business. The terminus of the Northern Pacific Railroad, it was also a steamboat stop and the jumping-off place for miners and prospectors heading for the Black Hills during the gold rush of 1874-77. Even more important to Casino was the presence of the Seventh Cavalry of the U.S. Army, stationed just across the Missouri at Fort Abraham Lincoln.

Her establishment, separated from the town's business district by the railroad tracks, was not far off Fourth Street, widely known as "Murderer's Gulch" or "Bloody Fourth" because of the shootings that erupted almost daily in its drinking places. A newspaper reporter of the time wrote: "There was no cessation in the daily and nightly routine of revelry and wickedness." The saloon in "Casino's Place" was one of 18 in the settlement of 1,200 inhabitants; their doors never closed.

In this atmosphere Casino prospered. The house marked with the deuce of spades soon became the town's premier emporium of its type. Contributing to its popularity was its ornate decor and the fact that Casino had acquired one of the first pianos in the territory. Every few days a seamstress replaced the gold tassels cut from the velvet window draperies by mule-skinner patrons who adorned the bridles of the lead animals of their pack trains with the "pretties."

A tiny, demure woman who loved elegant but conservative clothing, Little Casino attracted no unusual attention in her frequent trips about town. She avoided publicity, but was sometimes forced to appear in court to bail out her "girls" when they got in trouble — usually for drunkenness or disturbing the peace. The fledgling *Bismarck Tribune* duly reported such appearances in its columns. Among her "regulars" were Canada Nell, Big Rose, Gentle Annie and BeJesus Lil. The more prosaically-named Nell Watson died of inflammatory rheumatism while in Casino's employ, her illness complicated by alcohol and morphine addiction. Casino supported her drug habit, maybe out of pity or in order to keep the woman working.

Little Casino made money — a great deal of it, by several accounts — but she also spent it. She was generous to people in trouble and supported civic and religious enterprises. During the successful campaign to secure the Dakota Territorial Capital for Bismarck, she gave $1,200 for the cause, though her name does not appear on the list of donors. She chartered a private railroad car to travel to the St. Louis World's Fair, and used it as luxurious living quarters during her stay. While her private life is mostly a mystery, it was known that she did not always travel alone. In those days of prosperity, Casino bought some rural property about 20 miles north of Bismarck, some say as a favor to a friend. But predictably, her prosperity did not continue. As Bismarck changed from a roaring frontier settlement to a respectable family town and state capital, public opinion forced the red-light houses to close.

In 1893 Little Casino lost her Bismarck holdings through a mortgage foreclosure. Aware of the town's increasingly hostile climate toward her, and with her health failing, she decided to move to her rural property in an area that had proved to be rich in lignite deposits. There she operated a small coal mine, known to everyone as "The Little Casino Mine." The mine never made much money, partly because of her generous nature toward transients and loafers, some of whom always stayed the winter, supposedly digging enough coal for their keep, but most likely not. A local farmer seeded the crop land on the property on shares.

People who had known the fashionable woman in her early Bismarck days would have had trouble recognizing the haggard crone Casino became. A local historian who often saw her shopping in nearby Wilton wrote this unflattering description: "She reminded me of a little bedraggled bird. She was always dressed in rusty black clothes of yesteryears — skirts full and touching the ground. She was old and looked weak, and had a rattling cough, and I would guess that she didn't weigh more than 80 pounds. She looked dirty and unkempt. She would smear white liquid face paint over her wizened features, which showed up the dirty furrows in her scraggly neck. Her tiny, brownish hands with uneven, dirty nails made me think of a bird's claws." Her raspy harsh voice was said to frighten little children. Boys dubbed her "Dirty Casino," and hooted at her when she passed in her buggy, followed by the procession of hounds she kept. As if conscious of her marked status in the rural community she wasted no time in conducting her business, buying groceries and mining supplies that she always paid for in cash.

Conditions at her home deteriorated also. Trash is said to have littered the yard, and her house was referred to as a hovel, complete with thriving bedbugs and lice.

The hangers-on who shared her quarters occupied the main level; Casino climbed the ladder-like steps to an attic enclosure where she slept on a bed of rags. It was there she died, on September 16, 1916, of a "stroke of paralysis," according to the obituary in the *Wilton News*. Under the headline "Pioneer Passes," she was identified as "Mrs. Elizabeth McClellan, 76," with no reference to her past. The *Bismarck Tribune*, which years earlier had carried accounts of her coming to court with her girls, did not print an obituary.

The town undertaker had considerable difficulty in removing her body through the small attic opening. He also reported removing, from a grimy ribbon around her neck, a beautiful diamond. The minister of the Wilton Presbyterian Church arranged a "Christian burial" for Casino, attended by nine persons including the pallbearers, who were local businessmen. No women were present. A small boy who had been afraid of the old woman with the raspy voice watched the procession. Years later, he recalled that what he remembered most were "her hound dogs trotting along behind the buggy. They waited outside during the service, and then when the men started for the cemetery with the body, the dogs trotted right along. It looked so pitiful." She is buried in an unmarked grave in Riverview Cemetery just outside of Wilton, overlooking the Missouri.

The entrance to the Casino Mine, along with some sinkholes and caves from the digging were visible until recently. Not long ago, however, workers of the Soil Conservation Service filled the excavations. The only evidence left of Casino's tenure on the land is the depression in the earth where the house stood. There is even less evidence of Little Casino having lived in Bismarck. The new home of the *Bismarck Tribune* at 701 Front Avenue, stands where the deuce of spades once identified Little Casino's place of business. The newspaper is in a modern, efficient building where a visitor will look in vain for tasseled window draperies.

References

Bird, George F., and Edwin J. Laylor Jr. *History of the City of Bismarck, North Dakota*. Bismarck, N.D., 1972.

Slaughter, Linda Warfel. *From Fortress to Farm*. Reprint. Bismarck, N.D.: *The Bismarck Tribune*, 1947.

Williams, Mary Ann Barnes. Pioneer Days of Washburn, North Dakota and Vicinity. Bismarck, N.D., 1953.

Information also acquired from issues of *The Bismarck Tribune* of the 1880s and 1890s, from *The Wilton News* of October 6, 1916, and from conversations with older Wilton residents over the years who remembered Little Casino when she lived near the town.

Frances Wold is a journalist and historian living in Bismarck, N.D.

Emma McDonald's claim shanty. Photo courtesy of Floy Higgens, Sarles, N.D.

Cecil Nickelson's claim shanty, Grouse Coolie, McKenzie County. Photo courtesy of Maxine Carley, Casselton, N.D.

The homestead sod house of Henry and Mary Budke, near Sherwood, N.D. in 1905. Photo courtesy of Aurora Seehofer, Drake, N.D.

Drive Your Oxen, Ride Your Plows: Homesteading Women in North Dakota

by H. Elaine Lindgren and William C. Sherman

Miss Emma Williams has one of the finest claims on the James River, and has about 15 acres ready for crop next year. Her improvements, plowing, well and buildings are valued at about $1,500.00. Besides her homestead, Miss Williams has a beautiful timber claim in sight of her new home.

— *Port Emma Times,* December 27, 1883.

A century ago, one hundred and thirty-five quarter sections were claimed by settlers in Dakota Territory's newly platted township, T129-R59. Of that number, 22 quarter sections, or about 16 percent, were taken by women. Indeed, the nearby trading center of Port Emma was named after Emma Williams, whose claim was just beyond the township boundries.

Settlement in this locality occurred at an early date, 1883-86, a few years prior to statehood. Only twenty years before that, soldiers and Sioux had fought a battle on the nearby Whitestone Hills, but in 1882 the township was virtually without inhabitants. The Sioux no longer hunted the region, and European settlers had not yet arrived. It was a remote area, the nearest railroads were at least 20 miles away. There were no schools, no churches, no physicians, only trails and lush grasslands. But a number of women committed themselves to build some sort of a house, break up the prairie sod, and live on their claim long enough to "prove up."

This essay is an attempt to look closely at the women on that 36 square miles labeled T129-R59, land which was eventually called Lovell Township. Who were they? Where did they come from? Why did they come? How did they manage? Why did they leave? Although women filed on claims throughout North Dakota,

Lovell Township was of particular interest because of the relatively high proportion of women taking land at such an early settlement date. These women were all of Anglo-American background, one of the earliest ethnic groups to settle in Dakota Territory. Their experiences may suggest the settlement experience of other homesteading women.

Along its western edge, the township was dominated by the presence of the James River, which arose in North Central Dakota and coursed southward to the Sioux and finally the Missouri rivers. The terrain was almost flat, part of the glaciated region of prehistoric times. A few potholes dotted the landscape, left over from ancient ice chunks which melted, leaving their special impressions. The entire region, however, was in more recent times the bed of Lake Dakota, a glacial backwater that covered large parts of Dakota. In this case, it embraced all of Lovell Township and extended a dozen miles to the north and west.

Though rail transportation was still some miles away in northern South Dakota, the region was surprisingly accessible. During summer months, the river would provide a somewhat dependable freight and passenger service; but winter and summer, there were military and post office trails which proved to be thoroughfares for wagons and buggies. Settlers looked to the area with a special fondness because there appeared to be an abundance of water. The ancient lake bed encouraged a growth of lush grasses, and the presence of the river seemed to speak of a temperate and well watered corridor through the often dry plains of Dakota. The region was truly an unknown and deceptive environment, a fact that may excuse the excessive rhetoric of a local editor writing on December 6, 1883, in the *Port Emma Times*. (The first settler had arrived 8 months earlier):

> Nowhere on earth can the agriculturist take so great advantage of the improved facilities for seeding and harvesting as in the James River Valley. Its unbroken surface, free from rocks, pure water and embracing cool air and large amount of nutriment in the vegetation. . . .The months of May, June and July bring periodical rains that gives a more rapid vegetation than in any other climate. When the grass and grain put forth a beautiful deep, heavy green foliage, all nature smiles with fortune .

The nearby town of Port Emma, a village a mile northwest of Lovell Township, dominated the early life of the area. Port Emma was founded on June, 1882, when T. W. Bush from Grenville County, Ontario, built a house along the James River at what was called the "fish hook bend." Bush could say, in later years, that no habitation existed within a radius of fifteen miles (*Port Emma Times*, 20 November 1883). By the spring of 1883, a general store had been built on the townsite, along with a rather spacious hotel (appropriately called, by Mr. Bush, the Ottawa House). That same year saw the arrival of a great number of squatters, some 40 before mid-July, who guessed where the surveyors' lines would run and quickly erected a shack on the plot of land which they hoped the land office would recognize as their claim when the township officially was opened for occupation. In 1883 the Nettie Baldwin steamboat began to move goods and people from Columbia, 30 miles to the south, to Port Emma. The 40-mile river journey took 5 hours. The *Port Emma Times* looked forward to abundant times as in this glowing description of the James River: "The sparkling waters of the river and the green sward reaching either bank over thousands of acres of choicest land, called forth the good judgment of our fortune hunters . . ." (6 December 1883).

The first issue of the *Times* was printed on November 20, 1883, and continued until July 16, 1886, when it merged with a Ludden paper. The enthusiasm of its editors brings to life the people whose names otherwise only appear on the rather cold pages of official county and federal land records. Such reports need to be read cautiously, allowing for their having been written in the heat of particular moments, and with an eye to advancing the fortunes of those who were investing their time and money in the booming frontier. Nevertheless, the editor of the *Port Emma Times* had cause to be enthusiastic. Owning land along the James River promised health, "pure air" and invigorating surroundings. Of a man from New Hampshire, it was said, "Since coming to Dakota his health has wonderfully improved and instead of being simply able to cast a shadow he is now enjoying robust health" (28 August 1884). Some Lovell Township settlers came west to establish a new identity and escape the failures or scandals of the past. Most settlers came to the Dakota prairies to better themselves financially.

The United State Government owned all the land in Lovell Township and was giving it away "free" to all who would invest the time and the toil. Land acquisition laws allowed any person over 21, who was either single, widowed, divorced, or the head of a household, to take 160 acres of land. Three main procedures could be followed: (a) Homestead: This method involved a modest entry fee, five years of residency, the erection of some kind of "suitable habitation" and the breaking of

---

My great-grandmother, Lillie Maillard Vollmer, was born in France in 1858. She traveled with her parents to Quebec, and from there to Lowell, Massachusets, where, in her early teens, she began working in a textile mill. In 1890 she and her father both filed homesteads near Omemee, in Bottineau County. She always said that coming to North Dakota was better than any life she could have endured in Massachusets. She died near the homestead site in 1947.

Mark Vollmer
Grand Forks, N.D.

some crop land. Through commutation, which meant the payment of $1.25 to $2.50 per acre, the five year residency requirement could be shortened considerably, depending on which law was in effect at a given moment. (b) Preemption: this method insisted on prior occupancy and then allowed the outright purchase of the land; the price was the same as for commutation, $1.25 to $2.50 per acre. (c) Timber Culture provisions: this legal procedure meant the settler was required to plant and tend a specific number of trees; after an eight or ten year period the claimant received a patent. The tree claim did not require residence and could be held simultaneously with a homestead or a preemption. The laws applied equally to single women and men, widows and widowers. But if a couple was married the claim was filed under the husband's name unless his wife could prove she was head of the household. (For a more detailed discussion of land laws and policies see, *A History of the Public Land Policies*, Benjamin Hibbard, Macmillan Company, New York, 1924; *Our Landed Heritage; The Public Domain 1776-1936*, Roy M. Robbins, Princeton University Press, Princeton, 1942; *The Lure of the Land*, Evertt Dick, University of Nebraska Press, Lincoln, 1970 ; "The Homestead Act; Free Land, Policy in Operation, 1862-1935," Paul W. Gates in *Land Use Policy and Problems in the United States*, Ed. Howard W. Ottoson, University of Nebraska Press, Lincoln, 1963.)

The first residents of Lovell Township came on April 6, 1883. The *Port Emma Times*, with a sense of history, described the occasion nine months later:

> About April 6th, 1883, there might have been seen driving out of Columbia, Brown County, a wagon containing four gentlemen. Driving north through Brown County they struck the well known stage road, which has been the "beaten path towards the land of happiness and plenty" for so many a home-seeker. Following this road northwards, they reached the northern boundary of Brown [County] and passed into township 129 range 59 of Dickey County, and here they stopped, enchanted, as it were, by the beautiful stretch of country before them. No. 1 [said], "This is what we want" and the rest say "ditto." Let us see who these gentlemen were. The party consisted of Edward F. Kay, DeWitt C. Towne, Hiram M. Towne and that "guardian angel of the squatter," Henry A. Tice of Columbia.

> On April 7th these gentlemen took up their actual residence on their land, and few people who ride through the country today would believe that only nine months ago when these gentlemen settled, that there was not a person living in the township but themselves, while only a few shanties could be seen in any direction as far as the eye could reach (14 February 1884).

As was true of most western speculators, these men, all squatters, were not modest. The intersections of their land parcels received the name Ticeville. Mr. Kay appointed himself postmaster, school commissioner and road supervisor, and the four pioneers considered their spot civilized. Looking back over the experience of his first year, another squatter wrote in the *Times* of his initial impressions.

> This is a beautiful level prairie, gently sloping towards the river.... I and a young lady who came from Rankin [Iowa] with my wife and myself, located two adjoining quarters and built our house on the line. Miss Hanabery on the south quarter and

I on the north. She has a neat little room on her claim and boarded with us. When we located here there was no other house in sight on this side of the river; now you can stand in my door-yard and count over 100 houses, besides the two towns in sight. One is a mile and a half south [Ticeville] the other, Port Emma, two miles and a half north on the west bank of the river (31 July 1884).

The surveyor's final report (1883) revealed that forty-one individuals were in residence; of that number five were women. This meant that within two months after Mr. Tice and his three colleagues took land, a genuine rush of men and women had arrived; of the five women who squatted, four officially claimed their acreages. The *Port Emma Times* on January 17, 1884, said that Township 129-Range 59, "came in market Thursday of last week." The acquisition of claims could now officially take place. Already the paper noted, "A large part of the tree claims were secured by parties who were waiting around with a view to gaining the spoils." (A tree claim guaranteed hold on a piece of land without taking up a permanent residence.) The newspaper said on September 14, 1884, "The spring boom has commenced and the sound of the carpenters' hammers is heard in the land." The land rush was proceeding at a furious pace. Lovell Township would never be the same.

Settling on the land required some capital outlay. The newspaper suggested that about $650 would set one up in farming in grand style: "You can get a good team, say two pair of oxen, at a cost of $300. Your Government filing $14; your building that will be comfortable and answer for the first year until you get your crop, $200; two plows, breaking and back setting, $40; five months board for one man, $100 (20 December 1883). Even such a simple thing as choosing the right land could get complicated. The paper suggested using a land agent as a "locator": "Do not be afraid to call upon an agent, they are perfectly tame and will not hurt you. You may spend fifty dollars trying to locate yourself, and then not be satisfied, when an agent would locate you for ten dollars and do your business in better shape" (14 February 1884).

Even the matter of construction of a "suitable dwelling" allowed for various options. The $650 mentioned above pointedly avoids discussion of the type of house required; many dwellings in the area were of sod. A photographer from Chicago was in the Lovell Township area during the summer of 1885. The editor says, "Our sod houses and immense fields will be very interesting back east" (3 September 1885). Almost as frequent, however, were frame shelters. (Nowhere is there a mention of log cabins; timber was scarce in Dickey County.) Homesteaders purchased milled lumber in Ellendale or Columbia and brought it to the claim at their own expense. If friends or neighbors could not lend a hand it was possible to hire someone to construct the shack. Laborers were in abundance; the going price for the erection of a shelter was $15.

The size varied; some frame dwellings were as small as 8 x 10, some 8 x 12 and frequently 12 x 14. At Guelph, a few miles to the west, a family built a house 16 x 24 feet and a story and a half high. This building became a landmark and was termed a "castle" (Black 1930). Most shelters were considered temporary. The newspaper optimistically reported on August 28, 1884, "Sod and tarpaper shelters will give place to neatly painted houses now that the market of grain has commenced."

Spring 1884 was a busy time. "The Ottawa House is crowded with guests this week. There were many strangers present, and it seems that all eyes were turned toward Port Emma, the coming metropolis. . . .There seems to be a team on every quarter of land seeding or breaking. . . .Four new buildings in one week" (12 June, 5 June, and 8 May 1884). Women as well as men were caught up in this whirl of activity. Sixteen percent of the claimants in Lovell Township were women, a figure that is somewhat unusual for a township settled during the mid 1880s. Our recent studies indicate the proportion of women claimants in areas settled before 1900 tend to be under 15 percent while those settled after that date usually fall in the range between 15-30 percent. Just as newspapers give the social conditions of the moment, so it is possible to determine the basic details in the women's background from the Federal Land Office files concerning land claimants (in the National Archives) and the record of land transactions found in the Dickey County Register of Deeds office. Files were not available for squatters unless they eventually acquired title to the land.

In 1883, eight women arrived; in 1884, nine arrived; in 1885, four; in 1886, two. The proportions and time period coincide generally with the land rush activity elsewhere in that part of Dickey County, which was early in comparison to most central and western parts of Dakota. Of those whose origins were known, three women came from Iowa, two from Illinois; one each from Minnesota, Michigan, Wisconsin, New York and Maine. They did not arrive as part of a single organized group, rather, they came as members of many different groups or as friends and relatives of other settlers. This conclusion is supported by their varied time of arrival, the disparate home towns and the fact that their final filing papers showed no overlap in character witnesses. Ten women chose the preemption method for acquiring land, seven homesteaded, two had timber claims and one acquired a homestead by virtue of a Veteran Widow's privilege. One woman had both a homestead and a preemption quarter; another had a tree claim and a homestead acreage. Few homesteaders chose the five year residency course. Most commuted their homesteads, that is, paid a purchasing fee after at least six months of residency.

Land office records show that each homesteader or preemption claimant built a house. The structures varied in size: two women built a shack that was 10 feet x 14 feet; one built a house 8 x 16; four built 12 x 14; one built 7 x 12, four built 10 x 12, one was 9 x 12. Two were quite large in proportions: 14 x 30 and 12 x 24. Almost every one of the structures was described as "frame," usually with a shingle roof and often wrapped in tar paper. Two, however, appeared to be primarily of sod. The fact that most women chose the fastest land acquisition method, preemption and commutation, leads to the conclusion that many expected to stay in Dickey County for as short a time as possible.

Whether a woman saw homesteading in Dakota as a temporary or a permanent proposition may have had something to do with her marital status. An unmarried woman would probably look at the future in less than certain terms and would want to have her options as flexible as possible. The demands of an eight year tree claim or a five year homestead residency could seem excessively confining. Of the women claimants in Lovell Township nine were single when they filed on the land, and nine were widows. Four of the single women married within five years of the entry on their land. Six of the widows were between the ages of 26 to 49 while three were older than 50.

Only two women built barns. This fact also points to the rather temporary plans of the Lovell Township women. (Land laws never required construction of barns.) One woman, Mary Clark, twenty-eight years of age, built a 12 x 14 foot frame house and a 10 x 12 sod barn. Miss Clark was unmarried and left the land after eleven months of residence. A second woman, Mary Martin, built more substantially. Her frame house was 14 x 30 feet and was said to have ten rooms with a cellar. Her barn, also of frame materials, was 12 x 24. In addition, she had a storeroom which was 14 x 30. Mary Martin was a widow with three children. Quite clearly, she intended to stay on the land longer than the law required. Three women are of special interest; they were over sixty years of age. Two were single women, and one was a widow with four grown children who lived on land in the same township. All three probably came with other homesteading friends or relatives and saw life on the prairie as a permanent rather than a temporary situation.

The reports describing the boom period in the *Port Emma Times* stood in sharp contrast to the tales of misery and deprivation so common in frontier literature. The newspaper would have us believe that the "niceties" of civilization arose almost at the first moment of settlement. The rapid construction of one Dakota settlement is described in the *Port Emma Times* of August 23, 1884: "In one settlement which recently came into being, there were only two weeks after the receipt of the first load of lumber, a bank, a newspaper office, two hotels, the church, six stores, a market, five saloons, a telegraph office, a post office, and three lumber yards." While Port Emma never reached the size described above, by 1884 Port Emma, claiming that it was "the booming town of the James River Valley," had a hotel and the Ottawa House which was of considerable size, a feed mill, several stores, a real estate office, and a handful of frame residences. The *Port Emma Times* said in one Spring issue: "Five new buildings were erected last week." A few months earlier the paper reported "Dwelling houses in Port Emma rent for $20 and offices for $15 per month." In addition, speculator towns like Ticeville, Hudson, Coraton, Eaton, and Ludden were all located within six miles of the township's borders.

Already, in 1884, a bridge was proposed to replace the ferry across the James. By Spring of 1884, a stage line went three times a week to larger towns, such as Ellendale and LaMoure and brought mail from railroad centers in the north and south. Regularly the riverboat, Nettie Baldwin, made the trip from Port Emma to Columbia, the railroad town to the south, in half a day. (With proper water levels the boat would carry twenty tons of freight.) Well worn trails led in every direction. A buggy ride to a railhead city could be accomplished in five hours. So Lovell Township was no longer an isolated part of America. Even in the winter, sleighs, cutters and an occasional ice boat moved across the snowy landscapes.

Social life was lively and varied. As many inhabitants found themselves "waiting it out," and had time with little to do, comradeship was important. Men and women, single and married, were thrust together in a new environment and lived with a minimum of conveniences. Some were young, and usually free of farm chores. Every description of life in Port Emma and its surroundings stresses these facts, as in these childhood memories of an early day resident: "Everyone was a neighbor to everyone else. Social circles were limited mostly by distance. A neighborhood gathering meant attendance by everyone from as far as word-of-mouth could reach. Ten or twelve miles might be traveled by lumber wagon to attend one of these gatherings" (Black 1930).

The *Port Emma Times* abounds in reports of pleasant social activities, as this mid-summer evening in 1884: "Port Emma was visited by quite a cavalcade of ladies and gentlemen this [Thursday] evening. They were mounted upon ponies and presented a pretty and inspiring sight as they came galloping over the hill southwest of town" (31 July 1884). The same summer saw other events: "Wednesday evening a dance was given at the residence of Mrs. Hall, nearly all of the young people from this vicinity being present. A good time is reported" (14 August 1884). Dances in the fall included a supper and music by a traveling musical group. "A social dance will be given at Prof. Eaton's new granary, Tuesday, Sept. 8. Music by Emerson's Orchestra. Supper and dance tickets 75 cents. All are cordially invited" (3 September 1885). The *Times* editor also had an eye for the cultural features of the moment: on April 12, 1884, he notes, "Lady equestrianship is quite fashionable in this vicinity."

There were inter-town baseball games; the local boys versus Ellendale, Frederick or Columbia. Also small disasters: "The pet coyote belonging to Miss Cora Squires died suddenly this week, from an overdose of granulated plumbum, administered by Mr. Hembling" (2 July 1885). And things of the mind were not ignored: "An elocutionary entertainment will be given at the Metropolis Saturday by the young ladies" (6 August 1885). An organ was offered for sale in one of the *Port Emma Times* first issues. In mid-summer, 1885, the newspaper said, "Our Union Sunday School had purchased a library of fifty volumes" (13 August 1885).

And the distances did not retard the tempo of the times, for, with almost one shack on every quarter section, within a two mile radius there could be as many as twenty dwellings. Then, as now, people exercised their ingenuity in traveling on the plains. "We heard a man in Ellendale make the statement that he drove from Port Emma to that place, 19 miles, in one hour and fifty minutes," and "We admire the pluck of a young gentleman who walked twenty miles to hire a team to take a young lady to the Ellendale celebration" (20 November 1883 and 10 July 1884). Winter after harvest was the season when energies and imaginations were taxed to while away the hours. Many of the houses were made of frame, one inch of lumber and a thin layer of tarpaper. Stoves were primitive; pot-bellied affairs, with straw, or twigs for kindling and chunks of wood or store-bought coal for fuel. Keeping the fire going probably was the most time consuming task on the place. Other chores included melting snow for water or fetching it from a protected well. Outhouses and chamber pots were the rule of the day. Yet the local newspaper editor tended to view winter with a defiant eye:

> Chautauqua clubs, dramatic clubs and glee clubs are already forming, while the usual number of progressive eucher clubs, checker clubs, and clubs where they anty up etc. are not forgotten. In fact, people in general are looking forward to and preparing for three months of rest and pleasure, of long evenings and bright fires, and have rightly concluded that these joys will be greatly increased by assembling together (1 October 1884).

The editor also grew eloquent about snow:

It is difficult to conceive of scenery grander than that which presents itself here on a beautiful winter morning. Away to the east across the myriad of silvery flashes from the ice of the river, are the snow-rapped [sic] hills, which seem to stretch to meet the clear blue of the sky while to the southeast you may see a mirage that looks like a far-reaching lake, over all shines the soft, clear light of the morning sun, making this true picture of Nature sparkle and glisten with a beauty that is wonderful and sublime (20 December 1884).

Indoor gaiety matched outdoor beauty: "Mrs. A. B. Raleigh served ice cream to her callers Wednesday evening" (15 January 1885). The Christmas season, 1884, featured a three act play at Port Emma: "Flower of the Family." Local actors were involved. They were greeted "with repeated applause" (24 December 1884). Yet winters could be dangerous: "Last week during our coldest weather, a farmer living near Bath started to go to town for a doctor, his wife being sick, when he lost his way and was frozen to death." Near Aberdeen, a certain William Carlson "froze both feet so badly that it was necessary to amputate them above the ankles" (31 January 1884). Temperatures were cruel. When the mercury fell to 24 below on a December morning, even the *Times* editor weakened: "The sun is shining bright . . . and although nature is charming in her winter garb, one cannot but feel a tinge of regret for faded flowers, frozen roses and the want of a warmer temperature" (17 December 1883).

Yet life was still fun. "There has been skating on the river for some time and the boys and girls are having a delightful time. Prof. Eaton and Dr. Wilson paid Port Emma a visit Saturday. They sailed up in an ice boat" (6 December 1883). In mid-December the paper reported, "Miss Hilda Johnson and Mr. Eugene Grant enjoyed a sleigh ride to their homes, north of here Christmas." "Misses Nellie Walker and Jennie Graham took to the skating rink at Ellendale Wednesday and returned home Thursday" (30 November 1883 and 6 December 1883). Some of the men turned to hunting:

Messrs. D. N. Bailey, Frank Schofield, H. W. Devendorf, W. H. Devine and Charles Hofner started last Thursday for the Missouri River on a hunting expedition. Some of the party did not get further than Ellendale before they had killed buffalo, Elk and Deer enough to satisfy them so they returned (30 December 1883).

In January a drove of fifteen antelope passed west of town. By March, 1884, two notes appear in the *Times*: "Great excitement at the Headquarters House, Tuesday, by the appearance of a flock of geese." "Great rejoicing over the appearance of bare ground. May it not be many days before we are scattering the seed" (17 January 1884 and March 1884). By spring everyone was active: "Mrs. M. A. Pettibone has the southeast quarter of sections 23, and 33 acres ready for crop. Mrs. Pettibone is an estimable aged lady, well worthy of one of Dakota's richest boons — 160 acres of land." "Mrs. True, a lady aged sixty years, rode 100 miles last week through the cold to secure a tree claim in township 130-60, and we are glad to say that she was not disappointed" (31 July 1884 and 24 January 1884).

Yet even with the pleasant weeks of spring and summer there were dangers. Clara Rowe was left to homestead as a widow when her husband drowned while attempting to cross the James River in a rowboat. On June 16, 1885 a windstorm destroyed some homesteader shacks. The storm with its rain and hail also toppled a few buildings in

Port Emma itself. But, the newspaper reported "it will not be long before they are rebuilt." The rains disappeared at times and the prairie grass became tinder dry. Fires then became a problem:

> Burned — The starting of a prairie fire on Tuesday resulted in the burning of Miss Belle Empsy's house, with all its contents, which consisted of clothing, bedding, and the necessary outfit for successfully holding down a claim (24 April 1884).

Even in November fires could threaten the entire rural community and frame shanties would burn in an instant.

> On Wednesday evening a terrible prairie fire was raging west of town, and we understand some of the farmers in the neighborhood have met with some heavy losses. Many of the residents of this place sat up most of the night, not daring to go to bed for fear the fire would run towards town, but happily towards morning the wind changed to a northeasterly course, and threw the fire away from us (20 November 1884).

The always present threat of illness and injury existed, aggravated by the remoteness of the region. A Ticeville news item reports on July 9, 1885: "Mrs. Case is dangerously sick but at present writing is slightly better. Dr. Mathews is attending her." At the Hudson settlement, five miles north of Lovell Township, diphtheria struck the home of a couple who resided on their claim. They had eight children who

---

My grandmother Agnes Elizabeth Jacobson Ekrem was born at Brattholmen, Norway. She lived not far from the home of Edvard Grieg, and later was employed in his home as a domestic. They took walks together, but she was not aware of his fame as a composer until many years later when she saw his name on the concert program of the New Rockford, North Dakota high school band.

She immigrated to America with a girlfriend in 1908. Among her belongings were a silver watch on a chain, two autograph books, several hardanger pieces, a hand-woven coverlet, a rosemaled sewing chest, a Norwegian primary reading book, and a vest, which had been in her mother's family for five generations. When she left, her mother gave her a gold locket and ring.

After working for one year for a family in South Dakota to pay for her boat passage, she married and moved to a homestead near Wellsburg, North Dakota.

Agnes Elizabeth died in 1981 at the age of 100, without seeing her native land and family again. Later, my mother and I visited her home in Norway. I saw the fish market where she shopped, the shoreline where she walked. What I remember most are the forget-me-nots she planted before she left for America.

Jocelyn Scriba
Bemidji, Minnesota

ranged from 15 years to infancy. Within a week, the seven older children were dead, only the baby and its parents were alive (27 December 1883). Life could be cruel at anytime. An April 1885 report described a family who lived ten miles north of Lovell Township. A man names B. K. Mooney died of consumption at his residence. The paper said, "He leaves wife and a large family in embarrassing circumstances" (23 April 1885).

Whether winter or summer, a certain amount of routine housekeeping matters, simple as they were, occupied the minds of the claim dwellers. Sugar was selling at what was called bargain prices in the summer of 1884: 13 pounds for $1.00. In winter, potatoes were $1.00 per bushel. At certain times during the year oysters were advertised as a special treat. In the spring an array of setting plants were available for the yard and garden: apple trees, roses, grape shoots, vines of various sorts. Flour, feed and lumber could be obtained locally. The nearby Ludden store sold bolts of cotton and cotton flannel for 15 cents a yard. A good horse could be purchased for $200 and flour was $3.50 per hundredweight (12 June 1885).

School was not a high priority, as most settlers were without children. No classes were held in 1883. A school district was forming in the spring of 1884 by combining Lovell and a neighboring township (28 February 1884). By fall of 1885, classes did begin, in the home of a local widow who was both teacher and janitor. The newspaper gives the impression that parents had to be coaxed to tear the younger ones away from chores and send them to school. "It will not be necessary to remind our worthy pioneers that at best the school term for farmer boys and girls

---

In Langdon, on a sunny day in 1915, Nellie Sparling showed up on the Cavalier County Courthouse steps to bid on a piece of land she had selected to be "her farm." Acreages known as "school land," set aside at the time of North Dakota statehood to provide for school funds, were put up for auction periodically. When Nellie put in her bid, the men were so surprised to see a woman enter the bidding, unheard of in those days, that they let her bid stand. Not one made a bid to raise it. So the land was hers.

Audrey Mahoney Will
Dayton, Ohio

is very short, and that if they go to school it must be during the winter months" (13 December 1883).

Church likewise, at least in the initial settlement period, received little emphasis. A preacher came to the Ottawa House for Sunday services several times a month: "Rev. Mr. Wells came regularly" during the summer months of 1884. He left to "resume his theological studies at Andover" back East. Reverend Davidson came, as did Rev. Mr. Hooks. Again, at the Ottawa House, a temperance lecture was given one winter night. The newspaper editor complained that it was a "hackneed subject" (14 February 1884).

When a church did become established in Port Emma, women were crucial in its construction. The newspaper reported, "The Ladies Aid are making vigorous efforts for a church in Port Emma, which is sure to win" (20 May 1884). By fall of 1887, a Methodist church was erected at Ludden, four miles east of the township. This structure, only the second to be built in all of Dickey County, was used regularly for services by Baptists, Methodists and Presbyterians (*The Ludden Times* 14 October 1887).

The high point of the summer's activities was the Fourth of July. In 1885, for example, the newspaper advertised the event weeks before its time. A "parade and a picnic" would be held "on the hills near the Baldwin's Springs on the east line of the township." There was to be a choir, a reading and an address by a war veteran (*Port Emma Times*, 25 June 1885). When the big day arrived, the paper said: "The Fourth of July passed off gloriously," a "six horse bandwagon, 13 girls dressed in white with Miss May Towne in the center around the goddess of liberty, and Miss Alice Devlin as Dakota." Two or three hundred people were present, with songs, chorus and addresses, and the singing of "Marching through Georgia" (9 July 1885).

But summer was mainly a time for work. Land had to be broken, wells dug, gardens planted, poultry and animals cared for. There were federal agents who "checked up" on things. The *Times* of May 20, 1884, warned residents that they had to be honest and genuinely try to fulfill government requirements:

> Don't swear!!! to please a neighbor that a hencoop is a habitable dwelling and a couple of naps on the land, six months of continuous residence. We don't want any U.S. Detectives interviewing people around here.

The pages of the *Port Emma Times* continuously proclaim that the classic democratic virtues of independence, self-determination, egalitarianism, practicality, and hard work characterized Lovell Township and the neighboring areas of Dickey County.

> There is a dignity attached to Dakota farming which can be found nowhere else. We have here doctors, preachers, professors, lawyers and even editors, as owners and actual tillers of the soil. You do not see here the ignorant, ragged, washed-once-a-year farmer that the East produces, but here you find the intelligent, well-dressed farmers coming to town with their 'spanking pair of bays,' and vehicles to match. It seems strange to think that Washington has not heard of Dakota when he said that "Agriculture is the most noble, the most useful and the most healthful employment of man," or something to that effect (*Port Emma Times*, 6 December 1883).

The newspaper reports with approval the comments of a widow who came from the East and after 18 months owned 320 acres: "Instead of the rude, ignorant class I expected to meet, I found people of cultivation, many of whom one would be glad to number among friends in any community. . . .There is so much enterprise, energy and push in every direction. This is eminently a land of workers" (3 September 1885). But there is more than just a frontier *esprit d'corps* involved. The writings and saying of the time embody what seems to be a kind of populist attitude, the sense that Eastern America was soft and even corrupt, that the West was the land of true American virtue. An editorial of December 13, 1883, proclaims:

> Come to the James River Valley. With economy and industry, about $800 and one year's time will place a man in a more comfortable and independent position than $8,000 and 60 years hard toil will in most any of the Eastern states.

Later editorials continue the theme:

> Every day we realize more and more that we live in the finest country in the world—truly the fair "land of the Dakota's," and that when she enters the sisterhood of states it will be as the queen of them all (15 May 1884).

> No wonder the eyes of the staid Yankee stick out when for the first time he beholds the wonderful progress made in the rapidly developing and developed West. The hotel accommodations, the mammoth farms of finest soil, stretching out mile after mile, the metropolitan cities with their churches, high schools, opera houses, and, by no means least, the daily papers, for which Dakota and Montana are famous. The bustle and activity, the energy and force with which enterprises are conceived and executed, all tend to surprise and astonish, and the never-failing result of a personal examination of the West, is the victim pulling stakes in his Eastern home and making all haste to cast his lot with those of this favored part (6 March 1884).

Whatever the noble words about virtue and democracy, it was land people came for; the mere possession of a claim meant profit. The first issue of the *Port Emma Times* contained a one line advertisement: "Money on loan on final proof, T. W. Bush" (20 November 1883). Many hopeful men and women were forced into debt in order to maintain their hold on their claim. "Large proportions of settlers now 'proving up' on their claims are obliged to mortgage and thus receive money required to pay Uncle Sam for the land, the expenses and commissions charged by attorneys . . . also for aid in procuring a team, tools, seed and other requisites." A quarter of land in Lovell Township in the 1890s was worth anywhere from $700 to $1200, and several settlers had "tied up their lands on five year loans of $225 to $300" (22 May 1884). Land claimants, then, who hoped to make a quick profit by selling soon after proving up could be disappointed when expenses diminished their gains by one-fourth or more.

Lovell Township settlers generally were not immigrants to America. Available land office records indicate that 17 of the woman who took land were born in the United States. One seems to have been Canadian-born and another was from Great

Britain. A sense of confidence, a touch of superiority, can be detected in almost every issue of the *Port Emma Times*. Not once in its first three years of publication did the paper discuss in detail a person who was not a "Yankee." The readers were aware of the flood of "rude immigrants" who were taking land elsewhere, but the James River people saw themselves differently. In a news article, John Kendall and son are described as "true Englishmen, they believe in mixed farming, beans, corn, rutabagas." The Eaton neighborhood, only four miles west of Lovell Township, is described as being made up of "Yankees [sic] of the intelligent pushing class, and deserving of squatters' privileges" (31 July 1884 and *Jim River Journal*, 5 October 1883). Foreign-born individuals are never mentioned in the *Times* by their specific name, they are reported in a generic sense. "A Swede came near drowning Thursday." "A Finlander, living between Eaton and Frederick, was frozen to death on his way home last week. A Norwegian south of Eaton was obliged to kill a valuable ox, on account of having a foot cut off" (*Port Emma Times*, 10 January 1884 and 11 September 1884).

The Yankee origins of the settlers may explain the relatively relaxed relationship that seems to have existed between men and women in the Lovell Township social scene. There were no signs of Old Country restraints, no rigid male-female division of labor. Again there seemed to be a kind of frontier equality, almost modern in its emphasis. The newspaper of January 3, 1884, reported, "Port Emma Ladies acted nobly and gallantly under their leap year privileges New Years Day, and harassed all the town boys with calls." Two weeks later on January 17 the paper said, "Girls, engage your boys for the entertainment to-morrow evening." Several months later the *Port Emma Times* described a dance held in the home of a bachelor:

> Last Thursday evening the young people of Port Emma and vicinity assembled at the residence of Mr. Bernard Cook and indulged in dancing for several hours. The bachelor quarters were tastefully decorated; clean, nicely scalloped papers were put upon the shelves by the "genial hostess," Charley McDonald, who is mother, wife, chamber maid and cook in the happy establishment. . . .The party dispersed at an "early hour," and all reached home without any noticeable incident (1 May 1884).

Young men and young women, each living apparently on their own claim, came together regularly for special events: a performance of "Dora, or Driven from Home" by a traveling troop, a corn husking party, a "pound sociable" which hoped to assist the Methodist minister who periodically held local services. In October it was for a skating party, and in January a sleigh ride and a dance in which "all formality was thrown aside" (9 October 1884 and 17 January 1884). An overnight riverboat excursion took place on June 5, 1884. The Nettie Baldwin left Port Emma at 10 a.m. with twenty-six men and women aboard. Their destination was the village of Columbia, 40 miles downstream. The newspaper describes the manner in which the young folks "sailed out upon the bosom of the deep" for two days of "unalloyed pleasure." On the way down there were generous servings of cake, ice cream and sandwiches. At Columbia the party proceeded to the Grand Hotel where the evening was occupied with a dance and entertainment. The next morning the fortunate excursionists reluctantly took leave of their quarters in the Grand Hotel and journeyed back, amid the splendid June foliage, to their Port Emma residences.

All this, at a time when only two years had elapsed since the first dwelling was erected (5 June 1884)!

In its first years of publication, the *Times* never decried a shortage of women in the community. The 1890 Dickey County census did report that there were more men (2051) than women (1795) in the county, but the difference in the totals is slight, a variance of only 165 individuals. Women were complaining, in mid-summer, 1885, that there were too few men in the community, additional bachelors were needed. "Port Emma bachelors [sic], attention, Just at present our social circles might be improved by the addition of more young men. At it is now, there are not quite half enough to go around. Hard on the girls, you bet" (9 July 1885). Regardless of the extent and pace of their social life, many women combined a zest for life with old fashioned "grit." A mid-winter report describes such a woman:

> Mrs. Pickard, a soldier's widow from Kilbourn City, Wis., is holding down a claim fifteen miles south of here....She was a week on the way from Wisconsin, and froze both of her feet going from Frederick to her claim. She is surmounting every difficulty, and after all her trouble thinks Dakota is the place to live. It is just such enterprise and pluck as this that will develop a new country. We want more plucky women and less effeminate men (28 February 1884).

Pluck and "grit" were character traits which allowed many women to think "big." They devoted their energies to expanding and improving their land holdings. A report in Spring 1884 said that the next year Miss Cora Devendorf: " will have 300 acres of wheat." Several months later: "Mrs. H. F. Eaton promises soon to become the bonanza farmer of the James Valley. She has recently purchased the Mrs. McFarlin claim and a choice lot of cattle from Mr. Hermanson's herd. This recent land purchase taken in connection with Mr. Eaton's quarters will give two solid miles of river front and will make one of the finest farms in this section" (27 March 1884 and 1 October 1884).

Apparently it was becoming clear, even at an early date, that part of the secret to success in Dickey County was diversity in farming efforts. Straight wheat farming might be all right over a short time for the opportunist and the speculator, but it could be disaster in a year of drought and bad crops. The *Times* hails a woman with such foresight: "Mrs. Mary Hall is one of the women of Dakota who makes a success of farming. Has 480 acres; 200 under cultivation. Does a big business in butter and eggs; has a fine showing of young stock growing up. She is certainly succeeding" (4 May 1888). Women held their own, took charge of their financial affairs and displayed dedication to improving their property. Yet there was still the sense that women in comparison to men, should be treated with an extra degree of respect; that they should be protected. In May 1884, a newcomer to the Port Emma community tried to usurp the rights of a woman's claim. This gave rise to an outcry of indignation of special intensity:

> It was a matter of no little surprise to many of our citizens to learn that one John N. Martin had filed a homestead upon the quarter section of land one mile west of town which Miss Anna Payne has so faithfully held as a pre-emption for over one year, being absent but a short time this winter on a visit to her former

home in Des Moines. We think Mr. Martn could not have posted himself very thoroughly in regard to the claim, and hope to be able to report the matter a mistake rather than an intentional effort to rob the young lady of that for which she has so long and faithfully worked and waited, and to which she is so justly entitled. It seems to us that no man would endeavor to cheat a lady, or make her unnecessary trouble. Our people feel justly indignant (8 May 1884).

On December 27, 1883, the *Times* editor urged women of all backgrounds to consider this new territory: "School teachers do not hesitate to come to Dakota. Your aspirations can be met. Drive your oxen, ride your plows — there is room for all." The phrase "drive your oxen," "ride your plow" were not made in jest. Yet it is not clear from our evidence that women in the Dakotas were doing these sorts of tasks regularly. Other studies suggest that while there was considerably more cooperation and interchange of roles than previously depicted, a preference still existed among many groups for more traditional arrangements. Women were more likely to be found managing the household, preparing food, caring for gardens, raising poultry, milking cows, and tending to the needs of men and children. Men took care of the plowing, planting, cultivating and caring for the stock. When labor was short women helped out often shocking grain and stacking hay during the harvest. Often a single woman hired a neighbor or relative to do her field work. Older widows usually had sons or relatives to help them.

The descriptions presented throughout this essay imply that the sojourn in North Dakota was seen as a temporary interlude for many homesteaders whether by choice or circumstance. Indeed the local newspaper regularly reported that this or that resident, male or female, was saying good-bye and returning to their home. Their time was up; their task had been fulfilled or they had come face to face with failure. Through the records of the Dickey County Register of Deeds it is possible to trace the land transactions for much of the land claimed by women in Lovell Township. The eventual dispersement of the land of 17 of 19 women reveals a pattern which is probably fairly representative of what happened in the rest of the state.

Nine women sold their land within five years of proving up. Some sold immediately. The profit on their investments varied considerably. Selling prices included, $650, $750, $900, $1300, $2,000. Many of these women probably left the area and perhaps the state after the sale of their land but some undoubtedly moved to other parts of the state and became permanent residents. Alice Eaton filed on a tree claim in 1889, proved up February 1901 and sold the property in April 1901. In the meantime she had married C. S. Brown and the couple moved to Oakes where they became active members of the community. Two women sold their land after a longer period of time had elapsed. Sarah Rowland held on to hers for nine years and Mary Clark for 32. Whether they remained in the community is not known. Four women lost their land in a sheriff's sale, although they had been successful in proving up. Libbie Ralyen inherited her claim from her brother who died before proving up. Clara Rowe, the widow whose husband drowned, lived out her life on her homestead and her land was passed on to heirs. Recollections by her grand-daughters (Ruth Rowe and Clara Saewert, Westminster, California) indicate that life was not easy and she often worried about financial matters: "She wrote many letters back to New York where she had a brother. He gave much encouragement — no money." Nevertheless at a later date Clara's financial situation allowed her to purchase an additional lot in the town of Ludden.

While a few like Clara stayed to establish permanent homes, many saw homesteading as a temporary situation and a good way to make a few dollars. Speculation was commonplace. The temporary nature of such an enterprise seems to be particularly true of the Lovell area. The Anglo-Americans came to the area early but did not stay, and, although the names of places in and around the area still reflect its Anglo-roots, no living relatives of these early women homesteaders can be found still residing in the community. What these women also left behind are insights into early settlement patterns. Homesteading has for the most part been portrayed as a masculine activity, initiated and carried out by men sometimes with the aid of a female helpmate, but records from Lovell Township as well as other areas show that women were active participants in settlement, a part of which included "taking" and "proving up" on homesteads. Some even "jumped the gun." They arrived to "squat" on land before the surveyors came. Not all the dreams came true. Some failed, but the cancelation rate on homesteads for women was no greater than that for men. Many succeeded, expanding their holdings or selling at a profit.

Women of all ages and marital status took advantage of the opportunity to homestead. Young women came looking for adventure and an investment. Widows often sought a permanent residence for themselves and their children. The Anglo-American women who helped settled Lovell Township along with women of many other ethnic backgrounds who homesteaded throughout the territory brought with them the courage and optimism necessary to forge the foundations of today's North Dakota.

References

Black, R. M., ed. *Dickey County*. Ellendale, N.D.: Dickey County Historical Society, 1930.
The Eleventh Census 1890, Part I - Population United States.
Jim River Journal, October 5, 1883.
Lindgren, H. Elaine. "Ethnic Women Homesteading on the Prairies of North Dakota,"
     to be published in *Great Plains Quarterly*, July 1989.
Port Emma Times, **1883**: November 20; December 6, 13, 17, 18, 20, 27, 30; **1884**: January 3, 10,
     17, 24, 31; February 14, 28; March 6, 27, 30; April 12, 24; May 1, 8, 15, 20; June 5, 12; July
     10, 31; August 14, 28, 29; September 11, 14; October 1; November 20; December 20, 24;
     1885: January 15; April 23; June 12, 16, 25; July 2, 9; August 6, 9, 13; September 3; **1888**:
     May 4.
The Ludden Times, October 14, 1887.

H. Elaine Lindgren is Associate Professor in the Department of Sociology/ Anthropology at North Dakota State University. She is studying homesteading women.

William C. Sherman is Associate Professor of Sociology at North Dakota State University and pastor of St. Michael's Church in Grand Forks. He is the author of *Prairie Mosaic* (1982) and co-author of *Plains Folk* (1988).

Nancy Hendrickson planting corn, about 1930.
Photo courtesy of North Dakota State Historical Society.

How Women Support Family Farms

by Polly A. Fassinger and Richard W. Rathge

What do women contribute to contemporary North Dakota family farms? To find out, we conducted a survey of North Dakota farm and ranch women that describes work done in farming households, including farm tasks, housework, and off-farm employment. This paper outlines our findings and develops a qualitative portrait of women's involvement in agriculture by examining what percentage of women independently run agricultural operations, are partners with their spouses, or have little direct involvement in farm work. We also have compared our information on North Dakota farm women's work with data now available on U.S. farm women's labor.

For the most part, women's involvement in agriculture has been poorly documented and poorly understood. Except for a report by Light, Hanson, and Hertsgaard (1983) published after our survey was conducted, we could find no systematic attempts to study the labor of North Dakota farm women. Nonetheless, our review of even the limited literature on farm women's history made us aware of the multifaceted, fluctuating nature of women's involvement in U.S. agriculture. In colonial times, women mainly produced goods for their families, like soap, candles, and clothes. Yet they also cultivated and harvested with other family members and in some cases were responsible for the barter and sale of crops (Kessler-Harris 1981). In the 1800s, when fewer women and men were involved in agriculture because of industrialization, women worked on the land as farm wives, farm managers, daughters of farmers, slaves, sharecroppers, or migrants (Brownlee and Brownlee 1976). During this era, women also were responsible for cooking, housework, child care, clothes making, and for growing from one third to one half of their families' food (Faragher 1981).

In the 1920s, home economists and extension agents conducted what were called "time budget" studies of farm wives. They asked women to keep daily diaries of they way they used their time. Women in those days, as was true in the 1800s, tended wood stoves, carried water to and from the house, and washed and wrung clothes by hand. These tasks were in addition to child care and daily housekeeping, including food preservation and preparation, which took as much as 50 percent of a woman's work time (Wasson 1930). By examining four well-documented time studies (Crawford 1927, Studley 1931, Wasson 1930, Wilson 1929), we found farm women averaged about 53 hours per week doing housework. This represented roughly 82 percent of their work week. The other 18 percent was spent doing farm tasks (about 12 hours per week). Wasson's (1930) study of 100 South Dakota farm wives showed women's work weeks ranged from 35 hours to 95 hours; the average was more than 66 hours. More than 50 hours were devoted to weekly housework. These wives also spent an average of more than 11 hours per week with such farm chores as field work, gardening, poultry care, and dairying. Similarly, Wilson's (1929) research in Oregon revealed that more than 97 percent of women on farms did farm work regularly, usually for about 11 to 15 hours per week.

As the United States industrialized in the 1800s, farm work came to be increasingly market-oriented, and only those activities that directly produced goods or services for the marketplace were seen by researchers as being relevant to farming. However, we think that market-oriented farm tasks, while important, are only one element of the economics of family farming and ranching. Other supportive activities like family care and home maintenance work, though hidden from the marketplace, contribute to the financial stability of farming families and to the success of agricultural operations.

The Study

We are interested in the multifaceted nature of women's work for family farms, including their unpaid farm labor, housework, family care, and off-farm work. (We realize also that women might work for organizations that promote family farming, or help neighbors by exchanging labor and other resources, but we have not investigated these possibilities.) We focused on the eastern part of the state because we felt that the western region, which has recently undergone some dramatic changes due to energy development, might present an atypical view of farming and ranching in North Dakota.

In 1983, we mailed a questionnaire to a random sample of eastern North Dakota farm women, having obtained their names from an agency that had a listing of more than 95 percent of all eastern North Dakota farmsteads. About 70 percent, or 120, responded. The questionnaire listed 28 common farm chores and asked women which person on their farms normally did each task, and who normally helped with these tasks. We also listed 21 home and family-care tasks and asked who normally did them, and who helped. All the women responding were married and averaged 46 years of age; they had been farming with their husbands for an average of 22 years. Their farms averaged 1,005 operated acres, mainly devoted to wheat and barley. More than 90 percent of the operations we surveyed involved field work (such as planting and combining small grains, preparing fields for planting, applying fertilizer, and hauling grain to the elevator); maintenance work (such as minor machinery repair and getting machine parts); and managerial tasks (such as paying farm bills, bookkeeping, and planning crop schedules).

Farm Work

More than three-quarters of the women in our survey are regularly involved with paying farm bills, doing farm bookkeeping, and buying or getting machine parts on farms where these tasks are done. Almost half the women haul grain and fix fences. In fact, at least 44 percent of the women we surveyed are involved in half of the farm tasks about which we inquired (see Table 1).

Husbands are much more involved with the group of 28 tasks than are wives, although none of the farm chores are done solely by men. At least 75 percent of the husbands do, or help with, 20 of the 28 chores. More than 90 percent of the men are commonly involved with buying and getting machine parts, checking market prices, doing minor machinery repairs, planning the cropping schedule, buying farm equipment, and planting small grains for operations on which these tasks are done.

Off-farm Work

While 57 percent of the wives have worked off-farm at some time since their marriage, currently 26 percent do so. Seventeen percent of the husbands also work off-farm. More than half of the women who have worked off-farm said they did so primarily because of their families' financial need.

At present (in 1988) American farmers are experiencing the worst financial crisis since the 1930s. Low commodity prices, high interest rates, declining land values, and increasing production costs have placed many farm families in severe financial hardship. As many as 41 percent of North Dakota's farms with annual sales over $40,000 are in poor economic condition, with more than 40 cents of debt for every dollar of total assets (Leistritz et al. 1987). When financial strain hits, farm women often seek off-farm employment, in North Dakota as elsewhere. The sum of all off-farm earnings of North Dakota farm women has risen sharply in recent years; by 31 percent in 1983-1984 and by 34 percent in 1984-1985 (Leistritz et al. 1986). However, as wives leave to work off-farm, farm families may feel unexpected impacts, because women's off-farm work often does not offset the associated costs of the many household and farm tasks not done by these working women. Estimates of the value of women's household and child care duties range as high as $20,000 annually (Hefferan 1982). Data suggest that in 1985, 58 percent of North Dakota farm women were employed in low paying sales and service occupations. Roughly one-fourth of working farm women earned under $3,000 (Goreham et al. 1987, Leistritz et al. 1986). Thus, for many farm families, women's off-farm work may be an ineffective strategy for offsetting financial obligations, due to the families' loss of potential labor at home and on the farm and the small incomes women earn off-farm. This could help explain why a panel study of 933 randomly selected North

Table 1: Percent of sample involved in common farm tasks

Task	Wives		Husbands	
	do	help	do	help
Plan cropping schedule	01	24	97	01
Minor machinery repair	02	16	89	03
Buy, get machine parts	11	66	85	06
Pay farm bills	38	38	62	11
Plant small grains	00	05	90	04
Prepare fields for planting	06	16	81	05
Combine small grains	05	22	80	02
Haul grain to elevator	10	43	81	03
Do farm bookkeeping	46	30	53	09
Apply fertilizer	03	05	84	04
Buy farm equipment	01	17	97	01
Apply chemicals	00	07	84	04
Work summer fallow	07	16	74	05
Haul small grains	23	37	59	04
Check market prices	09	35	87	06
Major machinery overhauls	01	07	59	04
Plant row crops	00	04	79	07
Cultivate row crops	00	07	73	06
Haul row crops	15	29	66	05
Combine row crops	04	17	78	05
Fix fences	04	42	84	03
Cut, put up hay	07	29	85	02
Feed livestock	12	41	81	05

Table 2: Percent of sample involved in common household tasks

Task	Wives		Husbands	
	do	help	do	help
Cook dinner	100	00	00	07
Canning and freezing	100	00	00	05
Baking	99	00	00	04
Clothing care	99	00	00	07
Vacuuming, floor care	99	00	00	09
Wash dishes	98	00	00	17
Grocery shopping	97	02	03	26
Child care	97	01	01	33
Child transportation	95	02	02	38
Dust furniture	94	02	00	04
Fix breakfast	85	11	13	07
Pay household bills	84	08	15	18
Tend vegetable garden	83	12	13	18
Yard work	76	14	17	28

Dakota farm households shows that farm couples who worked off-farm reported lower net farm incomes and higher debt-to-asset ratios than their counterparts who did not work off-farm (Leistritz et al. 1986).

Household and Family Care

Housework and child care in these farming families are mainly done by the wives. We asked the women to say who normally "does" and who normally "helps" with 21 common household and family chores. More than 90 percent of the wives report that they are involved often in 18 of these 21 tasks. Most husbands help with or do three tasks: repairing small appliances, carpentry repairs, and plumbing work. However, these three tasks are not commonly done in most of the households (see Table 2).

Overall then, we can say that household work and family care overwhelmingly fall on women's shoulders in these farm homes. And if anyone works off-farm, it is more likely the wife. Women also are quite involved in the duties we identified as farm tasks, since about 44 percent of the women usually do or help with half of the tasks done on their farms or ranches.

A Qualitative Portrait

While these findings provide some quantitative assessment of farm women's work, we also wondered about the qualitative differences that might be hidden within our sample. Among the "average" portraits, were there women extensively involved in farm work? Were there many women who rarely, or perhaps never, engage in farm tasks? In order to discern farm women's different work patterns, we used a typology developed by Pearson (1979) and modified by Lodwick and Fassinger (1979). These researchers hypothesized that women's involvement in their farming operations may exist on a continuum. On one end of the continuum we could expect to find "independent agricultural producers," women who perform most tasks on their farms. According to Pearson (1979), women commonly become independent producers because of the loss of their spouse. In a sample of mostly married couples, one would expect to find few independent agricultural producers. Only one woman in our sample of 120 households is an independent producer.

The term "agricultural partners" applies to women who, usually with their spouses, are responsible for carrying out many farm tasks. A management role is integral to agricultural partners, so most management tasks such as planning a cropping schedule, paying farm bills, checking market prices, buying farm machinery, and bookkeeping are usually done by agricultural partners. In addition, agricultural partners tend to do or help with many other farm chores, such as cultivating or hauling grain. There are six agricultural partners in our sample.

The third group, the "agriculturally active," are involved daily in farm work. They may do many of the tasks agricultural partners do, but these women tend not to be primarily responsible for management decisions. Much of the time they do farm work by "helping" others with chores. In our sample, women who are engaged in at least seven farm tasks are considered agriculturally active; their involvement in farm chores is above average compared to other North Dakota farm women. Our sample contains 48 agriculturally active farm women.

"Farm helpers" (38 women in our sample) are women who participate in some farm chores (usually three to six different tasks). Their work tends to increase during busy times, such as harvests when tasks include combining small grains, hauling crops, and running errands (such as getting machine parts). Women who do no field work but who support their farming operations through other farm tasks such as bookkeeping, paying farm bills, and running errands are "farm homemakers." There were 19 women in our sample. The eight "household helpers" in our sample do no farm tasks, but their homemaking enables others to do their farm chores more efficiently. In this typology, women are not classified according to their involvement in housework and family care, because the vast majority of farm women do most of their families' housework. Women's housework activities remain constantly high throughout the six types.

In comparison to Lodwick and Fassinger's (1979) exploratory study of two Michigan townships, North Dakota farm women are less likely to be independent operators (2% in Michigan versus .8% in North Dakota) and agricultural partners (15% versus 5%). Yet North Dakota women are more likely to be agriculturally active (21% versus 40%) and farm helpers (17% versus 32%). The largest proportion of Michigan women were farm homemakers (35%) while only 16 percent of North Dakota farm women are similarly involved. Of course, farming is different in Michigan. The operations studied by Lodwick and Fassinger (1979) were much smaller and both women and men were much more likely to work off-farm.

North Dakota and the United States: A Comparison

How do North Dakota farm women compare to farm women in the rest of the United States? Rosenfeld (1985) acquired data from a 1980 national telephone survey of farm women. Farm women were asked about their involvement in 15 home and farm tasks — whether they were regularly involved, occasionally involved, or never involved in each of 15 duties. Almost all women (97%) said they were regularly involved with housework activities and in looking after children (87%), as one might expect (although not all households had young children living at home). Additionally, more than three-quarters of United States farm women said they regularly or occasionally do farm bookkeeping (78%), run farm errands, such as picking up repair parts (85%), and care for a garden or animals for family use (88%). Thirty-one percent of the women Rosenfeld surveyed in 1980 worked off-farm, mostly because of financial need.

While the questions we asked North Dakota farm women are not identical to those of Rosenfeld, we can make some comparisons between the two studies. To begin with, bookkeeping, paying bills, and running errands for the operation are the tasks most often done both by women in North Dakota and the nation as a whole. This finding is interesting because previous researchers mainly have thought of farming as work done in fields or barns. Even the time studies of the 1920s and 1930s assumed this. Yet bookkeeping and paying bills may be done at home and errands are done away from home. Because these chores are not traditional outdoor farm tasks, we wonder how often researchers may overlook their significance. For example, when the United States Bureau of the Census (1980) records unpaid family laborers, they look for persons who worked on the farm for 15 or more hours per week. This definition implies that farm work is done *on* the land and not in or away from the home. Until we better understand the nature of farm women's work, contributions like these will be ignored and undocumented.

Of course, many United States and North Dakota farm women do perform field and barn work. Around one-third of these women (37% in the nation and 32% in the state) participate in the initial stages of growing crops by plowing, planting, and cultivating. Additionally, more than half of all farm women in North Dakota and the nation do harvest work, such as combining and hauling crops. These tasks are more traditional types of farm work. Still, as we noted earlier, few researchers have taken a serious look at the overall contributions women make to their families' farming operations.

We believe there are two primary reasons for researchers' inattention to farm women's work. First, these authors do not fully appreciate the various tasks (not always related to field or barn work) women do to support their farm families. Work that enables others to do direct market-oriented activities (such as feeding hired hands) often goes unnoticed. In the future, we need to expand common notions of what farm work is and acknowledge that family farms' market-oriented labor is supported by many hidden factors of production (Oakley 1974). Second, researchers have too readily accepted notions of the division of labor on farms which relegate women to housework and men to farm work. Yet as Kohl (1977) discovered, even when men and women uphold a segregated division of labor as "the way things are done," many women can be observed doing a great deal of field work and other farm chores. By only listening to people's descriptions of daily life and not watching their behavior, we may get a distorted view of what occurs on farms.

The notion of separate jobs for women and men is pervasive. This was displayed in Rosenfeld's (1985) study of United States farm women's self-perceptions. She asked farm women how they identified themselves on their tax forms. Sixty percent of all farm women called themselves mother, wife, or housewife. Only eight percent labeled themselves as either farm wife, farmer, or rancher. However, Rosenfeld also asked each woman whether she was a main operator of her farm (i.e., a daily decision-maker); Rosenfeld discovered that most women (55%) felt they were. Yet 59% of these main farm operators had listed their occupations as wife, mother, or housewife on their tax forms. Only 12 percent listed themselves as either farm wife or farmer/rancher. The remainder stated "other" occupations. On the surface, these two responses seem contradictory. Farm women consider themselves very actively involved in and responsible for their families' operations, but often do not see themselves as farmers. Instead, their family or homemaking roles seem more central to their self-concepts. This centrality makes sense, given that women do the vast majority of family care and housework. Still, while women may say they are homemakers, their lives are heavily embedded in daily farm work. By failing to acknowledge their multiple occupations or roles, farm women unintentionally could be enabling researchers and the general public to overlook their labor.

Conclusion

According to our data, farm women in North Dakota do most of the housework for their households, are more likely than their husbands to work off-farm, and often do farm work (since almost half of all women regularly do about half of the farm tasks we studied). In comparison with other areas of the nation, it is likely that women in our state are more actively involved in outdoor farm tasks (as agriculturally active or farm helpers); however, North Dakota farm women are similar to most farm women in their extensive involvement in farm tasks such as bookkeeping, running errands, and paying bills.

Women's contributions to North Dakota agriculture are substantial. However, in part because of a still pervasive ideology that rigidly separates men's work and women's work, we believe women's contributions to North Dakota agriculture are undervalued. The federal government's farm policies often assume farming operations are run by an individual, rather than by a marital partnership. According to Brodshaug (1986), payments by government agencies are generally given to a sole registered producer. If the wife wishes to be included in the money transfer, she must provide proof of her participation in farming, but her husband need not prove his participation. Additionally, many farm cooperatives and farm credit organizations regard farms as units with single proprietors. Thus the Production Credit Association gives voting rights to only one person, even when both spouses sign a loan with that organization (Brodshaug 1986). Too, North Dakota has yet to adopt the Uniform Marital Property Act which would automatically recognize half of all farmland acquired after a marriage as the wife's property. We need to revise policies and programs that undervalue women's contributions to North Dakota agriculture. Farm women deserve this recognition from their communities and state.

References

Brodshaug, J. Women in Agriculture, Full Partners on the Family Farm: Myth or Reality? Master's Thesis. Moorhead, Minn.: Moorhead State University, 1986.

Brownlee, W. and M. Brownlee. *Women in the American Economy.* New Haven, Conn.: Yale University Press, 1976.

Crawford, I. *The Use of Time by Farm Women.* Bulletin 146. Moscow: University of Idaho Agricultural Experiment Station, 1927.

Faragher, J. "History from the Inside-out: Writing the History of Women in Rural America." *American Quarterly.* 33, 1981.

Goreham, G., R. Rathge and F. Leistritz. "Value of Off-farm Employment as a Strategy to Meet Farm Financial Obligations." Paper presented at the annual meeting of the Southern Regional Science Association, Atlanta, Ga., 1987.

Hefferan, C. "What is a Homemaker's Job Worth? Too Many Answers." *Journal of Home Economics.* 74 , 1982.

Kessler-Harris, A. *Women Have Always Worked.* Old Westbury, N.Y.: The Feminist Press, 1981.

Kohl, S. "Women's Participation in the North American Family Farm." *Women's Studies International Quarterly,* January 1977.

Leistritz, F., A. Leholm, H. Vreugdenhil, and B. Ekstrom. "Effect of Farm Financial

Stress on Off-farm Work Behavior of Farm Operators and Spouses in North Dakota." *North Central Journal of Agricultural Economics,* July 1986.

Leistritz, F., W. Hardie, B. Ekstrom, A. Leholm and H. Vreugdenhil. *Financial, Managerial, and Attitudinal Characteristics of North Dakota Farm Families: Results of the 1986 Farm Survey.* Agricultural Economics Report No. 22. Fargo: North Dakota State University, 1987.

Light, H., D. Hanson and D. Hertsgaard. "The Work of North Dakota Farm and Ranch Women." *North Dakota Farm Research Bimonthly Bulletin.* September/ October 1983.

Lodwick, D. and P. Fassinger. "Variations in Agricultural Production Activities of Women on Family Farms." Paper presented at the annual meeting of the Rural Sociological Society, Burlington, Vt., 1979.

Oakley, A. *Woman's Work.* New York: Vintage Books, 1974.

Pearson, J. "Note on Female Farmers." *Rural Sociology.* 44, 1979.

Rosenfeld, R. *Farm Women.* Chapel Hill: University of North Carolina Press, 1985.

Studley, L. *Relationship of the Farm Home to the Farm Business.* Bulletin 279. St Paul: University of Minnesota Agricultural Experiment Station, 1931.

U.S. Bureau of the Census. *Census of Population: 1980.* Volume 1. Chapter C. General Social and Economic Characteristics. Washington, D.C.: U.S. Government Printing Office, 1980.

Wasson, G. *Use of Time by South Dakota Farm Homemakers.* Bulletin 247. Brookings: South Dakota State College Agricultural Experiment Station, 1930.

Wilson, M. *Use of Time by Oregon Farm Homemakers.* Bulletin 256. Corvallis: Oregon State University Agricultural College Experiment Station, 1929.

Polly Fassinger is Assistant Professor of Sociology at Concordia College in Moorhead, Minnesota. She received her doctorate from Michigan State University where she specialized in the areas of gender, work and families.

Richard Rathge is Associate Professor of Sociology and Agricultural Economics at North Dakota State University and directs the State Census Data Center. He received his doctorate from Michigan State University where he specialized in demography, rural sociology, and social organizations.

Jessie Webb Corwin in a 1915 photograph wearing a broad-brimmed black beaver hat. Picture courtesy of the Fred Hultstrand "History in Pictures" Collection, North Dakota Institute for Regional Studies, North Dakota State University, Fargo.

A Record in Fabric

by Shirley E. Friend

Looking at clothes worn in the past — what they were made of and how they were made, what materials were used and what styles and colors and designs were favored most — adds to what we can know about how women lived and worked day by day, and how they adapted prevailing styles of living to their particular circumstances. For example, knowing that prairie women wore bustles in the 1880s tells us of their desire to duplicate the styles of their eastern counterparts. Katherine Winslow studied changes Norwegian immigrants made in their clothing that would give evidence of their acculturation. Between 1870 and 1900, she found, clothing worn in cities in Norway varied considerably from what was worn in the country: urban women wore fashionable dress and rural women favored traditional costumes (Winslow 1983). Letters written by immigrants in the U.S. to correspondents in Europe revealed that new immigrants looked different to people from their own country who had arrived earlier. Norwegians already in North Dakota advised anyone planning to come to bring a good supply of cloth; prices were higher in the U.S. than in Norway and fabric was of lower quality. Later advice changed, and new travelers were urged to bring only what they needed for the trip because transporting large quantities of clothing was expensive and difficult. Newcomers who planned to be servants and seamstresses were advised to adopt American dress styles because American employers wanted anyone working in their homes to wear American styles. But, Winslow found, those who settled in predominantly Norwegian areas were less likely to alter their style of dress than those who lived in communities of mixed ethnic backgrounds.

In a study of the clothing worn more generally by immigrant women on the northern plains, Gerilyn Tandberg interviewed children of four families who had come to Dakota Territory from Sweden and Norway. She also looked at photographs taken between 1880 and 1907, and at a few garments dated from 1892 to 1910. Like Winslow, Tandberg thought immigrants wanted to conform quickly to American dress styles, and found that in her group even those who settled in communities dominated by their own ethnic group (Swedish or Norwegian) quickly changed to "American" clothes. Social class, she thought, had less to do with determining how members of these four families dressed than did their individual "personalities, taste, self perceptions and aspirations."

Joyce Marie Larson (1978) describes clothing worn in the Territory between 1861 and 1889, and now in museums and private collections in South Dakota. She points out that rail transportation ended the need for women to make all of their own clothing. She and others show that by the 1870s weaving essentially was a thing of the past. People bought clothes locally, ordered by mail, hired a dressmaker, or sewed themselves. Sewing machines were available after 1850. By the time of statehood, fabric production by North Dakota women was, as elsewhere, pretty much limited to knitting. Susan Armitage (1979) studied descriptions of housework between 1895 and 1920 in oral histories in Colorado, and said this about clothing construction:

> Women made clothes for themselves and for their children; men's work clothes were usually store-bought. For years flour sacks were printed in calico so that they could be recycled into boys' shirts or little girls' dresses. For women, clothing styles were extremely simple and easy to sew. Fashionable clothes, requiring skilled dressmaking, were completely out of the reach of most women. Women also knitted stockings and mittens. None of the clothesmaking was supplemental or ornamental; it was essential, basic provision of clothing.

The most easily available evidence about women's clothing comes, not surprisingly, from the preserved wardrobes of middle and upper middle class urban women, who dressed in much the same way as their contemporaries did in more settled parts of the U.S. The dresses and coats and other garments that are the basis of this study are now preserved in such collections as the Emily Reynolds Costume Collection (Department of Apparel, Textiles and Interior Design, North Dakota State University, Fargo), and show what was worn as well as how clothing was made and marketed. While commercially produced dress patterns were available before statehood (1889), some women continued to cut patterns from existing garments. (In the early nineties, when she was married and homesteading in Garborg Township, Richland County, Kari Williamson owned the only sewing machine in the community, and used it until her death at age 90.)

Dressmakers often used a drafting model, such as one labeled "French A La Mode Modesta Pattern" distributed by a dealer in Cavalier for $5. Both the Butterick and McCall companies were producing commercial tissue patterns by the late 1800s, and women's publications like *Godey's Lady's Book, The Delineator*, and *Peterson's Magazine* printed sewing information.

Clothing was sold first in general stores, and as population increased, so did the numbers of stores specializing in clothing. Fargo's first general store opened in 1871 in a tent, but by 1879 J. deLendrecies opened as The Chicago Dry Goods Store. In

1882 the Straus Company opened a store in Valley City and another in Fargo in 1899; the Straus establishment is still managed by the same family. In Bismarck, Daniel Eisenberg opened a general merchandise store in 1875 which sold clothing, furniture and groceries, and by 1878 four more stores had opened in Bismarck. (Silverman's in Grand Forks, according to family legend, was begun by the father and grandfather of the present owners. He had been a peddler, walking from town to town with a push-cart, and when he got to Grand Forks decided he had walked enough and opened a men's clothing store.)

The sheer number and variety of activities women were enjoying in North Dakota towns at the turn of the century suggest full wardrobes. Letters, diaries, and newspapers report operas and minstrel shows, dances and costume parties, and sports such as skating, baseball, sleighing, horseback riding and croquet, as well as buggy and wagon rides. The town of Brinsmade instituted a Gopher Day in 1902, paying a penny a tail to rid the community of gophers, considered pests. Brinsmade's Gopher Day became a social event, with races, prizes, a merry-go-round, games, speakers, and a dance, "a day to be dressed up. The boys exchanged their overalls for a suit and the girls wore their best dresses, in pastel colors, over two or three stiffly starched petticoats" (Foy). May Bethia Roberts, while she was a student at UND in 1888, described going to an "entertainment of songs, essays and recitations":

> After signing a paper to mind Miss Allen our chaperone, we were allowed to go to the party in the big bus; 13 went down and about 40 were there. We played games & enjoyed ourselves until 11:00 PM, had a lovely repast of cakes, sandwiches, and fruits, and as it was the first time I have seen Grand Forks society & thought it very nice, wore my black silk and Elena her black dress (and she didn't look as well as usual), Miss Todd's pale blue silk & swan's down, Miss Anderson red cashmere, Miss Wettington green and yellow, Miss Creeks dark dress & lace collar (Hampsten 1979).

Although most of the clothing that we can see people wearing in photographs generally follows fashion, some descriptions and photographs tell how fashionable clothing was modified in cold weather. Men can be seen wearing a sweater under their jacket rather than a vest. Mary Dodge Woodward, who farmed with her sons near Fargo, writes in *The Checkered Years* of astrakkan and buffalo coats, and says her son Walter wore two coats for one trip to Fargo. She and her daughter Katie wore "shoes made of woolen braid woven basket-fashion, lined with wool in the fleece" for warmth in the house, and more than once Mary Woodward referred to wearing her hood, shawl and mittens while cooking because the kitchen was so cold.

Clothing from the settlement period in the Emily Reynolds Costume Collection also indicates the quality of clothing available as well as the varied social life even at such an early period of the region's history. Amelia Mickle was born in Berlin, Germany, emigrated with her family to Canada and moved to Park River at age 18. She married George Henry Walker, a blacksmith. Her dress, still in excellent condition, is in the fashionable styling of the mid-1880s: of finely woven wool, silk lace and ribbon trims, with a cotton sateen underlining. Pleated detailing and crochet-covered buttons show the skill and care that went into its construction, and suggest that blacksmithing in Park River was a prosperous and socially prestigious occupation.

A two-piece dress worn in 1893 by Mrs. Peter Stockstead, who with her husband farmed near Milner, is of loosely woven coarse wool yarns, the neckline filled with silk moire. Braid trims the bodice. The skirt is lined with a cotton sateen to provide more body and is worn with a small bustle pad covered in the same fabric. Mrs. Stockstead's daughter Alma Gilbertson, of Kindred, remembers the dress, that it was her mother's "best dress, both winter and summer," and that after her mother no longer wore it, she used the skirt to warm rising bread. Both pieces of the dress show signs of heavy use, with patched holes in the skirt. Alma Gilbertson believes her mother made the dress, because she was an excellent seamstress and sewed all of the family's clothing.

Although labels on some items of clothing indicate that they were purchased, most can be assumed to have been hand-sewn, either by their owners, or by seamstresses, and demonstrate the high level of skill that went into high fashion. A woman named Mary Hannaher sewed for the Rindlab-Woolege family of Fargo, providing them with lingerie decorated with rows of tucks and lavish use of lace, including silk pegnoirs, a lace and ribbon corset cover, cotton nightgown, cotton open drawers, and cotton petticoat. Rural people of modest means tried to keep at least one approximately fashionable costume.

Because people tend only to preserve or describe or take pictures of clothing for special occasions — wedding gowns, christening dresses, burial clothing — it is more difficult to know what people wore for work. Work clothes seldom last long enough to be preserved in museums. Work clothes for men and women shown in pictures include heavy boots, rough pants and shirts for men, Mother Hubbards (loose, shapeless dresses sometimes worn with a belt) for women. Mary Dodge Woodward hints at the controversy over women's unrestricted clothing (the more acceptable being the fashionable silhouettes).

> I have cut out the dress which Nellie sent me. Were I farther west, I should not dare to make it "Mother Hubbard" as the paper says that in Pendleton, Oregon, that type of costume is prohibited unless worn belted. Bills to that effect have been posted in the town, ladies who violate the ordinance being fined heavily. The alleged reason is that such garments "scare horses, cause accidents, and ruin business."

Very poor people in these same years did not display, or feel "grand" about their clothing, but struggled to keep clean and warm. Pauline Diede, of Hebron, in *Homesteading on the Knife River Prairies* (1983), has described how her parents' and her aunt and uncle's families arrived in 1909 from Russia with "meager" supplies. They had to discard bedding because it had become infested with bedbugs during the sea voyage. Arriving in Ashley in the middle of the winter, Pauline's father borrowed a sheepskin coat because he had no money to buy a coat, and he marveled at the riches that permitted another man to have an extra coat to lend. During their early days, the two families "did not have enough for a complete change for each person." Rags were used to diaper babies, and children "had little more than what they wore, and were barefoot."

But for those who could afford good clothing, prevailing fashions nation-wide were important to people in towns and farms from the earliest days of North Dakota settlement, and they reflect the way many settlers bridged two worlds, the one of elegance and improving conveniences of eastern urban sections, and the other of more primitive living conditions — and hard work. Younger women and those with active social lives felt a greater need for fashionable clothes than did older, less social women, but even farm women and men had a "good" dress or suit for Sunday best.

References

Armitage, S. H. "Household Work and Childrearing on the Frontier: The Oral History Record," *Sociology and Social Research*, Vol. 63, No. 3, April 1979.

Diede, P. N. *Homesteading on the Knife River Prairies*, Elizabeth Hampsten, ed. Bismarck, ND: Germans from Russia Heritage Society, 1983.

Emily Reynolds Costume Collection. Fargo: Department of Apparel, Textiles and Interior Design, North Dakota State University.

Foy, S. R. Memories of Brinsmade. Fargo: North Dakota Institute for Regional Studies, North Dakota State University, 1976.

Jonason, L. N. Dressmaking in North Dakota Between 1890 and 1920: Equipment, Supplies and Methods. Master's Thesis. Fargo: North Dakota State University, 1977.

Larson, J. M. Clothing of Pioneer Women of Dakota Territory, 1861-1889. Master's Thesis. Brookings: South Dakota State University, 1978.

Tandberg, Gerilyn. "New World -- Old Fashions? Immigrant Clothing on Northern Plains. *Dress*, 13. Storrs: University of Connecticut, 1987.

Winslow, K. Dress of Norwegian Immigrants to North Dakota. Master's Thesis. Fargo: North Dakota State University, 1983.

Woodward, Mary Dodge. *The Checkered Years*, M. B. Cowdrey, ed. Reprint. West Fargo: Cass County Historical Society, 1984.

Shirley Friend is Professor and Chair of the Department of Apparel, Textiles and Interior Design at North Dakota State University in Fargo, where she supervises the Emily Reynolds Costume Collection of historic garments.

AIRPLANE RIDES

FLY WITH HOWARD BURLESON
In A New 1937 Five Passenger STINSON
RELIANT --- with Electric Controlable
Propeller and Vacuum Landing Flaps

AND EVELYN BURLESON
Only Woman Transport Pilot in North Dakota
IN HER REARWIN SPORTSTER

1c Per Lb.   Maximum $1.50

Place *Carrington*
Date *Sun. Aug. 22nd*

Photos courtesy of 99's Resource Center.

Up and Away Over the Barn

by Judy Logue

Evelyn Waldren was a barnstormer in North Dakota during the Depression. She and her husband managed flight operations at the Jamestown airport, and flew a variety of other jobs to pay the aircraft expenses. Evelyn logged 23,000 hours in a fifty-seven year career as she ferried, instructed, hunted coyotes, flew fire patrol, and even flew record-setting flights. But it was barnstorming that made her notorious. Her friend Dorothy Hester Stenzel spoke about barnstorming during the Depression: "We'd all get together in one car, drive out to the field where the planes were landing, share a fried chicken picnic and wait for someone to kill themselves." In an oral history recorded by the Ninety-Nines, an international organization of women pilots, Evelyn described her career as a barnstormer:

> We'd go out every weekend during the season. We had an advance man who would find a suitable field (we liked stubble fields), and he'd pass out bills advertising that we'd be in town, and then that weekend he'd decorate the fences with balloons and crepe paper to show where we'd be landing.
>
> Well for the entire weekend we'd put on a show every two hours. We usually had five or six planes. We'd do aerobatics, and we usually had a parachute jumper. He'd use the time between shows to re-pack his chute. Then we'd sell airplane rides for $1 a ride. We got so we could give a ride in just about six minutes.
>
> Oley had a chance wheel like you see on television now. He had it set up on a table made out of two oil barrels and some planks. The wheel had numbers from one to ten and then there were corresponding numbers from one to ten down on the surface of the table. People would come up and put a dime down on a number and that would pay for a spin of the wheel. If their number came up they'd have won a $1 ride for 10 cents. It was Oley's idea and it was a good one. We always had at

least fifty rides paid up and waiting. Sometimes we'd fly way after dark and land by the light of car headlights.

In those days Evelyn flew a Wright Jr, a fragile ship with the pusher propeller behind the pilot. One of her adventures might have turned out worse than it did, and was fairly typical of the strange, unsettled life of a barnstormer, and of many people who found odd, but imaginative and sometimes dangerous ways of earning a living during the Depression. The story that Evelyn tells is about a man who had paid for an airplane ride:

> So we got up to four or five hundred feet and he decided to crawl up into the cockpit with me. Well, it overbalanced the airplane and the nose went down and I couldn't hold it up, and I thought well, we're going to die here, that's all. So I gave him a great big shove and got him back in his seat and he stayed there. I thought, ye gods, I've never had an experience like that before. Then all of a sudden I heard a clatter-clatter and I thought, Oh oh, he's waved at somebody, he's put his hand in the propeller behind him and he's got his hand cut off. But, that wasn't the cause. He'd thrown his hat out and the hat went into the propeller. I'll bet that hat was in a million pieces by the time it got to the ground.
>
> I thought, I've got to find some way to get rid of this guy. He's a pain in the neck. But he'd bought $26 worth of tickets and that was a couple of hours more flying time than the range of the airplane. So, I thought real fast and said, "How would you like a little trip and fly to some of the towns around here?" and he said, "Sure." So I figured that if I charged him 20 cents a mile instead of the usual 10 cents that we'd just about fly out the $26. So we flew around to some of the little towns, then I took him back and I hoped that he wouldn't be unhappy because we got back so soon. But he was happy. He was so happy that he reached into his pocket and gave me a silver dollar tip.

Later that night after all the flying for the day was done, Evelyn went to the general store, which was the local evening hang-out, and there was her unruly passenger (who she thought "may have been drinking"). He handed her a large sack and said, "Here, this is for my pilot." She examined the contents after she got home.

> Why, there was cake, cookies, candy, bananas, oranges, apples, grapes, gum, everything imaginable. And at the very bottom of the sack were five more silver dollars. Well, I really felt foolish about having cheated the man, but whenever we went back to that town, he was always there. He always bought rides, and I always gave him extra flying time to make up for cheating him that first time.

Evelyn Waldren's career was marked by the contradictions displayed in that story: professional accomplishment and physical courage in flying, mixed sometimes with human weakness, all colored by very difficult economic times, when ingenuity could mean survival, but at personal cost.

Her early life prepared her well for hard times, but not for stable relationships. The ten years she barnstormed in Jamestown were her longest stay anywhere. She was born in 1908 in a small town in central Nebraska. Her mother, Mary, was a first-generation German immigrant, and her father, named Bill Nichols, she described as a wheeler-dealer in livestock sales. He gambled, and for that reason Mary left him when Evelyn was still a small child. Mary married a man who worked as dragline operator with the railroad. Evelyn remembered a Gypsy-like childhood, as her step-father built and repaired railroads in Nebraska, Kansas, Colorado, Utah, Wyoming and the Dakotas. Often their home was the crew train. It was hard to make friends, and Evelyn and her younger sister invariably were the new kids in town; worse, they were thought part of a threatening itinerant population and referred to as "those damned Dagos." The two girls often were shipped back to Nebraska to live with relatives for months at a time, and usually separated to make it easier for the families who took them in. Evelyn graduated from eighth grade in Bonneville, Wyoming, but constant moving kept her from finishing high school.

In the 1920s, when Evelyn was a teenager, aviation was gaining public attention, particularly record-setting flights — who could fly the highest, the longest, or perform the most continuous loops. Women attracted a share of the public's thirst for sensationalism; flying created heroes who were women that young girls could look up to, like Amelia Earhart, Ruth Elder, Phoebe Omilie, Louise Thaden, Viola Gentry. These were Evelyn's heroes too, and she wanted flying lessons. After months of Evelyn's pleading, her mother agreed to pay for lessons. That was the beginning of a life-long career in aviation. Evelyn began working in the office of the Lincoln Flying Service for $14 and one hour of flying per week. Soon she moved to the Arrow Aircraft factory and covered wings for the same salary and flying time. In 1929, when she was 20, Evelyn married her flight instructor, Howard Burleson.

The couple moved to Jamestown, North Dakota, to operate the Jamestown airport, and to take advantage of the job opportunities of this new, and often exotic industry. Evelyn was primarily interested in long-distance flying and in setting records of her own, which she did, establishing a world's time/distance record for small aircraft. But more often she and Howard were faced with less heroic and rather more bizarre errands, as in this account, which took place after a snowstorm, and was written up in the *Jamestown Sun:*

> The Burlesons, both of whom are licensed transport pilots, have been busy for several days answering emergency calls for transportation. When the hearse of a local mortuary was unable to reach Woodworth recently, the body of the deceased was brought into Jamestown by plane.

Other ways of earning money with an airplane now seem odd as well as dangerous. Coyote hunting brought a bounty of $2.50 for each coyote, plus rewards from sheep and cattlemen's associations. Some ranchers were so grateful to have the predators controlled that they invited the flyers to home-cooked meals and even siphoned gas from their farm machinery into the airplane used in the hunt. After shooting a coyote, the flyers would land to pick it up, tie a hind leg to each side of the propeller, and skin the animal on the spot. They might collect five or six hides in a day to sell to a furrier. Evelyn said, "We'd tie those skins up real tight in a bag and keep them as far back in the plane as we could because the fur was full of fleas. One day I had to go into the bank after hunting coyotes and I could just feel a flea walking up my neck, and I could see that the lady behind the counter was staring at it. Oh, I just about died from embarrassment."

Coyote hunting from an airplane requires low, slow flight, made especially dangerous by power lines and other obstacles. In the Ninety-Nines' oral histories, Evelyn described one hunt:

> One day a sheep rancher up by Pingree called us and said he'd lost a fourth of his flock to a killer-coyote and he offered a nice reward. So we took off, found the ranch, and saw a man on horseback trailing the coyote. I was the pilot and my husband was the gunner. So, we took after the coyote. Well, this was an experienced coyote. He'd been hunted before. You had to really watch him. He'd make 180-degree turns and was real smart. We were flying along, trying to get this coyote, and I looked up and there was a rise in the ground higher than I was! I was flying as slow as the aircraft would go and I didn't dare bank either way or I'd dig a wing in the ground, so I stayed just a few feet off the ground all the way up the side of the hill.

> But right on top, there was this pile of rocks where this farmer had cleared his field and my left gear hit into this pile of rocks and broke off. It also took off about two inches of the tip of the propeller so it shook like it had malaria. Well, we forgot about getting the coyote and flew back to Jamestown and worried about how we were going to get that aircraft landed on one wheel. The plane was shaking and our teeth were chattering, but outside of that we were OK. This aircraft had almost six hours of gas and we wanted to burn off all of our gas before we landed, so we flew around and around. And people began to notice that something was haywire. They could see that part of the gear was missing. Pretty soon there was a string of cars from town going out to the airport. They all wanted to see the crash. They hoped you wouldn't crash, but if you did, they didn't want to miss it.

> The whole airport was covered with people by the time our gas was used up. So, we yelled down at them to clear a swath in those people so that we could land. They cleared a swath, and at the far end was a photographer. My husband said he'd land it, so he took the cushion out of his seat so that I could hold it in front of my face in case we nosed over. He landed the aircraft on the remaining wheel and kept the wing up real high. The switch was cut, and the gas, what little we had left, was turned off. It rolled on for quite a ways on that one wheel and gradually it lost speed. Finally the wing came down, made contact with the ground, and swung us around about eighty degrees, stopped and didn't hurt a thing. The photographer was so excited about all this that he forgot to take his picture. It cost us $27 to fix up the airplane, $17 for the prop and the rest for welding the gear back on.

Evelyn Waldren's best years were in Jamestown, when she was a partner in the "Flying Burlesons" and the darling of the barnstorming circuit. For many years she was the only woman pilot in North Dakota. She not only enjoyed the celebrity status, but for the first time in her life, was finding the stability she never had as a child. These were busy years. She was station agent for Northwest Airlines, observer for the Weather Bureau, and immersed in civic activities of Jamestown. She formed model airplane clubs, and promoted, managed and sponsored air shows and fly-ins. She spoke to women's groups about flying, and was politically active as a member of the Stutsman County Young Democrats. She wrote a regular aviation column in the *Jamestown Sun*, and her work appeared in other newspapers as well. In the May 1931, *Kensal Times*, she described her first solo flight with Howard as her instructor:

So he [Howard] climbed out and examined the radiator. Then he said, "Take 'er."
I was so surprised I was speechless and so happy I began beating the cowling of the
cockpit with my hands. I was fifty feet in the air before I realized that I did not have
my goggles pulled down over my eyes. The ship landed wonderfully and I was so
happy. I sang and recited poetry. I believe that is the height of joy.

As long as Evelyn and Howard worked and flew together, they maintained a
high professional standard — they had to to stay alive. But the marriage did not last.
After the "Flying Burlesons" moved their operation to Oregon, Howard left Evelyn,
and they divorced. After she left North Dakota, Evelyn Waldren did reconnaissance
flying for the State of California, for the State of Washington's Department of
Natural Resources, and the U.S. Forest Service. In California she also flew charter
for construction companies, and instructed in the Civilian Pilot Training program
during World War II. She established a world's time/distance record for small
aircraft, flying a tiny, overloaded, 65 horsepower airplane that carried eighty
gallons of fuel from Vancouver to Tijuana in sixteen and a half hours. However, her
other record-setting plans were shut down because of the attack on Pearl Harbor.
During the war she directed the aviation education program for the Oregon State
Board of Aeronautics, and continued writing aviation columns for local newspapers. She even had a radio show called "Flying Time."

Evelyn married two more times. In the early days of World War II, she walked
into the office of a young army officer she had known for a few months and
announced: "I want to get pregnant. Let's get married." Evelyn described him as
a "jealous sort" who cut the pictures of Howard Burleson out of her scrapbooks. By
the time the baby was born, the father was overseas — she said she "didn't see much
of him again." Evelyn went to Jamestown for the birth to be near her sister, and then
left her son with her sister and returned to Oregon. She saw little of him until late
in her life; he was passed among relatives as he grew up, much as she and her sister
had been.

**Judy Logue is director of the oral history program for the 99's Resource Center,
and an advocate for the Domestic Violence and Sexual Assault Center in Casper,
Wyoming, where she lives and also sculpts.**

Mrs. Bettenhausen with canned goods.
North Dakota, November 1940.
John Vachon. FSA 130.
Special Collections, University of North Dakota.

North Dakota Women During World War II

by Barbara Honeyman Pierce

World War II brought changes to the way many women in North Dakota lived and worked. As men entered the service, such male-dominated jobs as welding, driving taxi cabs, working on assembly lines in air craft factories, or harvesting crops now were being handled by women. We have known in a general way about the kinds of work women did in the war, and how the war affected our families, but I discovered that it was not easy to learn more specifically what women's lives were like in those years in North Dakota. Little research material is available about that time, and I was told it is rare to find anything about women during World War II. So I knew I would have to rely on personal recollections from women, but when I started interviewing women, I was surprised to find so many reluctant to talk about themselves. They would freely talk about the men and what they did, but it was hard for me to get them to talk about themselves. Most refused to answer personal questions about their feelings during this time, or about war in general. There were, fortunately, a few exceptions, and I found wonderful sources in women who were strangers to me and wrote letters, from which I will quote at length, beginning with one of the many women who traveled to the west coast to work in a defense plant.

Clara Dramstad: The men at the aircraft plant were mostly older, or younger men who were 4Fs and didn't make it into the service There were a lot of women who were GI wives like me who filled their waiting time with producing things for war. I began in the burring and filing department, then I moved up to riveting. From there, I transferred to right wing electrical on the Constellation where we strung wires and soldered on lugs and put them in boxes. I remember how we ran out to see a Constellation fly over the hangar and how proud we were of it. There were only

13 of them made at that time.

There was "some" over hiring on the part of Lockheed because they were subsidized by the government according to the number of workers. So there were times when we didn't have enough work to keep people busy. There were times when I took my crocheting along and stood with my head and shoulders up in the wing and crocheted. "Look busy," the overseers would say. We carried our lunch buckets, which were inspected as we came and went.

I remember my pay was higher out on the floor than that of the office workers. I think my pay was around $1.75 with raises real often up to $2.15. That was good pay in those days. I proudly took my weekly check and deposited it in the bank, for savings for us when my husband came home.

One way women could obtain work in defense plants was to join the National Youth Administration (NYA) for training before leaving North Dakota.

Lillian Holden: In February of 1942 I signed up with the National Youth Administration which was training people to work in a defense plant. I was transferred to work at Boeing Aircraft Co. in Seattle, Washington. I was happy to have the opportunity to do something for my country. I had learned to run a lathe and drill press. I drilled holes in brackets for the wing section of the airplane. We worked on the B-17, B-19, and B-29.

Our work hours were not always to our liking. I worked two years on graveyard shift, and one year on swing shift. They tried to accommodate us workers in every way. They would have swing shift dances for the workers, which started at 1 AM Saturday nights and ended at 5AM Sunday morning.

The women who stayed in North Dakota also found themselves doing jobs that previously had been the responsibility of men. The combination of the lack of males and the emphasis on increasing food production forced farmers to use any hands available to harvest crops: women, children, troops, prisoners of war, businessmen and others who had never farmed before. Women moved back with their parents to help in the fields; schools ended their year earlier so the adolescents could also work.

June Nelson: I learned to drive the tractor and ride the binder in harvest. The hardest work was shucking the grain on a hot day.

Edna Belisle: During the harvest season a Basic Training Camp was set up in tents in our small town. That was an exciting thing for the local girls who were old enough to date. They would put on marching drills and demonstrations that the public were invited to watch. The boys were sent to local farmers to help with the combining. This was not too successful because most of the boys had never been on a farm before and knew nothing about the machinery. As children we were needed to help with farm chores, since farm workers were scarce. I learned to milk cows, rake hay, and haul grain with a team of mules. It was very uncommon for girls in our area to join the service. I remember seeing only one woman in uniform in our hometown. She was thought to be a "loose woman" by my family.

Ruth Fisher: The threshing crew was made up of anyone who was willing to work for a day, a part of a day or a few hours. Because of the war there were few men left to do the ordinary work. The rural mail carrier and the superintendent of Pettibone School came out to help after their regular hours were over. At that time I was living at home so I could help with all farming operations evenings and week-ends, as time permitted. I was also teaching.

Gerry Clarey Deutch said that after a Statewide Elks Navy-WAVE campaign had recruited 65 women, a special ceremony was held at the Fargo Elks Club complete with patriotic band music, speeches and a parade to escort the women to the train station. Many considered the recruitment of women important since the work these women did in the service released more servicemen from noncombat positions and allowed them to be sent overseas.

In North Dakota as elsewhere there were shortages of consumer goods, a price freeze, and rationing.

Lydia Bechtold: I will never forget those ration books, and those tokens. Each member of the family had to have a ration book to get certain foods. With a large family, we were always running out of sugar. And our oldest son was always wearing out his shoes. We were not supposed to sell or trade stamps, but we could not let a little boy go bare-footed in the winter, so we did trade stamps to a friend for her shoe stamps, as she cooked on a little kerosene stove, and also heated her small room with kerosene. When my youngest son was born I was in the hospital, and my doctor always made me stay until the tenth day, but this time he came in on the 9th day and said you can go home today. If you stay until tomorrow you will lose your sugar stamp for this month. Naturally I went home.

Phyllis Nordwall: Preparing meals was a challenge. Each person was allowed 5 pounds of sugar per coupon and we used it sparingly, trying to save some for the canning season. White syrup was more readily available and I baked many cakes using syrup instead of sugar. Living on a farm we had eggs and cream so we indulged in simple desserts quite often. I remember so well making up a recipe for lemon pudding using lemons, egg, syrup and corn starch. My father in law said it was "so refreshing." Many food items were in short supply and when a shipment did come to the store the grocer was often quite selective as to who got to buy it. The regular customers were the most favored. This practice did not promote good public relations and sometimes caused hurt feelings.

Lydia Bechtold: (She and her sister owned a grocery store.) Sugar was purchased in bulk one hundred pound sacks. It was sold by scooping into paper sacks — one, two, five pound or whatever the customer had stamps for. Before we could buy more sugar we had to have stamps as well as money. Somehow when the inspector came, our sugar supply and the number of stamps we had didn't match. Some sugar could have been damaged or spilled or probably there was a shortage when [my sister and I bought the store and] the inventory was taken in June. Anyway we were both called into court to try to explain why the numbers didn't coincide. I don't remember much else about the ordeal. I suppose my sister who is a little older and much braver did most of the talking. As a result we were penalized for whatever we had done wrong by not being allowed to sell sugar for a number of weeks.

Ruth Fisher: Conservation and collection were the key words of the war period. People were urged to conserve. Conserve gas, sugar, tires, shoes, and money. Gasless Sundays were announced and the speed limit was lowered to 35 miles per hour.

Edna Belisle said that war bond drives were common and many put every penny they could in war bonds and stamps: saving for a victory, saving for the end of war, saving for when their husbands and boyfriends returned. Food was conserved by the raising of Victory Gardens and chickens. Ironically, the utilization of home grown food was limited because canning jars and lids were in short supply.

A new pair of shoes had to be very practical and serviceable. I hated them. Mom would buy large sacks of flour which came in flowered cotton. These sacks became our school dresses and also aprons which we wore for home chores. Conservation and recycling led to a local contest for teens. They were asked to collect old shoes to be turned in to the local department store. My second oldest sister joined the contest and she spent a lot of time on the phone getting promises of shoes which we would go around the country on Sunday afternoons and pick up. She won second prize in the contest which was a beautiful red wagon with battery operated headlights made to look like a car.

June Rindahl Nelson: My students and I filled the grain bin with papers and magazines which had accumulated. It was my job to stand in this sea of papers, arranging them some way to best use the space. I threw my non-rationed shoes out on the ground because they kept falling off my feet. I have often wondered if a truck ever did arrive to recycle the paper that granary held.

Women also wrote to me how, with shortages of men, gasoline, money, and food, social activities changed in small towns. Single women spent dateless weeks stuck in small communities with no money or gas to go anywhere. According to Agnes Wanek, some women envied servicemen their travel and adventure, in spite of the knowledge of the danger they faced. Social events centered around the war or a war-related conservation effort. North Dakota women picked ergot from rye (a mold used in medications) with tweezers, "even," according to Enid Bern, "to the extent of carrying their rye with them to coffee parties" (Bern 1975).

Lenore Nordwall: I joined the Army Mothers in 1944. This was a new organization whose members served the veterans in any way they could. We sewed bibs and ditty bags for the hospitals. Later when there was a VA hospital in Minot, the Army Mother posts took turns serving cookies and coffee to the patients there. We also sent packages and cards to the boys overseas.

Lydia Bechtold: One of the things I recall most is how the letters were censored; from the one in the Navy his letters looked like paper doilies with all the parts cut out.

Women's lives changed in many ways.

Irene Pommier: I went to the old homestead where my parents were living and helped there on the farm and next year taught a school in the home district. It was a lonely time for wives of servicemen. At first we did not receive an allotment as it took an act of Congress before we were granted this support. I'll never forget the first allotment I got included back pay, and I got it all in cash, stuffed it in my purse and came home to my parents and my brothers. I walked into the front room and to their surprise said money, money, and took handsful of bills and threw them up in the air in the front room and they fell to the floor while my people looked at me like I had gone crazy and then we all laughed till we cried. When we complained to some other women in the community we did not get much sympathy as many were wives of World War I veterans and they said they had gone through the same thing. I continued teaching and put money in bonds to buy a home when my husband came back or when the war was over.

Sylvia Botnen: Summer came and I drove to Kansas to spend some time with my husband. I packed my infant son's crib in the back seat of the car and tied the ironing board to the back bumper. There was no polyester on the market and pressing must be done. Around the army bases, housing was difficult to find. Women and children flocked into the area to spend a short time with loved ones. They lived in tents, barn lofts, garages and whatever was available. We found a one room apartment. Troops marched by our door and one day ate their lunch in our front yard. When they finished eating lunch, the mess sergeant asked me if I could use some sliced pineapple. I was glad to receive some, but didn't quite know what to do with a dishpan full of slices.

Gas was becoming scarce and I had a hard time getting coupons for my return home. A few times I remember station managers not taking coupons if they knew you were service connected. Some gas was bought on the Black Market and also tires.

I went to visit my husband one more time before he went overseas. I arrived in Nebraska one evening and the next day he was shipped to Cheyenne. I remember with amazement the great number of women and children who were at the railroad station the next morning ready to leave for Cheyenne. Every moment together was so precious. In those days there were no disposable diapers, so as the women arrived at the station, they draped wet, washed diapers on the steaming radiators to get them dry. There was so much commotion.

In many ways, World War II was a good time for North Dakota (as Elwyn Robinson has described in his *History of North Dakota*). Weather was good and crops flourished. Land prices were low and crop prices high. The war economy snatched up all the food that was produced and paid well for it. Personal income for North Dakotans rose 145% between 1940 and 1945. Per capita income rose from $350 in 1940 to $1009 in 1943. The state government got out of debt and built up reserves. Farmers operated on a cash basis. Because of the constant demand for food products, workers were needed to farm and ranch. Many North Dakota men obtained draft deferments to stay on the farm. North Dakota had the second highest percentage of draft deferments; only 34% of those eligible entered the service. Many men who stayed in the state during the war flourished, but those who served did not have the advantage of those who stayed and farmed. The war ended, the surviving servicemen returned to North Dakota, saw the opportunities they had missed, and their resentment grew. With the end of the war came other changes.

Sylvia Botnen: My husband came home to very few jobs and little money. It was a discouraging time for us because people not in the service seemed financially secure.

Margery Underdahl: Always at the back of each person's mind, was, when will this war end, but I don't think anyone gave any thought that it would be a possibility that we could lose the war. The only thought was when will it end? September 2, 1945, when it was announced that Japan had surrendered we were joyous that we were victorious over Japan in this war, but one cannot help but think of all the service men who did not come back or came back with injuries both mental and physical, all the sacrifices the many people of our country made in the name of freedom.

Helen Baker: I think now there's always a certain fear of another war.

References

Bern, Enid. "Memories of a Prairie School Teacher," *Journal of the Northern Plains* : 42, Summer 1975.
Robinson, Elwyn B., *History of North Dakota*. Lincoln: University of Nebraska Press, 1966.

Barbara Honeyman Pierce is from Reeder, North Dakota. She now lives in Bismarck, where she is the grants and contract officer in the Historic Preservation and Archeology Division of the North Dakota State Historical Society.

The Profession of Law

by Alice R. Senechal

Ida M. Crum, the first woman to practice law in North Dakota, was admitted to the Bar on September 7, 1897. Since then the number of women licensed to practice law in the state has grown to 215. Since 1981, both the number of women licensed to practice law and the percentage of licensed attorneys who are women have approximately doubled. In 1981, 100 licensed attorneys, or 7.8 percent of the total number in the state, were women. Between 1981 and 1988, both the number of licensed women attorneys and the percentage of licensed attorneys who are women grew each year. These 215 attorneys comprised 13.7 percent of the total number of licensed attorneys in the state in 1988. In 1987, according to the American Bar Association, 20 percent of attorneys nationwide were women.

Seventy-three women attorneys responded to a summer 1987 survey (conducted by the Women Lawyers Section, State Bar Association of North Dakota) of licensed North Dakota women attorneys in which each was asked to identify her primary area of practice. Forty-four of those responding were in private practice. Ten were employed in governmental agencies, five were employed as corporate counsel, three in legal services positions, two held teaching positions, one was a judge, one was in an accounting firm, and seven were not currently employed in law-related fields.

During the past decade, several North Dakota women have reached significant milestones in the judiciary, in political and governmental positions, and in the private sector. Beryl Levine was the first woman appointed to the North Dakota Supreme Court, in January 1985. Justice Levine graduated from the University of North Dakota Law School in 1974, ranking first in her class. She practiced with a large Fargo law firm prior to her appointment to the Court. Cynthia Rothe, who had been a county judge, became the first woman to serve as a district judge when she was appointed to the East Central Judicial District in March 1988. Karen K. Klein was appointed the first full-time United States magistrate in North Dakota in 1986. She had previously served as a part-time U.S. magistrate while practicing law in Fargo-Moorhead, and had worked as a judicial law clerk to Chief Judge Paul Benson. Jonal H. Uglem took office as county court judge in 1983, Gail Hagerty in 1987, and Georgia Pope Dawson in 1988.

Women attorneys have also sought and held statewide offices during the past decade. In 1986, Heidi Heitkamp was appointed to the office of State Tax Commissioner and in 1988 ran for election to that office. Sarah Vogel, nationally recognized for her representation of farmers in a class action lawsuit against the Farmers Home Administration, in 1988 campaigned for the office of commissioner of agriculture. In 1980, Alice Olson ran for the office of attorney general. In 1988, of the 53 States Attorneys in North Dakota, eight were women.

While women in North Dakota have made numerical progress in the legal profession, there is still much to be done before their integration into the profession could be considered complete. In 1987, a Women Lawyers Section was recognized by the state bar association which in 1987 also established a task force to consider issues of gender fairness in the state's legal system.

Alice Senechal is an attorney practicing in Grand Forks.

[A Turtle Mountain Chippewa, Leona Patnaude has been Chief Judge of the Court of Indian Offenses, Turtle Mountain Agency, Executive Director of the Associates for Progress, and on the staff of the United Tribes Employment Training Center in Belcourt, North Dakota.]

There has been a significant increase in the number of Indian people from my tribe who are involved in off-reservation partisan politics, primarily within the Democratic party. Thirty years ago, the people who had such an involvement could have been counted on a person's fingers.

Being a woman and a Native American has been both a hinderance and an asset. When I was first becoming involved, there were not many Native American women (or men) doing the kinds of things that I was. I felt that I had to work harder than everyone else to be accepted. In recent times, being both a woman and Native American seems to have become an asset. Many employers, boards, committees, governments seem to be looking for and actively recruiting persons who can qualify as a double minority. I feel that things have got much better for Native American women.

Leona Patnaude
Belcourt, N.D.

"Dearest Inventor of Joy"

by Thomas Matchie

My mother died last spring. She was ninety. I thought how much more frail she looked in death from the woman I knew in life — with the strength to teach when she was young, marry a farmer she loved against the advice of her family, and to start her own business school during the Depression when the farm failed. And through it all, she raised a family of teachers.

"You're too young to teach in that school, Gat," her mother had said, the summer of 1915 after Agatha graduated from Lidgerwood High School. Catherine Agatha Dewey (she never used her first name) had just returned from an excursion with some girl friends to Spiritwood Lake and was on her way to teach at Vaplon School a few miles from home. Agatha's sister Mabel is good at quoting their mother, and loves to take me through my mother Agatha's scrapbook, pointing out pictures like those of the seven girls on that lake trip. One of those girls was Marion "Toots" Eckes (now ninety and living in Fargo) who also taught country school. "You didn't have to have any fancy qualifications in those days," said Toots, "just a six-weeks' permit."

Agatha was an independent sort, the oldest of five living children — Mabel and Ethel, sisters a few years younger, and twin six-year-old brothers. Two years later she had her one-year elementary diploma from Valley City Normal School and it was now clear she intended to make teaching her career.

According to Mabel (now eighty-seven and at home in Alexandria, Minnesota), Agatha was a lot like her mother Theresa. Theresa was aggressive, an organizer, sometimes domineering. She wanted Agatha to succeed, but she wanted it her way. Theresa and her husband Andrew Dewey were Irish-Canadian immigrants who settled in Lidgerwood. As a boy I remember Grandpa (after Grandma had died) doing dishes in our house in Jamestown. He was an easy-going, bushy-haired gentleman who lacked his wife's Irish temper. We called him "Bank" because he gave us nickels when he could. Mom said he did odd jobs in Lidgerwood — driving horses for Dr. Sasse, serving as a policeman, selling real estate — to keep the family in food, clothes and college.

Agatha worked hard at everything, including helping her mother garden and plant flowers in the city park, but she wanted something different and more exciting. Teaching seemed natural to her and she had determined, said Mabel, to make it an avenue of freedom. During the summers, Agatha combined business courses at Dakota Business College in Fargo with more college in Valley City so she could teach commercial subjects in high school. Agatha's teens were disturbing times in North Dakota; farmers were organizing the Non-Partisan League, and men were going to war. She followed such events, especially the personalities involved. She would get me to read about Franklin Roosevelt when I was in high school, and later she wouldn't let me miss a Jack Kennedy press conference. These political interests came a little later, for on the threshhold of the 1920s, she was for the first time entirely on her own and had to worry about making a living. At first she tried bookkeeping in the mill at Casselton, where she got her first taste of living alone, eating downtown, and finding something to do at night to keep from going stir crazy. But then the mill burned — December 19, 1919. The pictures of that fire are in her scrapbook, and Mabel says it was a frightful experience. In the summer of 1920

In July 1985 I retired after teaching school in Cavalier County for 38 years. In these years I traveled by airplane, car, farm truck, horseback and on foot. Once, on March 15, 1951, it took me an hour and ten minutes to drive on State Highway 5 from the Easby corner where a sign says "Langdon 5 miles," into town. Usually, when I drove under snowy conditions I guided myself by fence posts at the edges of farmers' fields, grass protruding through the snow at the edges of the ditches, or the center of the highway yellow line. But that day I could not see anything and lost my sense of direction.

When I realized that I did not know whether my car was still on the road, I braked to a complete stop, opened the car door and fumbled for footing. When I could stand up, I tried to determine whether or not I was standing on the blacktop. Being careful not to lose sight of the car, I aimed straight to the left, until by feeling what was underfoot I discovered where the left edge of the highway was. Then just as carefully I retraced my steps and, going in front of the car, did the same to discover where the right edge of the highway was. I came to the conclusion that the car was about in the middle of the road. That was not a safe place to be when visibility was zero. I knew I should get back into the car and move it more to the right so that if there were other moving cars I would not be in the wrong lane. When I did get home, people in Langdon were amazed that I had driven in that snowstorm.

Elsie Schrader
Langdon, N.D.

Agatha finished school at Valley City and headed across the state to Cando to teach for the first time commercial subjects, and for the first time students in high school.

Miss Dewey, as her students called her, was at home in the classroom. Her students thought her smile contagious; they saw her as kind and felt she identified with them. Luella Allickson, a high school student in the '20s, writes:

> Your unchanging character, wonderful personality & disposition win the friendship of many... I never never shall forget you and your smile. When a student enters the classroom and is met with a "smile" — why shouldn't she feel like working the rest of the day?...Miss Dewey, allow me to say that if anyone ever loved you more than I do (which covers all that word love means) they would certainly have to go some.

Administrators, too, saw in her a gifted person, and wrote recommendations saying she was simply good for the school. Her only "fault" was going to dances, especially barn dances. Out of those dances came numerous friendships. Her letters show she was a close friend of Clayton Smith in Casselton, went out often with Stirling Thom in Cando, and the next year, teaching in Kenmare, even pondered marriage with R.A. Shonberg, who worked in the Northern Pacific Depot. According to her sister Mabel, Agatha hesitated because of her career, and the next year he married an old girlfriend, saying "Take care of yourself" as he left. Always one to move ahead, Agatha applied the next fall at Carrington, where Mabel, after attending dramatic school in Chicago, was also hired to teach. It promised to be an exciting

---

My father and mother are both teachers in North Dakota. My father saw education as a means to owning a small business; my mother heard a call to professionalism. Although career possibilities for women were rapidly expanding in the fifties when my mother was entering the job market, rural America still turned out predominantly one kind of woman professional — teachers.

Being a teachers' kid, I learned about things in teachers' lives that most students never see. I spent countless nights sitting beside my mother as she read and graded essays and tests. For a time, she didn't teach and I learned that life for four on one teacher's salary meant a tight budget. When my mother returned to teaching, I learned about the big workload and small benefits for a part-time teacher, and about re-entering the job market as a middle-aged woman.

I also learned the in and outs of small town academic culture as well as local and state politics. We knew which candidates would push bills to benefit education. At social gatherings, we assessed whether the town was for or against a new school building.

I found doors open for me that weren't for my father, and especially my mother. Their education helped them up, and now they boost me even higher.

Carmen Retzlaff
Minneapolis, Minn.

year.

Gat always was close to her sisters, Mabel and Eck. Mabel said that Agatha felt a deep love for her sisters all of her life. But, added Mabel, "she was also our ring leader" as she organized dances for the whole town, often inviting friends from other towns to come join in the fun. One fellow wrote back after one of her suppers at Beaty's Cafe, followed by dancing at the Jap's (later the Rainbow Gardens), calling her "Dearest Inventor of Joy." And so she was successful as a teacher, fun-loving outside of school, and close to her sisters who did her bidding as they gave her their support.

Agatha was also an adventurer. To the dismay of her family, she left in 1923 for Bridger, Montana. Mom often talked about the beauty of that little town nestled among the Rockies. In less than a month she orchestrated a dinner party at the old Palace Cafe, which she and two others renovated along the theme of Goldsmith's Deserted Village. People came from Fromberg and Red Lodge and even Billings to share in the gaiety, and letters in the paper showed the entire town appreciated the event. One signed "the men" read:

> While we natives were bewailing the lack of entertainment, three of our energetic lady teachers, Misses Mildred Dick, Agatha Dewey and Ollie May Chandler, conceived and executed the idea of the above novel and delightful little dance party, bearing all expense themselves, and doing all the work necessary to put the room in condition.

Agatha left Bridger in the spring, and by the mid-1920s settled in Jamestown — a larger town with a bigger school. Though women could now vote, the rule in school was still that a woman couldn't be married and teach, so Agatha continued to delay marriage in favor of her career. After two years, however, she began to get anxious, for she had met Timothy Matchie, who farmed near Spiritwood. Dad had nearly graduated in engineering at Marquette University in Milwaukee, but at the outbreak of World War I had come home to help his folks on the farm. He said that, because Agatha and he were nearly thirty, they decided that if they were going to have children they shouldn't wait forever. Gat's mother opposed the marriage. Though my father pointed out to her that he was a "good Catholic," Theresa still didn't like the idea.

They were married secretly in Jamestown in the summer of 1927. The school board found out in November and told her they would terminate her contract in the spring. So Agatha became a farmer's wife. Dad said she never liked the role, but she was a realist and soon learned to feed cows and pigs and chickens. She also became a good cook, feeding shockers and threshers. But after seven crop failures Tim and Agatha lost the farm. Taking Eck and Harper Brush's two children into their family (Eck had died in childbirth), my folks then moved to town, but Dad could not find work. Mom got him to take a civil service test for an opening at the Post Office — he got the highest score and the job. Gat decided to go back into teaching, but this time on her own terms.

She couldn't teach public school, so she found another way. Selling her diamond ring to buy typewriters, she opened her own business school, the Central Dakota Commercial College, above Preds' Ladies' Wear in Jamestown, journeying to the countryside to recruit her first students, even "carrying" many of those students until they got their first paycheck. Bernice Bagan, a student in 1937, said she had no money, but Agatha, who charged little anyway, let her go to school and pay afterwards.

In the 1940s Agatha moved the school to rooms above Woolworth's (later the Haroldson Office Supply), where she continued to educate most of the secretaries and young business executives in Jamestown. Many of her students were veterans —from World War II, the Korean War, and even into the Vietnam era. Ernie Young, who was there in 1946, said "she was really considerate of us guys." When I was eight years old I learned to type and take shorthand there, and I marvelled at my mother. Never loud or teachy, she got students to practice whatever they were doing, hardly ever corrected a test, but got them to work on their own. The atmosphere was a communal one, a kind of academic Cannery Row, and whether you were a high school graduate trying to get a job, a veteran collecting your GI Bill, or a teenager learning to type in the summertime, you felt at home in Agatha's school. Downstairs on Main Street the Palace Cafe became an extension of the school, for here the students could relax with their teacher and each other, and Agatha was able to make contact with future employers. Lucille Hehr (now working at the Senior Citizen Center in Jamestown), was a waitress at the Palace Cafe in the 1940s; she said, "Agatha was such a delight, so much more a human being than the other teachers who ate there; because of her I wanted to go to that school."

But Agatha was also a homebody. Though Mom had to teach each day, and often at night, she insisted the whole family meet at home for hamburgers at noon—this was a communal event, she said, important to keep us all together. In the 1950s when Mike and I were in high school, my folks trusted us with the car out of town, and came to all our basketball and football games at home. When we were in college at St. John's University Mom wrote to us almost every day. I was a little embarrassed at this, but one day Bucky Morgenson, who roomed next door in St. Mary's Hall, said, "Geez, she must love you two guys." School and church were central to our lives; all four kids went to St. John's Academy (the high school closed in the mid 60s) and all four of us graduated from college; you couldn't be in this family and not value education. In the 1960s, after thirty years at the business school, Agatha retired with Tim to their home on 4th Avenue, a block from Jamestown High where she had first taught when she came to town.

Agatha inspired her family as well as her students toward independence, the men as much as the women. She taught us how to be always inventive, and to feel joy because we felt alive. One day after turning eighty-six, she read an ad in the Jamestown Sun advertising for a teaching position in typing and business law, and quipped, "I could fill that spot in a minute." It was fitting that at her funeral seven granddaughters carried her body into St. James Church. The funeral director tried to help, but they insisted it was their job.

Thomas Matchie teaches American Literature and the Humanities at North Dakota State University, Fargo. He grew up in Jamestown, the third of four children of Agatha and Tim Matchie.

Protestant Women In Ministry

by Christyann Ranck Maxfield

On my first day as pastor of a small Congregational church in White Shield, on the Fort Berthold Reservation, I found on a shelf the portrait of Emma Calhoun Hall. The frame was dusty, the glass cracked. On the wall was the picture of her husband, Charles L. Hall. Emma and Charles were the missionary founders of this church which once stood in Nishu and had its roots in Like-a-Fishhook Village.

There are two main accounts of those early days: *100 Years at Fort Berthold* (1977) by Rev. and Mrs. Harold W. Case, and Charles L. Hall's "The Story of Fort Berthold" (unpublished manuscript, 1932). These describe Emma stepping off a steamboat, arm in arm with her bridegroom. The boat had been loaded with ammunition for Custer's last stand, but the missionaries came, they said, bringing "the Bible, not swords," according to Case, and convinced, in Hall's words, that "we had come for a great purpose."

Education was highly valued in the Congregational tradition. Emma Calhoun Hall graduated in 1871 from Western Female Seminary in Oxford, Ohio, and could consider herself well educated for a woman in the late Nineteenth Century. Yet her education at a school training aspiring missionaries was not as prestigious as her husband's education at two theological seminaries, Andover and Union. He, the pastor, was ordained and called a missionary. She was the unordained missionary teacher and at best she could be called "assistant missionary." However, although she had been recruited primarily to teach women and children, she also taught young men to read, and occasionally found herself doing marriage counseling. The Halls left evidence of an egalitarian marriage when Charles Hall was seen pushing the baby carriage among the homes of Like-a-Fishhook Village. Emma Hall succeeded in one of the criteria for judging missionary work, native adoption of white ways. She wrote (in *Life and Letters, A Sketch,* Santee Press, 1895): "There has been a great change in dress from blankets to citizen clothes."

Nearly a hundred years later, traveling by U-Haul truck, my husband and I came also from the east with our books, our Bibles, and our educations to encounter people of a different culture. But we were far less sure of ourselves than those early missionaries seemed. They had a plan, and absolute confidence that God was with them. They saw themselves bringing light to people who did not have the Gospel, and assumed something we no longer do, that Native Americans were living in darkness.

But some things haven't changed. Many people still subscribe to limiting ideas of "women's place," especially when it comes to the church (even though we repeatedly hear that in not more than 16% of American families does the father support a non-wage-earning mother and children). Many contemporary Protestant female clergy, I found, can report experiences of prejudice and rejection based on their gender, and most established church groups still are more likely to be led by a man than a woman. There are some exceptions: the state's six Salvation Army units are led by seven women and five men, and the state's two Unitarian-Universalist Fellowship pastors are woman. There is also only one woman Episcopalian minister. The American Lutheran Church, Western District, has the highest percentage of female clergy in N.D., 14 percent.

The Evangelical Free Church of America reported that it believes it "not biblical" for a woman to be the "main pastor." The church is "considering a credential for women in the fields of Christian Education, youth, and children." The Seventh Day Adventists license women for specific ministries but do not ordain them, although Bertha Jorgenson served as a licensed pastor in Velva, N.D., in 1907.

Such practices are at odds with other trends: women tend to be in the majortiy in Protestant church pews, and comprise nearly half of seminary student bodies.

Christyann Ranck Maxfield is an ordained pastor in the United Church of Christ, presently serving the Arickara Congregational Church on Fort Berthold Reservation. She has published articles on local history in *The Carson Press, Grant County News, Mandan News, REC Magazine,* and *The Back Forty.* She is the author of *Goodbye to Elbowoods: The Story of Harold and Eva Case,* published by the State Historical Society of North Dakota, 1986.

Jon-Paul, Bill, Theresa Brien sitting on North American Bison by Bennett Brien, Grand Forks, N.D.

Working at Wahpeton Indian School

by Angie Erdrich

The Wahpeton Indian School (WIS) has been in my family for a long time. My grandfather, a Chippewa from Turtle Mountain attended school there in the early 1900s. My father taught eighth grade at WIS for almost three decades and my family lived in a government house on campus for many years. My mother has worked at the school in several different capacities; she is currently working as a teaching assistant in the special needs program.

The WIS campus is located near the center of Wahpeton, yet is somewhat an island unto itself. At the time the school was founded, it was on the outskirts of town surrounded by large fields, used in the teaching of agriculture and the management of domesticated animals. Over the years much of the land previously owned by WIS has been donated to the North Dakota State School of Science and to the city to build a local high school, a sports arena and a hockey stadium among other things.

My work as a counselor's aide/dormitory aide at WIS began in February 1988. Now I can see first hand what my mother and father have been discussing at home since before I was born. Although I grew up around the Indian School, I went to public school and never knew very much about the students who attended school there. I wondered about their daily schedule, why they attended a boarding school away from home, and whether they had freedom or felt locked in.

When I was young, a gigantic lopsided barn stood in the field north of campus. That was the 1970s and by then it was teaming with rats and pigeons and no longer in use. In earlier days "barn detail" was one of the many chores assigned to the Native children entering school in Wahpeton. Other chores included work in the boiler room and in the kitchen and laundry room.

The seventh and eighth grade girls who live in the dorm in which I now work,

Sacajawea Hall, are also assigned "details" throughout the day: vacuuming, dusting, sorting linen, cutting out newspaper circles to place in the bottom of garbage cans, more vacuuming. Each day the girls' rooms are graded for orderliness and cleanliness; each month a weekend is designated "scrub day." On scrub Saturday, the students wax and buff tile floors in the building, clean walls, shelves, drawers, sanitize the bathroom, and on Sunday they clean their own rooms. The "Sac Hall" matrons are the ultimate judge of what is clean and what is not. If anyone gets in trouble for not obeying the (many) dorm rules they are given "hours" by the matrons. The only way to get rid of hours is to work them off, so the dorm is in a constant state of cleaning and more cleaning.

The Wahpeton Indian School used to be run on military discipline and aspects of that era linger on, particularly in the language. Certain areas of campus are "out of bounds," and visiting off-campus is considered going "on leave." When a student goes home for the weekend, the log reads "Tracey Smith, duty to leave"; on return, it is "leave to duty." (Once, when I sent some girls over to get pizza at the cafeteria, I wrote on their permission slip "duty to pizza.")

Students seldom have unsupervised contact with the greater Wahpeton community; a dormitory aide, such as myself, accompanies students to the park, on shopping trips, to the movies. Leaving the school campus without permission is termed "going AWOL." There is a rash of AWOLs every year at the first sign of spring. Although it might seem that students couldn't possibly cause any harm in a small town like Wahpeton, I know that girls have got into trouble when they went AWOL — and the dormitory employees feel responsible. In early March a group spent four days in an abandoned house eating shoplifted lunch meat sandwiches and sniffing gas. Sniffing gas causes brain damage and can result in death. One of the girls told me flippantly, "I'm glad I sniffed gas because I used to be too smart and now I'm just average."

So, I understand why dormitory employees must enforce the many rules at Sac Hall: to protect students from themselves and one another. For the most part, dormitory employees enjoy their work and spend extra time with students when off-duty.

As a new-comer to Sac Hall, I made my mistakes the first few months. As well as the military terminology, I have yet to master "dorm speak." I reported a boy to his matron for trying to "pass out." The correct phrase is "blacking out," a way of obtaining a brief feeling of unconsciousness by pressing one's fingers over the jugular vein and momentarily cutting off the oxygen supply to the brain. Blacking out can cause brain damage too.

"Dorm speak" also includes phrases like "who's on our wing?" (which matron is working in our hallway?) and "GI," which stands for Government Issue and generally denotes anything that is cheap or shoddy. Students who do not have money are issued GI shampoo and GI toothpaste, which comes in a blue and white tube reading *Kontrol Foam*.

Students who do have the money to buy these things must do so. This is called "budgeting." Students fill out a budget slip, listing all the things they need to buy and the estimated cost, and on the weekend they go with a dormitory aide and spend their money. Now to me, budgeting always meant saving money, not spending it, but after a few months in the dorm that distinction has become unclear in my mind. Once a student said to me, "I have no money at all. Can you believe I had $30 once and spent it all in one weekend?" "Edna," I said, "How did you manage that?" "Well," she said, "I budgeted."

The seventh and eighth grade girls have kitchen detail every other month. If they do not have detail, the girls go to dinner every night at 5:15 p.m. (The other day, as I was in line for dinner, the girl who was serving commodity cheese looked at me and asked, "Yellow or orange?") After dinner they go back to the dorms and shower and then turn in their linen. They must check off when they shower and show their particular number when they turn in their panties, socks and bras to be washed. A girl's number is written on everything she brings to the dorm; this prevents stealing and facilitates the sorting of laundry. After showers, the girls can play outside, watch TV, bead in the craft room, or attend a dorm outing or counseling activity. At 8:30 p.m. the matrons serve a bedtime snack which is referred to as "lunch" in dorm speak. Then the girls do their night time details and get ready for school the next day. They are in bed by 9:15 p.m. on weeknights. This is the routine and the rules are usually followed closely. When major rules are broken (stealing, going AWOL, "failure to comply," etc.) the girls are put on restriction and placed in the restriction room, where they sit for four to seven days when the others have free time.

Blacking out and sniffing gas are two forms of self destructive behavior that are classified as "Bodily Harm" and punished by four days restriction. Another is the practice of tattooing, done by poking a needle dipped in ink into one's skin. The marks are permanent. I have seen girls with names of friends written across their arms and various symbols carved into their hands. An entire family of girls from South Dakota, I am told, once tattooed black crosses into their foreheads. One girl scratched a boy's name deeply into her arm. When they broke up, she scratched "fuck you" next to it and ended up carving the skin on her arm to pieces to hide it. Quite a few students have scars of one kind or another, and I have wondered where they came from.

There are problems with understaffing and lack of professionally trained employees among the dorm staff. On the other hand, some matrons are wonderful counselors even though they haven't had any formal training. Some, who went to boarding schools, are able to relate to the students in a way that can resolve conflicts without resorting to unnecessary discipline. Most of the people with whom I have worked seem to truly care about the students and enforce the rules for the students' own welfare.

The counseling program that employs me consists of three counselors and three dormitory counseling aides for the whole school. In order to enroll students into the program there must be a either a psychologist's evaluation recommending counseling or a documented past history of a student's prolonged disruptive behavior. Working in the dormitory I have realized that every student, whether involved in the counseling program or not, seems to have a particular story. All are survivors of one abusive situation or another. I fear that many of the students would not be attending school at all if they did not come to Wahpeton.

I find myself thinking about the girls in my dorm all the time, wishing so much that they would all go on to do what they might do best in life, to have a happy family, to provide for their children the things that they haven't had. I wish so much that there was nothing dragging them down and they were all free to reach their potential. Many of them will make it I am sure and I will be happy to hear from them in the future. The emotional burden may be too much for some, however, and those are the students I worry about most.

In addition to working at the Wahpeton school, Angie Erdrich has studied art and art history at Dartmouth College in Hanover, New Hampshire. She works primarily in watercolors and uses Ojibwe floral beadwork designs in her paintings.

Making Less Than the Rest

by Beth Benson Schmidt

One out of every six families in the United States has a woman head of household who is the sole wage earner (Mazur 1984). One in three families with a female-headed household is below the poverty line, in contrast to one in eighteen for families with male-headed households. Half of these female-headed families would be brought above the poverty level if women were paid for the real value of their jobs (Grune and Reder 1984). The situation in North Dakota is not very different. The undervaluation of women in our society may at first seem to suggest a lower cost of wages, but actually it results in increased welfare costs, lost taxes, and a lower purchasing power for women. Welfare recipients are 93 percent women and children, 70 percent of people on food stamps are women, and two thirds of all medicaid and legal aid recipients are women (Philosophy and Public Policy 1983).

Comparable worth has been an important and controversial employment issue in the 1980s. The Equal Pay Act of 1963 did much to remedy instances where women were being paid less for doing the same work as men, and yet, despite gains made in equal pay for the same work, women continue to earn 60 to 65 percent of what men earn. The United States has a long tradition of social justice and fairness that is rooted in action to redress perceived inequities. Abolishing slavery, extending suffrage to minorities and women, ending racial segregation are just a few examples of times when we have acted on behalf of equality. However, this traditional championing of equality has not so far extended to the economic position of women, perhaps because the basic premise of comparable worth, that there should be equal pay for work of comparable value and that pay should be free of sex bias, is one that conflicts with the way wages often are determined.

Indeed the wage gap is one of the oldest and most persistent symptoms of sexual inequality. The 1851 Census in England showed that roughly half the women between the ages of 20 and 40 were unsupported by a husband. Those able to find employment (the largest occupation was domestic worker) still couldn't earn enough to support them and their children (Rose 1986).

None of the major economic, demographic, and political changes of the past twenty years has had any impact on the wage gap. Contrary to the popular belief that the situation of employed women has improved, especially with the movement of women into traditionally male jobs, the fact is that women still generally do different work than men and get paid less because women's work is undervalued relative to men's. The growth of white collar industry and the ensuing demand for female labor, the massive entry of women into the labor force, and the development of anti-discrimination laws have not made a dent in the wage gap between men and women (Grune and Reder, 1984). According to Remick (1984), "Recent research by sociologists and economists indicates that the wage difference between men and women is only partly explained by worker or job characteristics. The remaining wage difference, about half of the total, is associated with the sex of the people doing the work. In fact, the sex of the workers performing a job is the best single predictor of the compensation for that job, surpassing in importance education, experience, or unionization." Sex segregation in the labor market has a long and consistent history — among the 427 occupations listed by the *Dictionary of Occupational Titles*, 80 percent of women work in occupations in which at least 75 percent of the employees are women. Whether you examine the labor force at the turn of the century or at the present, two-thirds of the work force would have to change jobs to eliminate sex segregation in the work force (Hartmann and Reskin 1983).

The wage gap also can be accounted for by the systemic undervaluing of women's work, or the artificial depression of wages paid to women and men in jobs that historically have been considered women's work, as compared to what wages would be if these jobs were performed by white males (Steinberg 1984). All cultures, without any known exception, value male activity more highly than female activity. Regardless of whether an activity performed by men is performed by women in another culture, it is valued more when it is performed by men (Mead 1974). Thus proponents of comparable worth argue that the Equal Pay Act of 1963 did not reduce the wage gap between men and women because it did not erase the sex segregation of the work force and the undervaluation of work done primarily by women.

Opponents of comparable worth argue that in a free and fair market wages are determined automatically and accurately based on the laws of supply and demand (Lindsay, 1980), and that wages match productivity because employers will not pay workers less than their productivity is worth (they would be lured away to higher paying jobs), nor more (resulting in reduced net income). In theory, laws of supply and demand ensure that wages are set objectively and impersonally by forces beyond the control of individuals. But critics claim that this model is too artificial to explain the complexities of the wage setting process.

Achieving pay equity presumably involves job evaluation, yet current systems sustain rather than counter inequities. The general thinking in rules widely accepted today was set in a 1939 Westinghouse *Industrial Relations Manual* that ostensibly described a gender-neutral job-rating system. The *Manual* awarded points to each job, even though the jobs were sex-segregated, and then intentionally set lower wage rates for jobs occupied by women than for male dominated jobs with equal points. According to the manual, the wage curve was lower for women than for men "because of the more transient character of the service of the former, the relative shortness of their activity in industry, the differences in environment required, the extra services that must be provided, overtime limitations, extra help needed for the occasional heavy work, and the general sociological factors not requiring discussion herein" (Heen, 1984). Although job evaluation in the United States too often is used to sustain sex discrimination because "some employers are changing job evaluation systems, redesigning jobs and redrafting job descriptions to avoid the economic costs of righting past wrongs" (Manual on Pay Equity 1981), job evaluation techniques have been used successfully to implement comparable worth policies in other democracies and at the state and local level. In Australia legislation passed in 1969 and 1972 has raised the base pay of women from 74 percent of that of men in 1970, to 94 percent by 1980, and even opponents of comparable worth are surprised at the lack of negative impact on labor demand and the economy in general in Australia (Mitchell 1984). In Canada, the public sector has been actively supporting comparable worth since the passage in 1977 of the Human Rights Act. Progress in the United States has been slower — none of the 16 bills introduced at the federal level between 1983 and 1985 passed both houses. Comparable worth bills were introduced in 38 state legislatures between 1981 and 1985; 16 agreed to study the issue. Eight states funded the implementation of comparable worth policies and 13 states defeated or tabled the bills.

My grandmother, Anne Marie Danielson Christopherson (1866-1920), bonded herself as an indentured servant to pay for her right to passage to what she thought of as the "land of the free." She was born the second day of 1866 on a farm in Vermeland, Sweden. At fourteen, she left her home to tend goats on a neighboring farm at Tvangeberje gaard. In the spring, she drove goats twenty miles into the saeters, or flatlands, to graze, milking them and churning the milk into cheese, and living in the open on roots and berries. In late summer, she hauled the cheese down the mountain in a wheelbarrow.

After six years of working as a goatherder, Anne Marie set out on foot for Kristiana, now Oslo, 28 miles away. There she found work as a cook in a hotel. She was determined to follow her cousin to America; he found a farmer in North Dakota, Ole Sand, who was willing to pay her passage in exchange for two years of service. And so, in 1887, she came to work for him on his farm 20 miles from Grand Forks.

She married John Christopherson, a farmer and a widower with an eight-year-old daughter, on November 26, 1889, at Crary, N. D. They had nine children. The farm grew, eventually to 800 acres. Anne Marie's work grew as well. She managed the dairy, hogs and poultry, marketed eggs and produce from her vegetable garden, baked many loaves of bread to feed her growing brood. She cared for the sick and ailing and the children of mothers too weak to care for their own.

Jo Ann Palmer
Gainesville, Florida

To see how national trends manifest themselves in North Dakota I analyzed the state personnel system, partly because 51 percent of public sector jobs are held by women (Bureau of Labor 1985). There are further advantages to selecting jobs in the public sector as a basis for an analysis of pay equity issues: 1) jobs paid for by the government are not involved in the profit motive (government goods and services are not for sale), making it difficult to apply traditional market standards to measure the value of workers (Aaron and Lougy 1986). 2) Goals of representation and equity are generally accepted as inherent to employment practices, and information about the public sector is more readily accessible than information about the private sector.

In North Dakota the public employee system is coordinated through the Central Personnel Division which is a branch of the Office of Management and Budget, and this personnel system is required to use a point method to determine the value of jobs, rank ordering them according to pay grade. The system, which uses market wages in addition to the point factor method and could be seen as a version of comparable worth, has been determining wages since 1982.

My study analyzes employees who are classified under the Central Personnel Division of North Dakota, but while all state agencies use the central personnel classification system, it does not apply to Job Service of North Dakota, the Bank of North Dakota, and institutions of higher education, all of whom have their own personnel departments. But, while they are not included in this study, they could be, for the same job classes and wage structure are in fact applied to them. Higher education faculty, however, are not covered by the state classification system and are not addressed in this study. I am considering only full time, year around salaries. I am using entry level annual salaries and entry level job requirements to control for individual differences in labor force experience. Central personnel assigns each job class to a pay grade and each pay grade has minimum and maximum salaries. New workers generally start at the entry level pay grade for the job class they have been hired in. I am considering a job class to be dominated by gender if at least 80 percent of class occupants are of one gender.

The descriptions that follow are based on 584 job classifications under the Central Personnel Division. Based on 1987 data supplied by Central Personnel there were a total of 5,773 classified employees in these job classes (in 1986-87). Of these job classes, 57 percent are male dominated, 26.7 are female dominated, and 16.3 percent are mixed gender classes. Just over half (51.5 percent) of the job classes have no females, while 20.4 have no males. Women make up 50.7 percent of the labor force, but they are not equally dispersed among the jobs. Women are clustered in fewer jobs than men and there are substantially more gender dominated jobs than mixed gender jobs, and although there are slightly fewer men in the labor force, the majority of jobs are male dominated.

The average starting salary for male dominated jobs is $22,095 and for female dominated jobs it is $15,970, a difference of $6,125. The average starting salary for all jobs is $19,680 which is approximately $3,710 higher than the average for female dominated jobs. The average starting salary for men is $17,898 and for women it is $13,522, a difference of $4,376.

Average Starting Salaries By Job Incumbents

Annual Salaries	Men	Women
Less than $11,000	13.5%	34.8%
Less than $15,000	36.6%	73.8%
Less than $20,000	64.2%	92.0%
More than $20,000	35.8%	8.0%
More than $25,000	10.1%	1.1%
More than $30,000	3.9%	.4%

Although 35.8 percent of the men are in jobs where the starting salary is $20,000 or higher, only 8 percent of the women are in such jobs. At the lower end of the spectrum the percentages practically reverse, with 34.8 percent of women in jobs where the starting salary is less than $11,000 per year while only 13.5 percent of the men are in such jobs. Jobs with average starting salaries of less than $15,000 per year are held by 73.8 percent of the women and by 36.6 percent of the men.

The differences in the salaries of women in female dominated jobs and men in male dominated jobs are even more striking. Only .5 percent of men in male dominated jobs earn less than $11,000 per year while 24.8 percent of women in female dominated jobs earn less than $11,000 per year. Of the men in male dominant jobs, 27.9 percent are in jobs where the starting salary is less than $15,000 and 80.4 percent of the women in female dominant jobs are in jobs where the starting salary is less than $15,000 per year. Just over 42 percent of the men are in male dominated jobs where the starting salary is more than $20,000 per year compared to 4.4 percent of women in female dominated jobs where the starting salary is more than $20,000 per year. In jobs where the starting salary is more than $25,000 there are 12.9 percent of men in male dominated jobs and .5 percent of women in female dominated jobs. Overall women come out worse than men in male dominated jobs as well as in female dominated jobs.

In mixed gender jobs — where neither gender is dominant — the difference between men and women aren't quite as startling but they are still there. For instance, 43.7 percent of the men are in jobs where the starting salary is less than $11,000 and 53 percent of the women are in such jobs.

Women in male dominated jobs don't fair as well as men do in those jobs. Among male dominated jobs 41.3 percent of the women are in jobs with starting salaries less than $15,000 per year, and only 27.9 percent of men in male dominated jobs are in such jobs. Seventy-two percent of the women in male dominated jobs are in jobs that start at less than $20,000 per year, compared to 57.5 percent of men in male dominated jobs. At the top of the spectrum women do slightly better, with 14.6 percent of women in male dominated jobs earning more than $25,000 per year as compared to 12.9 percent of men. However, women only account for 3.8 percent of the incumbents in male dominated jobs.

All jobs are classed into eight broad skill areas. Of those jobs classed as "officials

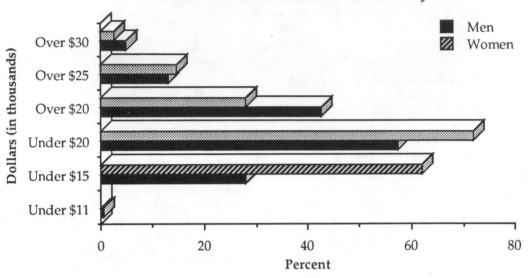

Incumbents in Male Dominate Jobs

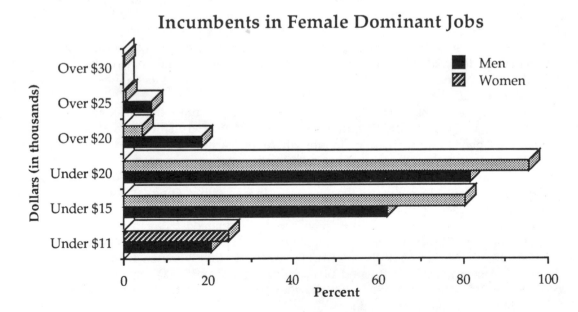

Incumbents in Female Dominant Jobs

Incumbents in Mixed Gender Jobs

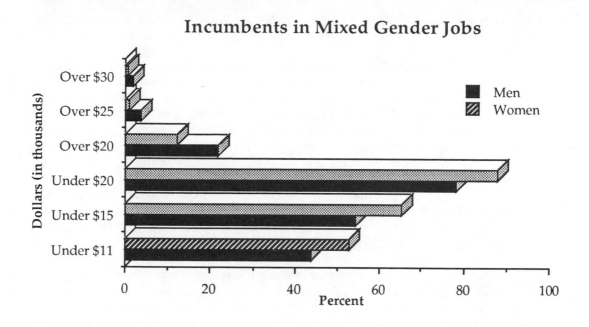

and administrators," 82.7 percent of them are male dominated and 10.8 percent are female dominated. Among those jobs classed as "office and clerical workers," 87.5 percent are female dominated and 4.2 percent are male dominated. Jobs classed as "skilled craft workers" are 93.3 percent male dominated and only 3.3 percent are female dominated jobs.

When jobs are divided according to minimum educational requirements while controlling for sex, women still end up with a substantial disadvantage. The differences in starting salaries for male dominated and female dominated jobs ranges from $2,290 — for jobs requiring 14 years of education, to $5,100 — for jobs requiring 17 years or more of education. On the average, male dominant jobs and female dominant jobs requiring equal levels of education and entry level experience still have substantial differences in compensation levels. Starting annual salaries for male dominated jobs average $6,125 more than female dominated jobs and after controlling for education as well as experience male dominated jobs still average $4,042 more than female dominated jobs. Differences in education and experience may account for one third of the wage gap between men and women in the North Dakota state labor force. The average years of education required for male domi-nated jobs is 14.86 years and the average starting salary for these jobs is $22,041. For female dominated jobs the average educational requirement is 14.10 years and the average starting salary for these jobs is $15,936. Among mixed gender jobs the average educational requirement is 14.55 years and the average starting salary for these jobs is $17,551. Overall, male dominated jobs that require three-quarters of a year more education than female jobs, and one-third more education than mixed gender jobs, pay substantially more than female dominated jobs or mixed gender jobs.

In North Dakota, while women constitute half of the state labor force, and laws and policies governing state personnel system require that classified employees be treated fairly without regard to "an individual's sex, race, age, color, religion, national origin, handicapped condition, political affiliation," or other non-merit factors, women in fact, on the average, earn $6,100 less than men in the state work force. Not more than a third of that difference can be accounted for by level of education and experience, leading to the plausible conclusion that the wage structure and job classification system discriminates against women.

Pay equity for state employees would necessarily involve leadership and cooperation among the State Personnel Board, the Governor's Commission on the Status of Women; the Legislative Council, the state legislature; the governor; public employees, the Central Personnel Division; and an attentive public. In 1988 the state legislature passed a study resolution (SCR 4016) on comparable worth in the state employee system, and the Commission on the Status of Women has identified it as a major agenda item.

Arguments about justice and fairness in wages, however, need to be redefined, and should focus on pay equity rather than on comparable worth. Comparable worth can be a useful tool for achieving pay equity, but the phrase has aroused so much controversy as to mask the deeper problem of pay equity. Public education on the economic inequities for women, and on the consequences of women's being more likely than men to experience poverty, could go a long way toward increasing public support for pay equity. If women's "work" were paid comparable to men's, the labor force would perhaps become more integrated, and what women have done might not seem as marginal.

References

Aaron, Henry J., and Cameran Lougy. *The Comparable Worth Controversy*. Washington, D.C.: The Brookings Institute, 1986.

Center for Philosophy and Public Policy. "Paying Women What They're Worth." QQ — *Report from the Center for Philosophy and Public Policy*, Spring 1985.

England, Paula. "Socioeconomic Explanations of Job Segregation," *Comparable Worth and Wage Discrimination*. Helen Remick, ed. Philadelphia: Temple University, 1984.

Grune, Joy Ann, and Nancy Reder. "Pay Equity: An Innovative Public Policy Approach to Eliminating Sex-Based Wage Discrimination," *Public Personnel Management Journal*, Spring 1984.

Hartmann, Heidi, and Barbara Reskin. "Job Segregation: Trends and Prospects," *Occupational Segregation and its Impact on Working Women: A Conference Report*. Albany, New York: Center for Women in Government, 1983.

Heen, Mary. "A Review of Federal Court Decisions under Title VII of the Civil Rights Acts of 1964," *Comparable Worth and Wage Discrimination*. Philadelphia: Temple University Press, 1984.

Lindsay, Cotton Mather. *Equal Pay for Comparable Work.* Coral Gables, Fla.: University of Miami Law and Economics Center, 1980.

Mazur, Rhoda. "Pay Equity: End the Discrimination." *National Forum,* 1984.

Mead, Margaret. "On Freud's View of Female Psychology," *Women and Analysis.* New York: Grossman, 1974.

Rose, Lionel. *The Massacre of Innocents.* London, Boston: Routledge and Kegan Paul, 1986.

Steinberg, Ronnie. "'A Want of Harmony': Perspectives on Wage Discrimination and Comparable Worth," *Comparable Worth and Wage Discrimination.* Philadelphia: Temple University Press, 1984.

U.S. Department of Labor. Bureau of Labor Statistics, Report 673, September 1982.

____. Bureau of Labor Statistics, "Employment and Earnings," January 1985.

Beth Benson Schmidt is Executive Director of the Abuse and Rape Crisis Center in Grand Forks, North Dakota.

Ancient Earth Series, Raku, by Katie McCleery, Grand Forks, N.D.

IV

There is a point in the distance where the road meets itself,
where coming and going must kiss into one.
She is always at that place, seen from behind,
motionless, torn forward, living in a zone
all her own.

Louise Erdrich
from "The Lady in the Pink Mustang," *Jacklight,* **1984**

"... My Momma can't (fancy) dance ... and my daddy don't rock 'n roll!" Silkscreen by Linda Brown, Valley City, N.D.

I Think I'll Make . . .
Women in the Visual Arts

by Laurel Reuter

"I think I'll build an art museum." It seemed like a whim at the time. Uncounted years later, I stand at a construction site under a burning June sun, watching new pilings being eased into the ground. My old wistful notion, sometimes set aside and seemingly forgotten, now appears as the benchmark for years of study, writing, and travel all over the world; of love and friendship; of concentrated work and concentrated pleasure. It is hotter than it should be this time of year, too uncomfortable for ruminating, and I am made miserable by the endless and awful wind that has marked this drought ridden summer. Still, I am pleased. Over the course of these few months I have watched this old gymnasium emerge into a small jewel, an exquisite little art museum. It was built in 1907, less than twenty years after North Dakota was entered into statehood. Now, after eighty years in the service of physical education, the building will have a second life as North Dakota's official art museum, opening just as the state's centennial celebration begins.

O yes, to stand here, I have warred with everyone. "Your dream is too large for North Dakota." "We hear you're very good, but . . . " "You should be satisfied hanging pictures in the halls of the theater, or in the Student Union." "Students can learn all they need to know from the art of local artists. They don't need this expensive stuff."

Truman Capote gave me the only answer I would ever need in response to those warring voices when he named a collection of essays *The Dogs Bark . . . But the Caravans Move On.* It is, of course, only an answer of consolation after battle. And scattered across North Dakota is a handful of allies, members of the caravan, people who have experienced the power of visual life. More diplomatic than I, they defend the idea of the museum at social gatherings and funding meetings, in circles of commerce and politics, and surprisingly often among people identified with the arts.

Why build an art museum? Maybe because it fell into my lap, the way running their farms fell into the laps of my grandmother and great grandmother. I remember reading somewhere that our grandfathers were cobblers and peddlers, so that our fathers could become doctors and lawyers, so that we could become artists and writers. I wonder, did my North Dakota grandmothers become farmers so that I could build an art museum in North Dakota? I would have been a architect if I had known that women could. I would have been a farmer, but I had brothers. No, my work was to build an art museum.

"I think I'll make a garden," again, said lightly. Halfway into the making of this art museum, the university administration that employs me decided that my art museum was expendable — $50,000, all the money I had at the time for exhibiting and collecting art, for shipping and insuring art, gone. Only a meager salary for myself and a secretary remained. Too weary to give up, I went home. I walked all the way through the house, not even seeing the rooms stacked floor to ceiling with books and paintings, and into the back property. Without thought, I began to dig in the soil. "I think I'll make a garden."

Months later, I wrote to a beloved aunt, "I feel so guilty. All my time and money are going into this garden." She and I always said the important things to each other by letter, so she responded, "Laurel Jean, you dig in that soil until your soul is at peace and then you make your decisions."

I decided to get on with making an art museum.

I am invited to write about the history of the visual arts in North Dakota. Instead I write about myself. I give you personal biography and call it art history. But isn't art history always private biography once it is stripped of commerce? In North Dakota there is no commerce in art. There is little visual history. There have only been individuals who have said to themselves, "I think I'll make . . ."

Where did my passion for art come from? My mind wanders back. I remember a watercolor of a single rose painted by my aunt, Suzanne Wallace. When I first saw it I was six and it was beautiful to me; my schooled eye tells me it is beautiful still. It hung in our house then; it hangs in my house now. She became a nurse and died at the age of twenty-seven in Globe, Arizona, from a sinus infection while attending a patient who needed desert air. There are no other known works of art by her.

I remember a book, *World Famous Paintings.* Now I know it was edited by Rockwell Kent and published in New York in 1939. Then I knew that all the pictures were in color. Today it is in my library, its binding broken, its pages barely hanging together, worn out by my child fingers. Years later, confined to a hotel in London while waiting out an inflamed hip, I hobble across the street to the Wallace Collection, I find Fragonard's *The Swing,* the painting I dreamed in as a kid. In Milan I stumble upon *The Last Supper,* again a picture from my book, but now almost hidden behind scaffolding as a dozen conservators go about their business of saving it for more generations. I crisscross Europe finding my paintings. At the Huntington Gardens in San Marino, California, I come upon Gainsborough's *The Blue Boy.*

That aristocratic child is as remote to me now as he was then. The book taught me to love the northern European painters of domestic life; as an adult I seek them out. The book also gave me my first lessons in stripping faces of their fashions, of their concealing makeup. Through studying those pictures, I came to understand that only one's trappings identify one's slot in history.

I have since seen Millet's peasants in my own family of farmers. I have seen Van Kyck's *Charles I*, that sneering, unhappy man, in many a modern malcontent. I have also come to live peacefully in North Dakota's Red River Valley with its flat landscape and orderly shelter belts. I am at home here because I know this landscape from an earlier time, from Hoblema's paintings of rural Holland in the seventeenth century. Yes, that was a wonderful book. How did I come to possess it? Probably it came through the mail, ordered from a book club by an aunt I lived with, maybe the only art book on the whole Fort Totten Sioux Indian Reservation — but what an art book for a child learning to see.

I remember a woman, probably just barely a woman, but in the eyes of a youngster, a creature of wonder. I do not remember what she looked like but I can recall how she felt in a room — cool, clean, magical, other-worldly. Her name was Betty Cutting and she came from Boston. Those are the only facts I know except that she was Roman Catholic and therefore one of "them." She was a missionary of sorts to the Indians, I suppose. St. Michael's Mission with its small surrounding village lay five miles to the north of Tokio, my hometown. A couple of times a week she came from the Mission to visit us in our two-room school house.

She had a big trunk that she brought with her on her visits. She would open it up and our time with her would begin. The most wonderful things would come out of that trunk: classical ballet costumes that she put on to dance for us. (Can you imagine being seven and having a ballerina dance for you, at a time, before television, when you did not even know that ballerinas existed? However, you did know about fairies.) Pastel crayons, beautiful papers, sheet music for singing and for the piano, and more dance costumes would come tumbling out of the trunk. We would make things, she and I and my companions. For me, the arts had little chance of ever becoming ordinary after Betty Cutting.

A year went by and she returned East, some said to enter a convent. She left behind a taste for magic tucked away in a little girl's head, and a mural painted in the entrance of St. Michael's Church. The mural disappeared in some general house-cleaning long before my adult eyes could find it.

Finally I remember a teacher, Douglas Kinsey. He taught art at the University of North Dakota, where I attended on scholarship. I hated university. I flunked my courses. I hated "other-directed activity." I never would learn to like it. The university decided to give me one more chance and a wise advisor sent me off to register for a semester of classes in anything that pleased me. The arts pleased me so I signed up for literature and art, nothing else. Douglas Kinsey taught Introduction to the Understanding of Art and he did it brilliantly. Once again I was completely enchanted by the power of pictures.

Twenty-five years later a nephew in his first year at Ohio State University called me: "Aunty, I am taking this art course and I just love it. I never knew people cared about things like line and color. I got an A on my final paper. Can I Fax it to you?"

This modern child, intent upon becoming a businessman like his father, had fallen into the hands of a teacher like my Mr. Kinsey. A couple of months later I arranged my travels to meet with him in Boston. We both knew we would spend all our time together in the art museums. What a fine time we had, a generation apart, but both mad about pictures.

I tell you my private history knowing it is generic. For all of us, passion for the arts is fed by small experiences that grow into magnificence; by encounters with parents, or teachers, or artists; by books, performances, and pictures. I know that it makes little difference what you care passionately about, only that you care passionately. However, I also know that certain passions are more important than others. To some of us the visual experience is the most essential, the most compelling. It is what takes us outside of ourselves and connects us with the rest of humanity. It is our link with the past and our reach toward the future.

Visual life always exists, at least for a small part of any population. Among the women of North Dakota the arts developed privately, as they always have — a lone venture for just a few. But here, as elsewhere, the arts grew out of seedlings planted in fertile ground.

Of all the visual arts, *to make a garden* is the most difficult. Line, form, mass, space, color — the formal elements — they are the same in all of the visual art forms. However, unlike every other art medium, the materials used to make a garden are eminently unstable. For instance, a batch of sweet peas may grow tall and lush, or not at all, depending upon the heat of early spring. They may sport, or mutate, or revert back to a parent strain. One year the color may be pale, the next year intense. They detest hot winds. They may feed the aphids rather than feast the eye, as they are supposed to. Passing deer or sudden hail may level them without warning. But cadmium red pigment is cadmium red for all time.

Making a garden was often the only visual art form available to the early settlers on the prairie. If they hungered for a complex visual life, they built gardens. Plants surrounded them; the tools of academic art were unreachable. North Dakota's first and probably most famous gardener, Fannie Heath, came to the Dakota Territories in 1881 to settle a farm five miles south and west of what is now Grand Forks. Seventy years later Erling Rolfsrud described her beginnings:

> On the grassy floor of the prairie squatted a homestead shanty. The flat horizon behind it was unrelieved by a single tree. There was not a shrub or thicket in sight. Only grass cloaked the earth stretching with appalling vastness on every side.
>
> When warm winds rustled the dead, brown grasses, Fannie Heath planted with eager hands. The weeks passed. A few spindly heads of green thrust upward from the soggy crust. Most of them withered, then died, and Fannie Heath knew a strange enemy that threatened the very foundation of her dreams: her soil was alkaline. Even the water from the new well was so alkaline it could not be used for garden purposes.
>
> She sought the help of the nearest nurseryman. "Give your farm away," he said. "You'll never get anything to grow on that alkali."

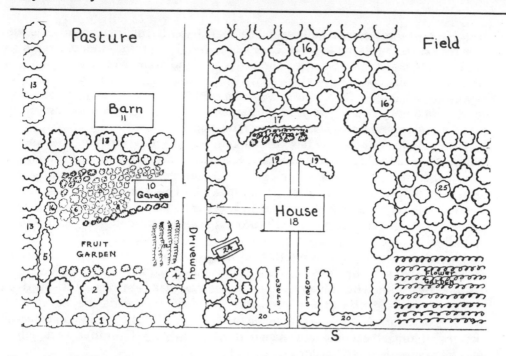

From Fannie Heath's manuscript of a gardening book, now at the North Dakota State Historical Society.

Fannie Heath succeeded in bringing her earth into bloom. Forsaking the cultivated plants of an earlier cultivated life, she turned to the native plants of the prairie to learn their survival lessons. She grew them by the thousands, and before she finished she was trading with the King's head gardener in England, as well as with unknown gardeners the world over. She taught herself the Latin names of plants, thus placing the common plants of North Dakota within the larger botanical world. She gave speeches about native wild flowers; she wrote magazine articles about them; finally her enthusiasm propelled her to the presidency of the National Horticulture Society. In 1923 Teddy Roosevelt's cabin was moved to the capital grounds in Bismarck and Fannie Heath was invited to landscape the surrounding area with native plants.

Fannie Heath was interested in growing plants; she wasn't interested in creating a splendid formal garden. She may or may not have created an important work of art — the evidence long ago having gone back to the earth — but she did show the way for others who would. Catherine Mulligan, an artist living in Fargo in the 1980s, might have been speaking of Fannie Heath when she summed up her own place in the arts: "When I reached the age of fifty, I realized I would never be a Willen De Kooning, but I knew I was important to the fabric of art in this place."

My own garden was several years old, and already stacked earth to sky with plants, before I went off to visit the great gardens of England. I had always known that my appetite for gardens was nourished by the beloved garden of my childhood, started by my grandmother but brought to perfection over the course of forty years by my aunt, Agnes Smith. What I did not know until I saw Sissinghurst, Hicote, and their kin, was that this aunt had created an English garden of great beauty in Tokio, North Dakota. She didn't know it either. But through her the aesthetic sensibilities of her Scottish ancestors emerged and thrived on the prairies of North Dakota — despite rock-infested, alkali soil; the most fierce of climates; and a water supply that was never adequate. In the early 1980s she sold the property and moved into a retirement home. Within two years the garden had gone back to prairie; only a few peonies, the rugosa roses, and the lilacs remained.

How fragile aesthetic life has been among women, how private, how anonymous. Survival makes harsh demands. Nevertheless, the drive to order the world in visual terms refuses to be submerged. "We quilted as fast as we could so our families wouldn't freeze, and as beautifully as we could so our hearts wouldn't break." Although credited to a woman in Texas, that much repeated summation of pioneer life might have been uttered by scores of women from the Northern Prairies and Great Plains.

Even they were not the true settlers of this land. Before them came American Indian women who for centuries had lived in this place that is now called North Dakota. By tradition these Native American women made abstract art. Using dyed porcupine quills, earth and plant pigments, and later glass beads, they covered the surfaces of an array of useful, animal-skin items with brightly colored geometric designs. (Unlike the women, the men of these tribes made figurative work, which was often used to record historical events.)

Today one finds in museums all over the world leggings and moccasins, gauntlets and robes, shirts and pants, amulets and decorated tools, even beautifully painted rawhide parfleche, or carrying bags, "collected in North Dakota." The identity and the lives of women-makers were lost long ago. To date, the name of no great female artist has risen from the legions of American Indians who made art on the vast Northern Plains before the Europeans moved in: no Sioux, no Mandan, no Hidatsa, no Chippewa, and no Arikara. Only the wonderful objects, still breathing with life, remain as testimony to art-filled existences.

In the last quarter of the 19th century, the European settlers arrived, thereby turning the great tribes of the Dakotas into displaced people. Driven onto reservations, barely able to sustain themselves or their culture, they could give little thought to art. It fell into the decline so often found among people in distress. Just as no great art has come out of Europe's ghettos or the world's concentration camps, so no great art has come from the American Indian women who suffered through the early reservation years.

Among the first European settlers were women like Fannie Heath, the prairie gardener. Hungering for visual life, they created from whatever lay at hand, or they tailored their creative drive to their duties at the time. For example, although many came from Scandinavian countries with strong home weaving traditions, few women in North Dakota wove on the loom. Yard-goods from the assembly line had become available with the industrial revolution; a woman's time was precious so she bought her cloth at the store. Instead the women of the prairies knitted. They sewed. They embellished their hand-sewn linens with fine embroidery, seldom creating their own patterns but ordering iron-on transfers from magazines. However, even factory-produced cloth remained precious for a long time. Scraps were carefully squirreled away in ragbags to be pieced into quilts. Very occasionally one of these was exceptionally beautiful, transcending utility to become a work of art.

But the urge to paint was not suppressed for long. In most families there was at least one woman like my Aunt Susie, an untrained artist who made modest paintings, drawings, or watercolors on paper. When canvas became available small paintings on stretched cloth began to appear. These domestic works — landscapes, flowers, or occasional portraits — were treasured by families and neighbors.

Mickie Stillwell was such an artist. In 1917 she was born in Vang, North Dakota, of parents who had grown up in Vang, a Norwegian community in the Pembina Hills near the Canadian border. Her grandparents had been brought to the Dakota Territories as small children. All five of Mickie Stillwell's children were in school before she began to paint, not late in a family where her own mother took up painting at age seventy. (Even Fannie Heath was not able to concentrate on her garden until the homestead was established and her children were raised.) Two of Mickie Stillwell's sisters painted. Her granddaughter graduated from art school in Denver in 1988.

Using oils and pastels she recorded the world around her: her family, the countryside, old barns, broken-down windmills, and log cabins. Sometimes she worked from photographs she had taken. Other times she sketched from life. The family ate in the kitchen; the dining room was her studio. Her family supported her life as an artist; so did her friends in the local art club. Painting was done in both stolen and empty moments. When she was not needed in the field she could stay home and paint. Winters were long on the farm so she worked on her pictures. She cared passionately about her art and her art sustained her. In 1984 Mickie Stillwell died, having lived out the classic story of the prairie woman who painted.

Today such gentle works of art from an earlier time occasionally show up at a farm or antique auction. Mostly they are passed on down through families. The tradition of making them continues, augmented by community art lessons, or group painting sessions for the amateur artist. Now, like then, the works are nostalgic and referential, growing out of past schools of art, drawing their subject from the lives of the artist's grandparents.

In 1982 Elizabeth Hampsten published a book about the private writings of Midwestern women from 1880-1910 (*Read This Only To Yourself*, Indiana Univ. Press). Her sources are from North Dakota, and she noted: "There are virtually no examples during the settlement period in North Dakota of women who entered professional and public life and continued these careers until retirement age, this in spite of the fact that the decades at the turn of the twentieth century were rather promising for women's education." This is true; survival makes harsh demands. It was not until 1910, at the very end of the settlement period, that North Dakota's first professional female artist arrived in the state. She was brought by John Babcock, the Dean of the School of Mines at the University of North Dakota, and the man who pioneered the exploration of high grade North Dakota clay for industrial ceramics. He had convinced the University President to establish a ceramics department, and to offer the artist Margaret Cable the position as chair. The choice was fortuitous. Margaret Cable, the daughter of one of Minnesota's first settlers, had pioneering in her blood. She accepted the position, one she was to hold for the next thirty-nine years. In the end it was *her* name and not John Babcock's that became synonymous with "Made of North Dakota Clay."

At first the department produced industrial and utilitarian objects; gradually Cable shifted the focus to the fine arts. With her students she began to incorporate motifs of North Dakota Indians, flora, and fauna onto the surfaces of hand-thrown or slip-molded pots. The department became infused with vitality as Miss Cable attracted many students and admirers. Most importantly, she opened lines of communication with the larger world through her travel and her demonstrations at such events as the 1929 Women's World's Fair in Chicago, and the Century of Progress Exposition in 1933 in Chicago. Her lecturing and consulting took her all over America in varied situations including a six-month tour with the United States Indian Field Service. Without fail she returned home to her studio for private revitalization. Margaret Cable made another important contribution to the future of women artists in the state. She hired women in her own department: Hildegarde Fried (1938-1963); her sister, Flora Cable Huckfield (1924-1949); Julia Mattson (1924-1963); Freida Hammers (1026-1939); and Margaret Pachl (1949-1970). At Margaret Cable's retirement, Alfred University's most prestigious Ceramics Department, in cooperation with the American Ceramic Society, bestowed upon her their highest award for her lifetime contribution to American ceramics.

Today Katie McCleery, a Michigan native, and Jackie McElroy-Edwards, formerly of Minnesota, continue the trend started by Miss Cable. Both came to the state to accept teaching jobs at the University of North Dakota — McCleery in the Ceramics Department, McElroy to teach printmaking and art history. Both have made their homes in Grand Forks, have developed their artistic lives in North Dakota, and are tenured teachers at the university. Later they were joined by Ellen Auyong, a jeweler, and Anita Kapaun, a weaver, also from other places.

North Dakota draws few of its working women in the visual arts from its native population. Most come here, education and profession in hand. Ann Solin, a native of Ohio, was chair of the North Dakota State University Art Department from 1934-1944. Kay Cann, an artist and an art critic who has worked in Fargo for three decades, came from Minnesota. Catherine Milligan came from Indiana. In the 1980s she is a vital force in the regional art world. Her dedication to her students at North Dakota State Universsity is widely admired. She cares deeply about the visual experience and continues daily to work on her own sculpture.

North Dakota has produced professional women artists, primarily for export. Lois Johnson, one of the finest, works and teaches in Philadelphia. Nancy Friese works and teaches in Connecticut. Lois took an undergraduate degree in art from the University of North Dakota in the early 1960s and then a Master of Fine Arts from Wisconsin in printmaking. Nancy graduated in nursing from the University of North Dakota in 1972 and after four years of working in various locations, the mountains, the desert, and near the ocean, she entered art school. She earned a Master of Fine Arts from Yale in painting and then began to teach on the college level "in order to support my life as an artist." Although she lives in Danbury, Connecticut, with her architect husband, North Dakota remains important to her. While never having painted the Dakota landscape, she credits its influence: "Growing up in North Dakota generated the idea of landscape for me." Like the writer Louise Erdrich whose subject is the physical and sociological terrain of her childhood, Lois Johnson has always incorporated images of North Dakota into her prints. Her early, growing up years are echoed in motifs of farm life, sheep, horses, grain elevators, and mechanical equipment. Her interest in urban architecture is counterpointed by the natural land masses of the North Dakota Badlands.

Lois Johnson and Nancy Friese were neither the first nor the last to leave, and the ranks are growing. Sara Hornbacker left her life in Fargo-Moorhead in 1975 to study media at the State University of New York at Buffalo. After graduation, she moved to New York to make her way as a video artist. Inclusion in a group exhibition at the Whitney Museum in 1982 marked her arrival as one of America's most promising young artists in the media field. For many of these artists the ties back to their North Dakota families are strong. It is their artistic lives that fully take place elsewhere.

If I want to be successful and influential in the art world I cannot build an art museum in North Dakota. I cannot work in North Dakota at all. Early on I needed to graduate from the best liberal arts college I could have gained entrance to, and then taken a doctorate from the likes of Harvard or Yale. Next I would have had to be willing to move, gaining experience in this museum or that as I worked my way up. Instead, I decided to build an art museum in North Dakota.

Nancy Friese, like Lois Johnson and Sally Hornbacker, wanted to establish her career in artistic circles; she wanted to play in the big league. She knew the game plan: "You have to start with top credentials so you go to the best schools. You need to support yourself so you find a teaching job in a good place. You also need to make very good art so you work at it all the time. Once you have paid your dues in the main center, which for artists is New York, you are free to move wherever you please, assuming you can afford it. But I look forward to the day I can return to North Dakota for a month each summer in order to paint" (conversation, August 1988).

The dilemma of cultural life: higher education policies dictate that faculty be hired who are educated out-of-state — supposedly they bring the most vitality to the system — and once native North Dakotans go away to college they seldom return. So college teaching positions, which are almost the only available means of good support for artists, are filled by people from other places, people who are apt to view North Dakota as the last stop on the bus. Artists do not flock to North Dakota because of the beauty of the natural landscape, or the magic of its mixed cultures, as they do to the Southwest. The state's population is sparse, and thinning. Outsiders see the landscape as spare and forbidding, the weather as fierce and foreboding. Neither male nor female artists seem to flourish here.

One hundred years after white settlement, North Dakota is still a pioneer place. The handful of serious women artists who have lived out their lives on the Northern Great Plains have been independent women of great energy and tenacity. Their audiences have been local. They have found their subject in the everyday, not in a nostalgic longing for a more eastern, civilized life, but through observing the world around them. The landscape has played little role in the art of these native women who stayed, a surprising difference from the art of women in either the West or the

Southwest. Teaching jobs have not been available to them. Instead they have lived with little comfort, patching finances together as best they could. They have rooted in this place called North Dakota, raised their families, and joined their communities. Nevertheless, in order to make their art, they have been willing to live outside the mainstream of both economic and cultural life — unless they married into affluence, a route none seem to have chosen.

Nancy Hendrickson was the first of these women. Born in 1889 on the family homestead thirteen miles southwest of Mandan, she was the youngest of six children. Despite having only one year of formal schooling, she became a literate woman, reading constantly and writing in a diary for forty years. While a young woman, Nancy discovered photography. It became her life passion as well as a sometimes occupation. Her subject was the peopled environment around her. Although she worked rodeos, country fairs, church gatherings, and the affairs of her friends and neighbors, it was her eccentric photographs of animals that were the most remarkable. She kept a menagerie of cats, which she dressed in human costumes to create theater. Having created sets or props to scale, she photographed her clothed creatures in appropriate domestic scenes. The resulting works are wonderful spoofs of human life as it unfolded in Mandan, North Dakota, in the 1920s.

Likewise, Emily Lunde chose to record in her paintings human life as she observed it at a critical moment in history. In 1973 Lunde published a book of her writings and drawings that she title *Uff Da*. The book (like Emily's paintings) is a smorgasbord of events and observations by a child who tagged her immigrant grandparents around a small farm in the early 1920s. The culture that they brought with them from Sweden was an everyday affair. The farm was located near Newfolden, Minnesota, thirty miles from the North Dakota border, where in 1914 the child, Emily Wilhelmina Dufke Olson, was born. She grew up to be, among other things, a painter; her manner of painting turned out to be both marvelous and genuine, for seldom do paintings so laced with humor escape from a university classroom. Today she is celebrated as North Dakota's most eminent folk artist. Her subject is still the everyday life of that first generation of Scandinavian settlers to the Red River Valley. Her hundreds of quickly-executed oil paintings function collectively as a "satire of human nature as I alternately roast and toast those I love," she writes in her second book *American Folk Art Album* (no date, self published).

Linda Brown is of the next generation of North Dakota women to forge her existence as an artist away from the center. She has known many passages: Linda, a girl from Fargo, marries young and moves to a rural community. She has a son, Ricky. To survive isolated circumstances, she takes a correspondence course in The History of Art from Jackie McElroy at the University of North Dakota. She becomes fascinated; years later she can still quote text and page from her "Jansen." Linda Brown divorces. She and her son move to Grand Forks where Linda enrolls in art at the university. To support the two of them she runs the University Sign Service. She meets a fellow artist, David Christy, and leaves the university one credit short of a Master's degree. She and her husband establish the Sanger Art Farm in the ghost town of Sanger, in western North Dakota. Linda makes art. She also raises goats for show and breeding. She and her goats win many prizes. She has two more children. The family are forced to move when their rented studio spaces (and home) become part of the Cross Ranch nature reserve. They buy a farm outside of Valley City and once again set up studios. Time passes. It is a good life and Linda, the artist, tracks her movements through the years in her silkscreen prints.

During the decade of the eighties she concentrates on the series *Prairie Women*. It contains such prints as " . . . the girls night out . . ." in which she deals with motherhood. "Having just had two children I felt the theme was appropriate. The image is three very pregnant women out for a stroll in their colorful maternity garb," she writes in her *Sanger Studios Newsletter* in the summer of 1988. The women include the artist and two friends from real life. All three have set aside their careers for a time in order to bear children. Once the children are a bit independent, the women have resumed professional life. Other prints deal with the "beautiful and brilliant costumes and the fascinating women and children who dance at the United Tribes Pow Wows" for the Scandinavian women of the Midwest accompanied by their intricately-designed quilts.

To become an artist in this wind-swept, lonely place called North Dakota seems both difficult and subject to happenstance. But somehow the numbers accumulate with each decade. For example, Dr. Marion Nelson of the Scandinavian American Museum in Decorah, Iowa, has curated an exhibition (to open in the summer of 1989) of the work of five Scandinavian-American women artists descending from one immigrant family. Nancy Friese is a member of that family. Her grandfather Benjamin Huset, a weatherman from western North Dakota, is the relative in common to all the women. Although the family farms in Hatton and Crosby are still owned by grandchildren and great-grandchildren, Nancy is the only one of the artists ever to have lived in North Dakota. In writing about her mother she writes about the plight of all women who might become artists: "My mother is an untrained artist in Wadsworth, Ohio. She tells me that when she was a freshman at North Dakota State University in home economics her women professors advised her to go to the Chicago Art Institute . . . but my mother's parents were divorced and she had no idea how to finance something like that. It must have been very hard to imagine being an artist for young women in the state. And I think that mind's eye vision of oneself as an 'artist' has to be seen before one takes the first step."

How does one come to make art? I wonder. How does one build an art museum? Probably one approaches these things the same way a prairie gardener tackles alkaline soil — with tenacity and endless experimentation, by taking one's commands from inside oneself, by rejecting failure. Fannie Heath learned to counter North Dakota's sweet soil by pouring qualities of vinegar into the earth, stopping only when it ceased to bubble. Today I dig truck loads of peat moss from the woods of Minnesota and Canada into my soil. Finally, after many seasons, I have begun to neutralize the alkali and my garden flourishes. And finally, after one hundred years of uprooting and resettlement, our Indian women are beginning to make art again and our young artists such as Fargo's Deb Wallwork are finding ways to survive professionally in North Dakota. It is in celebration of these private victories, won over a long century, that we open our first public art museum.

Laurel Reuter is Director of the North Dakota Museum of Art in Grand Forks.

"Shoe," by Angie Erdrich, Wahpeton, N.D.

Evidence of Having Lived in the State

by Kathleen Norris

I was raised a rootless person, even by modern American standards. My father was a Navy bandmaster, and I grew up in Washington, D.C., Chicago, and Honolulu. After college in Vermont I worked in New York City. My grandparents' house in a little Dakota town was the one constant in all those years, the place I understood to be most deeply mine. As the center of my childhood summers, where I learned to swim in the WPA pool and to play Monopoly on card tables set up in the backyard, the town over the years assumed an air of holiness. In 1973, when I decided to leave New York City for my grandparents' house in Dakota, I was aware of the move as a deliberate haunting, a plunge into my past. Like others who have written about childhood experiences in the Dakotas — Larry Woiwode, Lois Phillips Hudson and Margarethe Shank come to mind — I recognized Dakota as the place my stories came from, and in ways I was barely conscious of, I knew that here I would find the stories that needed to be written.

Like many who have written about North Dakota, I'm invigorated by the harsh beauty of the land, and feel a deep need to tell the human stories that come from this soil. We have been formed by the experiences of our ancestors on this last American frontier, where the clash between native and white cultures took the form of military encounters little more than a hundred years ago, and where the tensions between European homesteaders and the American "melting pot" ideal are still evident in our families. The Dakotas have become for us a place to return to, holy ground where our ghosts and stories reside. I'm unusual in that I returned in the literal sense; I now face difficulties trying to hold on here as a poet, essayist, and book reviewer.

The historian Frederick Jackson Turner suggested in 1901, just twelve years after

North Dakota entered the Union, that it would not be surprising "if the task of reducing the Province of the Lake and Prairie Plains to the uses of civilization should for a time overweigh art and literature." The state Centennial is an appropriate time to consider to what extent Turner's remark has proved true, and also to look at the difficulties women writers especially have had in establishing themselves here.

The isolation North Dakota writers often report is no illusion. Minnesota has roughly three-and-a-half times the professionally published poets and fiction writers per capita as North Dakota; New York State has fifteen times more (*A Directory of American Poets and Fiction Writers* 1987). And while I don't believe that there is an active conspiracy in the literary world to discredit writers from the Plains, I have found that human provincialism tends to reward writers for proximity to publishing centers, or for participation in the academic network of graduate writing programs. Even a writer such as Robert Bly, now strongly identified with Minnesota, paid his dues as a young poet in the New York City literary scene before moving back home. In my own case, I found that the relatively easy access to grants and literary awards I had enjoyed in New York from 1969 – 1973 pretty much dried up after I moved to the Plains. For me, the move was worth it, and my early publications earned me a name that helped me to continue publishing in literary journals across the country. But a young woman growing up in North Dakota who wants to "be a writer" and stay in North Dakota will have a hard time establishing her credentials.

North Dakota, from the earliest days of settlement, has been a state to be *from*. Some 70% of the first homesteaders left after ten years; 80% were gone after twenty. William Sherman, a student of North Dakota ethnic and demographic patterns, says that the state now ranks first in the nation in having natives who live elsewhere. Its writers are no exception. Of the North Dakota writers who have received the most national recognition — Richard Critchfield, Louise Erdrich, Lois Phillips Hudson, Thomas McGrath, and Larry Woiwode — not one currently resides in the state.

A minister, a third-generation North Dakotan, has described our region as "prairies of pain," where parents must raise their children "for the outside," encouraging them to leave in order to advance themselves professionally; and where young people return home from a year at college to find they are outsiders on their home ground, invisibly but indelibly marked as different from their friends who stay. These are uncomfortable truths, but this is where we must start, with who we are, not who we think we should be. Far fewer of us are farmers or ranchers than in 1889, but we're still a frontier people trying to survive in both a notoriously harsh climate and a fickle boom-and-bust economy. "Culture" as exemplified in the arts still commands both respect and disdain, as something hardy pioneers engaged in "real work" have little time for. How have women, who traditionally do so much of the real work of feeding and caring for others, fared in North Dakota when they have desired to write about their experiences? What do women writers in the state today say about living and working here?

What has become a traditional way for writers to earn a living, teaching at a college, is possible for very few writers in this state. While, as one North Dakota writer has pointed out, it is possible to earn $20,000 a year writing non-fiction articles, "no matter where you live," writers who wish to concentrate on serious fiction and poetry must find other ways to survive. The North Dakota Council on the Arts Artist-in-Residence Program pays writers to teach writing to school children, but for those living away from urban areas it requires that they be away from home — often hundreds of miles away — for weeks at a time. It's no surprise that people leave for jobs elsewhere, where they can spend more time with their families. Many writers here, myself included, find that they must put together a crazy-quilt of part-time jobs in order to remain in the region.

The program does take advantage of the writer's role both as an outsider and someone belonging to these plains, and offers students and teachers a chance to write and to hear some of their own literature: poems and stories about baling, calving, falling in love and raising families, being born and dying right here in Dakota. In my role as an outsider I relish taking poetry to a variety of audiences here (North Dakota state legislators and a bull sale crowd among them) and appreciate the surprised but pleased response of people who thought they hated poetry — especially contemporary poetry — discovering that they enjoy it. At the same time I recognize that to write the truth in rural areas and small towns, in a culture where women are supposed to be pleasing and acceptable, is a difficult and sometimes impossible act.

It should not surprise us that the earliest writing by the women of North Dakota is in the form of letters and diaries, fragmentary forms well-suited for a few stolen moments at the end of a long day's work on a homestead. In recent years there has been increased interest in collecting these early writings; many may be found in *To All Inquiring Friends: Letters, Diaries, and Essays in North Dakota 1880-1910*, edited by Elizabeth Hampsten (1979), who writes not only of the valuable record of everyday life these women have left us, but asserts that "what we might least realize without pages such as these, is how important was the act of writing; by their own account people have invested into what is written down a great deal of time, care, ingenuity, and affection. Writing is one of the complex strategies of their survival."

Such artists are a little like the trees in the dry, windswept North Dakota landscape: their urge to survive must be deep-rooted, and must translate into a single-minded and sustained effort. Other arts — notably dance and theater — seem to require urban centers, both for a labor pool and an audience. But writing is a solitary act and, ideally, North Dakota might be considered to provide a writer with ample solitude and quiet. But women often have a hard time finding solitude, even here. They have other roles to fill, as breadwinners, wives and mothers, as volunteers and club members, and too often their "solitude" becomes a crushing isolation that silences them. One West River writer, a ranch woman and mother, summed up the problem in describing the one time she was able to attend the annual Childrens Writing Workshop in Grand Forks. She said: "I regard that 8 hour drive as one of my great accomplishments. It was so neat to be by myself. I hadn't been alone for thirteen or fourteen years."

Women write against the odds here, and this should make us value the women writers who have written about North Dakota all the more. Much North Dakota literature is in the form of reminiscences of pioneer days, and one of the most remarkable is Aagot Raaen's *Grass of the Earth: Immigrant Life in the Dakota Country*. It witnesses to the "middle period of pioneer settlement," recording the "coming of the railroad, the saloon, the farm mortgage and the sales agent rather than the earlier days of unbroken prairie" (Blegen 1950). Written when she was in her 70s, the book is luminous with detail: candle-making, haying, yarn spinning, berry picking are all described with such care that the reader understands that a pioneer childhood was one of unremitting hard work but also satisfaction at living close to nature and the rhythm of the seasons.

Unlike Nina Morgan's *Prairie Star*, which mythologizes immigrant life into a fairy tale of "snug" tarpaper houses where "all was in order," and obstacles were faced and tidily overcome, *Grass of the Earth* is refreshing in its honesty. We feel the loss, and the waste, when a baby dies because the doctor is simply too far away. When Raaen's father, an idealistic man unsuited for farming, starts drinking in town for days on end, his wife tells the children he's gone "into the shadows." And when he mortgages the farm the children must give up their dreams of an education in order to keep the land.

The reader is made to understand what the desire for an education means to such children. They sacrifice for the land and for each other, "working out" so that another might attend school for a semester. In a moving passage describing her arrival at Mayville Teachers' College, Raaen writes:

> A kindly voice stopped her, "Are you looking for work? We have some scrubbing and cleaning to be done. Come this way."
> So this was the end of the big day! Good-bye to books...Ahead were miles and miles of houses to be cleaned and scrubbed...and far in the distance were the books, piles and stacks of books about beautiful, wonderful things — books she could never, never touch...
> Her courage was returning, but she kept her eyes on her worn dress and red hands as she spoke. "I like to scrub and clean, but I must go to school now. I simply must."

Morgan's book glorifies progress, and the cooperation between prairie people that popular mythology dictates has passed down to us unchanged to this day. In describing how the established Norwegian settlers helped newcomers (other Norwegians) build a claim shack, she writes: "It was the spirit of the pioneer, and every settler shared and helped so that the homesteaders could conquer the vast prairie. It was a chain building a new nation together." Aagot Raaen's perspective is different, and perhaps more valuable to us if we are to understand ourselves in the 1980s. Watching what happened as mercantile centers were established, she writes: "The settlers became intent on gain. As a spirit of rivalry developed, the helpful friendly pioneer spirit disappeared...Most of the pioneers wanted wealth for their children; many of them imagined that possessions would bring happiness, contentment, and ease."

Morgan and Raaen exemplify the two voices one hears in North Dakota literature. The first is an evangelical call to the prairie that began with Linda Slaughter, who came to Fort Rice in April of 1870 and began writing enthusiastic stories for Eastern newspapers. To Slaughter and other boosters who followed her, the prairie is a last frontier, where progress is inevitable and human endeavor must, like the sky, be larger than life. In her book *Rose Berries in Autumn* Nina Wishek begins a poem about Bismarck's Memorial Bridge: "We come today to honor you,/ Memorial Bridge/...stand strong above our Western plains." As late as 1938, when dreams of grandeur had turned to failure for many, Wishek writes with pride of "the march of pioneers."

The other voice in Dakota is that of the desert contemplative. It is a voice that considers the pain and failure these prairies so often bring their inhabitants. Another early North Dakota poet, Florence Borner, represents an interesting juxtaposition of both voices. In many ways she was a North Dakota booster, exceptional in her determination to write despite the obstacles. She got several newspapers in the state to print her poems, as well as articles on farming and public relations stories for the Non-Partisan League. But she lost money on a book of poems she had printed in 1919 and felt that she was working in a vacuum. Still, when she and her husband were forced off their farm in 1936, she refused to leave the state without leaving her mark. In presenting a 714-page volume of poems, as well as several typewritten manuscripts to the North Dakota State Historical Library, she said, "I would like to leave some evidence of my having lived in the state."

Lois Phillips Hudson is another writer whose family was forced out by the depressed farm economy of the 20s and 30s. The magnificent gift she returned to us is a novel of that period, *The Bones of Plenty*, which tells the truth about North Dakota as only great fiction can. The words of her dedication seem prophetic today: "For My Grandfather, the last man of his line to live and die on his own land — a man without successors, of a generation without successors."

This is a rich novel, and as its characters speak we realize that they still exist in North Dakota today: the conservative land-owning grandfather whose actions are determined by honesty and old-fashioned piety; his hot-headed son-in-law (named George Custer) who resents having to lease land from a storeowner in town and lambasts politicians, "Jew bankers," and grain speculators for his problems even while taking pride in his "Independence;" government officials who insult farmers as they explain the benefits of an acreage set-aside program.

Much of the novel's poignancy comes from the narrative of a girl, Custer's daughter, desperate for her father's love, who reveals that "every day she proved to God that she was worthy of being changed into a boy." The girl has not misread her situation. Her father does wonder, "Why hadn't she been a boy? He had not been too disappointed when she was first born, because he realized that one girl was an asset to a farm family, otherwise the mother had a hard time keeping up with the housework and the other babies as they came along." But no sons followed, and his daughter's sex represents yet another way the world has turned on George Custer.

George's wife Rachel might, in other hands, have been portrayed as the stereotypical, larger-than-life and long-suffering prairie woman whose main characteristic is silence, her life a litany told by others: dust got in the flour, but ma never complained; grasshoppers ate the baby, but ma never complained.

Hudson makes us reflect on the different ways in which Rachel and George experience their world. When blackbirds arrive in the spring, Rachel seems almost glad for their company, and goes outside to watch them come. She knows that while the birds will eat insects early on, they'll eat wheat later. Still, she admires them:

"She never ceased to wonder at the incredible power of birds for adaptation. These had flown perhaps a thousand miles from the South." The birds make her reflect on her own situation: "Perhaps people ought to migrate too, and never strive to put down roots at all. It often seemed to her that the desire of human beings to own land was the cause of all their troubles ...Yet how would a human being know who he was, without roots?" George is plowing when the birds arrive. They are not worth much thought, except as yet another of his enemies: "When the flock of birds passed between him and the clouds, he did look up for an instant. It wouldn't be long before they would be back to feed on the grain. Just one of the plagues visited upon the helpless earth by the busy sky."

It is a revelation to read Rachel's painful deliberations over oilcloth advertisements in the Ward's catalog. In placing her winter order she studies the rotogravure illustrations and tries to imagine "from reading the description what 'predominately green' might mean." She recalls the domestic trouble that followed when she ordered a tablecloth in a color George didn't like and reflects, "The oilcloth would not have been so important if it had not been almost the only thing that ever changed in the house." This is minutiae, the kind of "woman's concern" that our culture says doesn't matter in the grand scheme of things. But history begins in the everyday, and Rachel Custer knows that for a North Dakota farm family facing not only a housebound winter but an economy in which "money became more confusing every day," small things like the cost and color of an oilcloth matter a great deal.

We feel the price of Rachel's reticence, for the sake of propriety, as the anger she suppresses comes close to the surface. When a neighbor whose tubercular wife has just given birth to their sixth child comes for help, she rages inwardly: "Males! God save the world from males! How could that man come in here and confess that his own hideous lust had procreated another tragic child to grow up motherless?" All she says, however, as she prepares to go with him is "Well I never! Why in the world didn't somebody tell us?"

Rachel's pain on being forced to leave the land forces her to acknowledge her real values, and to realize that they are different than those of her husband. Her desperation is vividly portrayed:

> roots were as irreplaceable as lives...It would be better to stay here and lose her life than to leave and lose her roots....What did one do when one no longer had a bed, a stove, or a table? What did one do for an address? Without a mailing address, how did a person even know who she was? How did her children — oh God! — how would her children know who they were? And George had thought of none of these things.

Many a North Dakota farm woman has asked herself these questions in the 1980s, and Rachel's anguish might speak to them over fifty years. Her piano has been sold, and the family's departure for points West is imminent: "If I go over and touch it now...just touch the middle C above the golden lock again, I would be turned into a pillar of salt; I would never walk out of here and get into the front seat of the car beside my husband, where the world says I belong."

Other women writers have dealt with North Dakota politics and history. Lorna

Doone Beers includes in her novel *Prairie Fire* an important episode from the state's history, when a North Dakota legislator told protesting farmers who had come to the capitol in 1915 to speak on behalf of a state-owned grain cooperative, to "go home and slop the hogs." The incident led to the formation of the Non-Partisan League. Beers' book is critical of rural and small-town society as a narrow "condemnation of the unconventional," and paints a sharp picture of a girl, imagining herself "as a triumphant wife...[who] had no other climax for her dream. Stern Lutheranism and the pious monogamy of the farming community saw to that." Her reward is to be the "little wife" of a wealthy banker who is "conscious of her only as a part of an environment which he had created as a monument to his success." Her dreams of escape come to nothing, but as the author notes ironically, "Christine did not pine away. Civilization is too good a disciplinarian for that. She acquired a caustic tongue."

Other books dealing with "the power of convention in a rural society" include Sarah Comstock's *Speak to the Earth* and Margarethe Erdahl Shank's *The Coffee Train*. All of these books show that North Dakota society is complex, and that tolerance and intolerance, radical opinion and the conventional, often co-exist here in surprising ways.

A little-known book, Berneice Lunday's *The Unblessed*, is about the bitter fight that erupts in a family and pioneer community in the early 1900s when a mixed Catholic/Lutheran marriage takes place and the social fabric is torn. Beyond its fascinating study of the consequences of prejudice, the book reveals several serious problems North Dakota writers face. It took courage to write such a book — one

---

Alice Haarsager Peterson, my great-grand aunt, celebrated her 100th birthday in June 1987. She is known, although almost anonymously, through the book "Per," written by her nephew E. Palmer Rockswold, who depended on her for much of the story about his parents. She was his mother's younger sister.

Alice had immigrated from Norway to North Dakota with her parents when she was six years old. In 1909 she began her own homestead in South Dakota as "an adventure," but at her father's request (he didn't think she was safe) she returned to her parents' farm in LaMoure County, where she lived until well into her 80s. She ran the family farm, renting out land, doing the haying herself with a team of horses, and tending her own cows, sheep, chickens and pigs. That was when I knew her, staying with her and helping with all these tasks. She was married at age 49 to a much younger man, and she learned to drive a car when she was 60. She had no children of her own, but served as midwife to many of her neighbors. She helped to bring up her brother's children when their mother died after the birth of a seventh child. Her life has lent purpose and direction to mine.

Kathy Kramer Maruska
Alice, N.D.

senses that Lunday is telling a family story — and not many people are prepared to face the anger of family members or fellow citizens of small towns who resent having a story like this brought to light. The book is also badly in need of editing, and might stand as an example of what happens when writers are working, as many North Dakota writers are, not just in solitude but in real isolation from other writers or those who might offer professional editorial advice.

Era Bell Thompson's *American Daughter*, the memoirs of a black woman who grew up in North Dakota, offers witness to the general racial tolerance that existed — at least for a black farm family — on the frontier. During a Christmas get-together with another black family, "Out in the middle of nowhere, laughing and talking and thanking God for this new world of freedom and opportunity," she realizes suddenly that the fifteen of them constitute "four percent of the state's entire Negro population." White families stop in to join the festivities, and she writes, "the spell of race was broken, but not the spirit of Christmas."

Thompson attended the University of North Dakota and later worked for many years as an editor of *Ebony* magazine in Chicago. When her professional skills are brought to bear on her Dakota childhood, the result is a simple eloquence. In describing the aftermath of her mother's death when she was a girl, she writes: "I was afraid to go into the house, for I could see Mother everywhere." She is farmed out to an aunt, but comes back home on her own. "What are you doing here?" a brother asks. "'I came back home,' I tried to sound casual. 'Aunt Ann talks too much.'" Her description of her father during this period is literature any culture could be proud of: "For weeks Pop hardly spoke a word to us. He cooked the meals and cleaned the house, walking around in a halo of grief, whistling or humming the old hymns, the troubled hymns of Zion."

Writers such as Era Bell Thompson, or Louise Erdrich, who attain professional standing elsewhere and who write about North Dakota from a distance, do not have to cope on a day-to-day basis with North Dakota society, which especially in its rural areas and small towns, still reflects 19th century attitudes towards women who write. When Charlotte Bronte wrote to British poet laureate Robert Southey in 1837 for advice, he told her to "give up thoughts of becoming a poet...Literature cannot be the business of a woman's life and ought not to be." Even more distressing is Bronte's self-effacing reply: "I carefully avoid any appearance of pre-occupation and eccentricity...I have endeavored not only attentively to observe the duties a woman ought to fulfill but to feel deeply interested in them. I don't always succeed, for some times when I'm teaching or sewing I would rather be reading or writing; but I try to deny myself."

Jane Eyre is a miracle, then, and the books Charlotte Bronte might have written had she not died in childbirth constitute a grievous loss. It is impossible to know how much loss we still suffer in North Dakota, where women who want to write instead try hard to feel "deeply interested" in Tupperware parties and all the "ought-to-dos" of their daily lives. They know only too well the truth of novelist Kate Wilhelm's words, quoted in the aptly titled *How To Suppress Women's Writing*, "the world, everyone in it practically, will give more and more responsibility to any woman who will continue to accept it."

The loss to North Dakota culture is significant, although we may not recognize it. The stories of Belcourt society won't be found anywhere but in the Turtle Mountains; a farm woman forced to move to Fargo has her own tales to tell; and this unique witness is lost to us as literature unless someone has the time and inclination to write it. One is tempted to say that any woman writer who comes out of North Dakota soil is a miracle, because so many find it easier to lapse into silence, or else to write only what is socially approved — appropriate for reading at a Golden Wedding anniversary or Mother-Daughter banquet. We live too close to each other here, and often have too many family and social ties, to be willing to write the truth. "I'd like to write about my relatives," one rural woman says, "but I'm no good at disguising things." This constitutes self-censorship, and is a form of silencing that's very hard to overcome.

Often, when a woman first starts to write, "the family...will think it's cute or precocious, or at least not dangerous." But even this condescending acceptance may be short-lived. Storytelling can be dangerous, and family members are quick to realize this when it's "wife" or "mother" who is doing it. Once a farm woman in a writing workshop I taught reported that she had trouble doing the assignments I'd given because whenever her husband saw her writing in her notebook, he'd say, "that's enough of writing in that stupid thing." Another woman, whose life was bound up in church and volunteer work, confessed that she hadn't told anyone she was attending a writing workshop. She said she was going "to a meeting," because a writing workshop might sound frivolous or selfish. Is it any wonder that these women have a difficult time editing out the sentimentality and eagerness to please that mars much amateur writing, that they hesitate to take their work seriously enough to risk telling the truth?

Women writers face these difficulties in other states. But often, in more populated areas where physical isolation is less a factor, they stand a better chance of finding others in the same situation. In North Dakota it is only in the college towns that women are likely to find such support. In Bismarck, Nancy Olson has doggedly kept a writer's group afloat; in Fargo a group called Wordshop emerged from a college writing workshop and has been operating for several years. In such a group a woman might learn that the tough process of editing and revising frees her to discover her true voice. The paradox is that writing is hard work, and that the aim of all that work is simplicity, letting stories tell themselves. In Dakota, in the many volumes of family and regional history — mostly written by women — that appear each year, the voice of the booster and the desert contemplative are still very much in conflict, and truth often suffers at the hands of sentiment.

Many North Dakota women writers are either unpublished or they pay to have their books printed by subsidy publishers or local printers. Often their first publication is in a local newspaper column. Because they haven't received much outside recognition they are often too self-effacing to simply say, "I'm a writer," and to claim the privacy and time needed to write. But when a woman here does publish, she can find that the success that serves to validate her work also sets her apart and makes her an easy target for disapproval. Of course there are good responses, people who will offer encouragement and express real appreciation for her writing. A typical reaction is one of pride that someone "from here" is a writer. But one woman who began publishing a column of reminiscences in a local paper was surprised to find that she felt "more insecure than I did without it." She was also surprised that so many people reacted with a sullen silence. She said, "Something drives me to write. I'm possessed to do this. Maybe nothing drives them. Maybe it's a sin to be possessed in North Dakota."

Dorothy Dayton, a West River ranch woman whose feminist reworking of fairy tale motifs, *The Epic of Alexandra,* was published by a small press in 1979, doesn't speak in terms of possession but admits, "I feel restless and on edge when I don't write." She has had some magazine publications in *Country Woman News* and elsewhere since the book came out, but has been unable to sell the sequels to *Alexandra* or any of the nearly twenty book-length manuscripts she has turned out since then. She says, "Sometimes it's just drudgery and I wonder, Why am I doing this? *Any* recognition is satisfying."

Dorothy has been fortunate in finding an editor at a major children's publisher who offers specific criticisms of her work and encourages her to send more. "It's great," Dorothy says, "she hasn't accepted a book but she'll write and say what doesn't work, what's wrong with a certain character. Sometimes it's frustrating," she says, "but I need direction and this gives me something to work towards." Dorothy grew up in a small city in the Southwest, and while she finds that "North Dakota is OK for writing," she doesn't like "the lack of contact with other writers." Her research in *Writer's Market* and other publications has led to contact with an agent who has expressed some interest in her writing, but, she says, "I still feel as if I don't know what I'm doing in terms of marketing." She acknowledges that she's put some projects on hold just because of her physical isolation. "I'd like to do a historical novel," she says, "but it's hard to do the research when you're 400 miles away from a research library."

Still, she writes. Her persistence is telling, and while it's a characteristic writers need to survive anywhere, Dorothy does find it threatened by both her physical and social isolation. She is amused to find herself an oddity in her community: "I was never known for anything before," she says. "I was always rather shy and conventional. So I might as well be known as a little bit different. I'm raising my children with the idea that it's all right to be different." Dorothy began writing in earnest, she says, "after my first son was born and I was bored. I'd put Michael where I could keep my eye on him, and he'd sit there and watch Mommy write." As her family grew she found it difficult to find the time to write, or to have the "mental conversations with people" that lead to writing. "Mowing the grass is good for this," she says, "or walking early in the morning." Like many women writers, she tries to get up before the rest of the family to have some time for writing.

Tillie Olsen, a working-class California woman who found that the pressures of supporting her family forced her to stop writing for many years, reminds us in her book *Silences* that she and other writers often experience "not natural silences...that necessary time for renewal, lying fallow, in the natural cycle of creating" but rather "the unnatural thwarting of what struggles to come into being but cannot." Like most women writers with families, Dorothy knows this only too well. She had hoped to write full-time when her youngest child entered school but the farm economy made it necessary for her to get a job in town. "Now I have less time than when the kids were home," she says, and the office she had set up in her home "just sits there, and I get so I have no ideas." Her dream of writing "an elaborate fantasy like Ursula K. LeGuin, where you have to create the whole universe," seems more and more remote. "My real love is fantasy," Dorothy says, "but it takes time and it's hard to do well, and it's hard to get anyone to pay attention to it."

Jane Kohn, a second-generation North Dakotan who lives with her husband and brother on the land near Halliday that her father homesteaded, also began writing out of boredom; and she's found that a childhood mode of dealing with the world has served her well as a writer. "Whenever I got bored I retreated into my own world, where no one could touch me — they don't know what you're thinking."

In what might serve as an autobiography for many a woman writer, she says, "I was not a chosen child. The valuable ones were the two boys. I lived my own life and did a lot of thinking." In a memoir, one of her columns for the *Dunn County Herald*, she states: "Jane grew up the youngest member of her family. Half her best friends were horses and the rest were dogs." Jane's father was something of an outsider, an educated Irishman, a loner among close-knit Norwegians. "He was a farmer by choice," she says, "and he taught us that an education meant that whatever you are, you are by choice." Jane went off on her own at 18, and taught in several Western states before returning to North Dakota in the 1950s. She was divorced by then, and had a young daughter. "I didn't wear a scarlet letter," she says, "but there were some who hid their sons from me."

Jane is a Dakota native — "At the age of ten," she says, "I herded 100 cattle and rode a horse that could jump a 3-wire fence" — but her experiences as an outcast here, who married a Kansas combiner, "an outsider who came to stay," as she describes him, seem to have strengthened her resolve to write. "I knew when I was young," she says, "that I wasn't going to fill my life with women's meetings and things like that. I wasn't going to be part of anything that had nothing to give me." Minnesota writer Carol Bly, in *Letters from the Country,* speaks of the sense of mortality, a "sense of time left" that prompts many middle-aged people in small towns, "people who have dazedly accepted belonging to clubs for twenty years" to suddenly drop out, " [choosing] to topple into their own lives instead." This sense of "time left" that often results in choosing solitude over belonging, is one that writers seem to develop early and need to nurture all their lives. It does not necessarily make them popular in their families or in small towns.

Jane knows that women "have to be motivated to write," and they need to struggle against old-fashioned attitudes: "Dishwashing is still dishwashing," she says, "but at my house you don't say 'women's work.'" She adds, "Women have to walk around with dreams in their heads, even if they're working in manure. That's where my stories come from, that's when I start thinking." Like Dorothy Dayton and just about any other woman writer who has a family, she finds it hard to find blocks of time for thinking and writing: "There are too many other people counting on me," she says. But, she emphasizes, "Here and there a woman just has to step on a few toes and put her writing above other things." Jane thinks North Dakota is "full of good telling stories," that have yet to be tapped. "There's a mountain of potential, but people have to seize it." She says, "I let my mother die without realizing that the monotonous stuff she told me day after day was not a pain in the neck but a history."

And this is what any essay on North Dakota writing must be about: valuing who we are, and being willing to tell our stories, and above all being willing to tell them true. We might take inspiration from Louise Erdrich's eloquent novels, *Love Medicine*, *The Beet Queen*, and *Tracks*, which give voice to the most silenced of Dakota women: Indians, the poor and working class, whose stories are seldom seen as "history," as worth anything at all. Farm wives, too, are seldom heard, and we can only hope that women will write about their lives in today's farm economy as Lois Phillips Hudson wrote about the Dakota of the 1930's in *The Bones of Plenty*.

But North Dakotans suffer from a kind of schizophrenia when it comes to their literature. Unless our writings are validated by the literary standards of "back East," it can't be any good. Many people are surprised to find that good literary magazines are being published in North Dakota: *Bloodroot, North Dakota Quarterly, Plains Poetry Journal,* and *Plainswoman* among them. Libraries that do a brisk business in best-sellers often have to be coaxed into buying materials that are published within the region.

Still another dimension of the problem is that the work of some North Dakota women writers — their newspaper columns for dailies and weeklies, for example — does not receive the recognition it deserves even if it is of high quality. Such work may be dismissed because it's seen to be of purely local interest or because it's by and about women. We depend on women to be the bearers and keepers of culture — prairie schoolmarms and church builders among pioneer wives epitomize this — but we also tend to regard "women's concerns" as somehow less "universal" than the stories, and histories, of men.

Not all of the local histories, stories, and poems women write in North Dakota are well-written, but we can value these works for other things. Sometimes the very qualities that make them suspect to scholars make them valuable to us. The familial and nostalgic tone of a local history, for example, may reveal an important "shared ideology about the past" that offers us valuable insight into who we are today. Such local histories, most often written by women, tend to censor out conflict and controversy in order to serve up the past as a "harmonious whole," implying that the "past was better" or at least more stable "than the present" (Kohl 1988).

Some stories that are uniquely ours, such as an ode to soybeans (to the tune of "Home on the Range") or a paean to the Parent Teacher Organization that I ran across in a privately printed anthology, might be considered invaluable as folk art. That anthology, *Wild Prairie Roses: A Collection of Verses by North Dakotans*, edited by Shirley J. Mikkelson, offers an intriguing look at what people around the state were writing in 1980. Our "cowgirl poets" are also important. Their work, a folksy American adaptation of sophisticated British narrative forms, is often full of the "good telling stories" we love to hear and offers testimony to life on the land.

The telling of such stories has always been important to human beings, even before they had a written language. And such stories are being told in North

Dakota, by women who say, "I love the act of writing. It is essential to my whole self. It is what brings me to perfect pitch and whether or not what I write is ever published is almost of no account." This woman, Barb Crow, is a member of Fargo's Word-shop. She finds a peculiar freedom in the struggle to write in North Dakota, which she sees as "pure, almost virginal, spacious, strict in the old Presbyterian work ethic sense, restrictive, stuck on tradition, hard work and keeping to the lines." She finds that while it may be "a hard state to be placed in to suddenly find you want to break out of the mold," it may, conversely, "be the best, for reaction to the restrictions brings an almost predictable swing in the other direction."

I once spent a few days working in the Regent, North Dakota, public schools, and a teacher there said that having an artist in residence was a little like letting a cat into the school. The analogy pleased me, because I do see my role as artist as that of a subversive outsider who does some non-schoolish things in class in order to encourage students to "break out of the mold." I also respect the traditions and family stories these students bring with them, and try to help them see and value these "ordinary" things in a new way.

I had written a great deal in my notebook my first night in town, and wrote a poem about a butte outside Regent the next day at the school, typing the first draft in the principal's office. I read the poem to the students and told them that although I'd lived in New York and had seen Paris, I thought Regent was a pretty inspiring place. When I had them look up the origin of their town's name in the school library, we discovered that Regent got its name because people thought it would be the "Queen City," a railroad center and county seat. Well, I told them, Dickinson got the railroad, and Mott is the county seat, and Regent, bearing its grand name, is still waiting for glory.

A few seemed to think this was a strange pursuit, but the students did start to think about their town in a new way. I got very little of the standard complaint teenagers especially usually make: "This is a boring place, and I can hardly wait to leave." One little girl, a first grader, stared at me and the colorful clothes I wear when I work with kids, the red boots that have reminded more than one child of Dorothy in *The Wizard of Oz*. She raised her hand and asked, "Do you live in a country?" Of course, I told her, the same one you live in. The magic is here because we are, and the things that happen to us in our daily lives here are not a nothing, but a history that needs to be told.

References

Beers, Lorna Doone. *Prairie Fires*. New York: E.P. Dutton and Co., 1925.

Blegen, Theodore C., in Aagot Raaen, *Grass of the Earth: Immigrant Life in the Dakota Country*. Northfield, Minn.: Norwegian-American Historical Association, 1950, vii. Additional information on Aagot Raaen may be found in an unpublished paper by Eldri Salter.

Borner, Florence. *Modern Poems for Modern People*. Bismarck, N.D.: The Bismarck Tribune Co., 1919. Additional information on Florence Borner may be found in an unpublished paper by Frances Wold.

Bly, Carol. *Letters From the Country*. New York: Harper and Row, 1981.

Comstock, Sarah. *Speak to the Earth*. Garden City, N.Y.: Doubleday, Page and Co., 1927.

Dayton, Dorothy. *The Epic of Alexander.* Winston-Salem, N.C.: J.F. Blair, 1979.

Erdrich, Louise. *The Beet Queen,* 1986. *Love Medicine,* 1984. *Tracks,* 1988. New York: Holt, Rinehart and Winston.

Hampsten, Elizabeth, comp. *To All Inquiring Friends: Letters, Diaries and Essays in North Dakota.* Grand Forks: University of North Dakota, 1979.

Hanson, Nancy Edmonds. *How You Can Make $20,000 Writing, No Matter Where You Live.* Cincinatti: Writer's Digest Books, 1980.

Hudson, Lois Philips. *Bones of Plenty.* Boston: Little, Brown, 1962.

Kohl, Seena. "Making the Past A Harmonious Whole." *Plainswoman,* May 1988.

Lunday, Berneice. *The Unblessed.* Nashville, Tenn.: Southern Publishing Association, 1979.

Mikkelson, Shirley J., ed. *Wild Prairie Roses: A Collection of Verses by North Dakotans.* Minot, N.D.: Private Publisher, 1980.

Morgan, Nina. *Prairie Star.* New York: Viking, 1935.

Olson, Tillie. *Silences.* New York: Delacorte Press, 1978.

Russ, Joanna. *How To Suppress Women's Writing.* Austin: University of Texas Press, 1983.

Shank, Margarethe Erdahl. *Coffee Train.* Minneapolis: Augsburg Publishing Co., 1968.

Thompson, Era Bell. *American Daughter.* Chicago: University of Chicago Press, 1946. Reprint. St. Paul: Minnesota Historical Society Press, 1986.

Turner, Frederick Jackson. "The Middle West," in Jean A. Peyroutet, "The North Dakota Farmer in Fiction." *North Dakota Quarterly,* Winter, 1971.

Wishek, Nina Farley. *Rose Berries in Autumn.* Ashley, N.D.: Ashley Tribune, 1938.

Kathleen Norris is an Artist in Residence for the North Dakota Council on the Arts, and is on the faculty of the Great Plains Institute of Theology. Her work has appeared in numerous publications. She is the author of a book of poems, *The Middle of the World* (Univ. of Pittsburgh Press, 1981); in 1988 she won the Wayland Press Poetry Chapbook competition for *The Year of Common Things,* to be published in 1989. She lives in Lemmon, South Dakota.

For Further Reading

Armitage, Susan, and Elizabeth Jameson, editors. *The Women's West*. Norman and London: University of Oklahoma Press, 1987. Essays by presenters at the Women's West Conference, Sun Valley, Idaho, summer 1983. Topics include images of women in art (cowboy art and paintings of Indian women) and in literature; women in the fur trade and in mining towns; women's work, homesteading, prostitution; immigrant women, Chicanas, and members of other ethnic groups; women's suffrage and political activities.

Bently, Susan, and Carolyn Sachs. *Farm Women in the United States: An Updated Literature Review and Annotated Bibliography*. University Park, Pennsylvania: Department of Agricultural Economics and Rural Sociology (A.E. & R. S. 174). The Pennsylvania State University, 1984. Essay reviews the history of women's changing role in agricultural production and describes :sexual division of labor on farms, women's access to land, off-farm employment, farm workers, racial distinctions, and women in professional agricultural occupations. 76 pages, offset.

Degler, Carl N. *At Odds: Women and the Family in America from the Revolution to the Present*. New York: Oxford University Press, 1980. Stresses and changes in family life for the most part made women's lives especially difficult and often limited.

Diede, Pauline Neher. *Homesteading on the Knife River Prairies*. Edited by Elizabeth Hampsten. Bismarck, N.D.: Germans from Russia Heritage Society, 1983. Two German-Russian families settled in western North Dakota; interviews tell of the first two years, 1909-1911 when they broke sod, built houses, began farming, learned the language, and almost starved.

Edelman, Marian Wright. *Families in Peril: An Agenda for Social Change*. Cambridge, MA: Harvard University, 1987. A denunciation of Reagan's "pro-family" policies, written by the president of the Children's Defense Fund.

Faragher, John Mack. *Women and Men on the Overland Trail*. New Haven: Yale University Press, 1980. An account of how people behaved on the journeys to California and Oregon, based largely on letters and diaries of the travelers.

Fairbanks, Carol, and Sara Brooks Sundberg. *Farm Women on the Prairie Frontier: A Sourcebook for Canada and the United States*. Metuchen, N.J., and London: The Scarecrow Press, Inc., 1983. Four essays on land, people, history and the fiction of the grasslands of Canada and the United States; and annotated bibliographies of women's non-fiction and fiction writings in Canada and the United States. Illustrations.

Gilman, Carolyn and Mary Jane Schneider. *The Way to Independence: Memories of a Hidatsa Indian Family, 1840-1920*. St. Paul: Minnesota Historical Society, 1987. Catalog of an exhibition of Hidatsa culture at the Minnesota Historical Society in 1987.

Gjerde, Jon. *From Peasants to Farmers: The Migration from Balestrand, Norway, to the Upper Middle West*. New York: Cambridge University Press, 1985. How Norwegians became Norwegian-Americans, including intimate descriptions of courtships.

Hampsten, Elizabeth. *Read This Only to Yourself: The Private Writings of Midwestern Women,*

1880-1910. Bloomington: Indiana University Press, 1982. Discussions of letters and diaries and reminiscences by women, as they reveal their ideas and feelings about their daily lives — work, health, childbirth and child care, family relationships. Most sources are from North Dakota.

Hoffmann, Leonore, and Margo Culley, editors. *Women's Personal Narratives, Essays in Criticism and Pedagogy.* New York: The Modern Language Association of America, 1985. Essays by participants at an NEH Humanities Institute at the University of Alabama, summer 1979, discuss reading and teaching women's private writings, and analyze specific texts. A complete diary and a collection of letters are included as examples of women's personal writings.

Jeffrey, Julie Roy. *Frontier Women: The Trans-Mississippi West, 1840-1880.* New York: Hill and Wang, 1979. A general overview of women's move westward that emphasizes how, even in the face of dire frontier adversity, women tried to maintain their more eastern ideas about proper roles. A chapter on Mormon women.

Jensen, Joan M., editor. *With These Hands: Working Women on the Land.* Old Westbury, New York: The Feminist Press, 1981. Published and private writings by women about agriculture and gardening.

Kaufman, Polly Welts. *Women Teachers on the Frontier.* New Haven: Yale University Press, 1984. An analysis of a diary by an Iowa teacher, Arozina Perkins, and discussions of letters by other teachers describing daily living and work.

Kolodny, Annette. *The Land Before Her: Fantasy and Experience of the American Frontiers, 1630-1860.* Chapel Hill and London: The University of North Carolina Press, 1984. Whereas men approached the frontier with the idea of conquering land, women tended to domesticate it, and designed gardens. Discussions of captivity narratives, novels, and other publications by women that describe the landscapes they imagined as they settled the frontier.

Matthaei, Julie A. *An Economic History of Women in America: Women's Work, the Sexual Division of Labor, and the Development of Capitalism.* New York: Schocken Books, 1982. A survey of how the basic features of the American economy have affected women's lives.

Medicine, Beatrice, and Patricia Albers, editors. *The Hidden Half: Studies on Northern Plains Indian Women.* Washington, D.C.: University Press of America, 1983. Papers presented at a 1977 conference on women in Plains Indian cultures, on the topics of images of women, work, status, and identity.

Moynihan, Ruth Barnes. *Rebel for Rights, Abigail Scott Duniway.* New Haven: Yale University Press, 1985. Duniway was a suffragist, journalist, and national leader during the early settlement of Oregon. She ran a newspaper, the New Northwest and was important in the politics of the region.

Myres, Sandra L. *Westering Women and the Frontier Experience, 1800-1915.* Albuquerque: University of New Mexico Press, 1982. Descriptions of women's lives in the Southwest that refute traditional stereotypes of women on the frontier.

Peterson, Susan, and Courtney Roberson. *Women With Vision: The Presentation Sisters of South Dakota.* Urbana: University of Illinois Press, 1988. A group of Catholic nuns known as Presentations Sisters migrated in 1880 from Ireland to Dakota Territory where they founded schools and hospitals in Sioux Falls, Mitchell, and Aberdeen, South Dakota, and Miles City, Montana. Aberdeen is the site of their Presentation Junior College.

Powers, Marla N. *Oglala Women: Myth, Ritual, and Reality.* Chicago: University of Chicago,

1986. The lives of Oglala Sioux women, past and present, based on conversations and oral interviews.

Riley, Glenda. *Frontierswomen: The Iowa Experience*. Ames: Iowa State University, 1981. Chapters on women's migration, women's work, and women during the Civil War as well as studies of individual Iowa women.

_____. *Women and Indians on the Frontier, 1825-1915*. Albuquerque: University of New Mexico Press, 1984. Interactions between Anglo-European women and Native American women contrasted with the aggressive stance of frontier males toward Indians; women in the two cultures had more positive and less violent relationships than did men.

_____. *The Female Frontier: A Comparative View of Women on the Prairie and the Plains*. Lawrence: University Press of Kansas, 1988. While men's experiences differed between the prairie regions such as Minnesota and the plains such as the Dakotas, women's experiences were more similar from region to region and displayed characteristics that mark a distinctive "female frontier."

Rosenfeld, Rachel Ann. *Farm Women: Work, Farm, and Family in the United States*. Chapel Hill: University of North Carolina Press, 1987. A national study of women on farms based on the 1980 Farm Women's Survey of 2,509 farm operators and wives of farm operators.

Ryan, Mary P. *Womanhood in America: From Colonial Times to the Present*. New York: New Viewpoints, 1983. A general history of women's experiences in America.

Schlissel, Lillian. *Women's Diaries of the Westward Journey*. New York: Schocken Books, 1982. Examinations of women's migrations to California and Oregon, based on private writings.

Springer, Marlene, and Haskell Springer, editors. *Plains Woman: The Diary of Martha Farnsworth, 1882-1922*. Blomington, Indiana University Press, 1986. Daily recordings of an ordinary woman who was a teacher, photographer, and suffragist, and described her life somewhat in the style of sentimental novels.

Stauffer, Helen, and Susan Rosowski, editors. *Women and Western American Literature*. Troy: The Whitson Publishing Company, 1982. Essays on images of women in western myth and literature and on specific writers like Agnes Smedley, Hamlin Garland, Jean Stafford, Marie Sandoz, and Paula Gunn Allen.

Stratton, Joanna L. *Pioneer Women: Voices from the Kansas Frontier*. New York: Simon and Schuster, 1982. Stratton's grandmother had asked women to write to her of their settlement experiences, but she did not publish their responses as she had intended; Stratton describes daily lives based on those writings.

Sykes, Hope Williams. *Second Hoeing*. Introduction by Timothy J. Kloberdanz. 1935. Reprint. Lincoln and London: University of Nebraska Press, 1982. A novel about German-Russian sugar beet farmers and laborers in Northern Colorado in the early twentieth century. Both times it was published, this book stirred some controversy among German-Russians who thought it gave an unflattering portrait of the characters' hard lives.

Unger, Steven, editor. *The Destruction of American Indian Families*. New York: Association on American Indian Affairs, 1978. Essays on Indian family life.

Prepared by Larry Peterson, History Department, North Dakota State University, Fargo.

Index